REFLECTING ON NATURE

REFLECTING ON NATURE

Readings in

Environmental

Philosophy

Edited by

Lori Gruen &

Dale Jamieson

New York ∾ Oxford

Oxford

University

Press ∾ 1994

Oxford University Press

Oxford   New York   Toronto
Delhi   Bombay   Calcutta   Madras   Karachi
Kuala Lumpur   Singapore   Hong Kong   Tokyo
Nairobi   Dar es Salaam   Cape Town
Melbourne   Auckland   Madrid

and associated companies in
Berlin   Ibadan

Copyright © 1994 by Oxford University Press, Inc.

Published by Oxford University Press, Inc.
200 Madison Avenue, New York, New York 10016

Library of Congress Cataloging-in-Publication Data
Reflecting on nature: readings in environmental philosophy /
edited by Lori Gruen and Dale Jamieson.
p. cm.   Includes bibliographical references.
ISBN 0-19-508290-7
1. Environmental sciences—Philosophy.   I. Gruen, Lori.   II. Jamieson, Dale.
GE 40.R44   1994
363.7′001—dc20   93-26696

Pages v–vii constitute an extension of the copyright page.

2 4 6 8 9 7 5 3 1

Printed in the United States of America
on acid-free, recycled paper

The editors wish to express their appreciation to the following for permission to reprint the selections in this volume.

Terry L. Anderson and Donald R. Leal, from *Free Market Environmentalism*, pp. 162, 167–72. Boulder: Westview Press, 1991. Reprinted by permission of the publisher.

Aristotle, from *Physics* and *Politics*. Translated by Christopher Shields.

Murray Bookchin, from *Defending the Earth: A Dialogue Between Murray Bookchin and Dave Foreman*, pp. 95–99, 75–86. Boston: South End Press, 1991. Reprinted by permission of the publisher.

Daniel Botkin, from *Discordant Harmonies: A New Ecology for the Twenty-First Century*, pp. 188–92. Copyright © 1990 by Oxford University Press. Reprinted by permission of the publisher.

Robert D. Bullard, from "Environmental Blackmail in Minority Communities," from B. Bryant and P. Mohai, eds., *Race and the Incidence of Environmental Hazards*, pp. 82–83, 85–92, 94. Boulder: Westview Press, 1992. Reprinted by permission of the publisher.

J. Baird Callicott, from "The Wilderness Idea Revisited: The Sustainable Development Alternative," *The Environmental Professional*, volume 13, 1991, pp. 236–42, 245. Reprinted by permission of the publisher.

Commission on Developing Countries and Global Change, from *For Earth's Sake: A Report from the Commission on Developing Countries and Global Change*, pp. 16–30. Ottawa: International Development Research Centre, 1992. Reprinted by permission of the publisher.

Charles Darwin, from chapters 6 and 15 of *On the Origin of Species*, 6th ed., volumes 1 and 2, pp. 251, 304–5. New York: Appleton, 1898.

Bill Devall, from "Deep Ecology and Radical Environmentalism," *Society and Natural Resources*, volume 4, number 1, 1991, pp. 247–52, 257. Philadelphia: Taylor & Francis. Reprinted by permission of the publisher.

John Dryzek, from "Green Reason: Communicative Ethics for the Biosphere," *Environmental Ethics* 12, Fall 1990, pp. 195–210. Reprinted by permission of the publisher.

Anne H. Ehrlich and Paul R. Ehrlich, "Extinction: Life in Peril," from *Lessons of the Rainforest*, pp. 95–105. Copyright © 1990 by Suzanne Head and Robert Heinzman. Reprinted by permission of Sierra Club Books.

Paul R. Ehrlich and Anne H. Ehrlich, from *The Population Explosion*, pp. 13–23, 37–40. Copyright © 1990 by Paul R. Ehrlich and Anne H. Ehrlich. Reprinted by permission of Simon & Schuster.

From Genesis, Revised Standard Version of the Bible. Copyright © 1946, 1952, and 1971 by the Division of Christian Education of the National Council of the Churches of Christ in the USA.

Jonathan Glover, from *What Sort of People Should There Be?* pp. 109–10. New York: Penguin Books, 1984. Copyright © 1984 by Jonathan Glover. Reproduced by permission of the publisher.

Kenneth E. Goodpaster, from "On Being Morally Considerable," *The Journal of Philosophy*, 75:6, June 1978, pp. 308–9, 314–20, 322–25. Reprinted by permission of the publisher.

Stephen J. Gould, from "The Golden Rule—A Proper Scale for Our Environmental Crisis," *Natural History*, September 1990, pp. 30–31. Reprinted by permission of the author.

Lori Gruen, from "Animals," from P. Singer, ed., *A Companion to Ethics*, pp. 343–53. Oxford: Basil Blackwell, 1991. Reprinted by permission of the publisher.

Ramachandra Guha, "Radical American Environmentalism and Wilderness Preservation: A Third World Critique," *Environmental Ethics*, volume 11, Spring 1989, pp. 71–83. Reprinted by permission of the publisher.

This book is dedicated to all the people whose reflections on nature have led them to fight to defend the wild places of the Earth; and to Jeremy and Ludwig, loyal animal companions.

I swear the earth shall surely be complete to
*   him or her who shall be complete,*
The earth remains jagged and broken only to
*   him or her who remains jagged and*
broken.

> Walt Whitman,
> "A Song of the Rolling Earth"

Preface

Since the 1970s, when courses in environmental ethics were first taught in philosophy departments, the number of courses on the environment has steadily increased and their content expanded. During the 1980s, these courses became increasingly common in departments of politics, sociology, religion, geography, and biology, and even in professional schools such as business, engineering, and law. Nowadays the examination of our place in nature is occurring throughout the university. This book is intended to facilitate this examination.

Philosophical concern for the environment has become more sophisticated in the past decade. In compiling this anthology, we have been able to mine a much richer literature than was available in the early 1980s. As part of this process of maturation, philosophical writing about the environment has spilled beyond the borders of ethics and has involved explorations in the history of philosophy, political philosophy, and the philosophy of science, among other fields. Environmental ethics—the central concern of the 1970s and 1980s—is now just one important dimension of environmental philosophy. This shift is reflected in the structure and title of this book.

For too long environmental philosophy, as influential as it has been in some circles, has been practiced on the margins of its home discipline. Yet some of the questions that environmental philosophers have been struggling with are closely connected to traditional philosophical questions. By bringing the writings of such leading environmental philosophers as Holmes Rolston III and Paul Taylor together with texts by such prominent moral philosophers as Jonathan Glover and Bernard Williams, we have tried to illuminate some of the connections between environmental philosophy and the philosophical tradition.

Another important change from the 1980s is that the environment has become more central in the thought of diverse people all over the globe. The environment is no longer just the province of a few philosophers, historians, and scientists. The environmental issues that are now of major concern are global in scope—ozone depletion, climate change, and biodiversity loss, for example. These problems must be addressed in the context of a world characterized by radical inequality. The problem of international justice cannot be evaded if our environmental crises are to be solved. In this book, we have tried to reflect the changing global discourse by including voices that are not usually heard in philosophical discussions about the environment. A significant number of articles are by women and authors from the developing world.

With the demise of Reaganism and the restoration of mainstream environmentalism in the United States, space has been created for new thinking. Such movements as deep ecology, social ecology, and ecofeminism may move from the margins closer to the center in the 1990s. We have also included these voices in this volume.

In addition to hearing new voices, it is important for us to listen to echoes from the past. Such philosophers as John Stuart Mill and naturalists as John Muir still have important lessons to teach us. Moreover, understanding the diverse images of nature that are part of our cultural heritage is vital for appreciating the environmental crises that we face.

As we approach the end of the twentieth century, our environmental problems continue to worsen. It is difficult to select a few problems as more worthy of attention than others. In this book, we focus on wilderness because the very concept seems endangered, on animals because they continue to suffer in numbers that are almost unimaginable, and on overpopulation and overconsumption because a strong case can be made that they are at the root of our problems. Finally, we have chosen to address biodiversity loss because the issue is so complex and yet so urgent. Never before in the history of the planet has a single species been responsible for such a holocaust.

These problems cannot be solved by a book. A philosophy book is, after all, only a collection of words. Yet words are important to action, in part because in speaking and writing we are doing something. This is part of the reason why language about controversial issues is often itself controversial. In this book, we have adopted various linguistic conventions that we cannot fully defend here. The most that we can do is to make some of these choices explicit.

Like most philosophers, we often use the word "we" to refer to some vaguely defined community of readers. Our use of this term is not meant to be exclusive or patronizing; we use it to refer to our probable readership—college undergraduates in the United States, Canada, Britain, Australia, and New Zealand. Nor do we mean to suggest that this probable readership forms a homogenous group.

In a world of almost 200 countries, each with its own culture, traditions, and institutions, it is difficult to speak in sweeping terms. Yet sometimes it is necessary to do so. We have used the term "developed country" to refer to such countries as the United States, Germany, and Japan, and the term "developing country" to refer to such countries as Kenya, Indonesia, and Brazil because these terms reflect the usage that has become conventional in international forums. However, this vocabulary is controversial and is challenged with good reason by people in all parts of the world.

Occasionally, we use the term "animal" to refer to nonhuman animals. This usage is misleading because it suggests that humans are not animals, thus reinforcing one of the dualisms that may be implicated in our environmental problems. We have been careful to refer to nonhuman animals with gendered pronouns so as not to reinforce the prejudice that they are mere objects, like tables or chairs.

In many cases, we have taken significant liberties with the original texts. Most of the selections are drawn from discussions that are far more extensive and nuanced than the extracts might suggest. For the serious student, there is no substitute for reading the original publications. We have deleted many notes, and in at least one case, we have rearranged some material; however, the linguistic conventions adopted by the authors have not been changed. For example, some use gender-neutral language; some do not.

∽

Producing this anthology was a lot more work than we had anticipated, and many people helped in various ways. Unfortunately, we cannot remember them all here. But we would especially like to thank those whose words we have reproduced, both for their work on the articles presented here and for their larger contributions to environmental theory and practice. Our students—now numbering in the thousands at the University of Colorado, the University of British Columbia, and Cornell University—have been an invaluable source of insight and inspiration. Since 1980, D. J. has occasionally co-taught courses on the environment with Micky Glantz, whose influence on this project is deep, if indirect. Alison Jaggar, Linda Nicholson, David Rosenthal, Peter Singer, Bob Solomon, and especially David Tatom were sources of advice and encouragement when we began. Robin Attfield, Andrew Brennan, David Crocker, Robert Elliot, Alastair Gunn, Ned Hettinger, Holmes Rolston, and two anonymous referees made helpful suggestions. Lori Cohen generously provided a comfortable place for L. G. to work while in Vancouver. John A. Fisher suggested the title, and he, along with Christopher Shields, played supporting roles in this project with their usual flair. Dooley, Grete, Kenny, and Toby were unusually patient, even indulgent. Angela Blackburn and Rob Dilworth shepherded the project through the labyrinth of Oxford University Press, and Angela's enthusiasm for the project from the beginning was contagious and helped to sustain us.

Perhaps most important, this book grows out of a community of thought and action about the environment. Without the efforts, enthusiasm, and interest of many unnamed and unacknowledged people this book would not exist.

Boulder, Colo.   L. G.
April 1993   D. J.

Contents

PART I

Images of Nature

We live in a world of fax machines, MTV, electronic mail, and mass tourism. In such a world, it is easy to think that reality is what is happening now and that our lives are what we make of them. We can be whoever we want. History is the story of alien people who lived in a strange world. What could it possibly have to do with us here and now?

In an article published more than twenty-five years ago, the historian Lynn White, Jr., argued that our current ecological crisis is rooted in the Judeo-Christian cultural tradition. White's article touched off a spirited debate. Some thinkers have argued that White is too hard on the Judeo-Christian tradition. They insist that the God of the Bible did not give the Earth to humans for them to pillage and destroy. Even Vice President Al Gore has gotten into the act, writing in his book, *Earth in the Balance*, that "the biblical concept of dominion is quite different from the concept of domination," since having dominion over the earth requires believers to " 'care for' the earth even as they 'work' it." (p. 243). Others have thought that White gives too much credit to ideas. On their view, religions and philosophies are created to rationalize what we do for economic or political reasons. The Judeo-Christian tradition could no more be a cause of our ecological crisis than numbers can cause earthquakes.

While we cannot pretend to settle these controversies here, it is important to recognize that ideas have consequences. They shape the concepts and vocabularies that we use to approach the problems of our time. For this reason, if no other, it is important for us to examine our cultural heritage. We may be embarrassed by it or find it ugly or despicable. But through this examination we may also find important threads that can help illuminate our present problems. At the very least, from this examination we can learn to understand ourselves better.

In virtually all cultures and religious traditions, one can find creation myths. In the Judeo-Christian story, some have found a vindication of the value of nature, while others have seen a mandate for human dominance. We are told

1

that before creating Adam, God surveyed nonhuman nature and "saw that it was good"; he blessed the animals and commanded them to be "fruitful and multiply." In the peaceable kingdom before Adam's sin, both humans and animals ate only vegetables. But after violence and corruption swept the Earth, God decided to "make an end to all flesh." Before bringing the flood, however, he commanded Noah to take into his ark two of each animal. After the waters had receded, God gave the animals to Noah for food, but he promised both Noah and the animals that he would never again send a flood to destroy the Earth.

It may be that there is no single attitude toward nature that is expressed in the Bible. Nevertheless, it is undeniable that for most of its history Western culture has been characterized by a highly exploitative attitude toward nature, often justified by appeals to God's plans.

Another important influence on Western culture is the ancient Greek philosophical tradition. Artistotle (384–322 B.C.E.), who believed in "natural teleology," was a central figure. Natural teleology is the idea that everything in nature exists to serve some purpose; for example, the sky rains in order for corn to grow. According to Aristotle, there is a hierarchy in nature: plants exist for the sake of animals, and animals exist for the sake of humans.

The view that humans are at the pinnacle of nature and that everything exists for their sake has been an important influence on Western political and legal thought. The British philosopher John Locke (1632–1704) developed a theory of property that is often appealed to today. According to Locke, God gave all of nature, including the "inferior creatures," to mankind to hold in common. But land that was left idle was a waste and without value. By "mixing" his labor with land—tilling, cultivating, planting, and so on—a man improved the land and thereby came to own it.

The idea that humans are at the center of nature and everything was created to serve their purposes received a serious blow from the British naturalist Charles Darwin (1809–1882). Darwin showed how purposeless biological processes operating over geological time could have produced the diversity of life that seems so miraculous. Rather than God creating distinct, immutable species arranged in hierarchical order with humans at the top, Darwin argued for the continuity of all life. In his view, humans are not so much fallen angels as risen apes.

John Muir (1838–1914), born in Scotland, was the founder of the Sierra Club and has since become the patron saint of the environmental movement. He spent much of his life on long treks through various wilderness areas, writing about what he saw. In a more pointed way than Darwin, Muir ridiculed the idea that humans are the divinely appointed masters of nature and that it is nature's purpose to serve human interests. If God created nature solely to serve human interests, then what are we to make of human-eating animals, mosquitos, and poisonous plants?

If Muir was the patron saint of the early environmental movement, then Aldo Leopold (1887–1948) was its philosopher. Leopold was trained in wildlife management, but as his career unfolded he produced a remarkable series of essays exploring the profound values that exist in nature. He argued that our relationship with the land is fundamentally an ethical one and envisioned an expanding circle of morality that might one day lead us to see ourselves as citizens of the "land community" rather than conquerors of it.

A number of nineteenth-century thinkers had visionary views about the human relationship to nature. Henry David Thoreau (1817–1862)—vegetarian, antiwar activist, and all-around American eccentric—wrote movingly about nature. In both his life and work, Thoreau expressed his commitment to the strength, integrity, and life-promoting character of wildness. John Stuart Mill (1806–1873), the most famous of utilitarian philosophers, produced works on moral and political theory, language, logic, and science that are read and admired even today. Less well known are his views about the importance of reaching a "stationary state" in which population and economic growth stabilize, and we are free to devote ourselves to improving the quality of life. Mill warns of a future in which "solitude is extirpated," and every piece of land and field of flowers is brought into cultivation to feed the growing mass of humanity.

In recent years, there has been an explosion of writing about nature, from many different perspectives. Daniel Botkin, an American ecologist, has been in the forefront of rethinking the science of ecology. Instead of viewing nature as a machine and humans as its operators, Botkin argues that we need to regard nature as a living system, global in scale, in which humans are an active participant. Vandana Shiva is a feminist philosopher who left a career in India's nuclear-energy program in order to devote herself to political and social activism. She criticizes the traditions of Western science, which she sees as leading to "maldevelopment" and the exploitation of women and nature. Drawing on Hindu mythology, political analysis, and social movements, Shiva calls for major shifts in values and behavior. Stephen Jay Gould is a biologist, paleontologist, and historian of science who believes that humans have a remarkable proclivity for exaggerating their role in the natural world. Nature will survive our insults, but we may not. According to Gould, we have to make a pact with the planet, akin to the Golden Rule, in which we commit ourselves to treating the Earth as we wish to be treated ourselves.

This part of the book presents a sample of the vast array of threads that make up the tapestry that is our contemporary view of nature. Some of the views presented here may seem anachronistic, others enlightening, and still others may be so much a part of how we view nature that we have trouble seeing them at all. Whatever we may think about any particular part of the tapestry, it is important for us to occasionally stop and contemplate it. If we are to do better by nature, we will have to learn more about ourselves. Examining how we got into our present predicament is one way of doing that.

Further Reading

Attfield, Robin. *The Ethics of Environmental Concern*. 2nd ed. Athens: University of Georgia Press, 1992.

Part 1 is a survey of Judeo-Christian and Enlightenment attitudes toward nature.

Callicott, J. Baird, and Roger Ames, eds. *Nature in Asian Traditions and Thought: Essays in Environmental Philosophy*. Albany: State University of New York Press, 1989.

A collection of essays addressing attitudes toward nature in the Chinese, Japanese, and Indian traditions.

Engel, J. Ronald, and Joan Gibb Engel, eds. *Ethics of Environment and Development: Global Challenge and International Response*. Tucson: University of Arizona Press, 1990.

A volume of papers by scholars from all over the world that addresses environmental ethics in Africa, Asia, Latin America, Europe, and North America.

Glacken, Clarence. *Traces on the Rhodian Shore: Nature and Culture in Western Thought from Ancient Times to the End of the Eighteenth Century*. Berkeley: University of California Press, 1967.

A magisterial study of attitudes toward nature from the Greeks to the Enlightenment.

Gore, Al. *Earth in the Balance: Ecology and the Human Spirit*. Boston: Houghton Mifflin, 1992.

An extraordinary book in which the vice president of the United States argues that the world is on the brink of environmental catastrophe, and sketches the sort of worldwide mobilization that is required to save us from disaster.

Hargrove, Eugene C. *Foundations of Environmental Ethics*. Englewood Cliffs N.J.: Prentice-Hall, 1989.

Parts 1 and 2 discuss philosophical views of nature, land use, aesthetic and scientific attitudes toward the environment, and wildlife protection.

Merchant, Carolyn. *The Death of Nature: Women, Ecology, and the Scientific Revolution*. New York: Harper & Row, 1980.

The classic study of how the scientific revolution affected cultural attitudes toward women and nature.

Oelschlaeger, Max. *The Idea of Wilderness from Prehistory to the Age of Ecology*. New Haven, Conn.: Yale University Press, 1991.

A historical and philosophical defense of a postmodern conception of wilderness.

The Historical Roots of Our Ecologic Crisis

Lynn White, Jr.

A CONVERSATION with Aldous Huxley not infrequently put one at the receiving end of an unforgettable monologue. About a year before his lamented death he was discoursing on a favorite topic: man's unnatural treatment of nature and its sad results. To illustrate his point he told how, during the previous summer, he had returned to a little valley in England where he had spent many happy months as a child. Once it had been composed of delightful grassy blades; now it was becoming overgrown with unsightly brush because the rabbits that formerly kept such growth under control had largely succumbed to a disease, myxomatosis, that was deliberately introduced by the local farmers to reduce the rabbits' destruction of crops. Being something of a Philistine, I could be silent no longer, even in the interests of great rhetoric. I interrupted to point out that the rabbit itself had been brought as a domestic animal to England in 1176, presumably to improve the protein diet of the peasantry.

All forms of life modify their contexts. The most spectacular and benign instance is doubtless the coral polyp. By serving its own ends, it has created a vast undersea world favorable to thousands of other kinds of animals and plants. Ever since man became a numerous species he has affected his environment notably. The hypothesis that his fire-drive method of hunting created the world's great grasslands and helped to exterminate the monster mammals of the Pleistocene from much of the globe is plausible, if not proved. For six millennia at least, the banks of the lower Nile have been a human artifact rather than the swampy African jungle which nature, apart from man, would have made it. The Aswan Dam, flooding 5,000 square miles, is only the latest stage in a long process. In many regions terracing or irrigation, overgrazing, the cutting of forests by Romans to build ships to fight Carthaginians or by Crusaders to solve the logistics problems of their expeditions, have profoundly changed some ecologies. Observation that the French landscape falls into two basic types, the open fields of the north and the *bocage* of the south and west, inspired Marc Bloch to undertake his classic study of medieval agricultural methods. Quite unintentionally, changes in human ways often affect nonhu-

5

man nature. It has been noted, for example, that the advent of the automobile eliminated huge flocks of sparrows that once fed on the horse manure littering every street.

The history of ecologic change is still so rudimentary that we know little about what really happened, or what the results were. The extinction of the European aurochs as late as 1627 would seem to have been a simple case of overenthusiastic hunting. On more intricate matters it often is impossible to, find solid information. For a thousand years or more the Frisians and Hollanders have been pushing back the North Sea, and the process is culminating in our own time in the reclamation of the Zuider Zee. What, if any, species of animals, birds, fish, shore life, or plants have died out in the process? In their epic combat with Neptune have the Netherlanders overlooked ecological values in such a way that the quality of human life in the Netherlands has suffered? I cannot discover that the questions have ever been asked, much less answered.

People, then, have often been a dynamic element in their own environment, but in the present state of historical scholarship we usually do not know exactly when, where, or with what effects man-induced changes came. As we enter the last third of the twentieth century, however, concern for the problem of ecologic backlash is mounting feverishly. Natural science, conceived as the effort to understand the nature of things, had flourished in several eras and among several peoples. Similarly there had been an age-old accumulation of technological skills, sometimes growing rapidly, sometimes slowly. But it was not until about four generations ago that Western Europe and North America arranged a marriage between science and technology, a union of the theoretical and the empirical approaches to our natural environment. The emergence in widespread practice of the Baconian creed that scientific knowledge means technological power over nature can scarcely be dated before about 1850, save in the chemical industries, where it is anticipated in the eighteenth century. Its acceptance as a normal pattern of action may mark the greatest event in human history since the invention of agriculture, and perhaps in nonhuman terrestrial history as well.

Almost at once the new situation forced the crystallization of the novel concept of ecology; indeed, the word *ecology* first appeared in the English language in 1873. Today, less than a century later, the impact of our race upon the environment has so increased in force that it has changed in essence. When the first cannons were fired, in the early fourteenth century, they affected ecology by sending workers scrambling to the forests and mountains for more potash, sulfur, iron ore, and charcoal, with some resulting erosion and deforestation. Hydrogen bombs are of a different order: a war fought with them might alter the genetics of all life on this planet. By 1285 London had a smog problem arising from the burning of soft coal, but our present combustion of fossil fuels threatens to change the chemistry of the globe's atmosphere as a whole, with consequences which we are only beginning to guess. With the population explosion, the carcinoma of planless urbanism, the new geological deposits of sewage and garbage, surely no creature other than man has ever managed to foul its nest in such short order.

There are many calls to action, but specific proposals, however worthy as individual items, seem too partial, palliative, negative: ban the bomb, tear down the billboards, give the Hindus contraceptives and tell them to eat their sacred cows. The simplest solution to any suspect change is, of course, to stop it, or, better yet, to revert to a romanticized past: make those ugly gasoline stations look like Anne Hathaway's cottage or (in the Far West) like ghost-town saloons. The "wilderness-area" mentality invariably advocates deep-freezing an ecology, whether San Gimignano or the High Sierra, as it was before the first Kleenex was dropped. But neither atavism nor prettification will cope with the ecologic crisis of our time.

What shall we do? No one yet knows. Unless we think about fundamentals, our specific measures may produce new backlashes more serious than those they are designed to remedy.

As a beginning we should try to clarify our thinking by looking, in some historical depth, at the presuppositions that underlie modern technology and science. Science was traditionally aristocratic, speculative, intellectual in intent; technology was lower-class, empirical, action-oriented. The quite sudden fusion of these two, towards the middle of the nineteenth century, is surely related to the slightly prior and contemporary democratic revolutions which, by reducing social barriers, tended to assert a functional unity of brain and hand. Our ecologic crisis is the product of an emerging, entirely novel, democratic culture. The issue is whether a democratized world can survive its own implications. Presumably we cannot unless we rethink our axioms.

The Western Traditions of Technology and Science

One thing is so certain that it seems stupid to verbalize it: both modern technology and modern science are distinctively *occidental*. Our technology has absorbed elements from all over the world, notably from China, yet everywhere today, whether in Japan or in Nigeria, successful technology is Western. Our science is the heir to all the sciences of the past, especially perhaps to the work of the great Islamic scientists of the Middle Ages, who so often outdid the ancient Greeks in skill and perspicacity: al-Rāzī in medicine, for example; or ibn-al-Haytham in optics; or Omar Khāyyám in mathematics. Indeed, not a few works of such geniuses seem to have vanished in the original Arabic and to survive only in medieval Latin translations that helped to lay the foundations for later Western developments. Today, around the globe, all significant science is Western in style and method, whatever the pigmentation or language of the scientists.

A second pair of facts is less well recognized because they result from quite

recent historical scholarship. The leadership of the West, both in technology
and in science, is far older than the so-called scientific revolution of the seventeenth century or the so-called industrial revolution of the eighteenth century.
These terms are in fact outmoded and obscure the true nature of what they try
to describe—significant stages in two long and separate developments. By A.D.
1000 at the latest—and perhaps, feebly, as much as 200 years earlier—the West
began to apply water power to industrial processes other than milling grain.
This was followed in the late twelfth century by the harnessing of wind power.
From simple beginnings, but with remarkable consistency of style, the West
rapidly expanded its skills in the development of power machinery, laborsaving
devices, and automation. Those who doubt should contemplate that most
monumental achievement in the history of automation: the weight-driven mechanical clock, which appeared in two forms in the early fourteenth century.
Not in craftsmanship but in basic technological capacity, the Latin West of the
later Middle Ages far outstripped its elaborate, sophisticated, and esthetically
magnificent sister cultures, Byzantium and Islam. In 1444 a great Greek ecclesi-
astic, Bessarion, who had gone to Italy, wrote a letter to a prince in Greece. He
is amazed by the superiority of Western ships, arms, textiles, glass. But above
all he is astonished by the spectacle of waterwheels sawing timbers and pump-
ing the bellows of blast furnaces. Clearly, he had seen nothing of the sort in the
Near East.

By the end of the fifteenth century the technological superiority of Europe
was such that its small, mutually hostile nations could spill out over all the rest
of the world, conquering, looting, and colonizing. The symbol of this technological superiority is the fact that Portugal, one of the weakest states of the
Occident, was able to become, and to remain for a century, mistress of the East
Indies. And we must remember that the technology of Vasco da Gama and
Albuquerque was built by pure empiricism, drawing remarkably little support
or inspiration from science.

In the present-day vernacular understanding, modern science is supposed to
have begun in 1543, when both Copernicus and Vesalius published their great
works. It is no derogation of their accomplishments, however, to point out that
such structures as the *Fabrica* and the *De revolutionibus* do not appear overnight.
The distinctive Western tradition of science, in fact, began in the late eleventh
century with a massive movement of translation of Arabic and Greek scientific
works into Latin. A few notable books—Theophrastus', for example—escaped
the West's avid new appetite for science, but within less than 200 years effectively the entire corpus of Greek and Muslim science was available in Latin, and
was being eagerly read and criticized in the new European universities. Out of
criticism arose new observation, speculation, and increasing distrust of ancient
authorities. By the late thirteenth century Europe had seized global scientific
leadership from the faltering hands of Islam. It would be as absurd to deny the
profound originality of Newton, Galileo, or Copernicus as to deny that of the
fourteenth-century scholastic scientists like Buridan or Oresme on whose work

they built. Before the eleventh century, science scarcely existed in the Latin West, even in Roman times. From the eleventh century onward, the scientific sector of occidental culture has increased in a steady crescendo.

Since both our technological and our scientific movements got their start, acquired their character, and achieved world dominance in the Middle Ages, it would seem that we cannot understand their nature or their present impact upon ecology without examining fundamental medieval assumptions and developments.

Medieval View of Man and Nature

Until recently, agriculture has been the chief occupation even in "advanced" societies; hence, any change in methods of tillage has much importance. Early plows, drawn by two oxen, did not normally turn the sod but merely scratched it. Thus, cross-plowing was needed and fields tended to be squarish. In the fairly light soils and semi-arid climates of the Near East and Mediterranean, this worked well. But such a plow was inappropriate to the wet climate and often sticky soils of northern Europe. By the latter part of the seventh century after Christ, however, following obscure beginnings, certain northern peasants were using an entirely new kind of plow, equipped with a vertical knife to cut the line of the furrow, a horizontal share to slice under the sod, and a moldboard to turn it over. The friction of this plow with the soil was so great that it normally required not two but eight oxen. It attacked the land with such violence that cross-plowing was not needed, and fields tended to be shaped in long strips.

In the days of the scratch-plow, fields were distributed generally in units capable of supporting a single family. Subsistence farming was the presupposition. But no peasant owned eight oxen: to use the new and more efficient plow, peasants pooled their oxen to form large plow-teams, originally receiving (it would appear) plowed strips in proportion to their contribution. Thus, distribution of land was based no longer on the needs of a family but, rather, on the capacity of a power machine to till the earth. Man's relation to the soil was profoundly changed. Formerly man had been part of nature; now he was the exploiter of nature. Nowhere else in the world did farmers develop any analogous agricultural implement. Is it coincidence that modern technology, with its ruthlessness toward nature, has so largely been produced by descendants of these peasants of northern Europe?

This same exploitive attitude appears slightly before A.D. 830 in Western illustrated calendars. In older calendars the months were shown as passive personifications. The new Frankish calendars, which set the style for the Middle Ages, are very different: they show men coercing the world around them— plowing, harvesting, chopping trees, butchering pigs. Man and nature are two things, and man is master.

These novelties seem to be in harmony with larger intellectual patterns.

What people do about their ecology depends on what they think about them-selves in relation to things around them. Human ecology is deeply conditioned by beliefs about our nature and destiny—that is, by religion. To Western eyes this is very evident in, say, India or Ceylon. It is equally true of ourselves and of our medieval ancestors.

The victory of Christianity over paganism was the greatest psychic revolu-tion in the history of our culture. It has become fashionable today to say that, for better or worse, we live in "the post-Christian age." Certainly the forms of our thinking and language have largely ceased to be Christian, but to my eye the substance often remains amazingly akin to that of the past. Our daily habits of action, for example, are dominated by an implicit faith in perpetual progress which was unknown either to Greco-Roman antiquity or to the Orient. It is rooted in, and is indefensible apart from, Judeo-Christian teleology. The fact that Communists share it merely helps to show what can be demonstrated on many other grounds: that Marxism, like Islam, is a Judeo-Christian heresy. We continue today to live, as we have lived for about 1,700 years, very largely in a context of Christian axioms.

What did Christianity tell people about their relations with the environment?

While many of the world's mythologies provide stories of creation, Greco-Roman mythology was singularly incoherent in this respect. Like Aristotle, the intellectuals of the ancient West denied that the visible world had had a begin-ning. Indeed, the idea of a beginning was impossible in the framework of their cyclical notion of time. In sharp contrast, Christianity inherited from Judaism not only a concept of time as nonrepetitive and linear but also a striking story of creation. By gradual stages a loving and all-powerful God had created light and darkness, the heavenly bodies, the earth and all its plants, animals, birds, and fishes. Finally, God had created Adam and, as an afterthought, Eve, to keep man from being lonely. Man named all the animals, thus establishing his dominance over them. God planned all of this explicitly for man's benefit and rule: no item in the physical creation had any purpose save to serve man's purposes. And, although man's body is made of clay, he is not simply part of nature: he is made in God's image.

Especially in its Western form, Christianity is the most anthropocentric religion the world has seen. As early as the second century both Tertullian and Saint Irenaeus of Lyons were insisting that when God shaped Adam he was foreshadowing the image of the Incarnate Christ, the Second Adam. Man shares, in great measure, God's transcendence of nature. Christianity, in abso-lute contrast to ancient paganism and Asia's religions (except, perhaps, Zoroastrianism), not only established a dualism of man and nature but also insisted that it is God's will that man exploit nature for his proper ends.

At the level of the common people this worked out in an interesting way. In antiquity every tree, every spring, every stream, every hill had its own *genius loci*, its guardian spirit. These spirits were accessible to men, but were very unlike men; centaurs, fauns, and mermaids show their ambivalence. Before one cut a tree, mined a mountain, or dammed a brook, it was important to placate the spirit in charge of that particular situation, and to keep it placated. By destroying pagan animism, Christianity made it possible to exploit nature in a mood of indifference to the feelings of natural objects.

It is often said that for animism the Church substituted the cult of saints. True; but the cult of saints is functionally quite different from animism. The saint is not *in* natural objects; he may have special shrines, but his citizenship is in heaven. Moreover, a saint is entirely a man; he can be approached in human terms. In addition to saints, Christianity of course also had angels and demons inherited from Judaism and perhaps, at one remove, from Zoroastrianism. But these were all as mobile as the saints themselves. The spirits *in* natural objects, which formerly had protected nature from man, evaporated. Man's effective monopoly on spirit in this world was confirmed, and the old inhibitions to the exploitation of nature crumbled.

When one speaks in such sweeping terms, a note of caution is in order. Christianity is a complex faith, and its consequences differ in differing contexts. What I have said may well apply to the medieval West, where in fact technology made spectacular advances. But the Greek East, a highly civilized realm of equal Christian devotion, seems to have produced no marked technological innovation after the late seventh century, when Greek fire was invented. The key to the contrast may perhaps be found in a difference in the tonality of piety and thought which students of comparative theology find between the Greek and the Latin churches. The Greeks believed that sin was intellectual blindness, and that salvation was found in illumination, orthodoxy—that is, clear thinking. The Latins, on the other hand, felt that sin was moral evil, and that salvation was to be found in right conduct. Eastern theology has been intellectualist. Western theology has been voluntarist. The Greek saint contemplates; the Western saint acts. The implications of Christianity for the conquest of nature would change more easily in the Western atmosphere.

The Christian dogma of creation, which is found in the first clause of all the Creeds, has another meaning for our comprehension of today's ecologic crisis. By revelation, God had given man the Bible, the Book of Scripture. But since God had made nature, nature also must reveal the divine mentality. The religious study of nature for the better understanding of God was known as natural theology. In the early Church, and always in the Greek East, nature was conceived primarily as a symbolic system through which God speaks to men: the ant is a sermon to sluggards; rising flames are the symbol of the soul's aspiration. This view of nature was essentially artistic rather than scientific. While Byzantium preserved and copied great numbers of ancient Greek scientific texts, science as we conceive it could scarcely flourish in such an ambience.

However, in the Latin West by the early thirteenth century natural theology was following a very different bent. It was ceasing to be the decoding of the physical symbols of God's communication with man and was becoming the effort to understand God's mind by discovering how his creation operates. The rainbow was no longer simply a symbol of hope first sent to Noah after the Deluge: Robert Grosseteste, Friar Roger Bacon, and Theodoric of Freiberg produced startlingly sophisticated work on the optics of the rainbow, but they did it as a venture in religious understanding. From the thirteenth century onward, up to and including Leibnitz and Newton, every major scientist, in effect, explained his motivations in religious terms. Indeed, if Galileo had not been so expert an amateur theologian he would have got into far less trouble: the professionals resented his intrusion. And Newton seems to have regarded himself more as a theologian than as a scientist. It was not until the late eighteenth century that the hypothesis of God became unnecessary to many scientists.

It is often hard for the historian to judge, when men explain why they are doing what they want to do, whether they are offering real reasons or merely culturally acceptable reasons. The consistency with which scientists during the long formative centuries of Western science said that the task and the reward of the scientist was "to think God's thoughts after him" leads one to believe that this was their real motivation. If so, then modern Western science was cast in a matrix of Christian theology. The dynamism of religious devotion, shaped by the Judeo-Christian dogma of creation, gave it impetus.

An Alternative Christian View

We would seem to be headed toward conclusions unpalatable to many Christians. Since both *science* and *technology* are blessed words in our contemporary vocabulary, some may be happy at the notions, first, that, viewed historically, modern science is an extrapolation of natural theology and, second, that modern technology is at least partly to be explained as an occidental, voluntarist realization of the Christian dogma of man's transcendence of, and rightful mastery over, nature. But, as we now recognize, somewhat over a century ago science and technology—hitherto quite separate activities—joined to give mankind powers which, to judge by many of the ecologic effects, are out of control. If so, Christianity bears a huge burden of guilt.

I personally doubt that disastrous ecologic backlash can be avoided simply by applying to our problems more science and more technology. Our science and technology have grown out of Christian attitudes toward man's relation to nature which are almost universally held not only by Christians and neo-Christians but also by those who fondly regard themselves as post-Christians. Despite Copernicus, all the cosmos rotates around our little globe. Despite Darwin, we are *not*, in our hearts, part of the natural process. We are superior to nature, contemptuous of it, willing to use it for our slightest whim. The newly elected governor of California, like myself a churchman, but less troubled than I, spoke for the Christian tradition when he said (as is alleged), "When you've seen one redwood tree, you've seen them all." To a Christian a tree can be no more than a physical fact. The whole concept of the sacred grove is alien to Christianity and to the ethos of the West. For nearly two millennia Christian missionaries have been chopping down sacred groves, which are idolatrous because they assume spirit in nature.

What we do about ecology depends on our ideas of the man–nature relationship. More science and more technology are not going to get us out of the present ecologic crisis until we find a new religion, or rethink our old one. The beatniks, who are the basic revolutionaries of our time, show a sound instinct in their affinity for Zen Buddhism, which conceives of the man–nature relationship as very nearly the mirror image of the Christian view. Zen, however, is as deeply conditioned by Asian history as Christianity is by the experience of the West, and I am dubious of its viability among us.

Possibly we should ponder the greatest radical in Christian history since Christ: Saint Francis of Assisi. The prime miracle of Saint Francis is the fact that he did not end at the stake, as many of his left-wing followers did. He was so clearly heretical that a general of the Franciscan Order, Saint Bonaventura, a great and perceptive Christian, tried to suppress the early accounts of Franciscanism. The key to an understanding of Francis is his belief in the virtue of humility—not merely for the individual but for man as a species. Francis tried to depose man from his monarchy over creation and set up a democracy of all God's creatures. With him the ant is no longer simply a homily for the lazy, flames a sign of the thrust of the soul toward union with God; now they are Brother Ant and Sister Fire, praising the Creator in their own ways as Brother Man does in his.

Later commentators have said that Francis preached to the birds as a rebuke to men who would not listen. The records do not read so: he urged the little birds to praise God, and in spiritual ecstasy they flapped their wings and chirped rejoicing. Legends of saints, especially the Irish saints, had long told of their dealings with animals but always, I believe, to show their human dominance over creatures. With Francis it is different. The land around Gubbio in the Apennines was being ravaged by a fierce wolf. Saint Francis, says the legend, talked to the wolf and persuaded him of the error of his ways. The wolf repented, died in the odor of sanctity, and was buried in consecrated ground.

What Sir Steven Ruciman calls "the Franciscan docrine of the animal soul" was quickly stamped out. Quite possibly it was in part inspired, consciously or unconsciously, by the belief in reincarnation held by the Cathar heretics who at that time teemed in Italy and southern France, and who presumably had got it originally from India. It is significant that at just the same moment, about 1200, traces of metempsychosis are found also in western Judaism, in the Provençal *Cabala*. But Francis held neither to transmigration of souls nor to pantheism. His view of nature and of man rested on a unique sort of pan-psychism of all things animate and inanimate, designed for the glorification of their transcendent Creator, who, in the ultimate gesture of cosmic humility, assumed flesh, lay helpless in a manger, and hung dying on a scaffold.

I am not suggesting that many contemporary Americans who are concerned about our ecologic crisis will be either able or willing to counsel with wolves or exhort birds. However, the present increasing disruption of the global environment is the product of a dynamic technology and science which were originating in the Western medieval world against which Saint Francis was rebelling in so original a way. Their growth cannot be understood historically apart from distinctive attitudes toward nature which are deeply grounded in Christian dogma. The fact that most people do not think of these attitudes as Christian is irrelevant. No new set of basic values has been accepted in our society to displace those of Christianity. Hence we shall continue to have a worsening ecologic crisis until we reject the Christian axiom that nature has no reason for existence save to serve man.

The greatest spiritual revolutionary in Western history, Saint Francis, proposed what he thought was an alternative Christian view of nature and man's relation to it: he tried to substitute the idea of the equality of all creatures, including man, for the idea of man's limitless rule of creation. He failed. Both our present science and our present technology are so tinctured with orthodox Christian arrogance toward nature that no solution for our ecologic crisis can be expected from them alone. Since the roots of our trouble are so largely religious, the remedy must also be essentially religious, whether we call it that or not. We must rethink and refeel our nature and destiny. The profoundly religious, but heretical, sense of primitive Franciscans for the spiritual autonomy of all parts of nature may point a direction. I propose Francis as a patron saint for ecologists.

[From] Genesis

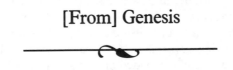

Chapter 1

In the beginning God created the heavens and the earth. 2 The earth was without form and void, and darkness was upon the face of the deep; and the Spirit of God was moving over the face of the waters.

3 And God said, "Let there be light"; and there was light. 4 And God saw that the light was good; and God separated the light from the darkness. 5 God called the light Day, and the darkness he called Night. And there was evening and there was morning, one day.

6 And God said, "Let there be a firmament in the midst of the waters, and let it separate the waters from the waters." 7 And God made the firmament and

separated the waters which were under the firmament from the waters which were above the firmament. And it was so. [8] And God called the firmament Heaven. And there was evening and there was morning, a second day.

9 And God said, "Let the waters under the heavens be gathered together into one place, and let the dry land appear." And it was so. [10] God called the dry land Earth, and the waters that were gathered together he called Seas. And God saw that it was good. [11] And God said, "Let the earth put forth vegetation, plants yielding seed, and fruit trees bearing fruit in which is their seed, each according to its kind, upon the earth." And it was so. [12] The earth brought forth vegetation, plants yielding seed according to their own kinds, and trees bearing fruit in which is their seed, each according to its kind. And God saw that it was good. [13] And there was evening and there was morning, a third day.

14 And God said, "Let there be lights in the firmament of the heavens to separate the day from the night; and let them be for signs and for seasons and for days and years, [15] and let them be lights in the firmament of the heavens to give light upon the earth." And it was so. [16] And God made the two great lights, the greater light to rule the day, and the lesser light to rule the night; he made the stars also. [17] And God set them in the firmament of the heavens to give light upon the earth, [18] to rule over the day and over the night, and to separate the light from the darkness. And God saw that it was good. [19] And there was evening and there was morning, a fourth day.

20 And God said, "Let the waters bring forth swarms of living creatures, and let birds fly above the earth across the firmament of the heavens." [21] So God created the great sea monsters and every living creature that moves, with which the waters swarm according to their kinds, and every winged bird according to its kind. And God saw that it was good. [22] And God blessed them saying, "Be fruitful and multiply and fill the waters in the seas, and let the birds multiply on the earth." [23] And there was evening and there was morning, a fifth day.

24 And God said, "Let the earth bring forth living creatures according to their kinds: cattle and creeping things and beasts of the earth according to their kinds." And it was so. [25] And God made the beasts of the earth according to their kinds and the cattle according to their kinds, and everything that creeps upon the ground according to its kind. And God saw that it was good.

26 Then God said, "Let us make man in our image, after our likeness and let them have dominion over the fish of the sea, and over the birds of the air, and over the cattle, and over all the earth, and over every creeping thing that creeps upon the earth." [27] So God created man in his own image, in the image of God he created him; male and female he created them. [28] And God blessed them, and God said to them, "Be fruitful and multiply, and fill the earth and subdue it; and have dominion over the fish of the sea and over the birds of the air and over every living thing that moves upon the earth." [29] And God said, "Behold, I have given you every plant yielding seed which is upon the face of all the earth, and every tree with seed in its fruit; you shall have them for food. [30] And to every beast of

the earth, and to every bird of the air, and to everything that creeps on the earth, everything that has the breath of life,I given every green plant for food." And it was so. ³¹ And God saw everything that he had made, and behold, it was very good. And there was evening and there was morning, a sixth day. . . .

Chapter 6

11 Now the earth was corrupt in God's sight, and the earth was filled with violence. ¹² And God saw the earth, and behold, it was corrupt; for all flesh had corrupted their way upon the earth. ¹³ And God said to Noah, "I have determined to make an end of all flesh; for the earth is filled with violence through them; behold, I will destroy them with the earth. ¹⁴ Make yourself an ark of gopher wood; make rooms in the ark, and cover it inside and out with pitch. ¹⁵ This is how you are to make it: the length of the ark three hundred cubits, its breadth fifty cubits, and its height thirty cubits. ¹⁶ Make a roof for the ark, and finish it to a cubit above; and set the door of the ark in its side; make it with lower, second, and third decks. ¹⁷ For behold, I will bring a flood of waters upon the earth, to destroy all flesh in which is the breath of life from under heaven; everything that is on the earth shall die. ¹⁸ But I will establish my covenant with you; and you shall come into the ark, you, your sons, your wife, and your sons' wives with you. ¹⁹ And of every living thing of all flesh, you shall bring two of every sort into the ark, to keep them alive with you; they shall be male and female. ²⁰ Of the birds according to their kinds, and of the animals according to their kinds, of every creeping thing of the ground according to its kind, two of every sort shall come in to you, to keep them alive. ²¹ Also take with you every sort of food that is eaten, and store it up; and it shall serve as food for you and for them." ²² Noah did this; he did all that God commanded him.

Chapter 7

Then the LORD said to Noah, "Go into the ark, you and all your household, for I have seen that you are righteous before me in this generation. ² Take with you seven pairs of all clean animals, the male and his mate; and a pair of the animals that are not clean, the male and his mate; ³ and seven pairs of the birds of the air also, male and female, to keep their kind alive upon the face of all the earth. ⁴ For in seven days I will send rain upon the earth forty days and forty nights; and every living thing that I have made I will blot out from the face of the ground." ⁵ And Noah did all that the LORD had commanded him.

6 Noah was six hundred years old when the flood of waters came upon the earth. ⁷ And Noah and his sons and his wife and his sons' wives with him went into the ark, to escape the waters of the flood. ⁸ Of clean animals, and of animals that are not clean, and of birds, and of everything that creeps on the ground, ⁹ two and two, male and female, went into the ark with Noah, as God

had commanded Noah. [10] And after seven days the waters of the flood came upon the earth.

11 In the six hundredth year of Noah's life, in the second month, on the seventeenth day of the month, on that day all the fountains of the great deep burst forth, and the windows of the heavens were opened. [12] And rain fell upon the earth forty days and forty nights. [13] On the very same day Noah and his sons, Shem and Ham and Japheth, and Noah's wife and the three wives of his sons with them entered the ark, [14] they and every beast according to its kind, and all the cattle according to their kinds, and every creeping thing that creeps on the earth according to its kind, and every bird according to its kind, every bird of every sort. [15] They went into the ark with Noah, two and two of all flesh in which there was the breath of life. [16] And they that entered, male and female of all flesh, went in as God had commanded him; and the LORD shut him in.

17 The flood continued forty days upon the earth; and the waters increased, and bore up the ark, and it rose high above the earth. [18] The waters prevailed and increased greatly upon the earth; and the ark floated on the face of the waters. [19] And the waters prevailed so mightily upon the earth that all the high mountains under the whole heaven were covered; [20] the waters prevailed above the mountains, covering them fifteen cubits deep. [21] And all flesh died that moved upon the earth, birds, cattle, beasts, all swarming creatures that swarm upon the earth, and every man; [22] everything on the dry land in whose nostrils was the breath of life died. [23] He blotted out every living thing that was upon the face of the ground, man and animals and creeping things and birds of the air; they were blotted out from the earth. Only Noah was left, and those that were with him in the ark. [24] And the waters prevailed upon the earth a hundred and fifty days.

Chapter 8

But God remembered Noah and all the beasts and all the cattle that were with him in the ark. And God made a wind blow over the earth, and the waters subsided; [2] the fountains of the deep and the windows of the heavens were closed, the rain from the heavens was restrained, [3] and the waters receded from the earth continually. At the end of a hundred and fifty days the waters had abated; [4] and in the seventh month, on the seventeenth day of the month, the ark came to rest upon the mountains of Ar'arat. [5] And the waters continued to abate until the tenth month; in the tenth month, on the first day of the month, the tops of the mountains were seen.

6 At the end of forty days Noah opened the window of the ark which he had made, [7] and sent forth a raven; and it went to and fro until the waters were dried up from the earth. [8] Then he sent forth a dove from him to see if the waters had subsided from the face of the ground; [9] but the dove found no place to set her foot, and she returned to him to the ark, for the waters were still on the face of the whole earth. So he put forth his hand and took her and brought

her into the ark with him. ¹⁰ He waited another seven days, and again he sent forth the dove out of the ark; ¹¹ and the dove came back to him in the evening, and lo, in her mouth a freshly plucked olive leaf; so Noah knew that the waters had subsided from the earth. ¹² Then he waited another seven days, and sent forth the dove; and she did not return to him any more.

13 In the six hundred and first year, in the first month, the first day of the month, the waters were dried from off the earth; and Noah removed the covering of the ark, and looked, and behold, the face of the ground was dry. ¹⁴ In the second month, on the twenty-seventh day of the month, the earth was dry. ¹⁵ Then God said to Noah, ¹⁶ "Go forth from the ark, you and your wife, and your sons and your sons' wives with you. ¹⁷ Bring forth with you every living thing that is with you of all flesh—birds and animals and every creeping thing that creeps on the earth—that they may breed abundantly on the earth, and be fruitful and multiply upon the earth." ¹⁸ So Noah went forth, and his sons and his wife and his sons' wives with him. ¹⁹ And every beast, every creeping thing, and every bird, everything that moves upon the earth, went forth by families out of the ark.

20 Then Noah built an altar to the LORD, and took of every clean animal and of every clean bird, and offered burnt offerings on the altar. ²¹ And when the LORD smelled the pleasing odor, the LORD said in his heart, "I will never again curse the ground because of man, for the imagination of man's heart is evil from his youth; neither will I ever again destroy every living creature as I have done. ²² While the earth remains, seedtime and harvest, cold and heat, summer and winter, day and night, shall not cease."

Chapter 9

And God blessed Noah and his sons, and said to them, "Be fruitful and multiply, and fill the earth. ² The fear of you and the dread of you shall be upon every beast of the earth, and upon every bird of the air, upon everything that creeps on the ground and all the fish of the sea; into your hand they are delivered. ³ Every moving thing that lives shall be food for you; and as I gave you the green plants, I give you everything. ⁴ Only you shall not eat flesh with its life, that is, its blood. ⁵ For your lifeblood I will surely require a reckoning; of every beast I will require it and of man; of every man's brother I will require the life of man. ⁶ Whoever sheds the blood of man, by man shall his blood be shed; for God made man in his own image. ⁷ And you, be fruitful and multiply, bring forth abundantly on the earth and multiply in it."

8 Then God said to Noah and to his sons with him,⁹ "Behold, I establish my covenant with you and your descendants after you, ¹⁰ and with every living creature that is with you, the birds, the cattle, and every beast of the earth with you, as many as came out of the ark. ¹¹ I establish my covenant with you, that never again shall all flesh be cut off by the waters of a flood, and never again shall there be a flood to destroy the earth." ¹² And God said, "This is the sign

of the covenant which I make between me and you and every living creature that is with you, for all future generations.

[From] *Physics*

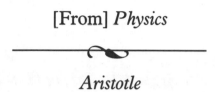

Aristotle

WHY SHOULDN'T nature operate not for the sake of something or because a result is better, but rather from necessity? That is, why shouldn't the sky rain not in order to make the corn grow, but rather of necessity (for, [as one might argue] what is taken up must cool, and what is cooled becomes water and comes down, with the result that the corn grows); similarly, if the corn rots on the threshing-floor, [we do not say that] it rains in order for the corn to rot, but that this [simply] happened. What prevents the parts of nature from being this way, e.g., why [shouldn't we ascribe] our teeth's coming up as they do to necessity? . . .

It is not possible that things should be this way. For teeth and all other natural things occur in a given way either always or for the most part; but nothing which occurs by chance or spontaneity [occurs always or for the most part]. . . . If then things occur either by coincidence or for the sake of something, it follows that [what occurs by nature] occurs for the sake of something. . . . Therefore, among the things which occur and exist in nature, [some things are] for the sake of something.

[From] *Politics*

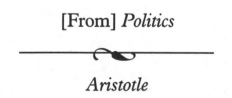

Aristotle

HENCE IT IS similarly clear that we must suppose that plants exist on account of animals . . . and the other animals for the sake of man, the tame ones because of their usefulness and as food, and if not all the wild ones, then most, on account of food and other assistance [they provide, in the form of] clothing and other tools which come from them. If, then, nature does nothing without an end and nothing in vain, it is necessary that nature made all these on account of men. Hence, the craft of war will be by nature a sort of art of acquisition (for hunting is a part of this), which one ought to use against wild beasts and those men who, those naturally ruled, do not submit, since this sort of war is just by nature.

[From] *The Second Treatise of Government*

John Locke

27. THOUGH THE EARTH and all inferior creatures be common to all men, yet every man has a property in his own person; this nobody has any right to but himself. The labor of his body and the work of his hands, we may say, are properly his. Whatsoever then he removes out of the state that nature has provided and left it in, he has mixed his labor with, and joined to it something that is his own, and thereby makes it his property.

28. He that is nourished by the acorns he picked up under an oak, or the apples he gathered from the trees in the wood, has certainly appropriated them to himself. Nobody can deny but the nourishment is his. I ask, then, When did they begin to be his? When he digested or when he ate or when he boiled or when he brought them home? Or when he picked them up? And it is plain, if the first gathering made them not his, nothing else could. That labor put a distinction between them and common; that added something to them more than nature, the common mother of all, had done; and so they became his private right. And will anyone say he had no right to those acorns or apples he thus appropriated because he had not the consent of all mankind to make them his? Was it a robbery thus to assume to himself what belonged to all in common? If such a consent as that was necessary, man had starved, notwithstanding the plenty God had given him. We see in commons, which remain so by compact, that it is the taking any part of what is common and removing it out of the state nature leaves it in which begins the property, without which the common is of no use. And the taking of this or that part does not depend on the express consent of all the commoners. Thus the grass my horse has bit, the turfs my servant has cut, and the ore I have digged in any place where I have a right to them in common with others, become my property without the assignation or consent of anybody. The labor that was

mine, removing them out of that common state they were in, has fixed my property in them. . . .

32. But the chief matter of property being now not the fruits of the earth and the beasts that subsist on it, but the earth itself, as that which takes in and carries with it all the rest, I think it is plain that property in that, too, is acquired as the former. As much land as a man tills, plants, improves, cultivates, and can use the product of, so much is his property. He by his labor does, as it were, enclose it from the common. Nor will it invalidate his right to say everybody else has an equal title to it, and therefore he cannot appropriate, he cannot enclose, without the consent of all his fellow commoners—all mankind. God, when he gave the world in common to all mankind, commanded man also to labor, and the penury of his condition required it of him. God and his reason commanded him to subdue the earth, i.e., improve it for the benefit of life, and therein lay out something upon it that was his own, his labor. He that in obedience to this command of God subdued, tilled, and sowed any part of it, thereby annexed to it something that was his property, which another had no title to, nor could without injury take from him. . . .

34. God gave the world to men in common; but since he gave it them for their benefit and the greatest conveniences of life they were capable to draw from it, it cannot be supposed he meant it should always remain common and uncultivated. He gave it to the use of the industrious and rational—and labor was to be his title to it—not to the fancy or covetousness of the quarrelsome and contentious. He that had as good left for his improvement as was already taken up needed not complain, ought not to meddle with what was already improved by another's labor; if he did, it is plain he desired the benefit of another's pains which he had no right to, and not the ground which God had given him in common with others to labors on, and whereof there was as good left as that already possessed, and more than he knew what to do with, or his industry could reach to.

35. . . . [H]ence subduing or cultivating the earth and having dominion, we see, are joined together. The one gave title to the other. So that God, by commanding to subdue, gave authority so far to appropriate; and the condition of human life which requires labor and material to work on necessarily introduces private possessions.

[From] *On the Origin of Species*

Charles Darwin

WITH RESPECT to the belief that organic beings have been created beautiful for the delight of man,—a belief which it has been pronounced is subversive of my whole theory,—I may first remark that the sense of beauty obviously depends on the nature of the mind, irrespective of any real quality in the admired object; and that the idea of what is beautiful, is not innate or unalterable. We see this, for instance, in the men of different races admiring an entirely different standard of beauty in their women. If beautiful objects had been created solely for man's gratification, it ought to be shown that before man appeared, there was less beauty on the face of the earth than since he came on the stage. Were the beautiful volute and cone shells of the Eocene epoch, and the gracefully sculptured ammonites of the Secondary period, created that man might ages afterwards admire them in his cabinet? Few objects are more beautiful than the minute siliceous cases of the diatomaceæ: were these created that they might be examined and admired under the higher powers of the microscope? . . .

Authors of the highest eminence seem to be fully satisfied with the view that each species has been independently created. To my mind it accords better with what we know of the laws impressed on matter by the Creator, that the production and extinction of the past and present inhabitants of the world should have been due to secondary causes, like those determining the birth and death of the individual. When I view all beings not as special creations, but as the lineal descendants of some few beings which lived long before the first bed of the Cambrian system was deposited, they seem to me to become ennobled. Judging from the past, we may safely infer that not one living species will transmit its unaltered likeness to a distant futurity. And of the species now living very few will transmit progeny of any kind to a far distant futurity; for the manner in which all organic beings are grouped, shows that the greater number of species in each genus, and all the species in many genera, have left no descendants, but have become utterly extinct. We can so far take a prophetic glance into futurity as to foretell that it will be the common and widely-spread species, belonging to the larger and dominant groups within each class, which will ultimately prevail and procreate new and dominant species. As all the living forms of life are the lineal descendants of those which lived long before the Cambrian epoch, we may feel certain that the ordinary succession by generation has never once been broken, and that no cataclysm has desolated the whole world. Hence we may look with some confidence to a secure future of great length. And as natural selection works solely by and for the good of each being, all corporeal and mental endowments will tend to progress towards perfection.

It is interesting to contemplate a tangled bank, clothed with many plants of many kinds, with birds singing on the bushes, with various insects flitting about, and with worms crawling through the damp earth, and to reflect that these elaborately constructed forms, so different from each other, and dependent upon each other in so complex a manner, have all been produced by laws acting around us. These laws, taken in the largest sense, being Growth with Reproduction; Inheritance which is almost implied by reproduction; Variability from the indirect and direct action of the conditions of life, and from use and disuse: a Ratio of Increase as to lead to a Struggle for Life, and as a consequence to Natural Selection, entailing Divergence of Character and the Extinction of less-improved forms. Thus, from the war of nature, from famine and death, the most exalted object which we are capable of conceiving, namely, the production of the higher animals, directly follows. There is grandeur in this view of life, with its several powers, having been originally breathed by the Creator into a few forms or into one; and that, whilst this planet has gone cycling on according to the fixed law of gravity, from so simple a beginning endless forms most beautiful and most wonderful have been, and are being evolved.

Anthropocentrism and Predation

John Muir

THE WORLD, we are told, was made especially for man—a presumption not supported by all the facts. A numerous class of men are painfully astonished whenever they find anything, living or dead, in all God's universe, which they cannot eat or render in some way what they call useful to themselves. They have precise dogmatic insight of the intentions of the Creator, and it is hardly possible to be guilty of irreverence in speaking of *their* God any more than of heathen idols. He is regarded as a civilized, law-abiding gentleman in favor either of a republican form of government or of a limited monarchy; believes in the literature and language of England; is a warm supporter of the English constitution and Sunday schools and missionary societies; and is as purely a manufactured article as any puppet of a half-penny theater.

With such views of the Creator it is, of course, not surprising that erroneous views should be entertained of the creation. To such properly trimmed people, the sheep, for example, is an easy problem—food and clothing "for us," eating grass and daisies white by divine appointment for this predestined purpose, on perceiving the demand for wool that would be occasioned by eating of the apple in the Garden of Eden.

In the same distant plan, whales are storehouses of oil for us, to help out the stars in lighting our dark ways until the discovery of the Pennsylvania oil wells. Among plants, hemp, to say nothing of the cereals, is a case of evident destination for ships' rigging, wrapping packages, and hanging the wicked. Cotton is another plain case of clothing. Iron was made for hammers and ploughs, and lead for bullets; all intended for us. And so of other small handfuls of insignificant things.

But if we should ask these profound expositors of God's intentions, How about those man-eating animals—lions, tigers, alligators—which smack their lips over raw man? Or about those myriads of noxious insects that destroy labor and drink his blood? Doubtless man was intended for food and drink for all these? Oh, no! Not at all! These are unresolvable difficulties connected with Eden's apple and the Devil. Why does water drown its lord? Why do so many minerals poison him? Why are so many plants and fishes deadly enemies? Why is the lord of creation subjected to the same laws of life as his subjects? Oh, all these things are satanic, or in some way connected with the first garden.

Now, it never seems to occur to these far-seeking teachers that Nature's object in making animals and plants might possibly be first of all the happiness of each one of them, not the creation of all for the happiness of one. Why should man value himself as more than a small part of the one great unit of creation? And what creature of all that the Lord has taken the pains to make is not essential to the completeness of that unit—the cosmos? The universe would be incomplete without man; but it would also be incomplete without the smallest transmicroscopic creature that dwells beyond our conceitful eyes and knowledge.

From the dust of the earth, from the common elementary fund, the Creator has made *Homo sapiens*. From the same material He has made every other creature, however noxious and insignificant to us. They are earth-born companions and our fellow mortals. The fearfully good, the orthodox, of this laborious patchwork of modern civilization cry "Heresy" on every one whose sympathies reach a single hair's breadth beyond the boundary epidermis of our own species. Not content with taking all of earth, they also claim the celestial country as the only ones who possess the kind of souls for which that imponderable empire was planned.

This star, our own good earth, made many a successful journey around the heavens ere man was made, and whole kingdoms of creatures enjoyed existence and returned to dust ere man appeared to claim them. After human beings have also played their part in Creation's plan, they too may disappear without any general burning or extraordinary commotion whatever.

Plants are credited with but dim and uncertain sensation, and minerals with positively none at all. But why may not even a mineral arrangement of matter be endowed with sensation of a kind that we in our blind exclusive perfection can have no manner of communication with?

But I have wandered from my object. I stated a page or two back that man claimed the earth was made for him, and I was going to say that venomous beasts, thorny plants, and deadly diseases of certain parts of the earth prove that the whole world was not made for him. When an animal from a tropical climate is taken to high latitudes, it may perish of cold, and we say that such an animal was never intended for so severe a climate. But when man betakes himself to sickly parts of the tropics and perishes, he cannot see that he was never intended for such deadly climates. No, he will rather accuse the first mother of the cause of the difficulty, though she may never have seen a fever district; or will consider it a providential chastisement for some self-invented form of sin.

Furthermore, all uneatable and uncivilizable animals, and all plants which carry prickles, are deplorable evils which, according to closet researches of clergy, require the cleansing chemistry of universal planetary combustion. But more than aught else mankind requires burning, as being in great part wicked, and if that transmundane furnace can be so applied and regulated as to smelt and purify us into conformity with the rest of the terrestrial creation, then the tophetization of the erratic genus *Homo* were a consummation devoutly to be prayed for. But, glad to leave these ecclesiastical fires and blunders, I joyfully return to the immortal truth and immortal beauty of Nature.

[From] The Land Ethic

Aldo Leopold

WHEN GOD-LIKE Odysseus returned from the wars in Troy, he hanged all on one rope a dozen slave-girls of his household whom he suspected of misbehavior during his absence.

This hanging involved no question of propriety. The girls were property. The disposal of property was then, as now, a matter of expediency, not of right and wrong.

Concepts of right and wrong were not lacking from Odysseus' Greece: witness the fidelity of his wife through the long years before at last his black-prowed galleys clove the wine-dark seas for home. The ethical structure of that day covered wives, but had not yet been extended to human chattels. During the three thousands years which have since elapsed, ethical criteria have been extended to many fields of conduct, with corresponding shrinkages in those judged by expediency only.

The Ethical Sequence

This extension of ethics, so far studied only by philosophers, is actually a process in ecological evolution. Its sequences may be described in ecological as well as in philosophical terms. An ethic, ecologically, is a limitation on freedom of action in the struggle for existence. An ethic, philosophically, is a differentiation of social from anti-social conduct. These are two definitions of one thing. The thing has its origin in the tendency of interdependent individuals or groups to evolve modes of co-operation. The ecologist calls these symbioses. Politics and economic are advanced symbioses in which the original free-for-all competition has been replaced, in part, by co-operative mechanisms with an ethical content.

The complexity of co-operative mechanisms has increased with population density, and with the efficiency of tools. It was simpler, for example, to define the anti-social uses of sticks and stones in the days of the mastodons than of bullets and billboards in the age of motors.

The first ethics dealt with the relation between individuals; the Mosaic Decalogue is an example. Later accretions dealt with the relation between the individual and society. The Golden Rule tries to integrate the individual to society; democracy to integrate social organization to the individual.

There is as yet no ethic dealing with man's relation to land and to the animals and plants which grow upon it. Land, like Odysseus' slave-girls, is still property. The land-relation is still strictly economic, entailing privileges but not obligations.

The extension of ethics to this third element in human environment is, if I read the evidence correctly, an evolutionary possibility and an ecological necessity. It is the third step in a sequence. The first two have already been taken. Individual thinkers since the days of Ezekiel and Isaiah have asserted that the despoliation of land is not only inexpedient but wrong. Society, however, has not yet affirmed their belief. I regard the present conservation movement as the embryo of such an affirmation.

An ethic may be regarded as a mode of guidance for meeting ecological situations so new or intricate, or involving such deferred reactions, that the path of social expediency is not discernible to the average individual. Animal instincts are modes of guidance for the individual in meeting such situations. Ethics are possibly a kind of community instinct in-the-making.

The Community Concept

All ethics so far evolved rest upon a single premise: that the individual is a member of a community of interdependent parts. His instincts prompt him to compete for his place in that community, but his ethics prompt him also to cooperate (perhaps in order that there may be a place to compete for).

The land ethic simply enlarges the boundaries of the community to include soils, waters, plants, and animals, or collectively: the land.

This sounds simple: do we not already sing our love for and obligation to the land of the free and the home of the brave? Yes, but just what and whom do we love? Certainly not the soil, which we are sending helter-skelter downriver. Certainly not the waters, which we assume have no function except to turn turbines, float barges, and carry off sewage. Certainly not the plants, of which we exterminate whole communities without batting an eye. Certainly not the animals, of which we have already extirpated many of the largest and most beautiful species. A land ethic of course cannot prevent the alteration, management, and use of these 'resources,' but it does affirm their right to continued existence, and, at least in spots, their continued existence in a natural state.

In short, a land ethic changes the role of *Homo sapiens* from conqueror of the land-community to plain member and citizen of it. It implies respect for his fellow-members, and also respect for the community as such.

In human history, we have learned (I hope) that the conqueror role is eventually self-defeating. Why? Because it is implicit in such a role that the conqueror knows, *ex cathedra*, just what makes the community clock tick, and just what and who is valuable, and what and who is worthless, in community life. It always turns out that he knows neither, and this is why his conquests eventually defeat themselves.

[From] Walking

Henry David Thoreau

I WISH to speak a word for Nature, for absolute freedom and wilderness, as contrasted with a freedom and culture merely civil,—to regard man as an inhabitant, or a part and parcel of Nature, rather than a member of society. I wish to make an extreme statement, if so I may make an emphatic one, for there are enough champions of civilization: the minister and the school-committee and every one of you will take care of that. . . .

Life consists with wildness. The most alive is the wildest. Not yet subdued to man, its presence refreshes him. One who pressed forward incessantly and never rested from his labors, who grew fast and made infinite demands on life, would always find himself in a new country or wilderness, and surrounded by the raw material of life. He would be climbing over the prostrate stems of primitive forest-trees.

Hope and the future for me are not in lawns and cultivated fields, not in towns and cities, but in the impervious and quaking swamps.

In literature it is only the wild that attracts us. Dullness is but another name for tameness. It is the uncivilized free and wild thinking in "Hamlet" and the "Iliad," in all the Scriptures and Mythologies, not learned in the schools, that delights us. As the wild duck is more swift and beautiful than the tame, so is the wild—the mallard—thought, which 'mid falling dews wings its way above the fens. A truly good book is something as natural, and as unexpectedly and unaccountably fair and perfect, as a wild flower discovered on the prairies of the West or in the jungles of the East. Genius is a light which makes the darkness visible, like the lightning's flash, which perchance shatters the temple of knowledge itself,—and not a taper lighted at the heartstone of the race, which pales before the light of common day.

English literature, from the days of the minstrels to the Lake Poets,—Chaucer and Spenser and Milton, and even Shakespeare, included,—breathes no quite fresh and, in this sense, wild stain. It is an essentially tame and civilized literature, reflecting Greece and Rome. Her wilderness is a greenwood, her wild man a Robin Hood. There is plenty of genial love of Nature, but not so much of Nature herself. Her chronicles inform us when her wild animals, but not when the wild man in her, became extinct.

In short, all good things are wild and free. There is something in a strain of music, whether produced by an instrument or by the human voice,—take the sound of a bugle in a summer night, for instance,—which by its wildness, to speak without satire, reminds me of the cries emitted by wild beasts in their native forests. It is so much of their wildness as I can understand. Give me for my friends and neighbors wild men, not tame ones. The wildness of the savage is but a faint symbol of the awful ferity with which good men and lovers meet.

I love even to see the domestic animals reassert their native rights,—any evidence that they have not wholly lost their original wild habits and vigor; as when my neighbor's cow breaks out of her pasture early in the spring and boldly swims the river, a cold, gray tide, twenty-five or thirty rods wide, swollen by the melted snow. It is the buffalo crossing the Mississippi. This exploit confers some dignity on the herd in my eyes,—already dignified. The seeds of instinct are preserved under the thick hides of cattle and horses, like seeds in the bowels of the earth, an indefinite period. . . .

I rejoice that horses and steers have to be broken before they can be made the slaves of men, and that men themselves have some wild oats still left to sow before they become submissive members of society.

[From] *Principles of Political Economy: With Some of Their Applications to Social Philosophy*

John Stuart Mill

THERE IS room in the world, no doubt, and even in old countries, for a great increase of population, supposing the arts of life to go on improving, and capital to increase. But even if innocuous, I confess I see very little reason for desiring it. The density of population necessary to enable mankind to obtain, in the greatest degree, all the advantages both of co-operation and of social intercourse, has, in all the most populous countries, been attained. A population may be too crowded, though all be amply supplied with food and raiment. It is not good for man to be kept perforce at all times in the presence of his species. A world from which solitude is extirpated, is a very poor ideal. Solitude, in the sense of being often alone, is essential to any depth of meditation or of character; and solitude in the presence of natural beauty and grandeur, is the cradle of thoughts and aspirations which are not only good for the individual, but which society could ill do without. Nor is there much satisfaction in contemplating the world with nothing left to the spontaneous activity of nature; with every rood of land brought into cultivation, which is capable of growing food for human beings; every flowery waste or natural pasture ploughed up, all quadrupeds or birds which are not domesticated for man's use exterminated as his rivals for food, every hedgerow or superfluous tree rooted out, and scarcely a place left where a wild shrub or flower could grow without being eradicated as a weed in the name of improved agriculture. If the earth must lose that great portion of its pleasantness which it owes to things that the unlimited increase of wealth and population would extirpate from it, for the mere purpose of enabling it to support a larger, but not a better or a happier population, I sincerely hope, for the sake of posterity, that they will be content to be stationary, long before necessity compels them to it.

It is scarcely necessary to remark that a stationary condition of capital and population implies no stationary state of human improvement. There would be as much scope as ever for all kinds of mental culture, and moral and social progress; as much room for improving the Art of Living, and much more likelihood of its being improved, when minds ceased to be engrossed by the art of getting on. Even the industrial arts might be as earnestly and as successfully cultivated, with this sole difference, that instead of serving no purpose but the increase of wealth, industrial improvements would produce their legitimate effect, that of abridging labour. Hitherto it is questionable if all the mechanical inventions yet made have lightened the day's toil of any human being. They have enabled a greater population to live the same life of drudgery and imprisonment, and an increased number of manufacturers and others to make fortunes. They have increased the comforts of the middle classes. But they have not yet begun to effect those great changes in human destiny, which it is in their nature and in their futurity to accomplish. Only when, in addition to just institutions, the increase of mankind shall be under the deliberate guidance of judicious foresight, can the conquests made from the powers of nature by the intellect and energy of scientific discoverers, become the common property of the species, and the means of improving and elevating the universal lot.

[From] *Discordant Harmonies: A New Ecology for the Twenty-First Century*

Daniel Botkin

In the Mirror of Nature, We See Ourselves

The answers to old questions—What is the character of nature undisturbed? What is the influence of nature on human beings? What is the influence of human beings on nature?—can no longer be viewed as distinct from one another. Life and the environment are one thing, not two, and people, as all life, are immersed in the one system. When we influence nature, we influence ourselves; when we change nature, we change ourselves. A concern with nature is not merely a scientific curiosity, but a subject that pervades philosophy, theology, aesthetics, and psychology. There are deep reasons that we desire a balance and harmony in the structure of the biological world and that we seek to find that structural balance, just as our ancestors desired and sought that kind of balance in the physical world.

Clearly, to abandon a belief in the constancy of undisturbed nature is psychologically uncomfortable. As long as we could believe that nature undisturbed was constant, we were provided with a simple standard against which to judge our actions, a reflection from a windless pond in which our place was both apparent and fixed, providing us with a sense of continuity and permanence that was comforting. Abandoning these beliefs leaves us in an extreme existential position: we are like small boats without anchors in a sea of time; how we long for safe harbor on a shore.

The change in perception of nature and the new answers to the ancient questions about nature arise from new observations and new ways of thinking that even now seem radical. The transition that is taking place affects us today and will continue to affect us deeply, in ways that may not be obvious, for decades. These changes strike at the very root of how we see ourselves. We have clouded our perception of nature with false images, and as long as we continue to do that we will cloud our perception of ourselves, cripple our ability to manage natural resources, and choose the wrong approaches to dealing with global environmental concerns. The way to achieve a harmony with nature is first to break free of old metaphors and embrace new ones so that we can lift the veils that prevent us from accepting what we observe, and then to make use of technology to study life and life-supporting systems as they are. A harmony between ourselves and nature depends on—indeed, requires—modern technological tools to teach us about the Earth and to help us manage wisely that we realize we have inadvertently begun to unravel.

Once we realize that we are part of a living system, global in scale, produced and in some ways controlled by life, and once we accept the intrinsic qualities of organic systems—with their ambiguities, variabilities, and complexities—we can feel a part of the world in a way that our nineteenth-century ancestors could not, but our ancestors before them did. We can leave behind the metaphors of the machine, which are so uncomfortable psychologically because they separate us from nature and are so unlifelike and therefore so different from ourselves, and we can arrive, with the best information available for us in our time, at a new organic view of the Earth, a view in which we are a part of a living and changing system whose changes we can accept, use, and control, to make the Earth a comfortable home, for each of us individually and for all of us collectively in our civilizations.

The machine-age view provided simple and immediate answers to the classic questions about the relationship between human beings and nature. Nature knew best; nature undisturbed was constant. Individuals, depending on which of the interpretations of nature they chose, had a certain fixed relationship to their surroundings. From the new perspective, nature does not provide simple answers. People are forced to choose the kind of environment they want, and a "desirable" environment may be one that people have altered, at least in some vicinities some of the time.

An awareness of the power of civilization to change and destroy the biological world has grown since the nineteenth century. We recognize that civilization has had a tremendous impact on nature, and it is tempting to agree with George Perkins Marsh that the absence of structural balance in the biological world is always, or almost always, the result of human activity, that "man is everywhere a disturbing agent. Wherever he plants his foot, the harmonies of nature are tuned to discords."[1] But we understand, in spite of our wishes, that nature moves and changes and involves risks and uncertainties and that our judgments of our own actions must be made against this moving image.

There are ranges within which life can persist, and changes that living systems must undergo in order to persist. We can change structural aspects of life within the acceptable ranges. Those changes that are necessary to the continuation of life we must allow to occur, or substitute for them at huge cost the qualities that otherwise would have been achieved. We can engineer nature at nature's rates and in nature's ways; we must be wary when we engineer nature at an unnatural rate in novel ways. To conserve well is to engineer within the rules of natural changes, patterns, and ambiguities; to engineer well is to conserve, to maintain the dynamics of the living systems. The answer to the question about the human role in nature depends on time, culture, technologies, and peoples. There is no simple, universal (external to all peoples, cultures, times) answer. However, the answer to this question for our time is very much influenced by the fact that we are changing nature at all levels—from the local to the global—that we have the power to mold nature into what we want it to be or to destroy it completely, and that we know we have that power. This leads us to a very different kind of answer from those of the Greek and Roman philosophers, their intellectual descendants in the Middle Ages and Renaissance, or the people of the early and mid-industrial–mechanical age.

Now that we understand that we are changing the environment at a global level, we must accept the responsibility for the actions we have taken and the changes these actions have wrought. It is prudent to minimize these effects and to slow down the rates of change as much as possible. This requires not only information and understanding, but also a political will and social and economic means and policies to accomplish what we need and desire, issues to which little attention has so far been paid. It is uncomfortable to us that the new perspective does not give the same simple answers to all questions, but requires that our management be specific and that answers to questions be dependent on the particular qualities of our goals and the actions open to us. Knowing what to do in each case requires considerable information, surveys, monitoring, knowledge, and understanding, which we as a society have been most reluctant to seek. Perhaps we have been too much like those people Peter Kalm met in eighteenth-century America, who believed that the study of nature was "a mere trifle, and the pastime of fools."[2]

A new awareness of biological nature is coming and is inevitable, and it can easily be misused. If we persist in arguing that what is natural is constant and what is constant is good, then those of us who value wilderness for its intrinsic characteristcs or believe that the biosphere must be maintained within certain bounds will have lost our ability to live in harmony with nature as it really is. If we do not understand the true nature of populations, biological communities, and ecosystems, how can we expect to husband them wisely? When we had less power, we could live with myths. But today, as Joseph Campbell recognized, "Science itself is now the only field through which the dimension of mythology can be again revealed."[3]

The task that I am encouraging the reader to join in continues that begun by George Perkins Marsh, a task that acknowledges the great destructive powers of human civilization but is optimistic that we may begin to choose as a prudent person would in our dealings with nature. The message of this book is consistent with the ethical outlook of Paul Sears, who wrote that "nature is not to be conquered save on her own terms."[4] I have tried simply to give a modern view of "her" terms. It is also consistent with the land ethic of Aldo Leopold: "Conservation is a state of harmony between men and land."[5] We have not abandoned that belief or Leopold's ethic, but have redefined "harmony." To achieve that new harmony, we must understand the character of nature undisturbed, that discordant harmony which has been the topic of this book.

The proper response to the problems we have created for the environment with our technology is not to abandon civilization or modern technology, as some have argued and as seems so comfortable and desirable a course of action to those who have suffered most the destructive effects of human actions against the natural world, or to cling to the belief that everything natural (that is, nonhuman) is desirable and good. Having altered nature with our technology, we must depend on technology to see us through to solutions. The task before us is to understand the biological world to the point that we can learn how to live within the discordant harmonies of our biological surroundings, so that they function not only to promote the continuation of life but also to benefit ourselves: our aesthetics, morality, philosophies, and material needs. We need not only new knowledge, but also new metaphors, which are arising from an amalgamation of the organic metaphor with a new technological metaphor, evolving from the old machine idea that we have been accustomed to using for the past 200 years.

. . . Could that most magnificent machine of the twentieth century, the airplane, serve as the proper model for the system of nature visible below? Machines can help us see nature, but they alone are not the proper model, the right metaphor for nature. We have things backward. We use an engineering metaphor and imagine that the Earth is a machine when it is not, but we do not take an engineering approach to nature; we do not borrow the cleverness and the skills of the engineer, which is what we must do. We talk about the spaceship Earth, but who is monitoring the dials and turning the knobs? No one; there are no dials to watch, only occasional alarms made by people peering out the window, who call to us that they see species disappearing, an ozone hole in the upper atmosphere, the climate change, the coasts of all the world polluted. But because we have never created the system of monitoring our environment or devised the understanding of nature's strange ecological systems, we are still like the passengers in the cabin who think they smell smoke or, misunderstanding how a plane flies, mistake light turbulence for trouble. We need to instrument the cockpit of the biosphere and to let up the window shade so that we begin to observe nature as it is, not as we imagine it to be.

Notes

1. G. P. Marsh, *Man and Nature,* ed. D. Lowenthal (1864; Cambridge, Mass.: Harvard University Press, 1967), 36.

2. P. Kalm, *Travels in North America*, 2 vols., trans. A. B. Benson (New York: Dover, 1966), 308–9.

3. J. Campbell, *The Masks of God: Primitive Mythology* (New York: Viking, 1959), 468.

4. P. Sears, *Deserts on the March* (Norman: University of Oklahoma Press, 1935), 3.

5. A. Leopold, *A Sand County Almanac, and Sketches Here and There* (New York: Oxford University Press, 1949), 207.

[From] *Staying Alive: Women, Ecology and Development*

Vandana Shiva

CONTEMPORARY western views of nature are fraught with the dichotomy or duality between man and woman, and person and nature. In Indian cosmology, by contrast, person and nature (Purusha-Prakriti) are a duality in unity. They are inseparable complements of one another in nature, in woman, in man. Every form of creation bears the sign of this dialectical unity, of diversity within a unifying principle, and this dialectical harmony between the male and female principles and between nature and man, becomes the basis of ecological thought and action in India. Since, ontologically, there is no dualism between man and nature and because nature as Prakriti sustains life, nature has been treated as integral and inviolable. Prakriti, far from being an esoteric abstraction, is an everyday concept which organises daily life. There is no separation here between the popular and elite imagery or between the sacred and secular traditions. As an embodiment and manifestation of the feminine principle it is characterized by (1) creativity, activity, productivity; (2) diversity in form and aspect; (3) connectedness and inter-relationship of all beings, including man; (4) continuity between the human and natural; and (5) sanctity of life in nature.

Conceptually, this differs radically from the Cartesian concept of nature as 'environment' or a 'resource'. In it, the environment is seen as separate from man: it is his surrounding, not his substance. The dualism between man and nature has allowed the subjugation of the latter by man and given rise to a new world-view in which nature is (1) inert and passive; (2) uniform and mechanistic; (3) separable and fragmented within itself; (4) separate from man; and (5) inferior, to be dominated and exploited by man.

The rupture within nature and between man and nature, and its associated transformation from a life-force that sustains to an exploitable resource characterises the Cartesian view which has displaced more ecological world-views and created a development paradigm which cripples nature and woman simultaneously.

The ontological shift for an ecologically sustainable future has much to gain from the world-views of ancient civilisations and diverse cultures which survived sustainably over centuries. These were based on an ontology of the feminine as the living principle, and on an ontological continuity between society and nature—the humanisation of nature and the naturalisation of society. Not merely did this result in an ethical context which excluded possibilities of exploitation and domination, it allowed the creation of an earth family.

The dichotomised ontology of man dominating woman and nature generates maldevelopment because it makes the colonising male the agent and model of 'development'. Women, the Third World and nature become underdeveloped, first by definition, and then, through the process of colonisation, in reality. . . .

Ecological ways of knowing nature are necessarily participatory. Nature herself is the experiment and women, as sylviculturalists, agriculturists and water resource managers, the traditional natural scientists. Their knowledge is ecological and plural, reflecting both the diversity of natural ecosystems and the diversity in cultures that nature-based living gives rise to. Throughout the world, the colonisation of diverse peoples was, at its root, a forced subjugation of ecological concepts of nature and of the Earth as the repository of all forms, latencies and powers of creation, the ground and cause of the world. The symbolism of Terra Mater, the earth in the form of the Great Mother, creative and protective, has been a shared but diverse symbol across space and time, and ecology movements in the West today are inspired in large part by the recovery of the concept of Gaia, the earth goddess.

The shift from Prakriti to 'natural resources', from Mater to 'matter' was considered (and in many quarters is still considered) a progressive shift from superstition to rationality. Yet, viewed from the perspective of nature, or women embedded in nature, in the production and preservation of sustenance, the shift is regressive and violent. It entails the disruption of nature's processes and cycles, and her inter-connectedness. For women, whose productivity in the sustaining of life is based on nature's productivity, the death of Prakriti is simultaneously a beginning of their marginalisation, devaluation, displacement and ultimate dispensability. The ecological crisis is, at its root, the death of the feminine principle, symbolically as well as in contexts such as rural India, not merely in form and symbol, but also in the everyday processes of survival and sustenance.

[From] The Golden Rule—A Proper Scale for Our Environmental Crisis

Stephen Jay Gould

. . . THIS DECADE, a prelude to the millennium, is widely and correctly viewed as a turning point that will lead either to environmental perdition or stabilization. We have fouled local nests before and driven regional faunas to extinction, but we have never been able to unleash planetary effects before our current concern with ozone holes and putative global warming. In this context, we are searching for proper themes and language to express our environmental worries.

I don't know that paleontology has a great deal to offer, but I would advance one geological insight to combat a well-meaning, but seriously flawed (and all too common), position and to focus attention on the right issue at the proper scale. Two linked arguments are often promoted as a basis for an environmental ethic:

1. That we live on a fragile planet now subject to permanent derailment and disruption by human intervention;

2. That humans must learn to act as stewards for this threatened world.

Such views, however well intentioned, are rooted in the old sin of pride and exaggerated self-importance. We are one among millions of species, stewards of nothing. By what argument could we, arising just a geological microsecond ago, become responsible for the affairs of a world 4.5 billion years old, teeming with life that has been evolving and diversifying for at least three-quarters of that immense span? Nature does not exist for us, had no idea we were coming, and doesn't give a damn about us. Omar Khayyám was right in all but his crimped view of the earth as battered when he made his brilliant comparison of our world to an eastern hotel:

> Think, in this battered Caravanserai
> Whose Portals are alternate
> Night and Day,

How Sultan after Sultan with his Pomp
Abode his destined Hour, and
went his way.

This assertion of ultimate impotence could be countered if we, despite our
late arrival, now held power over the planet's future (argument number one
above). But we don't, despite popular misperception of our might. We are
virtually powerless over the earth at our planet's own geological time scale. All
the megatonnage in our nuclear arsenals yield but one ten-thousandth the
power of the asteroid that might have triggered the Cretaceous mass extinction.
Yet the earth survived that larger shock and, in wiping out dinosaurs, paved
the road for the evolution of large mammals, including humans. We fear global
warming, yet even the most radical model yields an earth far cooler than many
happy and prosperous times of a prehuman past. We can surely destroy ourselves, and take many other species with us, but we can barely dent bacterial
diversity and will surely not remove many million species of insects and mites.
On geological scales, our planet will take good care of itself and let time clear
the impact of any human malfeasance. The earth need never seek a henchman
to wreak Henry's vengeance upon Thomas à Becket: "Who will free me from
this turbulent priest?" Our planet simply waits.

People who do not appreciate the fundamental principle of appropriate
scales often misread such an argument as a claim that we may therefore cease to
worry about environmental deterioration. . . . But I raise the same coun-
terargument. We cannot threaten at geological scales, but such vastness is
entirely inappropriate. We have a legitimately parochial interest in our own
lives, the happiness and prosperity of our children, the suffering of our fellows.
The planet will recover from nuclear holocaust, but we will be killed and
maimed by the billions, and our cultures will perish. The earth will prosper if
polar icecaps melt under a global greenhouse, but most of our major cities,
built at sea level as ports and harbors, will founder, and changing agricultural
patterns will uproot our populations.

We must squarely face an unpleasant historical fact. The conservation movement was born, in large part, as an elitist attempt by wealthy social leaders to
preserve wilderness as a domain for patrician leisure and contemplation
(against the image, so to speak, of poor immigrants traipsing in hordes through
the woods with their Sunday picnic baskets). We have never entirely shaken
this legacy of environmentalism as something opposed to immediate human
needs, particularly of the impoverished and unfortunate. But the Third World
expands and contains most of the pristine habitat that we yearn to preserve.
Environmental movements cannot prevail until they convince people that clean
air and water, solar power, recycling, and reforestation are best solutions (as
they are) for human needs at human scales—and not for impossibly distant
planetary futures.

I have a decidedly unradical suggestion to make about an appropriate environmental ethic—one rooted in the issue of appropriate human scale versus the majesty, but irrelevance, of geological time. I have never been much attracted to the Kantian categorical imperative in searching for an ethic—to moral laws that are absolute and unconditional and do not involve any ulterior motive or end. The world is too complex and sloppy for such uncompromising attitudes (and God help us if we embrace the wrong principle, and then fight wars, kill, and maim in our absolute certainty). I prefer the messier "hypothetical imperatives" that involve desire, negotiation, and reciprocity. Of these "lesser," but altogether wiser and deeper, principles, one has stood out for its independent derivation, with different words but to the same effect, in culture after culture. I imagine that our various societies grope toward this principle because structural stability, and basic decency necessary for any tolerable life, demand such a maxim. Christians call this principle the "golden rule"; Plato, Hillel, and Confucius knew the same maxim by other names. I cannot think of a better principle based on enlightened self-interest. If we all treated others as we wish to be treated ourselves, then decency and stability would have to prevail.

I suggest that we execute such a pact with our planet. She holds all the cards and has immense power over us—so such a compact, which we desperately need but she does not at her own time scale, would be a blessing for us, and an indulgence for her. We had better sign the papers while she is still willing to make a deal. If we treat her nicely, she will keep us going for a while. If we scratch her, she will bleed, kick us out, bandage up, and go about her business at her planetary scale. Poor Richard told us that "necessity never made a good bargain," but the earth is kinder than human agents in the "art of the deal." She will uphold her end; we must now go and do likewise.

PART II

Ethics and the Environment

SHOULD WE allow loggers to cut ancient forests and jeopardize the survival of the spotted owl? Is it wrong for producers to dump toxic waste into waterways? Must consumers refuse to purchase products that contribute to environmental degradation and animal suffering? These are some of the questions that lie at the heart of environmental ethics. Environmental ethics is the area of philosophy that explores our moral relations to the natural world and tries to answer these and other very difficult questions.

Questions about how we ought to think about and act toward the nonhuman world inevitably involve concerns about the status of moral values and the acceptibility of various principles. These concerns arise in discussions ranging from abstract ponderings about environmental ethics to everyday conversations about how we should interact with nature. Because philosophers who work in environmental ethics are interested in the practical application of abstract principles, they often find themselves addressing many of the traditional questions of ethics.

Fundamental to all areas of ethics are questions about moral values. It is important to identify and distinguish three central questions about moral values. First is the question about the *source* of moral values: Where do values come from? Would there be values if there were no valuers? The second question is about the *content* of values: What sorts of things are valuable? Are only human beings, their capacities, productions, and activities valuable or is nonhuman nature valuable as well? Finally there is the question about the *role* of particular values in our moral outlook: Do we value nonhuman nature for its own sake or because of its contribution to human interests?

The first question concerning the source of moral values is an ancient one; however, the lines were clearly drawn by two Cambridge philosophers of the late nineteenth and early twentieth centuries. Henry Sidgwick (1838–1900) held that values are mind-dependent. On his view, if there were no valuers, there would be no value. Arguing against this view, his student G. E. Moore (1873–

1958) posed the following "thought-experiment": imagine two worlds—one of the most beautiful you can possibly conceive, and the other "containing every-thing that is most disgusting to us." Moore claims that "quite apart from any possible contemplation by human beings," it would be rational to try to bring about the beautiful world rather than the ugly one. In this section, a contempo-rary Oxford philosopher, Jonathan Glover, offers a clear and amusing introduc-tion to this controversy.

It is important to see why the second question concerning the content of moral values is different from the first one. Even if Sidgwick is correct and all values are mind-dependent, it may still be the case that humans rightly value various aspects of nature. This is the view of another contemporary Oxford philosopher, Bernard Williams. He argues that we should refuse to be "anthro-pocentric" (human-centered) in the content of our values, but we should recog-nize that our refusal is a human one.

The third question concerns the role of particular values in our thought and action. We value much of what we value because it promotes some further end. For example, most of us value money—not for its own sake, but because it enables us to purchase various things that we want. Things, such as money, that are valuable because they are means to some further end are often described as having "instrumental value." In contrast, things that we regard as valuable in and of themselves, quite apart from any further good that they may promote, are often said to have "inherent value." Pleasure and happiness are examples of what many regard as inherent values. They are valuable in and of themselves, not just because of any further ends that they may promote. Although instrumental value and inherent value are distinct, one and the same thing can be valued in both ways. We might value a dog because he provides us with companionship and generally makes us happy, but we may also value the same dog as an end in himself, quite apart from the happiness that he brings us.

While all environmental ethicists recognize that values play distinct roles, not everyone uses the same language to describe them. Some speak of "intrinsic value" where we have spoken of "inherent value." Others use the term "extrin-sic" where we have used the term "instrumental." Still others distinguish be-tween inherent value and intrinsic value, and inherent value and inherent worth. We cannot explore the nuances of this debate here, but it is important to recog-nize that different philosophers often use different terms for the same kind of value, or the same terms for different kinds of value, and this can be confusing.

Peter Singer, a contemporary Australian philosopher and prominent de-fender of animals, has argued that the interests of nonhuman animals should figure in the content of our values. According to Singer, the interests of nonhu-man animals are valuable, just as the interests of humans are valuable. Interests are rooted in sentient experience—experiences of pleasure and pain—and non-humans have such experiences, just as humans do. Plants, however, cannot experience pleasure and pain and thus are not sentient. Any value that they have derives from the interests and preferences of sentient beings.

The contemporary American philosophers Kenneth Goodpaster and Holmes Rolston III argue that we must travel beyond the boundary of sentience in order to establish a sound environmental ethic. According to Goodpaster, non-sentient living things such as trees and plants are "self-sustaining" and have "independent needs" and "capacities for benefit and harm." For these reasons, they should be recognized as "morally considerable."

Rolston goes further. He believes that a sound environmental ethic must recognize as valuable not just individual plants and animals, but also species and ecosystems. Rolston distinguishes several kinds of value that he believes can be found in nature. Value, according to Rolston, is actually in nature and not just in the mind of the beholder. Indeed, human evaluators are one of the products of a valuable world.

The philosophers that we have discussed so far are mainly concerned with questions about where values come from, what sorts of things are valuable, and why. Another American philosopher, Paul Taylor, addresses how we respond to things that are valuable. He has developed an environmental ethic that has three parts: (1) an ultimate moral attitude of "respect for nature"; (2) a belief system, which he calls "the biocentric outlook"; and (3) a set of rules of duty that express the attitude of respect. The selection that follows develops these rules in detail.

Finally, the contemporary American philosopher Thomas Hill, Jr., suggests an entirely different approach to environmental ethics. In keeping with Williams's urging to pay close attention to our emotional relationship with nature as expressed in our feelings of gratitude, awe, and terror, Hill suggests that we turn away from questions about interests, utility, and rights, and even more general questions about values, and focus instead on questions about the kind of people we want to be. Rather than focusing on acts of environmental destruction, Hill asks us to think about the character of people who would treat nature with such contempt. Hill asks "what sort of person would destroy the environment?" His answer is nobody whom we would regard as embodying ideals of human excellence.

Two decades ago, the subject of environmental ethics barely existed. Today there is an impressive body of work in this field. Much of this work explores questions that are closely related to traditional philosophical writing about value, although these connections are not often developed. Studying the philosophical tradition can help guide our reflections on nature. But reflecting on nature can also contribute to our thinking about philosophy.

Further Reading

Brennan, Andrew. *Thinking about Nature.* Athens: University of Georgia Press, 1988.

A philosophical examination of the role that ecological science can play in addressing the moral challenges of the environment.

Callicott, J. Baird. *In Defense of a Land Ethic*. Albany: State University of New York Press, 1989.

A collection of essays on such topics as individualism, holism, and nonanthropocentric value theory.

Elliot, Robert, and Arran Gare, eds. *Environmental Philosophy*. University Park: Pennsylvania State University Press, 1983.

A collection of essays on environmental policy, duties to the nonhuman world, and attitudes toward nature.

Regan, Tom. *All that Dwell Therein*. Berkeley: University of California Press, 1982.

A collection of essays that span topics that include environmental ethics and animal rights.

Rolston, Holmes, III. *Environmental Ethics*. Philadelphia: Temple University Press, 1988.

A comprehensive analysis of values in the natural world.

Stone, Christopher. *Earth and Other Ethics*. New York: Harper & Row, 1987.

An argument for pluralism about environmental, moral, and legal ideals.

[From] *What Sort of People Should There Be?*

Jonathan Glover

. . . HENRY SIDGWICK supported a version of the mind-dependence view when he said, 'No one would consider it rational to aim at the production of beauty in external nature, apart from any possible contemplation of it by human beings.'[1] And G. E. Moore took a strongly opposed view in his comment on Sidgwick:

> Let us imagine one world exceedingly beautiful. Imagine it as beautiful as you can; put into it whatever on this earth you most admire—mountains, rivers, the sea; trees and sunsets, stars and moon. Imagine all these combined in the most exquisite proportions, so that no one thing jars against another, but each contributes to increase the beauty of the whole. And then imagine the ugliest world you can possibly conceive. Imagine it simply one heap of filth, containing everything that is most disgusting to us, for whatever reason, and the whole, as far as may be, without one redeeming feature. Such a pair of worlds we are entitled to compare: they fall within Prof. Sidgwick's meaning, and the comparison is highly relevant to it. The only thing we are not entitled to imagine is that any human being has, or ever, by any possibility, *can*, live in either, can ever see and enjoy the beauty of the one or hate the foulness of the other. Well, even so, supposing them quite apart from any possible contemplation by human beings: still, is it irrational to hold that it is better that the beautiful world should exist, than the one which is ugly? Would it not be well, in any case, to do what we could to produce it rather than the other? Certainly I cannot help thinking that it would: and I hope that some may agree with me in this extreme instance.[2]

(Moore puts the point in terms of human awareness, but it can be generalized to cover minds of any sort. And both Moore and Sidgwick discuss the issue in terms of rationality, which adds an extra complication. When that is eliminated, the mind-dependence issue remains.)

It is hard to see how to argue for or against the mind-dependence view when presented with Moore's alternatives. Neither Sidgwick nor Moore gives us much of an argument: Sidgwick tells us what he thinks no one would consider rational, while Moore tells us what he cannot help thinking. And Moore's thought experiment is problematic. If we feel disgust when we imagine the world full of filfth, we may not be quite clear what this is a reaction to. If our imagining it involves having images, we may be disgusted by them (experiences we *are* having) rather than by the possibility of an unseen heap of filth. This is not to make some Berkeleyan point about the impossibility of imagining unperceived things, but to suggest that our discrimination between the different potential objects of our dislike may be too crude for the thought experiment to be reliable.

Perhaps neither Sidgwick nor Moore is irrational or confused. The question is about what we value, and we may not all agree. My sympathies are strongly on the side of Sidgwick here, being quite unmoved by any of the excellences of universes eternally empty of conscious life. But, like Sidgwick and Moore, I have no argument to prove the other attitude wrong. If, travelling in a train through the middle of a ten-mile railway tunnel, I saw a man leaning out of the window into the darkness, I might wonder what he was doing. If it turned out to be G. E. Moore spraying the walls of the tunnel with paint, because painted walls are better than unpainted ones, even if no one ever sees them, I should not be able to prove him irrational. But I should not accept his offer of the use of a second paint spray, except possibly out of politeness.

Notes

1. H. Sidgwick, *The Methods of Ethics* (London: Macmillan, 1901), bk. 1, chap. 4. See also bk. 3, chap. 14, sec. 4 and 5.
2. G. E. Moore, *Principia Ethica* (Cambridge: Cambridge University Press, 1903), 83–84.

[From] Must a Concern for the Environment Be Centred on Human Beings?

Bernard Williams

IF WE ASK about the relations between environmental questions and human values, there is an important distinction to be made straight away between two issues. It is one thing to ask whose questions these are; it is another matter to ask whose interests will be referred to in the answers. In one sense—the sense corresponding to the first of these two issues—conservation and related matters are uncontestably human issues, because, on this planet at least, only human beings can discuss them and adopt policies that will affect them. That is to say, these are inescapably human questions in the sense that they are questions for humans. This implies something further and perhaps weightier, that the answers must be human answers: they must be based on human values, values that human beings can make part of their lives and understand themselves as pursuing and respecting.

The second issue then comes up, of what the content of those values can be. In particular, we have to ask how our answers should be related to our life. Few who are concerned about conservation and the environment will suppose that the answers have to be exclusively human answers in the further sense that the policies they recommend should exclusively favour human beings. But there are serious questions of how human answers can represent to us the value of things that are valued for reasons that go beyond human interests. Our approach to these issues cannot and should not be narrowly anthropocentric. But what is it that we move to when we move from the narrowly anthropocentric, and by what ethical route do we get there?

Many cases that we have to consider of course do directly concern human interests, and we shall perhaps understand our route best if we start with them. There is, first, the familiar situation in which an activity conducted by one person, A, and which is profitable and beneficial to A and perhaps to others as well, imposes a cost on someone else, B. Here the basic question is to decide whether B should be compensated; how much; by whom; and on what principles. A further range of problems arises when various further conditions hold. Thus there may be no specific B: the people affected are identified just as those who are exposed to the activity and affected by it, whoever they may be. When this is so, we have unallocated effects (all effects on future generations are unallocated). A different range of questions is raised when we ask whether B is affected in a way that essentially involves B's states of perception or knowledge. Thus B may be affected by the disappearance of song birds or the blighting of a landscape. These are experiential effects. It is important that an effect on B's experience may take the form of a deprivation of which, just because of that deprivation, B is never aware; living under constant atmospheric pollution, B may never know what it is to see the stars.

Beyond this, and leaving aside the experiential effects on human beings, there are effects on animals other than human beings. These are non-human effects. Finally, what is affected may be neither human nor a member of any other animal species: it may, for instance, be a tree or a mountain. These are non-animal effects.

It is of course a major question in very many real cases whether an activity that has one of these other effects on the environment may not also harm human beings: the cutting down of rain forests is an obvious example. To the extent that human interests are still involved, the problems belong with the well-known, if difficult, theory of risk or hazard. This aspect of the problems is properly central to political discussion, and those arguing for conservation and environmental causes reasonably try to mobilise human self-interest as far as possible. But the human concern for other, non-human and non-animal, effects is misrepresented if one tries to reduce it simply to a kind of human self-concern. Since, moreover, the concern for those other effects is itself a human phenomenon, humanity will be itself misrepresented in the process.

Our attitudes to these further kinds of effect are not directed simply to human interests, and in that sense they are not anthropocentric. But they are still our attitudes, expressing our values. How much of a constraint is that? What is involved in the ineliminable human perspective itself? Where might we look for an understanding of this kind of human concern?

There is a point to be made first about the experiences of non-human animals. I have so far mentioned experiential effects only in the context of effects on human beings, but, of course, there are also effects on the experience of other animals to be taken into account. This is also important, but it is not at the heart of the conservation and environmental concerns that I am considering, which focus typically on the survival of species. An experiential concern is likely to be with individual animals rather than with the survival of species, and it is bound to be less interested in the less complex animals; in these respects it is unlike a conservation concern. It also, of course, has no direct interest in the non-living. In all these ways an environmental concern in the sense relevant to conservation is at least broader than a concern with the experiences of other animals. This particularly helps to bring out the point that an environmental concern is not just motivated by benevolence or altruism. (Inasmuch as vegetarianism is motivated by those feelings, it is not the same as a conservation interest.)

There is a well-known kind of theory which represents our attitudes as still radically anthropocentric, even when they are not directed exclusively to human interests. On this account, our attitudes might be understood in terms of the following prescription: treat the non-animal effects, and also the non-human effects which do not involve other animals' experiences, simply as experiential effects on human beings, as types of state that human beings would prefer not to be in, in the case of what we call good effects, would prefer to be in. The badness of environmental effects would then be measured in terms of the effect on human experience—basically, our dislike or distaste for what is happening. It might be hoped that by exploiting existing economic theory, this way of thinking could generate prices for pollution.

This way of looking at things invovles some basic difficulties, which bring out the fairly obvious fact that this interpretation has not moved far enough from the very simply anthropocentric. This approach reduces the whole problem to human consciousness of these effects, but people's preferences against being conscious of some non-human or non-living effect are in the first instance preferences against the effect itself. A guarantee that no-one would further know about a given effect would not cheer anyone up about its occurring; moreover, if people simply ceased to care, this could not be counted an improvement. A preference of this kind involves a value. A preference not to see a blighted landscape is based on the thought that it is blighted, and one cannot assess the preference—in particular, one cannot decide what kind of weight to give to it—unless one understands that thought, and hence that value.

A different approach is to extend the class of things we may be concerned about beyond ourselves and the sufferings of other animals by supposing that non-animal things, though they have no experiences, do have interests. This directly makes the attitudes in question less anthropocentric, but I myself do not think that it is a way in which we are likely to make progress. To say that a thing has interests will help in these connections only if its interests make a claim on us: we may have to allow in some cases that the claim can be out-weighed by other claims, but it will have to be agreed that the interests of these things make some claim on us, if the notion of "interests" is to do the required work. But we cannot plausibly suppose that all the interests which, on this approach, would exist do make a claim on us. If a tree has any interests at all, then it must have an interest in getting better if it is sick; but a sick tree, just as such, makes no claim on us. Moreover, even if individual members of a species had interests, and they made some claims on us, it would remain quite unclear how a species could have interests: but the species is what is standardly the concern of conservation. Yet again, even if it were agreed that a species or kind of thing could have interests, those interests would certainly often make no claim on us: the interests of the HIV virus make no claim on us, and we offend against nothing if our attitude to it is that we take no prisoners.

These objections seem to me enough to discourage this approach, even if we lay aside the difficulties—which are obvious enough—of making sense in the first place of the idea of a thing's having interests if it cannot have experiences. The idea of ascribing interests to species, natural phenomena and so on, as a way of making sense of our concern for these things, is part of a project of trying to extend into nature our concerns for each other, by moralising our relations to nature. I suspect, however, that this is to look in exactly the wrong direction. If we are to understand these things, we need to look to our ideas of nature itself, and to ways in which it precisely lies outside the domestication of our relations to each other.

The idea of "raw" nature, as opposed to culture and to human production and control, comes into these matters, and fundamentally so, but not in any simple way. If the notion of the "natural" is not to distort discussion in a hopelessly fanciful way, as it has distorted many other discussions in the past, we have to keep firmly in mind a number of considerations. First, a self-conscious concern for preserving nature is not itself a piece of nature: it is an expression of culture, and indeed of a very local culture (though that of course does not mean that it is not important). Second, the disappearance of species is

itself natural, if anything is. Third, and conversely, many of the things that we
want to preserve under an environmental interest are cultural products, and
some of them very obviously so, such as cultivated landscapes, and parks.

Last of these general considerations, it is presumably part of the idea of the
natural that kinds of creatures have "natures," and we cannot rule out at the
beginning the idea that we might have one, and that if we have one, it might be
of a predatory kind. It is one of the stranger paradoxes of many people's
attitudes to this subject (and the same applies to some other matters, such as
animal rights) that while they supposedly reject traditional pictures of human
beings as discontinuous from nature in virtue of reason, and they remind us all
the time that other species share the same world with us on (so to speak) equal
terms, they unhesitatingly carry over into their picture of human beings a
moral transcendence over the rest of nature, which makes us uniquely able,
and therefore uniquely obliged, to detach ourselves from any natural determi-
nation of our behaviour. Such views in fact firmly preserve the traditional
doctrine of our transcendence of nature, and with it our proper monarchy of
the earth; they merely ask us to exercise it in a more benevolent manner.

Granted these various considerations, the concept of the "natural" is unlikely to serve us very well as anything like a criterion to guide our activities.
Nevertheless, our ideas of nature must play an important part in explaining our
attitudes towards these matters. Nature may be seen as offering a boundary to
our activities, defining certain interventions and certain uncontrolled effects as
transgressive.

Many find it appropriate to speak of such a conception as religious: a sense
that human beings should not see the world as simply theirs to control is often
thought to have a religious origin, and a "secular" or "humanist" attitude is
thought to be in this, as in other respects, anthropocentric. In one way, at least,
there must be something too simple in this association; while some traditional
religious outlooks have embodied feelings of this kind, there are some religions
(including many versions of Christianity) that firmly support images of human
domination of the world. However this may be, an appeal to religious origins
will in any case not be the end of the matter, for the question will remain of
why religious outlooks should have this content, to the extent that they do. In
particular, the religious sceptic, if he or she is moved by concerns of conservation, might be thought to be embarrassed by the supposed religious origin of
these concerns. Other sceptics might hope to talk that sceptic out of his or her
concerns by referring these attitudes back to religion. But they should reflect
here, as elsewhere, on the force of *Feuerbach's Axiom*, as it may be called: if
religion is false, it cannot ultimately explain anything, but itself needs to be
explained. If religion is false, it comes entirely from humanity (indeed if it is
true, it comes in good part from humanity). If it tends to embody a sense of
nature that should limit our exploitation of it, we may hope to find the source
of that sense in humanity itself.

I end with a line of thought about that source; it is offered as no more than a speculation to encourage reflection on the question. Human beings have two basic kinds of emotional relations to nature: gratitude and a sense of peace, on the one hand, terror and stimulation on the other. It needs to elaborate socio-biological speculation to suggest why these relations should be very basic. The two kinds of feelings famously find their place in art, in the form of its concern with the beautiful and with the sublime. We should consider the fact that when the conscious formulation of this distinction became central to the theory of the arts, at the end of the eighteenth century, at the same time the sublimity and the awesomeness of nature themselves became a subject for the arts, to a much greater extent than had been the case before. Art which was sublime and terrifying of course existed before, above all in literature, but its theme was typically not nature in itself, but rather, insofar as it dealt with nature, nature's threat to culture: in Sophocles, for instance,[1] or in *King Lear.* It is tempting to think that earlier ages had no need for art to represent nature as terrifying: that was simply what, a lot of the time, it was. An artistic reaffirmation of the separateness and fearfulness of nature became appropriate at the point at which for the first time the prospect of an ever-increasing technical control of it became obvious.

If we think in these terms, our sense of restraint in the face of nature, a sense very basic to conservation concerns, will be grounded in a form of fear: a fear not just of the power of nature itself, but what might be called Promethean fear, a fear of taking too lightly or inconsiderably our relations to nature. On this showing, the grounds of our attitudes will be very different from that suggested by any appeal to the interests of natural things. It will not be an extension of benevolence or altruism; nor, directly, will it be a sense of community, though it may be a sense of intimate involvement. It will be based rather on a sense of an opposition between ourselves and nature, as an old, unbounded and potentially dangerous enemy, which requires respect. "Respect" is the notion that perhaps more than any other needs examination here—and not first in the sense of respect for a sovereign, but that in which we have a healthy respect for mountainous terrain or treacherous seas.

Not all our environmental concerns will be grounded in Promethean fear. Some of them will be grounded in our need for the other powers of nature, those associated with the beautiful. But the thoughts which, if these speculations point in the right direction, are associated with the sublime and with Promethean fear will be very important, for they particularly affirm our distinction, and that of our culture, from nature, and conversely, the thought that nature is independent of us, something not made, and not adequately controlled.

We should not think that, if the basis of our sentiments is of such a kind, then it is simply an archaic remnant which we can ignore. For, first, Promethean fear is a good, general warning device, reminding us still appropriately of what we may properly fear. But apart from that, if it is something that many people deeply feel, then it is something that is likely to be pervasively connected to things that we value, to what gives life the kinds of significance that it has. We should not suppose that we know how that may be, or that we can be sure that we can do without those things.

As I said earlier, it is not these feelings in themselves that matter. Rather, they embody a value which we have good reason, in terms of our sense of what is worthwhile in human life, to preserve, and to follow, to the extent that we can, in our dealings with nature. But there are, undeniably, at least two large difficulties that present themselves when we try to think of how we may do that. First, as I also implied earlier, there is no simple way to put such values into a political sum. Certainly these philosophical or cultural reflections do not help one to do so. It may well be that our ways of honouring such values cannot take an economic form. The patterns must be political; it can only be the mobilisation, encouragement and expression of these attitudes, their manifest connection with things that people care about, that can give them an adequate place on the agenda.

The second difficulty concerns not the ways in which we might come to do anything about them, but what we might do. What many conservation interests want to preserve is a nature that is not controlled, shaped, or willed by us, a nature which, as against culture, can be thought of as just there. But a nature which is preserved by us is no longer a nature that is simply not controlled. A natural park is not nature, but a park; a wilderness that is preserved is a definite, delimited, wilderness. The paradox is that we have to use our power to preserve a sense of what is not in our power. Anything we leave untouched we have already touched. It will no doubt be best for us not to forget this, if we are to avoid self-deception and eventual despair. It is the final expression of the inescapable truth that our refusal of the anthropocentric must itself be a human refusal.

Note

1. As has been admirably shown by C. Segal, *Tragedy and Civilization* (Cambridge, Mass.: Harvard University Press, 1981).

[From] *Practical Ethics*

Peter Singer

THE ARGUMENT for extending the principle of equality beyond our own species is simple, so simple that it amounts to no more than a clear understanding of the nature of the principle of equal consideration of interests. . . . [T]his principle implies that our concern for others ought not to depend on what they are like, or what abilities they posses (although precisely what this concern requires us to do may vary according to the characteristics of those affected by what we do). It is on this basis that we are able to say that the fact that some people are not members of our race does not entitle us to exploit them, and similarly the fact that some people are less intelligent than others does not mean that their interests may be disregarded. But the principle also implies that the fact that beings are not members of our species does not entitle us to exploit them, and similarly the fact that other animals are less intelligent than we are does not mean that their interests may be disregarded.

. . . [M]any philosophers have advocated equal consideration of interests, in some form or other, as a basic moral principle. Few recognized that the principle has applications beyond our own species. One of the few who did was Jeremy Bentham, the founding father of modern utilitarianism. In a forward-looking passage, written at a time when black slaves in the British dominions were still being treated much as we now treat nonhuman animals, Bentham wrote:

> The day *may* come when the rest of the animal creation may acquire those rights which never could have been withholden from them but by the hand of tyranny. The French have already discovered that the blackness of the skin is no reason why a human being should be abandoned without redress to the caprice of a tormentor. It may one day come to be recognised that the number of the legs, the villosity of the skin, or the termination of the *os sacrum*, are reasons equally insufficient for abandoning a sensitive being to the same fate. What else is it that should trace the insuperable line? Is it the faculty of reason, or perhaps the faculty of discourse? But a full-grown horse or dog is beyond comparison a more rational, as well as a more conversable, animal

than an infant of a day, or a week, or even a month, old. But suppose they were otherwise, what would it avail? The question is not, Can they reason? nor Can they *talk?* but, *Can they suffer?*[1]

In this passage Bentham points to the capacity for suffering as the vital characteristic that entitles a being to equal consideration. The capacity for suffering—or more strictly, for suffering and/or enjoyment or happiness—is not just another characteristic like the capacity for language, or for higher mathematics. Bentham is not saying that those who try to mark 'the insuperable line' that determines whether the interests of a being should be considered happen to have selected the wrong characteristic. The capacity for suffering and enjoying things is a prerequisite for having interests at all, a condition that must be satisfied before we can speak of interests in any meaningful way. It would be nonsense to say that it was not in the interests of a stone to be kicked along the road by a schoolboy. A stone does not have interests because it cannot suffer. Nothing that we can do to it could possibly make any difference to its welfare. A mouse, on the other hand, does have an interest in not being tormented, because it will suffer if it is.

If a being suffers, there can be no moral justification for refusing to take that suffering into consideration. No matter what the nature of the being, the principle of equality requires that its suffering be counted equally with the like suffering—in so far as rough comparisons can be made—of any other being. If a being is not capable of suffering, or of experiencing enjoyment or happiness, there is nothing to be taken into account. This is why the limit of sentience (using the term as a convenient, if not strictly accurate, shorthand for the capacity to suffer or experience enjoyment or happiness) is the only defensible boundary of concern for the interests of others. To mark this boundary by some characteristic like intelligence or rationality would be to mark it in an arbitrary way. Why not choose some other characteristic, like skin colour?

Racists violate the principle of equality by giving greater weight to the interests of members of their own race when there is a clash between their interests and the interests of those of another race. White racists do not accept that pain is as bad when it is felt by blacks as when it is felt by whites. Similarly those I would call 'speciesists' give greater weight to the interests of members of their own species when there is a clash between their interests and the interests of those of other species. Human speciesists do not accept that pain is as bad when it is felt by pigs or mice as when it is felt by humans.

That, then, is really the whole of the argument for extending the principle of equality to nonhuman animals; but there may be some doubts about what this equality amounts to in practice. In particular, the last sentence of the previous paragraph may prompt some people to reply: 'Surely pain felt by a mouse just is not as bad as pain felt by a human. Humans have much greater awareness of what is happening to them, and this makes their suffering worse. You can't equate the suffering of, say, a person dying slowly from cancer, and a laboratory mouse undergoing the same fate.'

I fully accept that in the case described the human cancer victim normally suffers more than the nonhuman cancer victim. This in no way undermines the extension of equal consideration of interests to nonhumans. It means, rather, that we must take care when we compare the interests of different species. In some situations a member of one species will suffer more than a member of another species. In this case we should still apply the principle of equal consideration of interests but the result of so doing is, of course, to give priority to relieving the greater suffering.

Note

1. J. Bentham, *Introduction to the Principles of Morals and Legislation* (1789; New York: Hafner, 1948), 311.

[From] On Being Morally Considerable

Kenneth E. Goodpaster

> A thing is right when it tends to preserve the integrity, stability, and beauty of the biotic community. It is wrong when it tends otherwise.
>
> *Aldo Leopold*

WHAT FOLLOWS is a preliminary inquiry into a question which needs more elaborate treatment than an essay can provide. The question can be and has been addressed in different rhetorical formats, but perhaps G. J. Warnock's formulation of it is the best to start with:

> Let us consider the question to whom principles of morality apply from, so to speak, the other end—from the standpoint not of the agent, but of the "patient." What, we may ask here, is the condition of moral *relevance?* What is the condition of having a claim to be *considered,* by rational agents to whom moral principles apply?[1]

In the terminology of R. M. Hare (or even Kant), the same question might be put thus: In universalizing our putative moral maxims, what is the scope of the variable over which universalization is to range? A more legalistic idiom, employed recently by Christopher D. Stone,[2] might ask: What are the requirements for "having standing" in the moral sphere? However the question gets formulated, the thrust is in the direction of necessary and sufficient conditions on X in

   (1) For all A, X deserves moral consideration from A.

where A ranges over rational moral agents and moral 'consideration' is construed broadly to include the most basic forms of practical respect (and so is not restricted to "possession of rights" by X). . . .

   I

Let us begin with Warnock's own answer to the question, now that the question has been clarified somewhat. In setting out his answer, Warnock argues (in my view, persuasively) against two more restrictive candidates. The first, what might be called the *Kantian principle*, amounts to little more than a reflection of the requirements of moral *agency* onto those of moral considerability:

   (2) For X to deserve moral consideration from A, X must be a rational human person.

Observing that such a criterion of considerability eliminates children and mentally handicapped adults, among others, Warnock dismisses it as intolerably narrow.

   The second candidate, actually a more generous variant of the first, sets the limits of moral considerability by disjoining "potentiality":

   (3) For all A, X deserves moral consideration from A if and only if X is a rational human person or is a potential rational human person.

Warnock's reply to this suggestion is also persuasive. Infants and imbeciles are no doubt potentially rational, but this does not appear to be the reason why we should not maltreat them. And we would not say that an imbecile reasonably judged to be incurable would thereby reasonably be taken to have no moral claims (151). In short, it seems arbitrary to draw the boundary of moral *considerability* around rational human beings (actual or potential), however plausible it might be to draw the boundary of moral *responsibility* there.

   Warnock then settles upon his own solution. The basis of moral claims, he says, may be put as follows:

> . . . just as liability to be judged as a moral agent follows from one's general capability of alleviating, by moral action, the ills of the predicament, and is for that reason confined to rational beings, so the condition of being a proper

"beneficiary" of moral action is the capability of *suffering* the ills of the predicament—and for that reason is not confined to rational beings, nor even to potential members of that class. (151)

The criterion of moral considerability then, is located in the *capacity to suffer:*

(4) For all A, X deserves moral consideration from A if and only if X is capable of suffering pain (or experiencing enjoyment).

And the defense involves appeal to what Warnock considers to be (analytically) the *object* of the moral enterprise: amelioration of "the predicament."

Now two issues arise immediately in the wake of this sort of appeal. The first has to do with Warnock's own over-all strategy in the context of the quoted passage. Earlier on in his book, he insists that the appropriate analysis of the concept of morality will lead us to an "object" whose pursuit provides the framework for ethics. But the "object" seems to be more restrictive:

... the general object of moral evaluation must be to contribute in some respects, by way of the actions of rational beings, to the amelioration of the
human predicament—that is, of the conditions in which *these* rational beings,
humans, actually find themselves. (16; emphasis in the original)

It appears that, by the time moral considerability comes up later in the book, Warnock has changed his mind about the object of morality by enlarging the "predicament" to include nonhumans.

The second issue turns on the question of analysis itself. . . . [I]t is difficult to keep conceptual and substantive questions apart in the present con-
text. We can, of course, stipulatively *define* 'morality' as both having an object and having the object of mitigating suffering. But, in the absence of more argument, such definition is itself in need of a warrant. Twentieth-
century preoccupation with the naturalistic or definist fallacy should have taught us at least this much.

Neither of these two observations shows that Warnock's suggested criterion is wrong, of course. But they do, I think, put us in a rather more demanding mood. And the mood is aggravated when we look to two other writers on the subject who appear to hold similar views.

W. K. Frankena, in a recent paper, joins forces:

Like Warnock, I believe that there are right and wrong ways to treat infants,
animals, imbeciles, and idiots even if or even though (as the case may be) they
are not persons or human beings—just because they are capable of pleasure
and suffering, and not just because their lives happen to have some value to or
for those who clearly are persons or human beings.[3]

And Peter Singer writes:

If a being is not capable of suffering, or of experiencing enjoyment or happiness, there is nothing to be taken into account. This is why the limit of sentience (using the term as a convenient, if not strictly accurate, shorthand for

the capacity to suffer or experience enjoyment or happiness) is the only defensible boundary of concern for the interests of others.[4]

I say that the mood is aggravated because, although I acknowledge and even applaud the conviction expressed by these philosophers that the capacity to suffer (or perhaps better, *sentience*) is sufficient for moral considerability, I fail to understand their reasons for thinking such a criterion necessary. To be sure, there are hints at reasons in each case. Warnock implies that nonsentient beings could not be proper "beneficiaries" of moral action. Singer seems to think that beyond sentience "there is nothing to take into account." And Frankena suggests that nonsentient beings simply do not provide us with moral reasons for respecting them unless it be potentiality for sentience. Yet it is so clear that there *is* something to take into account, something that is not merely "potential sentience" and which surely does qualify beings as beneficiaries and capable of harm—namely, *life*— that the hints provided seem to me to fall short of good reasons.

Biologically, it appears that sentience is an adaptive characteristic of living organisms that provides them with a better capacity to anticipate, and so avoid, threats to life. This at least suggests, though of course it does not prove, that the capacities to suffer and to enjoy are ancillary to something more important rather than tickets to considerability in their own right. In the words of one perceptive scientific observer:

> If we view pleasure as rooted in our sensory physiology, it is not difficult to
> see that our neurophysiological equipment must have evolved via variation and
> selective retention in such a way as to record a positive signal to adaptationally
> satisfactory conditions and a negative signal to adaptationally unsatisfactory
> conditions. . . . The pleasure signal is only an evolutionarily derived indicator,
> not the goal itself. It is the applause which signals a job well done, but not the
> actual completion of the job.[5]

Nor is it absurd to imagine that evolution might have resulted (indeed might still result?) in beings whose capacities to maintain, protect, and advance their lives did not depend upon mechanisms of pain and pleasure at all.

So far, then, we can see that the search for a criterion of moral considerability takes one quickly and plausibly beyond humanism. But there is a tendency, exhibited in the remarks of Warnock, Frankena, and Singer, to draw up the wagons around the notion of sentience. I have suggested that there is reason to go further and not very much in the way of argument not to. But perhaps there is a stronger and more explicit case that can be made for sentience. I think there is, in a way, and I propose to discuss it in detail in the section that follows.

II

Joel Feinberg offers what may be the clearest and most explicit case for a restrictive criterion on moral considerability (restrictive with respect to life).[6] I should mention at the outset, however, that the context for his remarks is

1. the concept of "rights," which, we have seen, is sometimes taken to be narrower than the concept of "considerability"; and
2. the *intelligibility* of rights-attributions, which, we have seen, is problematically related to the more substantive issue of what beings deserve moral consideration.

These two features of Feinberg's discussion might be thought sufficient to invalidate my use of that discussion here. But the context of his remarks is clearly such that 'rights' is taken very broadly, much closer to what I am calling moral considerability than to what Passmore calls "rights." And the thrust of the arguments, since they are directed against the *intelligibility* of certain rights attributions, is *a fortiori* relevant to the more substantive issue set out in ([section] I). So I propose to treat Feinberg's arguments as if they were addressed to the considerability issue in its more substantive form, whether or not they were or would be intended to have such general application. I do so with due notice to the possible need for scare-quotes around Feinberg's name, but with the conviction that it is really in Feinberg's discussion that we discover the clearest line of argument in favor of something like sentience, an argument which was only hinted at in the remarks of Warnock, Frankena, and Singer.

The central thesis defended by Feinberg is that a being cannot intelligibly be said to possess moral rights (read: deserve moral consideration) unless that being satisfies the "interest principle," and that only the subclass of humans and higher animals among living beings satisfies this principle:

> . . . the sorts of beings who can have rights are precisely those who have (or can have) interests. I have come to this tentative conclusion for two reasons: (1) because a right holder must be capable of being represented and it is impossible to represent a being that has no interests, and (2) because a right holder must be capable of being a beneficiary in his own person, and a being without interests is a being that is incapable of being harmed or benefited, having no good or "sake" of its own. (51)

Implicit in this passage are the following two arguments, interpreted in terms of moral considerability:

(A1) Only beings who can be represented can deserve moral consideration.

Only beings who have (or can have) interests can be represented.

Therefore, only beings who have (or can have) interests can deserve moral consideration.

(A2) Only beings capable of being beneficiaries can deserve moral consideration.

Only beings who have (or can have) interests are capable of being beneficiaries.

Therefore, only beings who have (or can have) interests can deserve moral consideration.

I suspect that these two arguments are at work between the lines in Warnock, Frankena, and Singer, though of course one can never be sure. In any case, I propose to consider them as the best defense of the sentience criterion in recent literature.

I am prepared to grant, with some reservations, the first premises in each of these obviously valid arguments. The second premises, though, are *both* importantly equivocal. To claim that only beings who have (or can have) interests can be represented might mean that "mere things" cannot be represented because they have nothing to represent, no "interests" as opposed to "usefulness" to defend or protect. Similarly, to claim that only beings who have (or can have) interests are capable of being beneficiaries might mean that "mere things" are incapable of being benefited or harmed—they have no "well-being" to be sought or acknowledged by rational moral agents. So construed, Feinberg seems to be right; but he also seems to be committed to allowing any *living* thing the status of moral considerability. For as he himself admits, even plants

> . . . are not "mere things"; they are vital objects with inherited biological propensities determining their natural growth. Moreover we do say that certain conditions are "good" or "bad" for plants, thereby suggesting that plants, unlike rocks, are capable of having a "good." (51)

But Feinberg pretty clearly wants to draw the nets tighter than this—and he does so by interpreting the notion of "interests" in the two second premises more narrowly. The contrast term he favors is not 'mere things' but 'mindless creatures'. And he makes this move by insisting that "interests" logically presuppose *desires* or *wants* or *aims*, the equipment for which is not possessed by plants (nor, we might add, by many animals or even some humans?).

But why should we accept this shift in strength of the criterion? In doing so, we clearly abandon one sense in which living organisms like plants do have interests that can be represented. There is no absurdity in imagining the representation of the needs of a tree for sun and water in the face of a proposal to cut it down or pave its immediate radius for a parking lot. We might of course, on reflection, decide to go ahead and cut it down or do the paving, but there is hardly an intelligibility problem about representing the tree's interest in our deciding not to. In the face of their obvious tendencies to maintain and heal themselves, it is very difficult to reject the idea of interests on the part of trees (and plants generally) in remaining alive.

Nor will it do to suggest, as Feinberg does, that the needs (interests) of living things like trees are not really their own but implicitly *ours:* "Plants may need things in order to discharge their functions, but their functions are assigned by human interests, not their own" (54). As if it were human interests that assigned to trees the tasks of growth or maintenance! The interests at stake are clearly those of the living things themselves, not simply those of the owners or users or other human persons involved. Indeed, there is a suggestion in this passage that, to be capable of being represented, an organism must *matter* to human beings somehow—a suggestion whose implications for human rights (disenfranchisement), let alone the rights of animals (inconsistently for Feinberg, I think), are grim.

The truth seems to be that the "interests" that nonsentient beings share with sentient beings (over and against "mere things") are far more plausible as criteria of *considerability* than the "interests" that sentient beings share (over and against "mindless creatures"). This is not to say that interests construed in the latter way are morally irrelevant—for they may play a role as criteria of moral *significance*—but it is to say that psychological or hedonic capacities seem unnecessarily sophisticated when it comes to locating the minimal conditions for something's deserving to be valued for its own sake. Surprisingly, Feinberg's own reflections on "mere things" appear to support this very point:

> . . . mere things have no conative life: no conscious wishes, desires, and
> hopes; or urges and impulses; or unconscious drives, aims, and goals; or latent
> tendencies, direction of growth, and natural fulfillments. Interests must be
> compounded somehow out of conations; hence mere things have no interests.
> (49)

Together with the acknowledgment, quoted earlier, that plants, for example, are not "mere things," such observations seem to undermine the interest principle in its more restrictive form. I conclude, with appropriate caution, that the interest principle either grows to fit what we might call a "life principle" or requires an arbitrary stipulation of psychological capacities (for desires, wants, etc.) which are neither warranted by (A1) and (A2) nor independently plausible.

III

Thus far, I have examined the views of four philosophers on the necessity of sentience or interests (narrowly conceived) as a condition on moral considerability. I have maintained that these views are not plausibly supported, when they are supported at all, because of a reluctance to acknowledge in nonsentient living beings the presence of independent needs, capacities for benefit and harm, etc. . . .

Let us now turn to several objections that might be thought to render a "life principle" of moral considerability untenable quite independently of the adequacy or inadequacy of the sentience or interest principle.

(O1) A principle of moral respect or consideration for life in all its forms is mere Schweitzerian romanticism, even if it does not involve, as it probably does, the projection of mental or psychological categories beyond their responsible boundaries into the realms of plants, insects, and microbes.

(R1) This objection misses the central thrust of my discussion, which is *not* that the sentience criterion is necessary, but applicable to all life forms—rather the point is that the possession of sentience is not necessary for moral considerability. Schweitzer himself may have held the former view—and so have been "romantic"—but this is beside the point.

(O2) To suggest seriously that moral considerability is coextensive with life is to suggest that conscious, feeling beings have no more central role in the moral life than vegetables, which is downright absurd—if not perverse.

(R2) This objection misses the central thrust of my discussion as well, for a different reason. It is consistent with acknowledging the moral considerability of all life forms to go on to point out differences of moral significance among these life forms. And as far as perversion is concerned, history will perhaps be a better judge of our civilization's treatment of animals and the living environment on that score.

(O3) Consideration of life can serve as a criterion only to the degree that life itself can be given a precise definition; and it can't.

(R3) I fail to see why a criterion of moral considerability must be strictly decidable in order to be tenable. Surely rationality, potential rationality, sentience, and the capacity for or possession of interests fare no better here. Moreover, there do seem to be empirically respectable accounts of the nature of living beings available which are not intolerably vague or open-textured:

> The typifying mark of a living system . . . appears to be its persistent state of low entropy, sustained by metabolic processes for accumulating energy, and maintained in equilibrium with its environment by homeostatic feedback processes.[7]

Granting the need for certain further qualifications, a definition such as this strikes me as not only plausible in its own right, but ethically illuminating, since it suggests that the core of moral concern lies in respect for self-sustaining organization and integration in the face of pressures toward high entropy.

(O4) If life, as understood in the previous response, is really taken as the key to moral considerability, then it is possible that larger systems besides our ordinarily understood "linear" extrapolations from human beings (e.g., animals, plants, etc.) might satisfy the conditions, such as the biosystem as a whole. This surely would be a *reductio* of the life principle.

(R4) At best, it would be a *reductio* of the life principle in this form or without qualification. But it seems to me that such (perhaps surprising) implications, if true, should be taken seriously. There is some evidence that the biosystem as a whole exhibits behavior approximating to the definition sketched above, and I see no reason to deny it moral considerability on that account.[8] Why should the universe of moral considerability map neatly onto our medium-sized framework of organisms?

(O5) There are severe epistemological problems about imputing interests, benefits, harms, etc., to nonsentient beings. What is it for a tree to have needs?

(R5) I am not convinced that the epistemological problems are more severe in this context than they would be in numerous others which the objector would probably not find problematic. Christopher Stone has put this point nicely:

> I am sure I can judge with more certainty and meaningfulness whether and when my lawn wants (needs) water than the Attorney General can judge whether and when the United States wants (needs) to take an appeal from an adverse judgment by a lower court. The lawn tells me that it wants water by a certain dryness of the blades and soil—immediately obvious to the touch—the appearance of bald spots, yellowing, and a lack of springiness after being walked on; how does "the United States" communicate to the Attorney General?[9]

We make decisions in the interests of others or on behalf of others every day—"others" whose wants are far less verifiable than those of most living creatures.

(O6) Whatever the force of the previous objections, the clearest and most decisive refutation of the principle of respect for life is that one cannot *live* according to it, nor is there any indication in nature that we were intended to. We must eat, experiment to gain knowledge, protect ourselves from predation (macroscopic and microscopic), and in general deal with the overwhelming complexities of the moral life while remaining psychologically intact. To take seriously the criterion of considerability being defended, all these things must be seen as somehow morally wrong.

(R6) This objection, if it is not met by implication in (R2), can be met, I think, by . . . the distinction . . . between regulative and operative moral consideration. It seems to me that there clearly are limits to the operational character of respect for living things. We must eat, and usually this involves killing (though not always). We must have knowledge, and sometimes this involves experimentation with living things and killing (though not always). We must protect ourselves from predation and disease, and sometimes this involves killing (though not always). The regulative character of the moral consideration due to all living things asks, as far as I can see, for sensitivity and awareness, not for suicide (psychic or otherwise). But it is not vacuous, in that it does provide a *ceteris paribus* encouragement in the direction of nutritional, scientific, and medical practices of a genuinely life-respecting sort.

As for the implicit claim, in the objection, that since nature doesn't respect life, we needn't, there are two rejoinders. The first is that the premise is not so clearly true. Gratuitous killing in nature is rare indeed. The second, and more important, response is that the issue at hand has to do with the appropriate moral demands to be made on rational moral agents, not on beings who are not rational moral agents. Besides, this objection would tell equally against *any* criterion of moral considerability so far as I can see, if the suggestion is that nature is amoral.

~

I have been discussing the necessary and sufficient conditions that should regulate moral consideration. As indicated earlier, however, numerous other questions are waiting in the wings. Central among them are questions dealing with how to balance competing claims to consideration in a world in which such competing claims seem pervasive. Related to these questions would be problems about the relevance of developing or declining status in life (the very young and the very old) and the relevance of the part-whole relation (leaves to a tree; species to an ecosystem). And there are many others.

Perhaps enough has been said, however, to clarify an important project for contemporary ethics, if not to defend a full-blown account of moral considerability and moral significance. Leopold's ethical vision and its implications for modern society in the form of an environmental ethic are important—so we should proceed with care in assessing it.

Notes

1. G. J. Warnock, *The Object of Morality* (New York: Methuen, 1971), 148. All parenthetical page references to Warnock are to this book.

2. C. D. Stone, *Should Trees Have Standing? Toward Legal Rights for Natural Objects* (Los Altos, Calif.: William Kaufmann, 1974).

3. W. K. Frankena, "Ethics and the Environment," in *Ethics and Problems of the Twenty-first Century,* ed. K. Goodpaster and K. Sayre (Notre Dame, Ind.: University of Notre Dame Press, 1979).

4. P. Singer, "All Animals Are Equal," in *Animal Rights and Human Obligations,* 2nd ed., ed. T. Regan and P. Singer (Englewood Cliffs, N.J.: Prentice-Hall, 1989), 79 [this volume, 54].

5. M. W. Lipsey, "Value Science and Developing Society" (Paper presented to the Society for Religion in Higher Education, Institute on Society, Technology and Values, July 1973), 11.

6. J. Feinberg, "The Rights of Animals and Unborn Generations," in *Philosophy and Environmental Crisis,* ed. W. Blackstone (Athens: University of Georgia Press, 1974). All parenthetical page references to Feinberg are to this article.

7. K. M. Sayre, *Cybernetics and the Philosophy of Mind* (New York: Humanities Press, 1976), 91.

8. See J. Lovelock and S. Epton, "The Quest for Gaia," *New Scientist* 935 (February 1975): 304–9.

9. Stone, *Should Trees Have Standing?* 24.

Environmental Ethics: Values in and Duties to the Natural World

―――――――― ∽ ――――――――

Holmes Rolston III

ENVIRONMENTAL ethics stretches classical ethics to the breaking point. All ethics seeks an appropriate respect for life. But we do not need just a humanistic ethic applied to the environment as we have needed one for business, law, medicine, technology, international development, or nuclear disarmament. Respect for life does demand an ethic concerned about human welfare, an ethic like the others and now applied to the environment. But environmental ethics in a deeper sense stands on a frontier, as radically theoretical as it is applied. It alone asks whether there can be nonhuman objects of duty.

Neither theory nor practice elsewhere needs values outside of human subjects, but environmental ethics must be more biologically objective—nonanthropocentric. It challenges the separation of science and ethics, trying to reform a science that finds nature value-free and an ethics that assumes that only humans count morally. Environmental ethics seeks to escape relativism in ethics, to discover a way past culturally based ethics. However much our worldviews, ethics included, are embedded in our cultural heritages, and thereby theory-laden and value-laden, all of us know that a natural world exists apart from human cultures. Humans interact with nature. Environmental ethics is the only ethics that breaks out of culture. It has to evaluate nature, both wild nature and the nature that mixes with culture, and to judge duty thereby. After accepting environmental ethics, you will no longer be the humanist you once were.

Environmental ethics requires risk. It explores poorly charted terrain, where one can easily get lost. One must hazard the kind of insight that first looks like foolishness. Some people approach environmental ethics with a smile—expecting chicken liberation and rights for rocks, misplaced concern for chipmunks and daisies. Elsewhere, they think, ethicists deal with sober concerns: medical ethics, business ethics, justice in public affairs, questions of life and death and of peace and war. But the questions here are no less serious: The degradation of the environment poses as great a threat to life as nuclear war, and a more probable tragedy.

Higher Animals

Logically and psychologically, the best and easiest breakthrough past the traditional boundaries of interhuman ethics is made when confronting higher animals. Animals defend their lives; they have a good of their own and suffer pains and pleasures like ourselves. Human moral concern should at least cross over into the domain of animal experience. This boundary crossing is also dangerous because if made only psychologically and not biologically, the would-be environmental ethicist may be too disoriented to travel further. The promised environmental ethics will degenerate into a mammalian ethics. We certainly need an ethic for animals, but that is only one level of concern in a comprehensive environmental ethics.

One might expect classical ethics to have sifted well an ethics for animals. Our ancestors did not think about endangered species, ecosystems, acid rain, or the ozone layer, but they lived in closer association with wild and domestic animals than we do. Hunters track wounded deer; ranchers who let their horses starve are prosecuted. Still, until recently, the scientific, humanistic centuries since the so-called Enlightenment have not been sensitive ones for animals, owing to the Cartesian legacy. Animals were mindless, living matter; biology has been mechanistic. Even psychology, rather than defending animal experience, has been behaviorist. Philosophy has protested little, concerned instead with locating values in human experiences at the same time that it disspirited and devalued nature. Across several centuries of hard science and humanistic ethics there has been little compassion for animals.

The progress of science itself smeared the human–nonhuman boundary line. Animal anatomy, biochemistry, cognition, perception, experience, behavior, and evolutionary history are kin to our own. Animals have no immortal souls, but then persons may not either, or beings with souls may not be the only kind that count morally. Ethical progress further smeared the boundary. Sensual pleasures are a good thing; ethics should be egalitarian, nonarbitrary, nondiscriminatory. There are ample scientific grounds that animals enjoy pleasures and suffer pains; and ethically there are no grounds to value these sensations in humans and not in animals. So there has been a vigorous reassessment of human duties to sentient life. The world cheered in the fall of 1988 when humans rescued two whales from winter ice.

"Respect their right to life": A sign in Rocky Mountain National Park enjoins humans not to harass bighorn sheep. "The question is not, Can they reason, nor Can they talk? but, Can they suffer?" wrote Jeremy Bentham, insisting that animal welfare counts too.[1] The Park Service sign and Bentham's question increase sensitivity by extending rights and hedonist goods to animals. The gain is a vital breakthrough past humans, and the first lesson in environmental ethics has been learned. But the risk is a moral extension that expands rights as far as mammals and not much further, a psychologically based ethic that counts only felt experience. We respect life in our nonhuman but near-human animal cousins, a semianthropic and still quite subjective ethics. Justice remains a concern for just-us subjects. There has, in fact, not been much of a theoretical breakthrough, no paradigm shift.

Lacking that, we are left with anomaly and conceptual strain. When we try to use culturally extended rights and psychologically based utilities to protect the flora or even the insentient fauna, to protect endangered species or ecosystems, we can only stammer. Indeed, we get lost trying to protect bighorns, because, in the wild, cougars are not respecting the rights or utilities of the sheep they slay, and, in culture, humans slay sheep and eat them regularly, while humans have every right not to be eaten by either humans or cougars. There are no rights in the wild, and nature is indifferent to the welfare of particular animals. A bison fell through the ice into a river in Yellowstone Park; the environmental ethic there, letting nature take its course, forbade would-be rescuers from either saving or killing the suffering animal to put it out of its misery. A drowning human would have been saved at once. Perhaps it was a mistake to save those whales.

The ethics by extension now seems too nondiscriminating; we are unable to separate an ethics for humans from an ethics for wildlife. To treat wild animals with compassion learned in culture does not appreciate their wildness. Man, said Socrates, is the political animal; humans maximally are what they are in culture, where the natural selection pressures (impressively productive in ecosystems) are relaxed without detriment to the species *Homo sapiens*, and indeed with great benefit to its member persons. Wild animals cannot enter culture; they do not have that capacity. They cannot acquire language at sufficient levels to take part in culture; they cannot make their clothing or build fires, much less read books or receive an education. Animals can, by human adoption, receive some of the protections of culture, which happens when we domesticate them, but neither pets nor food animals enter the culture that shelters them.

Worse, such cultural protection can work to their detriment; their wildness is made over into a human artifact as food or pet animal. A cow does not have the integrity of a deer, or a poodle that of a wolf. Culture is a good thing for humans but often a bad thing for animals. Their biology and ecology—neither justice nor charity, nor rights nor welfare—provide the benchmark for an ethics.

Culture does make a relevant ethical difference, and environmental ethics has different criteria from interhuman ethics. Can they talk? and, Can they reason?—indicating cultural capacities—are relevant questions; not just, Can they suffer? *Equality* is a positive word in ethics, *discriminatory* a pejorative one.

On the other hand, simplistic reduction is a failing in the philosophy of science and epistemology; to be "discriminating" is desirable in logic and value theory. Something about treating humans as equals with bighorns and cougars seems to "reduce" humans to merely animal levels of value, a "no more than" counterpart in ethics of the "nothing but" fallacy often met in science. Humans are "nothing but" naked apes. Something about treating sheep and cougars as the equals of humans seems to elevate them unnaturally and not to value them for what they are. There is something insufficiently discriminating in such judgments; they are species-blind in a bad sense, blind to the real differences between species, valuational differences that do count morally. To the contrary, a discriminating ethicist will insist on preserving the differing richness of valuational complexity, wherever found. Compassionate respect for life in its suffering is only part of the analysis.

Two tests of discrimination are pains and diet. It might be thought that pain is a bad thing, whether in nature or culture. Perhaps when dealing with humans in culture, additional levels of value and utility must be protected by conferring rights that do not exist in the wild, but meanwhile we should at least minimize animal suffering. That is indeed a worthy imperative in culture where animals are removed from nature and bred, but it may be misguided where animals remain in ecosystems. When the bighorn sheep of Yellowstone caught pinkeye, they were blinded, injured, and starving as a result, and three hundred of them, more than half the herd, perished. Wildlife veterinarians wanted to treat the disease, as they would have in any domestic herd, and as they did with Colorado bighorns infected with an introduced lungworm, but the Yellowstone ethicists left the animals to suffer, seemingly not respecting their life.

Had those ethicists no mercy? They knew rather that, although intrinsic pain is a bad thing whether in humans or in sheep, pain in ecosystems is instrumental pain, through which the sheep are naturally selected for a more satisfactory adaptive fit. Pain in a medically skilled culture is pointless, once the alarm to health is sounded, but pain operates functionally in bighorns in their niche, even after it becomes no longer in the interests of the pained individual. To have interfered in the interests of the blinded sheep would have weakened the species. Even the question, Can they suffer? is not as simple as Bentham thought. What we ought to do depends on what is. The *is* of nature differs significantly from the *is* of culture, even when similar suffering is present in both.

At this point some ethicists will insist that at least in culture we can minimize animal pain, and that will constrain our diet. There is predation in nature; humans evolved as omnivores. But humans, the only moral animals, should refuse to participate in the meat-eating phase of their ecology, just as they refuse to play the game merely by the rules of natural selection. Humans do not look to the behavior of wild animals as an ethical guide in other matters (marriage, truth telling, promise keeping, justice, charity). Why should they justify their dietary habits by watching what animals do?

But the difference is that these other matters are affairs of culture; these are person-to-person events, not events at all in spontaneous nature. By contrast, eating is omnipresent in wild nature; humans eat because they are in nature, not because they are in culture. Eating animals is not an event between persons but a human-to-animal event; and the rules for this act come from the ecosystems in which humans evolved and have no duty to remake. Humans, then, can model their dietary habits from their ecosystems, though they cannot and should not so model their interpersonal justice or charity. When eating, they ought to minimize animal suffering, but they have no duty to revise trophic pyramids whether in nature or culture. The boundary between animals and humans has not been rubbed out after all; only what was a boundary line has been smeared into a boundary zone. We have discovered that animals count morally, though we have not yet solved the challenge of how to count them.

Animals enjoy psychological lives, subjective experiences, the satisfaction of felt interests—intrinsic values that count morally when humans encounter them. But the pains, pleasures, interests, and welfare of individual animals are only one of the considerations in a more complex environmental ethics that cannot be reached by conferring rights on them or by a hedonist calculus, however far extended. We have to travel further into a more biologically based ethics.

Organisms

If we are to respect all life, we have still another boundary to cross, from zoology to botany, from sentient to insentient life. In Yosemite National Park for almost a century humans entertained themselves by driving through a tunnel cut in a giant sequoia. Two decades ago the Wawona tree, weakened by the cut, blew down in a storm. People said, "Cut us another drive-through sequoia." The Yosemite environmental ethic, deepening over the years, answered, "No. You ought not to mutilate majestic sequoias for amusement. Respect their life." Indeed, some ethicists count the value of redwoods so highly that they will spike redwoods, lest they be cut. In the Rawah Wilderness in alpine Colorado, old signs read, "Please leave the flowers for others to enjoy." When the signs rotted out, new signs urged a less humanist ethic: "Let the flowers live!"

But trees and flowers cannot care, so why should we? We are not considering animals that are close kin, nor can they suffer or experience anything. Plants are not valuers with preferences that can be satisfied or frustrated. It seems odd to assert that plants need our sympathy, odd to ask that we should consider their point of view. They have no subjective life, only objective life.

Perhaps the questions are wrong, because they are coming out of the old paradigm. We are at a critical divide. That is why I earlier warned that environmental ethicists who seek only to extend a humanistic ethic to mammalian cousins will get lost. Seeing no moral landmarks, those ethicists may turn back to more familiar terrain. Afraid of the naturalistic fallacy, they will say that people should enjoy letting flowers live or that it is silly to cut drive-through sequoias, that it is aesthetically more excellent for humans to appreciate both for what they are. But these ethically conservative reasons really do not understand what biological conservation is in the deepest sense.

It takes ethical courage to go on, to move past a hedonistic, humanistic logic to a bio-logic. Pains, pleasures, and psychological experience will no further be useful categories, but—lest some think that from here on I as a philosopher become illogical and lose all ethical sense—let us orient ourselves by extending logical, propositional, cognitive, and normative categories into biology. Nothing matters to a tree, but much is vital to it.

An organism is a spontaneous, self-maintaining system, sustaining and reproducing itself, executing its program, making a way through the world, checking against performance by means of responsive capacities with which to measure success. It can reckon with vicissitudes, opportunities, and adversities that the world presents. Something more than physical causes, even when less than sentience, is operating within every organism. There is information superintending the causes; without it, the organism would collapse into a sand heap. This information is a modern equivalent of what Aristotle called formal and final causes; it gives the organism a telos, or end, a kind of (nonfelt) goal. Organisms have ends, although not always ends in view.

All this cargo is carried by the DNA, essentially a linguistic molecule. By a serial reading of the DNA, a polypeptide chain is synthesized, such that its sequential structure determines the bioform into which it will fold. Ever-lengthening chains are organized into genes, as ever-longer sentences are organized into paragraphs and chapters. Diverse proteins, lipids, carbohydrates, enzymes—all the life structures—are written into the genetic library. The DNA is thus a logical set, not less than a biological set, and is informed as well as formed. Organisms use a sort of symbolic logic, using these molecular shapes as symbols of life. The novel resourcefulness lies in the epistemic content conserved, developed, and thrown forward to make biological resources out of the physicochemical sources. This executive steering core is cybernetic—partly a special kind of cause-and-effect system and partly something more. It is partly a historical information system discovering and evaluating ends so as to map and make a way through the world, and partly a system of significances attached to operations, pursuits, and resources. In this sense, the genome is a set of conservation molecules.

The genetic set is really a propositional set—to choose a provocative term—recalling that the Latin *propositum* is an assertion, a set task, a theme, a plan, a proposal, a project, as well as a cognitive statement. From this, it is also a motivational set, unlike human books, because these life motifs are set to drive the movement from genotypic potential to phenotypic expression. Given a chance, these molecules seek organic self-expression. They thus proclaim a lifeway; and with this an organism, unlike an inert rock, claims the environment as source and sink, from which to abstract energy and materials and into which to excrete them. It takes advantage of its environment. Life thus arises out of earthen sources (as do rocks), but life (unlike rocks) turns back on its sources to make resources out of them. An acorn becomes an oak; the oak stands on its own.

So far we have only description. We begin to pass to value when we recognize that the genetic set is a normative set; it distinguishes between what is and what ought to be. This does not mean that the organism is a moral system, for there are no moral agents in nature; but the organism is an axiological, evaluative system. So the oak grows, reproduces, repairs its wounds, and resists death. The physical state that the organism seeks, idealized in its programmatic form, is a valued state. Value is present in this achievement. *Vital* seems a better word here than *biological*. We are dealing not simply with another individual defending its solitary life but with an individual having situated fitness in an ecosystem. Still, we want to affirm that the living individual, taken as a point-experience in the web of interconnected life, is per se an intrinsic value.

A life is defended for what it is in itself, without necessary further contributory reference, although, given the structure of all ecosystems, such lives necessarily do have further contributory reference. The organism has something it is conserving, something for which it is standing: its life. Though organisms must fit into their niche, they have their own standards. They promote their own realization, at the same time that they track an environment. They have a technique, a know-how. Every organism has a good of its kind; it defends its own kind as a good kind. In that sense, as soon as one knows what a giant sequoia tree is, one knows the biological identity that is sought and conserved.

There seems no reason why such own-standing normative organisms are not morally significant. A moral agent deciding his or her behavior ought to take account of the consequences for other evaluative systems. Within the community of moral agents, one has not merely to ask whether x is a normative system but also, because the norms are at personal option, to judge the norm. But within the biotic community, organisms are amoral normative systems, and there are no cases in which an organism seeks a good of its own that is morally reprehensible. The distinction between having a good of its kind and being a good kind vanishes, so far as any faulting of the organism is concerned. To this extent, everything with a good of its kind is a good kind and thereby has intrinsic value.

One might say that an organism is a bad organism if, during the course of pressing its normative expression, it upsets the ecosystem or causes widespread disease. Remember, though, that an organism cannot be a good kind without situated environmental fitness. By natural selection the kind of goods to which it is genetically programmed must mesh with its ecosystemic role. In spite of the ecosystem as a perpetual contest of goods in dialectic and exchange, it is difficult to say that any organism is a bad kind in this instrumental sense either. The misfits are extinct, or soon will be. In spontaneous nature any species that preys upon, parasitizes, competes with, or crowds another will be a bad kind from the narrow perspective of its victim or competitor.

But if we enlarge that perspective, we typically have difficulty in saying that any species is a bad kind overall in the ecosystem. An "enemy" may even be good for the "victimized" species, though harmful to individual members of it, as when predation keeps the deer herd healthy. Beyond this, the "bad kinds" typically play useful roles in population control, in symbiotic relationships, or in providing opportunities for other species. The *Chlamydia* microbe is a bad kind from the perspective of the bighorns, but when one thing dies, something else lives. After the pinkeye outbreak among the bighorns, the golden eagle population in Yellowstone flourished, preying on the bighorn carcasses. For the eagles, *Chlamydia* is a good kind instrumentally.

Some biologist-philosophers will say that even though an organism evolves to have a situated environmental fitness, not all such situations are good arrangements; some can be clumsy or bad. True, the vicissitudes of historical evolution do sometimes result in ecological webs that are suboptimal solutions, within the biologically limited possibilities and powers of interacting organisms. Still, such systems have been selected over millennia for functional stability, and at least the burden of proof is on a human evaluator to say why any natural kind is a bad kind and ought not to call forth admiring respect. Something may be a good kind intrinsically but a bad kind instrumentally in the system; such cases will be anomalous however, with selection pressures against them. These assertions about good kinds do not say that things are perfect kinds or that there can be no better ones, only that natural kinds are good kinds until proven otherwise.

In fact, what is almost invariably meant by a bad kind is an organism that is instrumentally bad when judged from the viewpoint of human interests, often with the further complication that human interests have disrupted natural systems. *Bad* as so used is an anthropocentric word; there is nothing at all biological or ecological about it, and so it has no force in evaluating objective nature, however much humanistic force it may sometimes have.

A vital ethic respects all life, not just animal pains and pleasures, much less just human preferences. The old signs in the Rawah Wilderness—"Please leave the flowers for others to enjoy"—were application signs using an old, ethically conservative, humanistic ethic. The new ones invite a change of reference frame—a wilder ethic that is more logical because it is more biological, a radical ethic that goes down to the roots of life, that really is conservative because it understands biological conservation at depths. What the injunction "Let the flowers live!" means is this: "Daisies, marsh marigolds, geraniums, and larkspurs are evaluative systems that conserve goods of their kind and, in the absence of evidence to the contrary, are good kinds. There are trails here by which you may enjoy these flowers. Is there any reason why your human interests should not also conserve these good kinds?" A drive-through sequoia causes no suffering; it is not cruel. But it is callous and insensitive to the wonder of life.

Species

Sensitivity to the wonder of life, however, can sometimes make an environmental ethicist seem callous. On San Clemente Island, the U.S. Fish and Wildlife Service and the Natural Resource Office of the U.S. Navy planned to shoot two thousand feral goats to save three endangered plant species (*Malacothamnus clementinus, Castilleja grisea*, and *Delphinium kinkiense*), of which the surviving individuals numbered only a few dozen. After a protest, some goats were trapped and relocated. But trapping all of them was impossible, and many thousands were killed. In this instance, the survival of plant species was counted more than the lives of individual mammals; a few plants counted more than many thousands of goats.

Those who wish to restore rare species of big cats to the wild have asked about killing genetically inbred, inferior cats presently held in zoos, in order to make space available for the cats needed to reconstruct and maintain a population that is genetically more likely to survive upon release. All the Siberian tigers in zoos in North America are descendants of seven animals; if these tigers were replaced by others nearer to the wild type and with more genetic variability, the species might be saved in the wild. When we move to the level of species, sometimes we decide to kill individuals for the good of their kind.

Or we might now refuse to let nature take its course. The Yellowstone ethicists let the bison drown, in spite of its suffering; they let the blinded bighorns die. But in the spring of 1984 a sow grizzly and her three cubs walked across the ice of Yellowstone Lake to Frank Island, two miles from shore. They stayed several days to feast on two elk carcasses, and the ice bridge melted. Soon afterward, they were starving on an island too small to support them. This time the Yellowstone ethicists promptly rescued the grizzlies and released them on the mainland, in order to protect an endangered species. They were not rescuing individual bears so much as saving the species.

Coloradans have declined to build the Two Forks Dam to supply urban Denver with water. Building the dam would require destroying a canyon and altering the Platte River flow, with many negative environmental consequences, including further endangering the whooping crane and endangering a butterfly, the Pawnee montane skipper. Elsewhere in the state, water development threatens several fish species, including the humpback chub, which requires the turbulent spring runoff stopped by dams. Environmental ethics doubts whether the good of humans who wish more water for development, both for industry and for bluegrass lawns, warrants endangering species of cranes, butterflies, and fish.

A species exists; a species ought to exist. An environmental ethics must make these assertions and move from biology to ethics with care. Species exist only instantiated in individuals, yet they are as real as individual plants or animals. The assertion that there are specific forms of life historically maintained in their environments over time seems as certain as anything else we believe about the empirical world. At times biologists revise the theories and taxa with which they map these forms, but species are not so much like lines of latitude and longitude as like mountains and rivers, phenomena objectively there to be mapped. The edges of these natural kinds will sometimes be fuzzy, to some extent discretionary. One species will slide into another over evolutionary time. But it does not follow from the fact that speciation is sometimes in progress that species are merely made up and not found as evolutionary lines with identity in time as well as space.

A consideration of species is revealing and challenging because it offers a biologically based counterexample to the focus on individuals—typically sentient and usually persons—so characteristic in classical ethics. In an evolutionary ecosystem, it is not mere individuality that counts; the species is also significant because it is a dynamic life-form maintained over time. The individual represents (re-presents) a species in each new generation. It is a token of a type, and the type is more important than the token.

A species lacks moral agency, reflective self-awareness, sentience, or organic individuality. The older, conservative ethic will be tempted to say that specific-level processes cannot count morally. Duties must attach to singular lives, most evidently those with a self, or some analogue to self. In an individual organism, the organs report to a center; the good of a whole is defended. The members of a species report to no center. A species has no self. It is not a bounded singular. There is no analogue to the nervous hookups or circulatory flows that characterize the organism.

But singularity, centeredness, selfhood, and individuality are not the only processes to which duty attaches. A more radically conservative ethic knows that having a biological identity reasserted genetically over time is as true of the species as of the individual. Identity need not attach solely to the centered organism; it can persist as a discrete pattern over time. From this way of thinking, it follows that the life the individual has is something passing through the individual as much as something it intrinsically possesses. The individual is subordinate to the species, not the other way around. The genetic set, in which is coded the telos, is as evidently the property of the species as of the individual through which it passes. A consideration of species strains any ethic fixed on individual organisms, much less on sentience or persons. But the result can be biologically sounder, though it revises what was formerly thought logically permissible or ethically binding. When ethics is informed by this kind of biology, it is appropriate to attach duty dynamically to the specific form of life.

The species line is the vital living system, the whole, of which individual organisms are the essential parts. The species too has its integrity, its individuality, its right to life (if we must use the rhetoric of rights); and it is more important to protect this vitality than to protect individual integrity. The right to life, biologically speaking, is an adaptive fit that is right for life, that survives over millennia. This idea generates at least a presumption that species in a niche are good right where they are, and therefore that it is right for humans to let them be, to let them evolve.

Processes of value that we earlier found in an organic individual reappear at the specific level: defending a particular form of life, pursuing a pathway through the world, resisting death (extinction), regenerating, maintaining a normative identity over time, expressing creative resilience by discovering survival skills. It is as logical to say that the individual is the species' way of propagating itself as to say that the embryo or egg is the individual's way of propagating itself. The dignity resides in the dynamic form; the individual inherits this form, exemplifies it, and passes it on. If, at the specific level, these processes are just as evident, or even more so, what prevents duties from arising at that level? The appropriate survival unit is the appropriate level of moral concern.

A shutdown of the life stream is the most destructive event possible. The wrong that humans are doing, or allowing to happen through carelessness, is stopping the historical vitality of life, the flow of natural kinds. Every extinction is an incremental decay in this stopping of life, no small thing. Every extinction is a kind of superkilling. It kills forms (species) beyond individuals. It kills essences beyond existences, the soul as well as the body. It kills collectively, not just distributively. It kills birth as well as death. Afterward nothing of that kind either lives or dies.

Ought species x to exist? is a distributive increment in the collective question, ought life on Earth to exist? Life on Earth cannot exist without its individuals, but a lost individual is always reproducible; a lost species is never reproducible. The answer to the species question is not always the same as the answer to the collective question, but because life on Earth is an aggregate of many species, the two are sufficiently related that the burden of proof lies with those who wish deliberately to extinguish a species and simultaneously to care for life on Earth.

One form of life has never endangered so many others. Never before has this level of question—superkilling by a superkiller—been deliberately faced. Humans have more understanding than ever of the natural world they inhabit and of the speciating processes, more predictive power to foresee the intended and unintended results of their actions, and more power to reverse the undesirable consequences. The duties that such power and vision generate no longer attach simply to individuals or persons but are emerging duties to specific forms of life. What is ethically callous is the maelstrom of killing and insensitivity to forms of life and the sources producing them. What is required is principled responsibility to the biospheric Earth.

Human activities seem misfit in the system. Although humans are maximizing their own species interests, and in this respect behaving as does each of the other species, they do not have any adaptive fitness. They are not really fitting into the evolutionary processes of ongoing biological conservation and elaboration. Their cultures are not really dynamically stable in their ecosystems. Such behavior is therefore not right. Yet humanistic ethical systems limp when they try to prescribe right conduct here. They seem misfits in the roles most recently demanded of them.

If, in this world of uncertain moral convictions, it makes any sense to assert that one ought not to kill individuals without justification, it makes more sense to assert that one ought not to superkill the species without superjustification. Several billion years' worth of creative toil, several million species of teeming life, have been handed over to the care of this late-coming species in which mind has flowered and morals have emerged. Ought not this sole moral species do something less self-interested than count all the produce of an evolutionary ecosystem as nothing but human resources? Such an attitude hardly seems biologically informed, much less ethically adequate. It is too provincial for intelligent humanity. Life on Earth is a many-splendored thing; extinction dims its luster. An ethics of respect for life is urgent at the level of species.

Ecosystems

A species is what it is where it is. No environmental ethics has found its way on Earth until it finds an ethic for the biotic communities in which all destinies are entwined. "A thing is right," urged Aldo Leopold, "when it tends to preserve the integrity, stability, and beauty of the biotic community. It is wrong when it tends otherwise."[2] Again, we have two parts to the ethic: first, that ecosystems exist, both in the wild and in support of culture; second, that ecosystems ought to exist, both for what they are in themselves and as modified by culture. Again, we must move with care from the biological assertions to the ethical assertions.

Giant forest fires raged over Yellowstone National Park in the summer of 1988, consuming nearly a million acres despite the efforts of a thousand fire fighters. By far the largest ever known in the park, the fires seemed a disaster. But the Yellowstone land ethic enjoined: "Let nature take its course; let it burn." So the fires were not fought at first, but in midsummer, national authorities overrode that policy and ordered the fires put out. Even then, weeks later, fires continued to burn, partly because they were too big to control but partly too because Yellowstone personnel did not really want the fires put out. Despite the evident destruction of trees, shrubs, and wildlife, they believe that fires are a good thing—even when the elk and bison leave the park in search of food and are shot by hunters. Fires reset succession, release nutrients, recycle materials, and renew the biotic community. (Nearby, in the Teton wilderness, a storm blew down fifteen thousand acres of trees, and some people proposed that the area be declassified from wilderness to allow commercial salvage of the timber. But a similar environmental ethic said, "No, let it rot.")

Aspen are important in the Yellowstone ecosystem. Although some aspen stands are climax and self-renewing, many are seral and give way to conifers. Aspen groves support many birds and much wildlife, especially beavers, whose activities maintain the riparian zones. Aspen are rejuvenated after fires, and the Yellowstone land ethic wants the aspen for their critical role in the biotic community. Elk browse the young aspen stems. To a degree this is a good thing, because it provides the elk with critical nitrogen, but in excess it is a bad thing. The elk have no predators, because the wolves are gone, and as a result the elk overpopulate. Excess elk also destroy the willows, and that destruction in turn destroys the beavers. So, in addition to letting fires burn, rejuvenating the aspen might require park managers to cull hundreds of elk—all for the sake of a healthy ecosystem.

The Yellowstone ethic wishes to restore wolves to the greater Yellowstone ecosystem. At the level of species, this change is desired because of what the wolf is in itself, but it is also desired because the greater Yellowstone ecosystem does not have its full integrity, stability, and beauty without this majestic animal at the top of the trophic pyramid. Restoring the wolf as a top predator would mean suffering and death for many elk, but that would be a good thing for the aspen and willows, the beavers, and the riparian habitat and would have mixed benefits for the bighorns and mule deer (the overpopulating elk consume their food, but the sheep and deer would also be consumed by the wolves). Restoration of wolves would be done over the protests of ranchers who worry about wolves eating their cattle; many of them also believe that the wolf is a bloodthirsty killer, a bad kind. Nevertheless, the Yellowstone ethic demands wolves, as it does fires, in appropriate respect for life in its ecosystem.

Letting nature take its ecosystemic course is why the Yellowstone ethic forbade rescuing the drowning bison but required rescuing the sow grizzly and her cubs, the latter case to insure that the big predators remain. After the bison drowned, coyotes, foxes, magpies, and ravens fed on the carcass. Later, even a grizzly bear fed on it. All this is a good thing because the system cycles on. On that account, rescuing the whales trapped in the winter ice seems less of a good thing, when we note that rescuers had to drive away polar bears that attempted to eat the dying whales.

Classical, humanistic ethics finds ecosystems to be unfamiliar territory. It is difficult to get the biology right and, superimposed on the biology, to get the ethics right. Fortunately, it is often evident that human welfare depends on ecosystemic support, and in this sense all our legislation about clean air, clean water, soil conservation, national and state forest policies, pollution controls, renewable resources, and so forth is concerned about ecosystem-level processes. Furthermore, humans find much of value in preserving wild ecosystems, and our wilderness and park system is impressive.

Still, a comprehensive environmental ethics needs the best, naturalistic reasons, as well as the good, humanistic ones, for respecting ecosystems. Ecosystems generate and support life, keep selection pressures high, enrich situated fitness, and allow congruent kinds to evolve in their places with sufficient containment. The ecologist finds that ecosystems are objectively satisfactory communities in the sense that organismic needs are sufficiently met for species to survive and flourish, and the critical ethicist finds (in a subjective judgment matching the objective process) that such ecosystems are satisfactory communities to which to attach duty. Our concern must be for the fundamental unit of survival.

An ecosystem, the conservative ethicist will say, is too low a level of organization to be respected intrinsically. Ecosystems can seem little more than random, statistical processes. A forest can seem a loose collection of externally related parts, the collection of fauna and flora a jumble, hardly a community. The plants and animals within an ecosystem have needs, but their interplay can seem simply a matter of distribution and abundance, birth rates and death rates, population densities, parasitism and predation, dispersion, checks and balances, and stochastic process. Much is not organic at all (rain, groundwater, rocks, soil particles, air), and some organic material is dead and decaying debris (fallen trees, scat, humus). These things have no organized needs. There is only catch-as-catch-can scrimmage for nutrients and energy, not really enough of an integrated process to call the whole a community.

Unlike higher animals, ecosystems have no experiences; they do not and cannot care. Unlike plants, an ecosystem has no organized center, no genome. It does not defend itself against injury or death. Unlike a species, there is no ongoing telos, no biological identity reinstantiated over time. The organismic parts are more complex than the community whole. More troublesome still, an ecosystem can seem a jungle where the fittest survive, a place of contest and conflict, beside which the organism is a model of cooperation. In animals the heart, liver, muscles, and brain are tightly integrated, as are the leaves, cambium, and roots in plants. But the so-called ecosystem community is pushing and shoving between rivals, each aggrandizing itself, or else seems to be all indifference and haphazard juxtaposition—nothing to call forth our admiration.

Environmental ethics must break through the boundary posted by disoriented ontological conservatives, who hold that only organisms are real, actually existing as entities, whereas ecosystems are nominal—just interacting individuals. Oak trees are real, but forests are nothing but collections of trees. But any level is real if it shapes behavior on the level below it. Thus the cell is real because that pattern shapes the behavior of amino acids; the organism, because that pattern coordinates the behavior of hearts and lungs. The biotic community is real because the niche shapes the morphology of the oak trees within it. Being real at the level of community requires only an organization that shapes the behavior of its members.

The challenge is to find a clear model of community and to discover an ethics for it: better biology for better ethics. Even before the rise of ecology, biologists began to conclude that the combative survival of the fittest distorts the truth. The more perceptive model is coaction in adapted fit. Predator and prey, parasite and host, grazer and grazed, are contending forces in dynamic process in which the well-being of each is bound up with the other—coordinated as much as heart and liver are coordinated organically. The ecosystem supplies the coordinates through which each organism moves, outside which the species cannot really be located.

The community connections are looser than the organism's internal interconnections but are not less significant. Admiring organic unity in organisms and stumbling over environmental looseness is like valuing mountains and despising valleys. The matrix that the organism requires to survive is the open, pluralistic ecological system. Internal complexity—heart, liver, muscles, brain—arises as a way of dealing with a complex, tricky environment. The skin-out processes are not just the support; they are the subtle source of the skin-in processes. In the complete picture, the outside is as vital as the inside. Had there been either simplicity or lockstep concentrated unity in the environment, no organismic unity could have evolved. Nor would it remain. There would be less elegance in life.

To look at one level for what is appropriate at another makes a mistake in categories. One should not look for a single center or program in ecosystems, much less for subjective experiences. Instead, one should look for a matrix, for interconnections between centers (individual plants and animals, dynamic lines of speciation), for creative stimulus and open-ended potential. Everything will be connected to many other things, sometimes by obligate associations but more often by partial and pliable dependencies, and, among other things, there will be no significant interactions. There will be functions in a communal sense: shunts and crisscrossing pathways, cybernetic subsystems and feedback loops. An order arises spontaneously and systematically when many self-concerned units jostle and seek to fulfill their own programs, each doing its own thing and forced into informed interaction.

An ecosystem is a productive, projective system. Organisms defend only their selves, with individuals defending their continuing survival and with species increasing the numbers of kinds. But the evolutionary ecosystem spins a bigger story, limiting each kind, locking it into the welfare of others, promoting new arrivals, increasing kinds and the integration of kinds. Species increase their kind, but ecosystems increase kinds, superposing the latter increase onto the former. Ecosystems are selective systems, as surely as organisms are selective systems. The natural selection comes out of the system and is imposed on the individual. The individual is programmed to make more of its kind, but more is going on systemically than that; the system is making more kinds.

Communal processes—the competition between organisms, statistically probable interactions, plant and animal successions, speciation over historical time—generate an ever-richer community. Hence the evolutionary toil, elaborating and diversifying the biota, that once began with no species and results today in five million species, increasing over time the quality of lives in the upper rungs of the trophic pyramids. One-celled organisms evolved into many-celled, highly integrated organisms. Photosynthesis evolved and came to support locomotion—swimming, walking, running, flight. Stimulus–response mechanisms became complex instinctive acts. Warm-blooded animals followed cold-blooded ones. Complex nervous systems, conditioned behavior, and learning emerged. Sentience appeared—sight, hearing, smell, taste, pleasure, pain. Brains coupled with hands. Consciousness and self-consciousness arose. Culture was superposed on nature.

These developments do not take place in all ecosystems or at every level. Microbes, plants, and lower animals remain, good of their kinds and, serving continuing roles, good for other kinds. The understories remain occupied. As a result, the quantity of life and its diverse qualities continue—from protozoans to primates to people. There is a push-up, lock-up ratchet effect that conserves the upstrokes and the outreaches. The later we go in time, the more accelerated are the forms at the top of the trophic pyramids, the more elaborated are the multiple trophic pyramids of Earth. There are upward arrows over evolutionary time.

The system is a game with loaded dice, but the loading is a pro-life tendency, not mere stochastic process. Though there is no Nature in the singular, the system has a nature, a loading that pluralizes, putting natures into diverse kinds: $nature_1$, $nature_2$, $nature_3$ . . . $nature_n$. It does so using random elements (in both organisms and communities), but this is a secret of its fertility, producing steadily intensified interdependencies and options. An ecosystem has no head, but it heads toward species diversification, support, and richness. Though not a superorganism, it is a kind of vital field.

Instrumental value uses something as a means to an end; intrinsic value is worthwhile in itself. No warbler eats insects to become food for a falcon; the warbler defends it own life as an end in itself and makes more warblers as it can. A life is defended intrinsically, without further contributory reference. But neither of these traditional terms is satisfactory at the level of the ecosystem. Though it has value *in* itself, the system does not have any value *for* itself.

Though it is a value producer, it is not a value owner. We are no longer confronting instrumental value, as though the system were of value instrumentally as a fountain of life. Nor is the question one of intrinsic value, as though the system defended some unified form of life for itself. We have reached something for which we need a third term: systemic value. Duties arise in encounters with the system that projects and protects these member components in biotic community.

Ethical conservatives, in the humanistic sense, will say that ecosystems are of value only because they contribute to human experiences. But that mistakes the last chapter for the whole story, one fruit for the whole plant. Humans count enough to have the right to flourish in ecosystems, but not so much that they have the right to degrade or shut down ecosystems, not at least without a burden of proof that there is an overriding cultural gain. Those who have traveled partway into environmental ethics will say that ecosystems are of value because they contribute to animal experiences or to organismic life. But the really conservative, radical view sees that the stability, integrity, and beauty of biotic communities are what are most fundamentally to be conserved. In a comprehensive ethics of respect for life, we ought to set ethics at the level of ecosystems alongside classical, humanistic ethics.

Value Theory

In practice the ultimate challenge of environmental ethics is the conservation of life on Earth. In principle the ultimate challenge is a value theory profound enough to support that ethics. In nature there is negentropic construction in dialectic with entropic teardown, a process for which we hardly yet have an adequate scientific theory, much less a valuational theory. Yet this is nature's most striking feature, one that ultimately must be valued and of value. In one sense, nature is indifferent to mountains, rivers, fauna, flora, forests, and grasslands. But in another sense, nature has bent toward making and remaking these projects, millions of kinds, for several billion years.

These performances are worth noticing, are remarkable and memorable— and not just because of their tendencies to produce something else; certainly not merely because of their tendency to produce this noticing in certain recent subjects, our human selves. These events are loci of value as products of systemic nature in its formative processes. The splendors of Earth do not simply lie in their roles as human resources, supports of culture, or stimulators of experience. The most plausible account will find some programmatic evolution toward value, and not because it ignores Darwin but because it heeds his principle of natural selection and deploys it into a selection exploring new niches and elaborating kinds, even a selection upslope toward higher values, at least along some trends within some ecosystems. How do we humans come to be charged up with values, if there was and is nothing in nature charging us up so? A systematic environmental ethics does not wish to believe in the special creation of values or in their dumbfounding epigenesis. Let them evolve. Let nature carry value.

The notion that nature is a value carrier is ambiguous. Much depends on a thing's being more or less structurally congenial for the carriage. We value a thing and discover that we are under the sway of its valence, inducing our behavior. It has among its strengths (Latin: *valeo*, "be strong") this capacity to carry value. This potential cannot always be of the empty sort that a glass has for carrying water. It is often pregnant fullness. Some of the values that nature carries are up to us, our assignment. But fundamentally there are powers in nature that move to us and through us.

No value exists without an evaluator. So runs a well-entrenched dogma. Humans clearly evaluate their world; sentient animals may also. But plants cannot evaluate their environment; they have no options and make no choices. A fortiori, species and ecosystems, Earth and Nature, cannot be bona fide evaluators. One can always hang on to the assertion that value, like a tickle or remorse, must be felt to be there. Its *esse* is *percipi*. To be, it must be perceived. Nonsensed value is nonsense. There are no thoughts without a thinker, no percepts without a perceiver, no deeds without a doer, no targets without an aimer.

Such resolute subjectivists cannot be defeated by argument, although they can be driven toward analyticity. That theirs is a retreat to definition is difficult to expose, because they seem to cling so closely to inner experience. They are reporting, on this hand, how values always excite us. They are giving, on that hand, a stipulative definition. That is how they choose to use the word *value*.

If value arrives only with consciousness, experiences in which humans find value have to be dealt with as appearances of various sorts. The value has to be relocated in the valuing subject's creativity as a person meets a valueless world, or even a valuable one—one able to be valued but one that before the human bringing of valuableness contains only possibility and not any actual value. Value can only be extrinsic to nature, never intrinsic to it.

But the valuing subject in an otherwise valueless world is an insufficient premise for the experienced conclusions of those who respect all life. Conversion to a biological view seems truer to world experience and more logically compelling. Something from a world beyond the human mind, beyond human experience, is received into our mind, our experience, and the value of that something does not always arise with our evaluation of it. Here the order of knowing reverses, and also enhances, the order of being. This too is a perspective but is ecologically better-informed. Science has been steadily showing how the consequents (life, mind) are built on their precedents (energy, matter), however much they overleap them. Life and mind appear where they did not before exist, and with them levels of value emerge that did not before exist. But that gives no reason to say that all value is an irreducible emergent at the human (or upper-animal) level. A comprehensive environmental ethics reallo-cates value across the whole continuum. Value increases in the emergent climax but is continuously present in the composing precedents. The system is value-able, able to produce value. Human evaluators are among its products.

Some value depends on subjectivity, yet all value is generated within the geosystemic and ecosystemic pyramid. Systemically, value fades from subjec-tive to objective value but also fans out from the individual to its role and matrix. Things do not have their separate natures merely in and for them-selves, but they face outward and co-fit into broader natures. Value-in-itself is smeared out to become value-in-togetherness. Value seeps out into the sys-tem, and we lose our capacity to identify the individual as the sole locus of value.

Intrinsic value, the value of an individual for what it is in itself, becomes problematic in a holistic web. True, the system produces such values more and more with its evolution of individuality and freedom. Yet to decouple this value from the biotic, communal system is to make value too internal and elemen-tary; this decoupling forgets relatedness and externality. Every intrinsic value has leading and trailing *and*'s. Such value is coupled with value from which it comes and toward which it moves. Adapted fitness makes individualistic value too system-independent. Intrinsic value is a part in a whole and is not to be fragmented by valuing it in isolation.

Everything is good in a role, in a whole, although we can speak of objective intrinsic goodness wherever a point-event—a trillium, for example—defends a good (its life) in itself. We can speak of subjective intrinsic goodness when such an event registers as a point-experience, at which point humans pronounce both their experience and what it is to be good without need to enlarge their focus. Neither the trilliums nor the human judges of it require for their respec-tive valuings any further contributory reference.

When eaten by foragers or in death resorbed into humus, the trillium has its value destroyed, transformed into instrumentality. The system is a value trans-former where form and being, process and reality, fact and value, are inseparably joined. Intrinsic and instrumental values shuttle back and forth, parts-in-wholes and wholes-in-parts, local details of value embedded in global structures, gems in their settings, and their setting-situation a corporation where value cannot stand alone. Every good is in community.

In environmental ethics one's beliefs about nature, which are based upon but exceed science, have everything to do with beliefs about duty. The way the world is informs the way it ought to be. We always shape our values in signifi-cant measure in accord with our notion of the kind of universe that we live in, and this process drives our sense of duty. Our model of reality implies a model of conduct. Differing models sometimes imply similar conduct, but often they do not. A model in which nature has no value apart from human preferences will imply different conduct from one in which nature projects fundamental values, some objective and others that further require human subjectivity superimposed on objective nature.

This evaluation is not scientific description; hence it is not ecology per se but metaecology. No amount of research can verify that, environmentally, the right is the optimum biotic community. Yet ecological description generates this valuing of nature, endorsing the systemic rightness. The transition from *is* to *good* and thence to *ought* occurs here; we leave science to enter the domain of evaluation, from which an ethics follows.

What is ethically puzzling and exciting is that an *ought* is not so much derived from an *is* as discovered simultaneously with it. As we progress from descriptions of fauna and flora, of cycles and pyramids, of autotrophs coordinated with heterotrophs, of stability and dynamism, on to intricacy, planetary opulence and interdependence, unity and harmony with oppositions in counterpoint and synthesis, organisms evolved within and satisfactorily fitting their communities, and we arrive at length at beauty and goodness, we find that it is difficult to say where the natural facts leave off and where the natural values appear. For some people at least, the sharp *is–ought* dichotomy is gone; the values seem to be there as soon as the facts are fully in, and both values and facts seem to be alike properties of the system.

There is something overspecialized about an ethic, held by the dominant class of *Homo sapiens*, that regards the welfare of only one of several million species as an object and beneficiary of duty. If the remedy requires a paradigm change about the sorts of things to which duty can attach, so much the worse for those humanistic ethics no longer functioning in, or suited to, their changing environment. The anthropocentrism associated with them was fiction anyway. There is something Newtonian, not yet Einsteinian, besides something morally naive, about living in a reference frame in which one species takes itself as absolute and values everything else relative to its utility. If true to its specific epithet, which means wise, ought not *Homo sapiens* value this host of life as something that lays on us a claim to care for life in its own right?

Only the human species contains moral agents, but perhaps conscience on such an Earth ought not to be used to exempt every other form of life from consideration, with the resulting paradox that the sole moral species acts only in its collective self-interest toward all the rest. Is not the ultimate philosophical task the discovery of a whole great ethic that knows the human place under the sun?

Notes

1. J. Bentham, *Introduction to the Principles of Morals and Legislation* (1789; New York: Hafner, 1948), 311.

2. A. Leopold, *A Sand County Almanac, and Sketches Here and There* (New York: Oxford University Press, 1949), 224–25.

[From] *Respect for Nature: A Theory of Environmental Ethics*

Paul W. Taylor

Having and Expressing the Attitude of Respect for Nature

The central tenet of the theory of environmental ethics that I am defending is that actions are right and character traits are morally good in virtue of their expressing or embodying a certain ultimate moral attitude, which I call respect for nature. When moral agents adopt the attitude, they thereby subscribe to a set of standards of character and rules of conduct as their own ethical principles. Having the attitude entails being morally committed to fulfilling the standards and complying with the rules. When moral agents then act in accordance with the rules and when they develop character traits that meet the standards, their conduct and character express (give concrete embodiment to) the attitude. Thus ethical action and goodness of character naturally flow from the attitude, and the attitude is made manifest in how one acts and in what sort of person one is.

The Biocentric Outlook and the Attitude of Respect for Nature

The attitude we think it appropriate to take toward living things depends on how we conceive of them and of our relationship to them. What moral significance the natural world has for us depends on the way we look at the whole system of nature and our role in it. With regard to the attitude of respect for nature, the belief-system that renders it intelligible and on which it depends for its justifiability is the biocentric outlook. This outlook underlies and supports the attitude of respect for nature in the following sense. Unless we grasp what it means to accept that belief-system and so view the natural order from its perspective, we cannot see the point of taking the attitude of respect. But once we do grasp it and shape our world outlook in accordance with it, we immediately understand how and why a person would adopt that attitude as the only appropriate one to have toward nature. Thus the biocentric outlook provides the explanatory and justificatory background that makes sense of and gives point to a person's taking the attitude.

The beliefs that form the core of the biocentric outlook are four in number:

1. The belief that humans are members of the Earth's Community of Life in the same sense and on the same terms in which other living things are members of that Community.
2. The belief that the human species, along with all other species, are integral elements in a system of interdependence such that the survival of each living thing, as well as its chances of faring well or poorly, is determined not only by the physical conditions of its environment but also by its relations to other living things.
3. The belief that all organisms are teleological centers of life in the sense that each is a unique individual pursuing its own good in its own way.
4. The belief that humans are not inherently superior to other living things.

To accept all four of these beliefs is to have a coherent outlook on the natural world and the place of humans in it. It is to take a certain perspective on human life and to conceive of the relation between human and other forms of life in a certain way. Given this world view, the attitude of respect is then seen to be the only suitable, fitting, or appropriate moral attitude to take toward the natural world and its living inhabitants.

The Basic Rules of Conduct

. . . I shall now set out and examine four rules of duty in the domain of environmental ethics. This is not supposed to provide an exhaustive account of every valid duty of the ethics of respect for nature. It is doubtful whether a complete specification of duties is possible in this realm. But however that may be, the duties to be listed here are intended to cover only the more important ones that typically arise in everyday life. . . . [I]n all situations not explicitly or clearly covered by these rules we should rely on the attitude of respect for nature and the biocentric outlook that together underlie the system as a whole and give it point. Right actions are always actions that express the attitude of respect, whether they are covered by the four rules or not. They must also be actions which we can approve of in the light of the various components of the biocentric outlook.

The four rules will be named (1) the Rule of Nonmaleficence, (2) the Rule of Noninterference, (3) the Rule of Fidelity, and (4) the Rule of Restitutive Justice.

1. *The Rule of Nonmaleficence.* This is the duty not to do harm to any entity in the natural environment that has a good of its own. It includes the duty not to kill an organism and not to destroy a species-population or biotic community, as well as the duty to refrain from any action that would be seriously detrimental to the good of an organism, species-population, or life community. Perhaps the most fundamental wrong in the ethics of respect for nature is to harm something that does not harm us.

The concept of nonmaleficence is here understood to cover only nonperformances or intentional abstentions. The rule defines a negative duty, requiring that moral agents refrain from certain kinds of actions. It does not require the doing of any actions, such as those that *prevent* harm from coming to an entity or those that help to *alleviate* its suffering. Actions of these sorts more properly fall under the heading of benefiting an entity by protecting or promoting its good. (They will be discussed in connection with the Rule of Restitutive Justice.)

The Rule of Nonmaleficence prohibits harmful and destructive acts done by moral agents. It does not apply to the behavior of a nonhuman animal or the activity of a plant that might bring harm to another living thing or cause its death. Suppose, for example, that a Rough-legged Hawk pounces on a field mouse, killing it. Nothing morally wrong has occurred. Although the hawk's behavior can be thought of as something it does intentionally, it is not the action of a moral agent. Thus it does not fall within the range of the Rule of Nonmaleficence. The hawk does not violate any duty because it *has* no duties. Consider, next, a vine which over the years gradually covers a tree and finally kills it. The activity of the vine, which involves goal-oriented movements but not, of course, intentional actions, is not a moral wrongdoing. The vine's killing the tree has no moral properties at all, since it is not the conduct of a moral agent.

Let us now, by way of contrast, consider the following case. A Peregrine Falcon has been taken from the wild by a falconer, who then trains it to hunt, seize, and kill wild birds under his direction. Here there occurs human conduct aimed at controlling and manipulating an organism for the enjoyment of a sport that involves harm to other wild organisms. A wrong is being done but not by the falcon, even though it is the falcon which does the actual killing and even though the birds it kills are its natural prey. The wrong that is done to those birds is a wrong done by the falconer. It is not the action of the Peregrine that breaks the rule of duty but the actions of the one who originally captured it, trained it, and who now uses it for his own amusement. These actions, it might be added, are also violations of the Rule of Noninterference, since the falcon was removed from its wild state. Let us now turn our attention to this second rule of duty.

2. *The Rule of Noninterference.* Under this rule fall two sorts of negative duties, one requiring us to refrain from placing restrictions on the freedom of individual organisms, the other requiring a general "hands off" policy with

regard to whole ecosystems and biotic communities, as well as to individual organisms.

Concerning the first sort of duty, the idea of the freedom of individual organisms[,] . . . freedom is absence of constraint, [and] a constraint is any condition that prevents or hinders the normal activity and healthy development of an animal or plant. A being is free in this sense when any of four types of constraints that could weaken, impair, or destroy its ability to adapt successfully to its environment are absent from its existence and circumstances. To be free is to be free *from* these constraints and to be free *to* pursue the realization of one's good according to the laws of one's nature. The four types of constraints, with some examples of each, are:

1. Positive external constraints (cages; traps).
2. Negative external constraints (no water or food available).
3. Positive internal constraints (diseases; ingested poison or absorbed toxic chemicals).
4. Negative internal constraints (weaknesses and incapacities due to injured organs or tissues).

We humans can restrict the freedom of animals and plants by either directly imposing some of these constraints upon them or by producing changes in their environments which then act as constraints upon them. Either way, if we do these things knowingly we are guilty of violating the Rule of Noninterference.

The second kind of duty that comes under this rule is the duty to let wild creatures live out their lives in freedom. Here freedom means not the absence of constraints but simply being allowed to carry on one's existence in a wild state. With regard to individual organisms, this duty requires us to refrain from capturing them and removing them from their natural habitats, *no matter how well we might then treat them.* We have violated the duty of noninterference even if we "save" them by taking them out of a natural danger or by restoring their health after they have become ill in the wild. (The duty is not violated, however, if we do such things with the intention of returning the creature to the wild as soon as possible, and we fully carry out this intention.) When we take young trees or wildflowers from a natural ecosystem, for example, and transplant them in landscaped grounds, we break the Rule of Noninterference *whether or not we then take good care of them and so enable them to live longer, healthier lives than they would have enjoyed in the wild.* We have done a wrong by not letting them live out their lives in freedom. In all situations like these we intrude into the domain of the natural world and terminate an organism's existence as a wild creature. It does not matter that our treatment of them may improve their strength, promote their growth, and increase their chances for a long, healthy life. By destroying their status as wild animals or plants, our interference in their lives amounts to an absolute negation of their natural freedom. Thus, however "benign" our actions may seem, we are doing what the Rule of Noninterference forbids us to do.

Of still deeper significance, perhaps, is the duty of noninterference as it applies to the freedom of whole species-populations and communities of life. The prohibition against interfering with these entities means that we must not try to manipulate, control, modify, or "manage" natural ecosystems or otherwise intervene in their normal functioning. For any given species-population, freedom is the absence of human intervention of any kind in the natural lawlike processes by which the population preserves itself from generation to generation. Freedom for a whole biotic community is the absence of human intervention in the natural lawlike processes by which all its constituent species-populations undergo changing ecological relationships with one another over time. The duty not to interfere is the duty to respect the freedom of biologically and ecologically organized groups of wild organisms by refraining from those sorts of intervention. Again, this duty holds even if such intervention is motivated by a desire to "help" a species-population survive or a desire to "correct natural imbalances" in a biotic community. (Attempts to save endangered species which have almost been exterminated by past *human* intrusions into nature, and attempts to restore ecological stability and balance to an ecosystem that has been damaged by past *human* activity are cases that fall under the Rule of Restitutive Justice and may be ethically right. These cases will be considered in connection with that rule.)

The duty of noninterference, like that of nonmaleficence, is a purely negative duty. It does not require us to perform any actions regarding either individual organisms or groups of organisms. We are only required to respect their wild freedom by letting them alone. In this way we allow them, as it were, to fulfill their own destinies. Of course some of them will lose out in their struggle with natural competitors and others will suffer harm from natural causes. But as far as our proper role as moral agents is concerned, we must keep "hands off." By strictly adhering to the Rule of Noninterference, our conduct manifests a profound regard for the integrity of the system of nature. Even when a whole ecosystem has been seriously disturbed by a natural disaster (earthquake, lightning-caused fire, volcanic eruption, flood, prolonged drought, or the like) we are duty-bound not to intervene to try to repair the damage. After all, throughout the long history of life on our planet natural disasters ("disasters," that is, from the standpoint of some particular organism or group of organisms) have always taken their toll in the death of many creatures. Indeed, the very process of natural selection continually leads to the extinction of whole species. After such disasters a gradual readjustment always takes place so that a new set of relations among species-populations emerges. To abstain from intervening in this order of things is a way of expressing our attitude of respect for nature, for we thereby give due recognition to the process of evolutionary change that has been the "story" of life on Earth since its very beginnings.

This general policy of nonintervention is a matter of disinterested principle. We may want to help certain species-populations because we like them or because they are beneficial to us. But the Rule of Noninterference requires that we put aside our personal likes and our human interests with reference to how we treat them. Our respect for nature means that we acknowledge the sufficiency of the natural world to sustain its own proper order throughout the whole domain of life. This is diametrically opposed to the human-centered view of nature as a vast piece of property which we can use as we see fit.

In one sense to have the attitude of respect toward natural ecosystems, toward wild living things, and toward the whole process of evolution is to believe that nothing goes wrong in nature. Even the destruction of an entire biotic community or the extinction of a species is not evidence that something is amiss. If the causes for such events arose within the system of nature itself, nothing improper has happened. In particular, the fact that organisms suffer and die does not itself call for corrective action on the part of humans *when humans have had nothing to do with the cause of that suffering and death*. Suffering and death are integral aspects of the order of nature. So if it is ever the case in our contemporary world that the imminent extinction of a whole species is due to entirely natural causes, we should not try to stop the natural sequence of events from taking place in order to save the species. That sequence of events is governed by the operation of laws that have made the biotic Community of our planet what it is. To respect that Community is to respect the laws that gave rise to it.

In addition to this respect for the sufficiency and integrity of the natural order, a second ethical principle is implicit in the Rule of Noninterference. This is the principle of species-impartiality, which serves as a counterweight to the dispositions of people to favor certain species over others and to want to intervene in behalf of their favorites. These dispositions show themselves in a number of ways. First, consider the reactions of many people to predator–prey relations among wildlife. Watching the wild dogs of the African plains bring down the Wildebeest and begin devouring its underparts while it is still alive, they feel sympathy for the prey and antipathy for the predator. There is a tendency to make moral judgments, to think of the dogs as vicious and cruel, and to consider the Wildebeest an innocent victim. Or take the situation in which a snake is about to kill a baby bird in its nest. The snake is perceived as wicked and the nestling is seen as not deserving such a fate. Even plant life is looked at in this biased way. People get disturbed by a great tree being "strangled" by a vine. And when it comes to instances of bacteria-caused diseases, almost everyone has a tendency to be on the side of the organism which has the disease rather than viewing the situation from the standpoint of the living bacteria inside the organism. If we accept the biocentric outlook and have genuine respect for nature, however, we remain strictly neutral between predator and prey, parasite and host, the disease-causing and the diseased. To take sides in such struggles, to think of them in moral terms as cases of the maltreatment of innocent victims by evil animals and nasty plants, is to abandon the attitude of respect for all wild living things. It is to count the good of some as having greater value than that of others. This is inconsistent with the fundamental presupposition of the attitude of respect: that all living things in the natural world have the same inherent worth. . . .

3. *The Rule of Fidelity.* This rule applies only to human conduct in relation to individual animals that are in a wild state and are capable of being deceived or betrayed by moral agents. The duties imposed by the Rule of Fidelity, though of restricted range, are so frequently violated by so many people that this rule needs separate study as one of the basic principles of the ethics of respect for nature.

Under this rule fall the duties not to break a trust that a wild animal places in us (as shown by its behavior), not to deceive or mislead any animal capable of being deceived or misled, to uphold an animal's expectations, which it has formed on the basis of one's past actions with it, and to be true to one's intentions as made known to an animal when it has come to rely on one. Although we cannot make mutual agreements with wild animals, we can act in such a manner as to call forth their trust in us. The basic moral requirement imposed by the Rule of Fidelity is that we remain faithful to that trust.

The clearest and commonest examples of transgressions of the rule occur in hunting, trapping, and fishing. Indeed, the breaking of a trust is a key to good (that is, successful) hunting, trapping, and fishing. Deception with intent to harm is of the essence. Therefore, unless there is a weighty moral reason for engaging in these activities, they must be condemned by the ethics of respect for nature. The weighty moral reason in question must itself be grounded on disinterested principle, since the action remains wrong in itself in virtue of its constituting a violation of a valid moral rule. Like all such violations, it can be justified only by appeal to a higher, more stringent duty whose priority over the duty of fidelity is established by a morally valid priority principle.

When a man goes hunting for bear or deer he will walk through a woodland as quietly and unobtrusively as possible. If he is a duck hunter he will hide in a blind, set out decoys, use imitative calls. In either case the purpose, of course, is to get within shooting range of the mammal or bird. Much of the hunter's conduct is designed to deceive the wild creature. As an animal is approaching, the hunter remains quiet, then raises his rifle to take careful aim. Here is a clear situation in which, first, a wild animal acts as if there were no danger; second, the hunter by stealth is deliberately misleading the animal to expect no danger; and third, the hunter is doing this for the immediate purpose of killing the animal. The total performance is one of entrapment and betrayal. The animal is manipulated to be trusting and unsuspicious. It is deliberately kept unaware of something in its environment which is, from the standpoint of its good, of great importance to it. The entire pattern of the hunter's behavior is aimed at taking advantage of an animal's trust. Sometimes an animal is taken advantage of in situations where it may be aware of some danger but instinctively goes to the aid of an injured companion. The hunter uses his knowledge of this to betray the animal. Thus when the hunting of shorebirds used to be legally permitted, a hunter would injure a single bird and leave it out to attract hundreds of its fellows, which would fly in and gather around it. This way the hunter could easily "harvest" vast numbers of shorebirds. Even to this day a similar kind of trickery is used to deceive birds. Crow hunters play recordings of a crow's distress calls out in the field. The recording attracts crows, who are then easy targets to shoot. This aspect of hunting, it should be repeated, is not some peripheral aberration. Much of the excitement and enjoyment of hunting as a sport is the challenge to one's skills in getting animals to be trusting and unsuspecting. The cleverer the deception, the better the skill of the hunter. . . .

It is not a question here of whether the animal being hunted, trapped, or fished has a *right* to expect not to be deceived. The animal is being deceived in order to bring advantage to the deceiver and this itself is the sign that the deceiver considers the animal as either having no inherent worth or as having a lower degree of inherent worth than the deceiver himself. Either way of looking at it is incompatible with the attitude of respect for nature. . . .

Besides breaking the Rule of Fidelity, hunting, trapping, and fishing also, of course, involve gross violations of the Rules of Nonmaleficence and Noninterference. It may be the case that in circumstances where the only means for obtaining food or clothing essential to human survival is by hunting, trapping, or fishing, these actions are morally permissible. The ethical principles that justify them could stem from a system of human ethics based on respect for persons plus a priority principle that makes the duty to provide for human survival outweigh those duties of nonmaleficence, noninterference, and fidelity that are owed to nonhumans. But when hunting and fishing are done for sport or recreation, they cannot be justified on the same grounds.

There are cases of deceiving and breaking faith with an animal, however, which can be justified *within* the system of environmental ethics. These cases occur when deception and betrayal must (reluctantly) be done as a necessary step in a wider action of furthering an animal's good, this wider action being the fulfillment of a duty of restitutive justice. If breaking faith is a temporary measure absolutely needed to alleviate great suffering or to prevent serious harm coming to an animal, such an act may be required as an instance of restitutive justice. Putting aside for the moment a consideration of the idea of restitutive justice as it applies to environmental ethics, it may be helpful to look at some examples.

Suppose a grizzly bear has wandered into an area close to human habitation. In order to prevent harm coming not only to people but also to the bear (when people demand that it be killed), the bear may be deceived so that it can be shot with harmless tranquilizer darts and then, while it is unconscious, removed to a remote wilderness area. Another example would be the live-trapping of a sick or injured animal so that it can be brought to an animal hospital, treated, and then returned to the wild when it is fully recovered. Still another kind of case occurs when a few birds of an endangered species are captured in order to have them raise young in captivity. The young would then be released in natural habitat areas in an effort to prevent the species from becoming extinct.

These human encroachments upon the wild state of mammals and birds violate both the rule of Noninterference and the Rule of Fidelity. But the whole treatment of these creatures is consistent with the attitude of respect for them. They are not being taken advantage of but rather are being given the opportunity to maintain their existence as wild living things. . . .

. . . Hunters and fishermen often argue that they show true respect for nature because they advocate (and pay for) the preservation of natural areas which benefit wild species-populations and life communities. And it is quite true that the setting aside of many "wildlife refuges," both public and private, has resulted from their efforts. Wild animals and plants have benefited from this. What is being overlooked in this argument is the difference between doing something to benefit oneself which happens also to benefit others, and doing something with the purpose of benefiting others as one's ultimate end of action. Hunters and fishermen want only those areas of the natural environment protected that will provide for them a constant supply of fish, birds, and mammals as game. Indeed, sportsmen will often urge the killing of nongame animals that prey on "their" (the sportsmen's) animals. In Alaska, for example, hunters have persuaded state officials to "manage" wolves—the method used is to shoot them from helicopters—so as to ensure that a large population of moose is available for hunting. The argument that hunters and fishermen are true conservationists of wildlife will stand up only when we sharply distinguish conservation (saving in the present for future consumption) from preservation (protecting from both present and future consumption). And if the ultimate purpose of conservation programs is future exploitation of wildlife for the enjoyment of outdoor sports and recreation, such conservation activities are not consistent with respect for nature, whatever may be the benefits incidentally brought to some wild creatures. Actions that bring about good consequences for wildlife do not express the attitude of respect unless those actions are motivated in a certain way. It must be the case that the actions are done with the intention of promoting or protecting the good of wild creatures as an end in itself and for the sake of those creatures themselves. Such motivation is precisely what is absent from the conservation activities of sportsmen.

4. *The Rule of Restitutive Justice.* In its most general terms this rule imposes the duty to restore the balance of justice between a moral agent and a moral subject when the subject has been wronged by the agent. Common to all instances in which a duty of restitutive justice arises, an agent has broken a valid moral rule and by doing so has upset the balance of justice between himself or herself and a moral subject. To hold oneself accountable for having done such an act is to acknowledge a special duty one has taken upon oneself by that wrongdoing. This special duty is the duty of restitutive justice. It

requires that one make amends to the moral subject by some form of compensation or reparation. This is the way one restores the balance of justice that had held between oneself and the subject before a rule of duty was transgressed.

The set of rules that makes up a valid system of ethics defines the true moral relations that hold between agents and subjects. When every agent carries out the duties owed to each subject and each subject accordingly receives its proper treatment, no one is wronged or unjustly dealt with. As soon as a rule is willfully violated, the balance of justice is tilted against the agent and in favor of the subject; that is, the agent now has a special burden to bear and the victim is entitled to a special benefit, since the doing of the wrong act gave an undeserved benefit to the agent and placed an unfair burden on the subject. In order to bring the tilted scale of justice back into balance, the agent must make reparation or pay some form of compensation to the subject.

The three rules of duty so far discussed in this section can be understood as defining a moral relationship of justice between humans and wild living things in the Earth's natural ecosystems. This relationship is maintained as long as humans do not harm wild creatures, destroy their habitats, or degrade their environments; as long as humans do not interfere with an animal's or plant's freedom or with the overall workings of ecological interdependence; and as long as humans do not betray a wild animal's trust to take advantage of it. Since these are all ways in which humans can express in their conduct the attitude of respect for nature, they are at the same time ways in which each living thing is given due recognition as an entity possessing inherent worth. The principles of species-impartiality and of equal consideration are adhered to, so that every moral subject is treated as an end in itself, never as a means only.

Now, if moral agents violate any of the three rules, they do an injustice to something in the natural world. The act destroys the balance of justice between humanity and nature, and a special duty is incurred by the agents involved. This is the duty laid down by the fourth rule of environmental ethics, the Rule of Restitutive Justice.

What specific requirements make up the duty in particular cases? Although the detailed facts of each situation of an agent's wrongdoing would have to be known to make a final judgment about what sorts of restitutive acts are called for, we can nevertheless formulate some middle-range principles of justice that generally apply. These principles are to be understood as specifying requirements of restitution for transgressions of *any* of the three rules. In all cases the restitutive measures will take the form of promoting or protecting in one way or another the good of living things in natural ecosystems.

In working out these middle-range principles it will be convenient to distinguish cases according to what type of moral subject has been wronged. We have three possibilities. An action that broke the Rule of Nonmaleficence, of Noninterference, or of Fidelity might have wronged an individual organism, a species-population as a whole, or an entire community. Violations of the Rules in all cases are ultimately wrongs done to individuals, since we can do harm to a population or community only by harming the individual organisms in it (thereby lowering the median level of well-being for the population or community as a whole). The first possibility, however, focuses on the harmed individuals taken separately.

If the organisms have been harmed but have not been killed, then the principle of restitutive justice requires that the agent make reparation by returning those organisms to a condition in which they can pursue their good as well as they did before the injustice was done to them. If this cannot wholly be accomplished, then the agent must further the good of the organisms in some other way, perhaps by making their physical environment more favorable to their continued well-being. Suppose, on the other hand, that an organism has been killed. Then the principle of restitutive justice states that the agent owes some form of compensation to the species-population and/or the life community of which the organism was a member. This would be a natural extension of respect from the individual to its genetic relatives and ecological associates. The compensation would consist in promoting or protecting the good of the species-population or life community in question.

Consider as a second possibility that a whole species-population has been wrongly treated by a violation of either nonmaleficence or noninterference. A typical situation would be one where most of the animals of a "target" species have been killed by excessive hunting, fishing, or trapping in a limited area. As a way of making some effort to right the wrongs that have been committed, it would seem appropriate that the agents at fault be required to ensure that permanent protection be given to all the remaining numbers of the population. Perhaps the agents could contribute to a special fund for the acquisition of land and themselves take on the responsibility of patrolling the area to prevent further human intrusion.

Finally, let us consider those circumstances where an entire biotic community has been destroyed by humans. We have two sorts of cases here, both requiring some form of restitution. The first sort of case occurs when the destructive actions are not only wrong in themselves because they violate duties of nonmaleficence and noninterference but are wrong, all things considered. They are not justified by a rule of *either* environmental ethics *or* of human ethics. The second sort of case is one in which the actions are required by a valid rule of human ethics though they are contrary to valid rules of environmental ethics. Even when greater moral weight is given to the rule of human ethics, so that the actions are justified, all things considered, they still call for some form of restitution on grounds of justice to all beings having inherent worth. This idea holds also within the domain of human ethics.

A duty of restitutive justice (as a corollary of the Rule of Reciprocity) arises whenever one of the other valid rules of human ethics is broken. Even if the

action was required by a more stringent duty, a human person has been unjustly treated and therefore some compensation is due her or him. That the
action was morally justified, all things considered, does not license our overlooking the fact that someone has been wronged. Hence the propriety of
demanding restitution. So in our present concerns, even if the destruction of a
biotic community is entailed by a duty of human ethics that overrides the rules
of environmental ethics, an act of restitutive justice is called for in recognition
of the inherent worth of what has been destroyed.

There are many instances in which human practices bring about the total
obliteration of biotic communities in natural ecosystems. Whether or not these
practices are justified by valid rules of human ethics, they all come under the
Rule of Restitutive Justice. A northern conifer woodland is cut down to build a
vacation resort on the shore of a lake. A housing development is constructed in
what had been a pristine wilderness area of cactus desert. A marina and yacht
club replace a tidal wetland which had served as a feeding and breeding ground
for multitudes of mollusks, crustacea, insects, birds, fish, reptiles, and mammals. A meadow full of wildflowers, both common and rare, is bull-dozed over
for a shopping mall. Strip mining takes away one side of a mountain. A prairie
is replaced by a wheat farm. In every one of these situations and in countless
others of the same kind, wholesale destruction of entire natural ecosystems
takes place. Unrestrained violence is done to whole communities of plants and
animals. Communities that may have been in existence for tens of thousands of
years are completely wiped out in a few weeks or a few days, in some cases in a
few hours. What form of restitution can then be made that will restore the
balance of justice between humanity and nature? No reparation for damages
can possibly be given to the community itself, which exists no more. As is true
of a single organism that has been killed, the impossibility of repairing the
damage does not get rid of the requirement to make some kind of compensation for having destroyed something of inherent worth.

If restitutive justice is to be done in instances of the foregoing kind, what
actions are called for and to whom are they due? Two possibilities suggest
themselves here. One is that compensation should be made to another biotic
community which occupies *an ecosystem of the same type* as the one destroyed. If
it is a northern conifer woodland, then the organizations or individuals who
were responsible for its destruction owe it to the life community of another
conifer woodland to help it in some way to further or maintain its well-being.
Perhaps a partially damaged area of woodland could be restored to ecological
health (removing trash that had been put there, cleaning up a polluted stream
flowing through the area, stopping any further contamination by acid rain or
other atmospheric pollution, and so on).

The other possible recipient of compensation would be any wild region of
nature that is being threatened by human exploitation or consumption. Compensatory action would be taken in behalf of a biotic community somewhere on

Earth that might be damaged or destroyed unless special efforts are made to protect it. Acquiring the land and giving it legal status as a nature preserve would be suitable measures.

These suggested middle-range principles are all derived from the one broad Rule of Restitutive Justice: that any agent which has caused an evil to some natural entity that is a proper moral subject owes a duty to bring about a countervailing good, either to the moral subject in question or to some other moral subject. The perpetrating of a harm calls for the producing of a benefit. The greater the harm, the larger the benefit needed to fulfill the moral obligation.

It is worth adding here that all of us who live in modern industrialized societies owe a duty of restitutive justice to the natural world and its wild inhabitants. We have all benefited in countless ways from large-scale technology and advanced modes of economic production. As consumers we not only accept the benefits of industrialization willingly, but spend much of our lives trying to increase those benefits for ourselves and those we love. We are part of a civilization that can only exist by controlling nature and using its resources. Even those who go out to a natural area to enjoy "the wilderness experience" are recipients of the benefits of advanced technology. (What marvels of modern chemistry went into the creation of plastics and synthetic fabrics in their backpacks, tents, sleeping bags, and food containers!) None of us can evade the responsibility that comes with our high standard of living; we all take advantage of the amenities of civilized life in pursuing our individual values and interests. Since it is modern commerce, industry, and technology that make these amenities possible, each of us is a consumer and user of what the natural world can yield for us. Our well-being is constantly being furthered at the expense of the good of the Earth's nonhuman inhabitants. Thus we all should share in the cost of preserving and restoring some areas of wild nature for the sake of the plant and animal communities that live there. Only then can we claim to have genuine respect for nature.

Ideals of Human Excellence and Preserving the
Natural Environment

————————— ❧ —————————

Thomas E. Hill, Jr.

I

A wealthy eccentric bought a house in a neighborhood I know. The house was surrounded by a beautiful display of grass, plants, and flowers, and it was shaded by a huge old avocado tree. But the grass required cutting, the flowers needed tending, and the man wanted more sun. So he cut the whole lot down and covered the yard with asphalt. After all it was his property and he was not fond of plants.

It was a small operation, but it reminded me of the strip mining of large sections of the Appalachians. In both cases, of course, there were reasons for the destruction, and property rights could be cited as justification. But I could not help but wonder, "What sort of person would do a thing like that?"

Many Californians had a similar reaction when a recent governor defended the leveling of ancient redwood groves, reportedly saying, "If you have seen one redwood, you have seen them all."

Incidents like these arouse the indignation of ardent environmentalists and leave even apolitical observers with some degree of moral discomfort. The reasons for these reactions are mostly obvious. Uprooting the natural environment robs both present and future generations of much potential use and enjoyment. Animals too depend on the environment; and even if one does not value animals for their own sakes, their potential utility for us is incalculable. Plants are needed, of course, to replenish the atmosphere quite aside from their aesthetic value. These reasons for hesitating to destroy forests and gardens are not only the most obvious ones, but also the most persuasive for practical purposes. But, one wonders, is there nothing more behind our discomfort? Are we concerned solely about the potential use and enjoyment of the forests, etc., for ourselves, later generations, and perhaps animals? Is there not something else which disturbs us when we witness the destruction or even listen to those who would defend it in terms of cost/benefit analysis?

Imagine that in each of our examples those who would destroy the environment argue elaborately that, even considering future generations of human beings and animals, there are benefits in "replacing" the natural environment which outweigh the negative utilities which environmentalists cite.[1] No doubt we could press the argument on the facts, trying to show that the destruction is shortsighted and that its defenders have underestimated its potential harm or ignored some pertinent rights or interests. But is this all we could say? Suppose we grant, for a moment, that the utility of destroying the redwoods, forests, and gardens is equal to their potential for use and enjoyment by nature lovers and animals. Suppose, further, that we even grant that the pertinent human rights and animal rights, if any, are evenly divided for and against destruction. Imagine that we also concede, for argument's sake, that the forests contain no potentially useful endangered species of animals and plants. Must we then conclude that there is no further cause for moral concern? Should we then feel morally indifferent when we see the natural environment uprooted?

II

Suppose we feel that the answer to these questions should be negative. Suppose, in other words, we feel that our moral discomfort when we confront the destroyers of nature is not fully explained by our belief that they have miscalculated the best use of natural resources or violated rights in exploiting them. Suppose, in particular, we sense that part of the problem is that the natural environment is being viewed exclusively as a natural *resource*. What could be the ground of such a feeling? That is, what is there in our system of normative principles and values that could account for our remaining moral dissatisfaction?

Some may be tempted to seek an explanation by appeal to the interests, or even the rights, of plants. After all, they may argue, we only gradually came to acknowledge the moral importance of all human beings, and it is even more recently that consciences have been aroused to give full weight to the welfare (and rights?) of animals. The next logical step, it may be argued, is to acknowledge a moral requirement to take into account the interests (and rights?) of plants. The problem with the strip miners, redwood cutters, and the like, on this view, is not just that they ignore the welfare and rights of people and animals; they also fail to give due weight to the survival and health of the plants themselves.

The temptation to make such a reply is understandable if one assumes that all moral questions are exclusively concerned with whether *acts* are right or wrong and that this, in turn, is determined by how the acts impinge on the rights and interests of those directly affected. On this assumption, if there is cause for moral concern, some right or interest has been neglected; and if the rights and interests of human beings and animals have already been taken into account, then there must be some other pertinent interests, for example, those of plants. A little reflection will show that the assumption is mistaken; but, in any case, the conclusion that plants have rights or morally relevant interests is surely untenable. We do speak of what is "good for" plants, and they can "thrive" and also be "killed." But this does not imply that they have "interests" in any morally relevant sense. Some people apparently believe that plants grow better if we talk to them, but the idea that the plants suffer and enjoy, desire and dislike, etc., is clearly outside the range of both common sense and scientific belief. The notion that the forests should be preserved to avoid *hurting* the trees or because they have a *right* to life is not part of a widely shared moral consciousness, and for good reason.[2]

Another way of trying to explain our moral discomfort is to appeal to certain religious beliefs. If one believes that all living things were created by a God who cares for them and entrusted us with the use of plants and animals only for limited purposes, then one has a reason to avoid careless destruction of the forests, etc., quite aside from their future utility. Again, if one believes that a divine force is immanent in all nature, then too one might have reason to care for more than sentient things. But such arguments require strong and controversial premises, and, I suspect, they will always have a restricted audience.

Early in this century, due largely to the influence of G. E. Moore, another point of view developed which some may find promising.[3] Moore introduced, or at least made popular, the idea that certain states of affairs are intrinsically valuable—not just valued, but valuable, and not necessarily because of their effects on sentient beings. Admittedly Moore came to believe that in fact the only intrinsically valuable things were conscious experiences of various sorts,[4] but this restriction was not inherent in the idea of intrinsic value. The intrinsic goodness of something, he thought, was an objective, nonrelational property of the thing, like its texture or color, but not a property perceivable by sense perception or detectable by scientific instruments. In theory at least, a single tree thriving alone in a universe without sentient beings, and even without God, could be intrinsically valuable. Since, according to Moore, our duty is to maximize intrinsic value, his theory could obviously be used to argue that we have reason not to destroy natural environments independently of how they affect human beings and animals. The survival of a forest might have worth beyond its worth *to* sentient beings.

This approach, like the religious one, may appeal to some but is infested with problems. There are, first, the familiar objections to intuitionism, on which the theory depends. Metaphysical and epistemological doubts about nonnatural, intuited properties are hard to suppress, and many have argued that the theory rests on a misunderstanding of the words *good*, *valuable*, and the like. Second, even if we try to set aside these objections and think in Moore's terms, it is far from obvious that everyone would agree that the existence of forests, etc., is intrinsically valuable. The test, says Moore, is what we would say when we imagine a universe with just the thing in question, without any effects or accompaniments, and then we ask, "Would its existence be better than its nonexistence?" Be careful, Moore would remind us, not to construe this question as, "Would you *prefer* the existence of that universe to its nonexistence?" The question is, "Would its existence have the objective, nonrelational property, intrinsic goodness?"

Now even among those who have no worries about whether this really makes sense, we might well get a diversity of answers. Those prone to destroy natural environments will doubtless give one answer, and nature lovers will likely give another. When an issue is as controversial as the one at hand, intuition is a poor arbiter.

The problem, then, is this. We want to understand what underlies our moral uneasiness at the destruction of the redwoods, forests, etc., even apart from the loss of these as resources for human beings and animals. But I find no adequate answer by pursuing the questions, "Are rights or interests of plants neglected?" "What is God's will on the matter?" and "What is the intrinsic value of the existence of a tree or forest?" My suggestion, which is in fact the main point of this paper, is that we look at the problem from a different perspective. That is, let us turn for a while from the effort to find reasons why certain *acts* destructive of natural environments are morally wrong to the ancient task of articulating our ideals of human excellence. Rather than argue directly with destroyers of the environment who say, "Show me why what I am doing is *immoral*," I want to ask, "What sort of person would want to do what they propose?" The point is not to skirt the issue with an ad hominem, but to raise a different moral question, for even if there is no convincing way to show that the destructive acts are wrong (independently of human and animal use and enjoyment), we may find that the willingness to indulge in them reflects the absence of human traits that we admire and regard morally important.

This strategy of shifting questions may seem more promising if one reflects on certain analogous situations. Consider, for example, the Nazi who asks, in all seriousness. "Why is it wrong for me to make lampshades out of human skin—provided, of course, I did not myself kill the victims to get the skins?" We would react more with shock and disgust than with indignation, I suspect, because it is even more evident that the question reveals a defect in the questioner than that the proposed act is itself immoral. Sometimes we may not regard an act wrong at all though we see it as reflecting something objectionable about the person who does it. Imagine, for example, one who laughs spontaneously to himself when he reads a newspaper account of a plane crash that kills hundreds. Or, again, consider an obsequious grandson who, having waited for his grandmother's inheritance with mock devotion, then secretly spits on her grave when at last she dies. Spitting on the grave may have no adverse consequences and perhaps it violates no rights. The moral uneasiness which it arouses is explained more by our view of the agent than by any conviction that what he did was immoral. Had he hesitated and asked, "Why shouldn't I spit on her grave?" it seems more fitting to ask him to reflect on the sort of person he is than to try to offer reasons why he should refrain from spitting.

III

What sort of person, then, would cover his garden with asphalt, strip mine a wooded mountain, or level an irreplaceable redwood grove? Two sorts of answers, though initially appealing, must be ruled out. The first is that persons who would destroy the environment in these ways are either shortsighted, underestimating the harm they do, or else are too little concerned for the well-being of other people. Perhaps too they have insufficient regard for animal life. But these considerations have been set aside in order to refine the controversy. Another tempting response might be that we count it a moral virtue, or at least a human ideal, to love nature. Those who value the environment only for its utility must not really love nature and so in this way fall short of an ideal. But such an answer is hardly satisfying in the present context, for what is at issue is *why* we feel moral discomfort at the activities of those who admittedly value nature only for its utility. That it is ideal to care for nonsentient nature beyond its possible use is really just another way of expressing the general point which is under controversy.

What is needed is some way of showing that this ideal is connected with other virtues, or human excellences, not in question. To do so is difficult and my suggestions, accordingly, will be tentative and subject to qualification. The main idea is that, though indifference to nonsentient nature does not *necessarily* reflect the absence of virtues, it often signals the absence of certain traits which we want to encourage because they are, in most cases, a natural basis for the development of certain virtues. It is often thought, for example, that those who would destroy the natural environment must lack a proper appreciation of their place in the natural order, and so must either be ignorant or have too little humility. Though I would argue that this is not necessarily so, I suggest that, given certain plausible empirical assumptions, their attitude may well be rooted in ignorance, a narrow perspective, inability to see things as important apart from themselves and the limited groups they associate with, or reluctance to accept themselves as natural beings. Overcoming these deficiencies will not guarantee a proper moral humility, but for most of us it is probably an important psychological preliminary. Later I suggest, more briefly, that indifference to nonsentient nature typically reveals absence of either aesthetic sensibility or a disposition to cherish what has enriched one's life and that these, though not themselves moral virtues, are a natural basis for appreciation of the good in others and gratitude.

Consider first the suggestion that destroyers of the environment lack an appreciation of their place in the universe. Their attention, it seems, must be focused on parochial matters, on what is, relatively speaking, close in space and time. They seem not to understand that we are a speck on the cosmic scene, a brief stage in the evolutionary process, only one among millions of species on Earth, and an episode in the course of human history. Of course, they know that there are stars, fossils, insects, and ancient ruins; but do they have any idea of the complexity of the processes that led to the natural world as we find it? Are they aware how much the forces at work within their own bodies are like those which govern all living things and even how much they have in common with inanimate bodies? Admittedly scientific knowledge is limited and no one can master it all; but could one who had a broad and deep under-standing of his place in nature really be indifferent to the destruction of the natural environment?

This first suggestion, however, may well provoke a protest from a sophisti-cated anti-environmentalist. "Perhaps *some* may be indifferent to nature from ignorance," the critic may object, "but *I* have studied astronomy, geology, biology, and biochemistry, and I still unashamedly regard the nonsentient environment as simply a resource for our use. It should not be wasted, of course, but what should be preserved is decidable by weighing long-term costs and benefits." "Besides," our critic may continue, "as philosophers you should know the old Humean formula, 'You cannot derive an *ought* from an *is*.' All the facts of biology, biochemistry, etc., do not entail that I ought to love nature or want to preserve it. What one understands is one thing; what one values is something else. Just as nature lovers are not necessarily scientists, those indif-ferent to nature are not necessarily ignorant."

Although the environmentalist may concede the critic's logical point, he may well argue that, as a matter of fact, increased understanding of nature tends to heighten people's concern for its preservation. If so, despite the objection, the suspicion that the destroyers of the environment lack deep understanding of nature is not, in most cases, unwarranted, but the argument need not rest here.

The environmentalist might amplify his original idea as follows: "When I said that the destroyers of nature do not appreciate their place in the universe, I was not speaking of intellectual understanding alone, for, after all, a person can *know* a catalog of facts without ever putting them together and seeing vividly the whole picture which they form. To see oneself as just one part of nature is to look at oneself and the world from a certain perspective which is quite different from being able to recite detailed information from the natural sci-ences. What the destroyers of nature lack is this perspective, not particular information."

Again our critic may object, though only after making some concessions: "All right," he may say, "*some* who are indifferent to nature may lack the cosmic perspective of which you speak, but again there is no *necessary* connec-tion between this failing, if it is one, and any particular evaluative attitude toward nature. In fact, different people respond quite differently when they move to a wider perspective. When *I* try to picture myself vividly as a brief, transitory episode in the course of nature, I simply get depressed. Far from inspiring me with a love of nature, the exercise makes me sad and hostile. You romantics think only of poets like Wordsworth and artists like Turner, but you should consider how differently Omar Khayyám responded when he took your wider perspective. His reaction, when looking at his life from a cosmic view-point, was 'Drink up, for tomorrow we die.' Others respond in an almost opposite manner with a joyless Stoic resignation, exemplified by the poet who pictures the wise man, at the height of personal triumph, being served a magnificent banquet, and then consummating his marriage to his beloved, all the while reminding himself, 'Even this shall pass away.' "[5] In sum, the critic may object, "Even if one should try to see oneself as one small transitory part of nature, doing so does not dictate any particular normative attitude. Some may come to love nature, but others are moved to live for the moment; some sink into sad resignation; others get depressed or angry. So indifference to nature is not necessarily a sign that a person fails to look at himself from the larger perspective."

The environmentalist might respond to this objection in several ways. He might, for example, argue that even though some people who see themselves as part of the natural order remain indifferent to nonsentient nature, this is not a common reaction. Typically, it may be argued, as we become more and more aware that we are parts of the larger whole we come to value the whole independently of its effect on ourselves. Thus, despite the possibilities the critic raises, indifference to nonsentient nature is still in most cases a sign that a person fails to see himself as part of the natural order.

If someone challenges the empirical assumption here, the environmentalist might develop the argument along a quite different line. The initial idea, he may remind us, was that those who would destroy the natural environment fail to *appreciate* their place in the natural order. "Appreciating one's place" is not simply an intellectual appreciation. It is also an attitude, reflecting what one values as well as what one knows. When we say, for example, that both the servile and the arrogant person fail to *appreciate* their place in a society of equals, we do not mean simply that they are ignorant of certain empirical facts, but rather that they have certain objectionable attitudes about their importance relative to other people. Similarly, to fail to appreciate one's place in nature is not merely to lack knowledge or breadth of perspective, but to take a certain attitude about what matters. A person who *understands* his place in nature but still views nonsentient nature merely as a resource takes the attitude that nothing is *important* but human beings and animals. Despite first appearances, he is not so much like the pre-Copernican astronomers who made the intellec-tual error of treating the Earth as the "center of the universe" when they made their calculations. He is more like the racist who, though well aware of other races, treats all races but his own as insignificant.

So construed, the argument appeals to the common idea that awareness of nature typically has, and should have, a humbling effect. The Alps, a storm at sea, the Grand Canyon, towering redwoods, and "the starry heavens above" move many a person to remark on the comparative insignificance of our daily concerns and even of our species, and this is generally taken to be a quite fitting response.[6] What seems to be missing, then, in those who understand nature but remain unmoved is a proper humility.[7] Absence of proper humility is not the same as selfishness or egoism, for one can be devoted to self-interest while still viewing one's own pleasures and projects as trivial and unimportant. And one can have an exaggerated view of one's own importance while grandly sacrificing for those one views as inferior. Nor is the lack of humility identical with belief that one has power and influence, for a person can be quite puffed up about himself while believing that the foolish world will never acknowledge him. The humility we miss seems not so much a belief about one's relative effectiveness and recognition as an attitude which measures the importance of things independently of their relation to oneself or to some narrow group with which one identifies. A paradigm of a person who lacks humility is the self-important emperor who grants status to his family because it is *his*, to his subordinates because *he* appointed them, and to his country because *he* chooses to glorify it. Less extreme but still lacking proper humility is the elitist who counts events significant solely in proportion to how they affect his class. The suspicion about those who would destroy the environment, then, is that what they count important is too narrowly confined insofar as it encompasses only what affects beings who, like us, are capable of feeling.

This idea that proper humility requires recognition of the importance of nonsentient nature is similar to the thought of those who charge meat eaters with "species-ism." In both cases it is felt that people too narrowly confine their concerns to the sorts of beings that are most like them. But, however intuitively appealing, the idea will surely arouse objections from our nonenvironmentalist critic. "Why," he will ask, "do you suppose that the sort of humility I *should* have requires me to acknowledge the importance of nonsentient nature aside from its utility? You cannot, by your own admission, argue that nonsentient nature *is* important, appealing to religious or intuitionist grounds. And simply to assert, without further argument, that an ideal humility requires us to view nonsentient nature as important for its own sake begs the question at issue. If proper humility is acknowledging the relative importance of things as one should, then to show that I must lack this you must first establish that one *should* acknowledge the importance of nonsentient nature."

Though some may wish to accept this challenge, there are other ways to pursue the connection between humility and response to nonsentient nature. For example, suppose we grant that proper humility requires only acknowledging a due status to sentient beings. We must admit, then, that it is logically possible for a person to be properly humble even though he viewed all nonsentient nature simply as a resource. But this logical possibility may be a psychological rarity. It may be that, given the sort of beings we are, we would never learn humility before persons without developing the general capacity to cherish, and regard important, many things for their own sakes. The major obstacle to humility before persons is self-importance, a tendency to measure the significance of everything by its relation to oneself and those with whom one identifies. The processes by which we overcome self-importance are doubtless many and complex, but it seems unlikely that they are exclusively concerned with how we relate to other people and animals. Learning humility requires learning to feel that something matters besides what will affect oneself and one's circle of associates. What leads a child to care about what happens to a lost hamster or a stray dog he will not see again is likely also to generate concern for a lost toy or a favorite tree where he used to live. Learning to value things for their own sake, and to count what affects them important aside from their utility, is not the same as judging them to have some intuited objective property, but it is necessary to the development of humility and it seems likely to take place in experiences with nonsentient nature as well as with people and animals. If a person views all nonsentient nature merely as a resource, then it seems unlikely that he has developed the capacity needed to overcome self-importance.

IV

This last argument, unfortunately, has its limits. It presupposes an empirical connection between experiencing nature and overcoming self-importance, and this may be challenged. Even if experiencing nature promotes humility before others, there may be other ways people can develop such humility in a world of concrete, glass, and plastic. If not, perhaps all that is needed is limited experience of nature in one's early, developing years; mature adults, having overcome youthful self-importance, may live well enough in artificial surroundings. More importantly, the argument does not fully capture the spirit of the intuition that an ideal person stands humbly before nature. That idea is not simply that experiencing nature tends to foster proper humility before other people; it is, in part, that natural surroundings encourage and are appropriate to an ideal sense of oneself as part of the natural world. Standing alone in the forest, after months in the city, is not merely good as a means of curbing one's arrogance before others; it reinforces and fittingly expresses one's acceptance of oneself as a natural being.

Previously we considered only one aspect of proper humility, namely, a sense of one's relative importance with respect to other human beings. Another aspect, I think, is a kind of *self-acceptance*. This involves acknowledging, in more than a merely intellectual way, that we are the sort of creatures that we are. Whether one is self-accepting is not so much a matter of how one attributes *importance* comparatively to oneself, other people, animals, plants, and other things as it is a matter of understanding, facing squarely, and responding appropriately to who and what one is, e.g., one's powers and limits, one's affinities with other beings and differences from them, one's unalterable nature and one's freedom to change. Self-acceptance is not merely intellectual awareness, for one can be intellectually aware that one is growing old and will eventually die while nevertheless behaving in a thousand foolish ways that reflect a refusal to acknowledge these facts. On the other hand, self-acceptance is not passive resignation, for refusal to pursue what one truly wants within one's limits is a failure to accept the freedom and power one has. Particular behaviors, like dying one's gray hair and dressing like those twenty years younger, do not *necessarily* imply lack of self-acceptance, for there could be reasons for acting in these ways other than the wish to hide from oneself what one really is. One fails to accept oneself when the patterns of behavior and emotion are rooted in a desire to disown and deny features of oneself, to pretend to oneself that they are not there. This is not to say that a self-accepting person makes no value judgments about himself, that he likes all facts about himself, wants equally to develop and display them; he can, and should feel remorse for his past misdeeds and strive to change his current vices. The point is that he does not disown them, pretend that they do not exist or are facts about something other than himself. Such pretense is incompatible with proper humility because it is seeing oneself as better than one is.

Self-acceptance of this sort has long been considered a human excellence, under various names, but what has it to do with preserving nature? There is, I think, the following connection. As human beings we are part of nature, living, growing, declining, and dying by natural laws similar to those governing other living beings; despite our awesomely distinctive human powers, we share many of the needs, limits, and liabilities of animals and plants. These facts are neither good nor bad in themselves, aside from personal preference and varying conventional values. To say this is to utter a truism which few will deny, but to accept these facts, as facts about oneself, is not so easy—or so common. Much of what naturalists deplore about our increasingly artificial world reflects, and encourages, a denial of these facts, an unwillingness to avow them with equanimity.

Like the Victorian lady who refuses to look at her own nude body, some would like to create a world of less transitory stuff, reminding us only of our intellectual and social nature, never calling to mind our affinities with "lower" living creatures. The "denial of death," to which psychiatrists call attention, reveals an attitude incompatible with the sort of self-acceptance which philosophers, from the ancients to Spinoza and on, have admired as a human excellence. My suggestion is not merely that experiencing nature causally promotes such self-acceptance, but also that those who fully accept themselves as part of the natural world lack the common drive to disassociate themselves from nature by replacing natural environments with artificial ones. A storm in the wilds helps us to appreciate our animal vulnerability, but, equally important, the reluctance to experience it may *reflect* an unwillingness to accept this aspect of ourselves. The person who is too ready to destroy the ancient redwoods may lack humility, not so much in the sense that he exaggerates his importance relative to others, but rather in the sense that he tries to avoid seeing himself as one among many natural creatures.

V

My suggestion so far has been that, though indifference to nonsentient nature is not itself a moral vice, it is likely to reflect either ignorance, a self-importance, or a lack of self-acceptance which we must overcome to have proper humility. A similar idea might be developed connecting attitudes toward nonsentient nature with other human excellences. For example, one might argue that indifference to nature reveals a lack of either an aesthetic sense or some of the natural roots of gratitude.

When we see a hillside that has been gutted by strip miners or the garden replaced by asphalt, our first reaction is probably, "How ugly!" The scenes assault our aesthetic sensibilities. We suspect that no one with a keen sense of beauty could have left such a sight. Admittedly not everything in nature strikes us as beautiful, or even aesthetically interesting, and sometimes a natural scene is replaced with a more impressive architectural masterpiece. But this is not usually the situation in the problem cases which environmentalists are most concerned about. More often beauty is replaced with ugliness.

At this point our critic may well object that, even if he does lack a sense of beauty, this is no moral vice. His cost/benefit calculations take into account the pleasure others may derive from seeing the forests, etc., and so why should he be faulted?

Some might reply that, despite contrary philosophical traditions, aesthetics and morality are not so distinct as commonly supposed. Appreciation of beauty, they may argue, is a human excellence which morally ideal persons should try to develop. But, setting aside this controversial position, there still may be cause for moral concern about those who have no aesthetic response to nature. Even if aesthetic sensibility is not itself a moral virtue, many of the capacities of mind and heart which it presupposes may be ones which are also needed for an appreciation of other people. Consider, for example, curiosity, a mind open to novelty, the ability to look at things from unfamiliar perspectives, empathetic imagination, interest in details, variety, and order, and emotional freedom from the immediate and the practical. All these, and more, seem necessary to aesthetic sensibility, but they are also traits which a person needs to be fully sensitive to people of all sorts. The point is not that a moral person must be able to distinguish beautiful from ugly people; the point is rather that unresponsiveness to what is beautiful, awesome, dainty, dumpy, and otherwise aesthetically interesting in nature probably reflects a lack of the opennesss of mind and spirit necessary to appreciate the best in human beings.

   The anti-environmentalist, however, may refuse to accept the charge that he
lacks aesthetic sensibility. If he claims to appreciate seventeenth-century minia-
ture portraits, but to abhor natural wildernesses, he will hardly be convincing.
Tastes vary, but aesthetic sense is not *that* selective. He may, instead, insist that
he *does* appreciate natural beauty. He spends his vacations, let us suppose,
hiking in the Sierras, photographing wildflowers, and so on. He might press
his argument as follows: "I enjoy natural beauty as much as anyone, but I fail
to see what this has to do with preserving the environment independently of
human enjoyment and use. Nonsentient nature is a resource, but one of its best
uses is to give us pleasure. I take this into account when I calculate the costs
and benefits of preserving a park, planting a garden, and so on. But the
problem you raised explicitly set aside to preserve nature as a means to enjoyment. I say, let us enjoy nature fully while we can, but if all sentient beings
were to die tomorrow, we might as well blow up all plant life as well. A
redwood grove that no one can use or enjoy is utterly worthless."
   The attitude expressed here, I suspect, is not a common one, but it represents a philosophical challenge. The beginnings of a reply may be found in the
following. When a person takes joy in something, it is a common (and perhaps
natural) response to come to cherish it. To cherish something is not simply to
be happy with it at the moment, but to care for it for its own sake. This is not
to say that one necessarily sees it as having feelings and so wants it to feel good;
nor does it imply that one judges the thing to have Moore's intrinsic value. One
simply wants the thing to survive and (when appropriate) to thrive, and not
simply for its utility. We see this attitude repeatedly regarding mementos. They
are not simply valued as a means to remind us of happy occasions; they come to
be valued for their own sake. Thus, if someone really took joy in the natural
environment, but was prepared to blow it up as soon as sentient life ended, he
would lack this common human tendency to cherish what enriches our lives.
While this response is not itself a moral virtue, it may be a natural basis of the
virtue we call "gratitude." People who have no tendency to cherish things that
give them pleasure may be poorly disposed to respond gratefully to persons
who are good to them. Again the connection is not one of logical necessity, but
it may nevertheless be important. A nonreligious person unable to "thank"
anyone for the beauties of nature may nevertheless feel "grateful" in a sense;
and I suspect that the person who feels no such "gratitude" toward nature is
unlikely to show proper gratitude toward people.
   Suppose these conjectures prove to be true. One may wonder what is the
point of considering them. Is it to disparage all those who view nature merely
as a resource? To do so, it seems, would be unfair, for, even if this attitude
typically stems from deficiencies which affect one's attitudes toward sentient
beings, there may be exceptions and we have not shown that their view of
nonsentient nature is itself blameworthy. But when we set aside questions of
blame and inquire what sorts of human traits we want to encourage, our
reflections become relevant in a more positive way. The point is not to insinu-

ate that all anti-environmentalists are defective, but to see that those who value such traits as humility, gratitude, and sensitivity to others have reason to promote the love of nature.

Notes

I thank Gregory Kavka, Catherine Harlow, the participants at a colloquium at the University of Utah, and the referees for *Environmental Ethics*, Dale Jamieson and Donald Scherer, for helpful comments on earlier drafts of this paper.

1. When I use the expression "the natural environment," I have in mind the sort of examples with which I began. There is also a broad sense, as Hume and Mill noted, in which all that occurs, miracles aside, is "natural." As will be evident, I shall use "natural" in a narrower, more familiar sense.

2. I assume here that having a right presupposes having interests in a sense which in turn presupposes a capacity to desire, suffer, etc. Since my main concern lies in another direction, I do not argue the point, but merely note that some regard it as debatable.

3. G. E. Moore, *Principia Ethica* (Cambridge: Cambridge University Press, 1903), and *Ethics* (London: Holt, 1912).

4. G. E. Moore, "Is Goodness a Quality?" in *Philosophical Papers* (London: George Allen & Unwin, 1959), 95–97.

5. T. Tildon, "Even this shall pass away," in *The Best Loved Poems of the American People*, ed. Hazel Felleman (Garden City, N.Y.: Doubleday, 1936).

6. An exception, apparently, was Kant, who thought "the starry heavens" sublime and compared them with "the moral law within," but did not for all that see our species as comparatively insignificant.

7. By "proper humility" I mean that sort and degree of humility that is a morally admirable character trait. How precisely to define this is, of course, a controversial matter; but the point for present purposes is just to set aside obsequiousness, false modesty, underestimation of one's abilities, and the like.

PART III

Alternative Perspectives on
Environmental Philosophy

H UMAN RELATIONS with nature pose profound philosophical and ethical questions that academics and activists alike are discussing, debating, formulating, and reformulating. Like John Muir, Aldo Leopold, and Rachel Carson before them, many environmentalists today believe that there must be a close link between environmental philosophy and environmental action. Behind protests and acts of civil disobedience lie philosophical principles about how humans ought to interact with the natural world. The essays in this part express new perspectives that in many cases emerge from environmental activism. While some of these selections are difficult and occasionally laden with jargon, they represent the struggle now under way to reconcile environmental theory and practice.

Deep ecology is perhaps the best known and most influential of the alternative environmental perspectives. The term "deep ecology" was coined by the Norwegian philosopher and activist Arne Naess, who characterizes it as "a normative, ecophilosophical movement that is inspired and fortified . . . by our experience as humans in nature." In his essay, sociologist and activist Bill Devall explains how deep ecologists seek to shift human thinking and action away from anthropocentrism (human-centeredness) toward ecocentrism. Deep ecologists are critical of "reform environmentalists" who view nature as valuable only because of the benefits it confers on humans. Some deep ecologists, such as those associated with Earth First!, insist that the natural world has value independent of its usefulness to humans. They advocate direct action and believe that there should be "no compromise in defense of Mother Earth."

Deep ecologists have been engaged in a long-standing debate with both social ecologists and ecological feminists. Social ecologists, like long-time activist Murray Bookchin, believe that in order to adequately resolve our ecological problems we must analyze the socioeconomic institutions that shape our world.

111

Social ecologists reject deep ecology because it fails to address the role of the state and capitalism in environmental destruction. Deep ecologists reply to this criticism by arguing that the social ecological perspective remains anthropocentric. Indeed it is. However, social ecologists believe that current ecological crises are direct results of the failure of human society to recognize and value the continuity, rather than the division, between nature and culture. By radically splitting nature and culture, deep ecologists perpetuate the evils they wish to eliminate. According to social ecologists, we must create decentralized, human-scale eco-communities in which decisions are reached through direct, participatory democratic processes.

Social ecologists argue that an essential part of building these eco-communities is the recognition that the domination of nature stems from the domination of humans by other humans. Thus a central component of social ecology is an examination of racism and sexism. Sociologist Robert Bullard, in his selection, confronts the problem of environmental racism through an examination of the growing movement against dumping environmentally hazardous toxic substances in poor and minority communities. "Toxic warriors" are a new kind of environmentalist who link resistance to ecological degradation to concerns about social justice, economic inequality, and civil rights. According to Bullard, mainstream American environmentalists must begin to practice a politics of inclusion, embrace social justice policies, and "reach out to the 'other' America."

Ecofeminists also argue for a politics of inclusion and share some of the concerns of social ecologists and those fighting environmental racism. Val Plumwood, an Australian philosopher and activist, specifically criticizes deep ecology for its failure to examine social institutions, such as patriarchy, that have contributed to ecological destruction. She also faults deep ecologists for failing to challenge the dualisms—such as those between nature and culture, feminine and masculine, and emotion and reason—that contribute to environmentally destructive attitudes. In addition, Plumwood argues that deep ecologists do not have a sophisticated enough conception of the self. While she agrees that in order to have a healthier and more just relationship to nature we have to develop different conceptions of ourselves, she argues against rejecting the boundary between self and other, as some deep ecologists suggest, or making the self as large or impartial as possible, as still other deep ecologists advocate. Instead, we should recognize that we are "relational selves"—continuous with nature while distinguishable from it. Ecofeminism, according to Plumwood, emphasizes the development of selves in community.

British political scientist John Dryzek argues that "instrumental reason," the type of rationality that is entirely a matter of choosing efficient means in pursuit of our ends, is at the heart of our destructive and dominating interactions with nature. However, Dryzek rejects attempts to replace instrumental reason with spirituality. Looking back at the Nazi cult of "blood and soil,"

Dryzek warns against the emergence of an "eco-fascism" that would sacrifice human values to an unreasoning worship of nature. As an alternative, Dryzek suggests that we develop a "communicative rationality" through which we think of ourselves as part of an ongoing dialogue that includes nature.

These alternative approaches to environmental philosophy are important not just as prescriptions for political action, but also as challenges to what has become the mainstream in environmental thinking. Although they are not as well developed as some traditional philosophical theories, these alternative perspectives bring fresh insights to our reflections on nature.

Further Reading

Bookchin, Murray. *The Ecology of Freedom*. Palo Alto, Calif.: Chesire Books, 1982.

Bookchin's major work examines hierarchy as an obstacle to social and natural progress.

Bullard, Robert D., ed. *Confronting Environmental Racism: Voices from the Grassroots*. Boston: South End Press, 1993.

These essays document how people of color are disproportionately endangered by toxic landfills, industrial dumping, and hazardous waste incinerators and what they are doing about this form of racism.

Gaard, Greta, ed. *Ecofeminism: Women, Animals, Nature*. Philadelphia: Temple University Press, 1993.

This collection of twelve articles explores connections and tensions among ecofeminists, animal liberationists, deep ecologists and social ecologists.

Goodin, Robert E. *Green Political Theory*. Cambridge, Mass.: Polity Press, 1992.

A philosophical discussion of green politics, arguing that it expresses a forceful, workable, and coherent moral vision.

List, Peter C. *Radical Environmentalism: Philosophy and Tactics*. Belmont, Calif.: Wadsworth, 1993.

A collection of writings by leading activists and theorists.

Merchant, Carolyn. *Radical Ecology: The Search for a Livable World*. New York: Routledge, 1992.

A survey of various movements and ideas addressing global environmental crises.

Naess, Arne. *Ecology, Community and Lifestyle: Outline of an Ecosophy*. Trans. and ed. David Rothenberg. New York: Cambridge University Press, 1989.

The major work in the philosophy of deep ecology.

[From] Deep Ecology and Radical Environmentalism

Bill Devall

DURING THE 1960s and early 1970s a new wave of environmental activism and policy issues attracted attention. These issues included the effects of the explosive growth of human population; the effects of toxic wastes and pollution on air, water, and soil as well as on human health and well-being; and deforestation and human-caused extinction of other species. Established conservation organizations such as the Sierra Club and newly established environmental organizations such as the Natural Resources Defense Council grew substantially in membership during the 1970s. However, during the 1970s, critics within the environmental movement saw these major national organizations as less and less responsive to grassroots demands for more rapid change in public policy, too bureaucratized and centralized, and too "shallow" in ideology. The major environmental groups were also criticized for their willingness to settle for reforms in government policy without changes in our society's basic culture, including the myths of economic growth, progress, belief that technology will save us from environmental problems, and humanism.

Deep ecology was a label put forward in the early 1970s for a philosophical tendency that provided both a critique of reform or shallow environmentalism and a critique of industrial society and the anthropocentric bias of that type of society. In the following pages, the major tenets of deep ecology and the relationship between deep ecology as philosophical perspective and the emerging radical wing of the environmental movement are discussed. Then, several radical groups and movements, including Earth First!, are described, providing an overview of radical environmentalism. Finally, relations among radical and reform environmental movement organizations, the anti-environmental counter-movement, and government agencies are discussed.

Deep Ecology

The terms *deep ecology* and *deep, long-range ecology movement* were originated by Norwegian philosopher and social activist Arne Naess. In a 1973 article, Naess asserted that shallow and deep ecology can be seen as two aspects of the environmental movement. He defined *shallow ecology* as the "fight against pollution and resource depletion. Central objective: The health and affluence of people in the developed countries."[1] He defined *deep ecology* as a normative, ecophilosophical movement that is inspired and fortified in part by our experience as humans in nature and in part by ecological knowledge. The literature on the deep–shallow distinction and on the historical and philosophical antecedents of the deep ecology movement has been extensively developed since 1973.[2]

The most distinctive aspect of deep ecology is the idea of *ecocentric identification*, which Naess calls the "ultimate norm" of self-realization. Humans are one of myriad self-realizing beings, and human maturity and self-realization come from broader and wider self-identification. Out of identification with forests, rivers, deserts, or mountains comes a kind of solidarity: "I am the rainforest" or "I am speaking for this mountain because it is a part of me."

Naess says that Rachel Carson showed this kind of self-identification combined with ecological understanding. According to Naess,

> The intense motivation of Rachel Carson was of a deep kind. It had to do with how she intuitively conceived herself, the human existence and the world. In short, a combined religious and philosophical motivation. She said: We cannot treat creation, God's creation, as we do. And it is in no way good for ourselves to behave as we do. Her Self was wide and deep. Her main motivation was religious and philosophical, *not* narrowly utilitarian.[3]

A second ultimate norm of deep ecology is *biocentrism*, or *ecocentrism* as some call it. In contrast with an anthropocentric or human-centered worldview, an ecocentric worldview suggests that humans are part of the "web of life"—not at the top of creation but equal with the many other aspects of creation. Naess calls this a *total-field image* and suggests that this image encourages respect for natural biodiversity and evolution. Speaking as a philosopher, Naess suggests that in an anthropocentric worldview every action is undertaken to protect present and future generations of humans. In an ecocentric worldview, future generations include generations of *all* living beings and "beings" are broadly defined to include living rivers as well as living species.

The supporters of the deep ecology movement, then, seek ways of living that are best for all living beings. "Do as little harm as possible" might be a slogan of those seeking a deep ecology–based lifestyle. Some taking of life is necessary to satisfy vital human needs, but the integrity, beauty, and stability of the native landscape is respected.

Realizing the goal of an ecocentric-based society requires *ecosophy* or wisdom. Ecosophy literally means wisdom of the household, or the place within which we dwell. Alan Drengson, editor of *The Trumpeter*, a widely read journal on deep ecology, explains that "ecosophy" for humans means ecological wisdom, which is not just discursive knowing, but a state of harmonious relationship with Nature. The Earth has wisdom, and each species has a wisdom peculiar to it, which is exemplified in continued flourishing, beyond bare survival. "Flourish" means an optimal state of self-fulfillment and self-realization. . . . Ecosophy is the wisdom of dwelling in a place and it is also the wisdom to dwell in a place harmoniously.[4]

There could be many articulations of a deep ecology type of position. Some of these could be based on Native American traditions, on Buddhist traditions, or on other cultural traditions and philosophical perspectives. Naess himself was greatly influenced by the philosopher Spinoza. Naess calls his own articulation of deep ecology "Ecosophy T."[5]

Sensing that some kind of platform or general statement was needed to show the unity among a diversity of deep ecology types of positions, Naess, along with philosopher George Sessions, formulated "8 points" as a modest suggestion for discussion. Naess insists that this platform is without great pretensions and has the primary function of stimulating dialogue about philosophy and strategies in politics and personal lifestyle decisions. Naess and other supporters of deep ecology have expanded and extensively commented on these principles in many publications.

1. The well-being and flourishing of human and nonhuman life on Earth have value in themselves. These values are independent of the usefulness of the nonhuman world for human purposes.
2. Richness and diversity of life forms contribute to the realization of these values and are also values in themselves.
3. Humans have no right to reduce this richness and diversity except to satisfy human needs.
4. The flourishing of human life and cultures is compatible with a substantial decrease of the human population. The flourishing of nonhuman life requires such a decrease.
5. Present human interference with the nonhuman world is excessive, and the situation is rapidly worsening.
6. Policies must therefore be changed. The changes in policies affect basic economic, technological, and ideological structures. The resulting state of affairs will be deeply different from the present.
7. The ideological change is mainly that of appreciating life quality (dwelling in situations of inherent worth) rather than adhering to an increasingly higher standard of living. There will be a profound awareness of the difference between big and great.
8. Those who subscribe to the foregoing points have an obligation directly or indirectly to participate in the attempt to implement the necessary changes.[6]

Although a wide variety of lifestyles and social policies are potentially compatible with a deep ecology position, the literature on deep ecology suggests that many supporters favor what has been called *green consumerism* (careful awareness both of the quality and quantity of products consumed, based on the principle of least harm to living beings and ecocentric identity), voluntary simplicity of lifestyle that maximizes rich experiences in nature, and bioregionalism or living in place. Supporters of deep ecology also tend to encourage the restoration movement, which seeks to enhance and restore native biodiversity within a bioregional context, and to favor protection of ancient forests, tropical rainforests, and all other types of ecosystems on the planet. Some supporters of deep ecology also favor vegetarianism based on principles outlined in John Robbins's (1987) *Diet for a New America*. Robbins emphasizes eating lower on the food chain. Generally speaking, the norm of nonviolence is widely accepted by deep ecologists. Naess himself wrote an explanation of Gandhi's principles of nonviolence and has been interested in Gandhian types of social movements since the 1930s.[7]

Deep Ecology and Green Politics

Supporters of deep ecology share with "greens" and green socialists a criticism of modern industrial societies and of the failure of reform environmental groups to make fundamental critical assessments of industrial society. Deep ecologists tend to differ from green socialists as well as from ecofeminists in assessing the reasons for the current environmental crisis. Although green socialists look to the conditions of capitalism and ecofeminist theorists focus on androcentrism as the cause of the environmental crisis, deep ecologists emphasize the dangerous tendencies of anthropocentrism, including the tendency toward hubris and narrow conceptions of the ego as a power-seeking entity. Deep ecologists also suggest that a rich life means exploring our "wild self" or ecological self and suggest that to do this we need to unmask the anthropocentrism that is part of the basic ideology of industrial society.

Warwick Fox, responding to critics of deep ecology, contrasts the deep ecology position with positions of other radical critical theories.[8] Deep ecology has strong affinities with established green parties and with emerging green political movements, as can be seen by comparing the deep ecology platform listed earlier with the principles and criteria of green parties and green activism.[9] The four pillars of green philosophy—ecology, grassroots democracy, social responsibility, and nonviolence—are variously interpreted, and healthy dialogue has occurred. The most revolutionary of the pillars, however, is ecology. Moreover, as Robyn Eckersley points out, the most radical and promising ecological insights have emerged in North America and Australasia rather than in Western Europe, where green parties are most fully established.[10]

Although supporters of deep ecology acknowledge the importance of developing compatible strategies for social justice and ecology, some green theorists have yet to accept that nature has inherent worth or even the importance of protecting ecosystem integrity—such as tropical rainforests—to enhance human well-being on the planet. Many supporters of deep ecology reject in turn any political strategy that ties economic growth to invasion of any remaining habitat of endangered species or massive developments of rainforests or other areas that provide habitat for native species. The uneasiness that many green socialists and social ecologists feel with deep ecology and the vitriolic criticisms that some green socialists and ecologists, including Murray Bookchin, have heaped on it reflect their unwillingness to accept its rejection of anthropocentrism for a truly ecocentric perspective.

Deep Ecology and Radical Environmentalism

As noted earlier, the deep, long-range ecology movement is a philosophical movement with implications for personal lifestyles and public policy as suggested in the platform presented by Naess and Sessions. Yet, deep ecology has increasingly become associated with radical environmental activism, or the use of tactics such as ecotage, sit-ins, guerrilla theater, demonstrations, and other forms of direct action. Although deep ecology does not provide a formal ideology for radical environmentalism, it offers a "diverse body of ideas . . . which taken as a whole express the vision behind the activism."[11] Part of this vision consists of a rejection of the shallow perspective and reformist tactics of the mainstream environmental movement.

Many radical environmentalists believe that, despite their anthropocentric orientation, reform environmental groups such as the Sierra Club, National Audubon Society, and Wilderness Society had a "window of opportunity" during the past few decades to work through conventional political channels for necessary changes. As noted by Peter Borrelli, editor of *The Amicus Journal*, particularly during the 1980s, many activists became increasingly disenchanted and alienated from mainstream environmental organizations. They were discouraged by the compromising attitude of mainstream groups, by the bureaucratization of the groups, by the professionalization of leaders and their detachment from the emerging concerns of grassroots supporters, and by the lack of success of mainstream organizations in countering the Reagan anti-environmental agenda.[12]

The emergence of so-called third-wave environmentalism during the 1980s especially discouraged and alienated many environmentalists. Third-wave environmentalism was based on the principle that environmental experts, usually lawyers and scientists, could and should negotiate directly with corporations and government agencies to achieve compromises on pollution controls, energy policies, and other environmental issues, preferably using the "market" mechanism. Third-wave environmentalism is narrowly rational and focuses on economics and public policy. No recognition is given to ecological sensibilities, the necessity of providing an ecocentric critique of industrial society, or of exploring the "wild self" and transforming society. Grassroots activists were not consulted in setting policy and, indeed, grassroots activists were frequently seen as burdened with too much emotion. The Environmental Defense Fund is sometimes cited as a prototypical third-wave group.[13]

Christopher Manes, in his book *Green Rage*, summarizes how reform environmentalism stimulated the development of radical environmentalism:

> The impetus for the radical environmental movement, at least in this country (USA), was not solely a response to the smug advocates of wilderness destruction and industrial development. . . . The mainstream, reformist environmental movement, embodied in national groups like the Sierra Club and the Wilderness Society, ensured an explosion of radical environmental forces by anxiously trying to restrain them.[14]

Led by the example of people like Dave Foreman and Howie Wolke, cofounders of Earth First! (both ex-staff members of mainstream environmental groups), a growing number of grassroots activists drew inspiration from the civil rights, anti-Vietnam, and women's movements and explored various forms of direct action—civil disobedience, guerrilla theater, monkey-wrenching, nonviolent demonstrations, and anarchism—in their efforts to open the minds and hearts of their fellow citizens to the plight of the planet under the domination of industrial society. In doing so they were continuing the radical amateur tradition that Fox sees as having been crucial throughout the history of the conservation movement.[15]

Radical environmentalists are also determined to reclaim their spiritual identity with nature, whether in the Buddhist tradition espoused by Gary Synder and Robert Aitken, in the tribal rituals of the early years of Earth First!, or in the "Council of All Beings" ritual. As described by John Seed, the purpose of a Council of All Beings is to change the perception of humans as *above* nature to that of humans *in* nature:

> What is described here should not be seen as merely intellectual. The intellect is one entry point. . . . For some people, however, this change of perspective follows from actions on behalf of mother Earth. "I am protecting the rain forest" develops to "I am part of the rain forest protecting myself. I am that part of the rain forest recently emerged into thinking." What a relief then! The thousands of years of imagined separation are over and we begin to recall our true nature. That is, the change is a spiritual one, thinking like a mountain, sometimes referred to as "deep ecology."[16]

Although radical environmentalism has been stimulated by the failures of reform environmentalism and by the philosophy and spirituality of deep ecology, ultimately "it is based on one simple but frightening realization: that our culture is lethal to the ecology that it depends on."[17] At root, then, radical environmentalism is a response to our existential condition. In a culture dominated by humanism and technology, radical environmental sensibilities come from a sense of the peril that all beings face because of human intervention in the biosphere. The agenda of radical environmentalism is less and less a reaction to the agenda of reform environmentalism (or the activities of industry and government) and more and more a reaction to the demands of our existence. Its concerns are acid rain, increasing rates of species extinction, the greenhouse effect, ozone depletion, and on and on. . . .

The ecocentric worldview and strong spiritual identification with the natural world represented by many people in the deep ecology movement promises to provide a potent source of inspiration for radical environmentalism and a challenge to the mainstream environmental movement as well as the rest of industrial civilization. Its ability to learn from earlier critiques by feminists and to absorb the insights of ecofeminism reflect the evolutionary strength of deep ecology. Participants in the deep, long-range ecology movement continue to learn and grow in a search for new meanings; to develop, explore, and integrate their embeddedness in nature; and to search for lifestyles and public policies that are less exploitative of nature than the conventional lifestyles of many people in the middle and upper-middle classes in advanced industrial societies. In interaction with supporters of other forms of environmental philosophy, Arne Naess and other supporters of deep ecology continually emphasize the importance of working with and finding common ground with those who speak from these different perspectives, an intellectual endeavor akin to the martial arts of Aikido.

Notes

1. A. Naess, "The Shallow and the Deep, Long-Range Ecology Movement," *Inquiry* 16 (1973): 97.

2. See, for example, W. Fox, *Toward a Transpersonal Ecology* (Boston: Shambhala, 1990), and G. Sessions, "The Deep Ecology Movement: A Review," *Environmental Review* 11 (1987): 105–25.

3. A. Naess, "Ecology and Ethics" (Manuscript, University of Oslo, 1989), 7.

4. A. Drengson, "In Praise of Ecosophy," *Trumpeter* 7 (1990): 101–2.

5. A. Naess, *Ecology, Community and Lifestyle: Outline of an Ecosophy,* trans. and ed. D. Rothenberg (New York: Cambridge University Press, 1989).

6. B. Devall and G. Sessions, *Deep Ecology: Living as if Nature Mattered* (Salt Lake City: Peregrine Smith, 1985), 70.

7. A. Naess, *Ghandi and Group Conflict: An Exploration of Satyagraha. Theoretical Background* (Oslo: Universitesforlaget, 1974).

8. W. Fox, "The Deep Ecology–Ecofeminism Debate and Its Parallels," *Environmental Ethics* 11 (1989): 5–25.

9. See, for example, F. Capra and C. Spretnak, *Green Politics,* rev. ed. (Santa Fe: Bear, 1986), and J. Porritt, *Seeing Green: The Politics of Ecology Explained* (New York: Basil Blackwell, 1985).

10. R. Eckersley, "Green Theory and Practice in Old and New Worlds: A Comparative Perspective" (Manuscript, University of Tasmania, 1990).

11. C. Manes, *Green Rage: Radical Environmentalism and the Unmaking of Civilization* (Boston: Little, Brown, 1990), 136.

12. P. Borrelli, ed., *Crossroads: Environmental Priorities for the Future* (Washington, D.C.: Island Press, 1988).

13. Ibid.

14. Manes, *Green Rage*, 44.

15. S. Fox, *John Muir and His Legacy: The American Conservation Movement* (Madison: University of Wisconsin Press, 1985).

16. Quoted in Devall and Sessions, *Deep Ecology*, 243.

17. Manes, *Green Rage*, 22.

[From] *Defending the Earth*

———————— ∽ ————————

Murray Bookchin

. . . ONE OF MY MAJOR complaints about "deep ecology" is that it lacks a clearly developed social analysis and ethics. It thus provides a "tolerant" philosophical home to profoundly conflicting ideas and sensibilities, from humanistic naturalists in the tradition of Thoreau to barely disguised racists. . . .

The problem, of course, is not deep ecology's stated commitment to foster a new sensibility towards the natural world. All radical ecologists agree on the need to go beyond the limited environmentalist perspective that sees "Nature" as merely a passive inventory of "natural resources" and defines appropriate human interaction with the natural world as merely using these resources "efficiently" and "prudently" without threatening the biological "sustainability" of the *human* species. Whatever our differences about nature philosophy, both deep and social ecologists call for a direct and profound respect for the biosphere, a conscious effort to function within its parameters, and an attempt to achieve harmony between society and the natural world. I believe that all social activists should embrace this new sensibility toward nature.

The main problem with deep ecology's philosophy, however, is that this is about as far as it goes. It does not highlight or systematically address the *social* roots of the ecological crisis. It does not document or interpret the historical emergence of society out of first, or biological, nature, a crucial development that brings social theory into organic contact with ecological theory. It presents no explanation of—indeed, it reveals little interest in—the emergence of hierarchy out of early organic society, of classes out of hierarchy, of the state out of classes—in short, the highly graded social as well as ideological developments which are at the roots of the ecological problem. Indeed, it is hardly more insightful about these questions than the reformist environmental movement. Thus, even when individual deep ecologists show concern for harmonizing relationships between races, genders, and classes, their concern does not stem from a coherent expression of deep ecology philosophy. Rather it is expressed only as an external ethical and social commitment that may—or may not, for that matter—be added to a deep ecology perspective.

Women, poor folks, and people of color are right, I think, to be very wary of a philosophy which interprets vital questions of human solidarity, democracy, and liberation as optional and secondary concerns, at best, and evidence of "anti-ecological" or "anthropocentric" selfishness, at worst. Ecological philosophy, if it is to provide a solid basis for alliance-building, must be a *social* ecology that critiques and challenges *all* forms of hierarchy and domination, not just our civilization's attempt to dominate and plunder the natural world. It must set as its overarching goal, the creation of a non-hierarchical *society* if we are to live in harmony with nature.

Our present society has a definite hierarchical character. It is a propertied society that concentrates economic power in corporate elites. It is a bureaucratic and militaristic society that concentrates political and military power in centralized state institutions. It is a patriarchal society that allocates authority to men in varying degrees. And *it is a racist society* that places a minority of whites in a self-deceptive sovereignty over a vast worldwide majority of peoples of color. While it is theoretically possible that a hierarchical society can biologically sustain itself, at least for a time, through draconian environmentalist controls, it is absolutely inconceivable that present-day hierarchical and particularly capitalist society could establish a non-domineering and ethically symbiotic relationship between itself and the natural world. As long as hierarchy persists, as long as domination organizes humanity around a system of elites, the project of dominating nature will remain a predominant ideology and inevitably lead our planet to the brink, if not into the abyss, of ecological extinction.

Social ecology provides a better foundation for alliance-building and a respectful unity-in-diversity because it understands that the very concept of dominating nature stems from the domination of human by human, indeed, of the young by their elders, of women by men, of one ethnic or racial group by another, of society by the state, of one economic class by another, and of colonized people by a colonial power. It thus stresses all the social issues that most deep ecologists and reform environmentalists tend to ignore, often downplay, or badly misunderstand. From this perspective, the fight against racism is not just a mere political item that can be added to "defending the Earth"; it is actually a vital and essential part of establishing a truly free and ecological society. . . .

One of the chief obstacles to building alliances across ethnic lines manifests itself at the programmatic level. One of the truisms of the environmental movement is that our society has reached ecological limits to its overall growth at the global level. Environmentalists thus call for limits on economic expansion, population growth, and individual consumption. There is a great deal of validity to such demands. I have long argued that we must transform our bloated, urbanized, and rapacious society into a confederation of eco-communities that are sensitively tailored in size, population, technology, and consumption to the specific ecosystems in which they are located. But when these demands are not set clearly within the context of a struggle for a non-hierarchical society, appeals for "limits to growth" are almost inevitably turned into racist and draconian measures by the powers-that-be to ensure the sustainability of hierarchical First World societies at the expense of the material needs of Third World people. It should not come as a surprise then, that for many activists of color environmentalism has come to mean little more than racist measures for blocking needed economic improvements and for intensifying austerity among people of color in this country and in Latin America, Asia, and Africa. It has also come to mean a vicious policy of limiting the "surplus" population of people of color throughout the world through starvation, disease, and forced sterilization. . . .

. . . Capitalist society, whether in Western corporate or Eastern bureaucratic forms, is fundamentally destructive. The power of this society to destroy has reached a scale unprecedented in the history of humanity—and this power is being used, almost systematically, to wreak havoc upon the entire world of life and its material bases. In nearly every region, air is being befouled, waterways polluted, soil washed away, the land desiccated, and wildlife destroyed. Coastal areas and even the depths of the sea are not immune to widespread pollution. More significantly in the long run, basic biological cycles such as the carbon cycle and nitrogen cycle, upon which all living things depend for the maintenance and renewal of life, are being distorted to the point of irreversible damage. The proliferation of nuclear reactors in the United States and throughout the world—some 1,000 by the year 2000 if the powers-that-be have their way—have exposed countless millions of people and other life forms to some of the most carcinogenic and mutagenic agents known. Some of these terrifying threats, like radioactive wastes, may be with us for hundreds of thousands of years.

To these radioactive wastes we also must add long-lived pesticides, lead residues, and thousands of toxic or potentially toxic chemicals in food, water, and air; the expansion of cities into vast urban belts, with dense concentrations of populations comparable in size to entire nations; the rising din of background noise; the stresses created by congestion, mass living, and mass manipulation; the immense accumulations of garbage, refuse, sewage, and industrial wastes; the congestion of highways and city streets with vehicular traffic; the profligate destruction of nonrenewable resources; the scarring of the earth by real estate speculators, mining and lumbering barons, and highway construction bureaucrats. Our lethal insults to the biosphere have wreaked a degree of damage in a single generation that exceeds the damage inflicted by thousands of years of human habitation on this planet. If this tempo of destruction is borne in mind, it is terrifying to speculate about what lies ahead in the generations to come.

In the face of such a crisis, efforts for change are inevitable. Ordinary people all over the globe are becoming active in campaigns to eliminate nuclear power plants and weapons, to preserve clean air and water, to limit the use of pesticides and food additives, to reduce vehicular traffic in streets and on highways, to make cities more wholesome physically, to prevent radioactive wastes from seeping into the environment, to guard and expand wilderness areas and domains for wildlife, to defend animal species from human depredation. The single most important question before the ecology movement today, however, is whether these efforts will be co-opted and contained within the institutional bounds of "reasonable" dissent and reformism or whether these efforts will mature into a powerful movement that can create fundamental, indeed revolutionary, changes in our society and our way of looking at the world.

I have long argued that we delude ourselves if we believe that a life-oriented world can be fully developed or even partially achieved in a profoundly death-oriented society. U.S. society, as it is constituted today, is riddled with patriarchy and racism and sits astride the entire world, not only as a consumer of its wealth and resources, but as an obstacle to all attempts at self-determination at home and abroad. Its inherent aims are production for the sake of production, the preservation of hierarchy and toil on a world scale, mass manipulation and control by centralized, state institutions. This kind of society is inexorably counterposed to a life-oriented world. If the ecology movement does not ultimately direct its main efforts toward a revolution in all areas of life—social as well as natural, political as well as personal, economic as well as cultural—then the movement will gradually degenerate into a safety valve for the established order.

Conventional reform efforts, at their best, can only slow down but they cannot arrest the overwhelming momentum toward destruction within our society. At their worst, they lull people into a false sense of security. Our institutional social order plays games with us to foster this passivity. It grants long-delayed, piecemeal, and woefully inadequate reforms to deflect our energies and attention from larger acts of destruction. Such reform measures hide the rotten core of the apple behind an appealing and reassuring artificially dyed red skin.

Ultimately, however, the key problem with the "pragmatic" political strategy of trade-offs, compromises, and lesser-evil choices is not that it can't take us as far as we want to go. An even more sinister effect of this strategy is that it conditions us to go where we do not want to go.

This "pragmatic" approach has had deadly consequences over the course of recent history. Fascism made its way to power in Germany, in part, because the radical labor movement moderated its revolutionary politics and sought to be "effective" by throwing its weight behind lesser-evil candidates. The movement thus surrendered its own initiative and leadership. Such a "realistic" approach, which seemed so practical at the time, led the German workers from making "realistic" choices between a moderate left and a tolerant center, to a tolerant center and an authoritarian right, and finally between the authoritarian right and totalitarian fascism. Not only did this moral devolution occur almost inevitably on a parliamentary level; a cruel dialectic of political degeneration and moral decomposition also occurred within the German labor movement itself. That the once militant and well-organized German working class permitted this political drift from one lesser evil to another without any act of direct resistance is perhaps the most dismal event in its history.

Environmental movements have not fared much better when they have placed their hopes on the nation-state and lesser-evil strategies. To the extent that European environmentalists have entered into national parliaments seeking state power as greens, they have generally attained little more than public attention for their self-serving parliamentary deputies and achieved very little to arrest environmental decay. . . . [W]ell-meaning environmentalists committed to strategies such as these have bartered away entire forests for token reserves of trees. Vast wilderness areas have been surrendered for relatively small national parks. Huge stretches of coastal wetlands have been exchanged for a few acres of pristine beaches. This is the inevitable result of "working within the system" when the system is *fundamentally* anti-ecological, elitist, and stacked against you. . . .

One of our chief goals must be to radically decentralize our industrialized urban areas into humanly scaled cities and towns artfully tailored to the carrying capacities of the eco-communities in which they are located. We need to transform the current pattern of densely populated urban sprawl into federations of much smaller cities and towns surrounded by small farms that practice diversified, organic agriculture for the local area and are linked to each other by tree belts, pastures, and meadows. In rolling, hilly, or mountainous country, land with sharp gradients should be left covered by timber to prevent erosion, conserve water, and support wildlife. Furthermore, each city and town should contain many vegetable and flower gardens, attractive arbors, park land, and streams and ponds which support fish and aquatic birds. In this way, the countryside would not only constitute the immediate environs of the city but would also directly infuse the city. Relatively close by, sizable wilderness areas would safely co-exist with human habitats and would be carefully "managed" to enhance and preserve their evolutionary integrity, diversity, and stability.

By decentralizing our communities, we would also be able to eliminate the present society's horribly destructive addiction to fossil fuels and nuclear energy. One of the fundamental reasons that giant urban areas and industries are unsustainable is because of their inherent dependency on huge quantities of dangerous and nonrenewable energy resources. To maintain a large, densely populated city requires immense quantities of coal, petroleum, or nuclear energy. It seems likely that safe and renewable energy sources such as wind, water, and solar power can probably not fully meet the needs of giant urban areas, even if careful energy conservation is practiced and automobile use and socially unnecessary production is curtailed. In contrast to coal, oil, and nuclear energy, solar, wind, and other alternative energy sources reach us mainly in small "packets," as it were. Yet while solar devices, wind turbines, and hydroelectric resources can probably not provide enough electricity to illuminate Manhattan Island today, such energy sources, pieced together in an organic energy pattern developed from the potentialities of a particular region, could amply meet the vital needs of small, decentralized cities and towns.

As with agriculture, the industrial economy must also be decentralized and its technology radically reworked to creatively utilize local resources in small-scale, multi-use facilities with production processes that reduce arduous toil, recycle raw materials, and eliminate pollution and toxic wastes. In this way, the *relatively* self-sufficient community, visibly dependent on its environment for its means of life, would likely gain a new respect for the organic interrelationships that sustain it. In the long run, the attempt to approximate local, or at least regional, self-sufficiency would prove more efficient than the wasteful and neo-colonial global division of labor that prevails today. Although there would doubtless be many duplications of small manufacturing and craft facilities from community to community, the familiarity of each group with its local environment and its ecological roots would make for a more intelligent and loving use of its environment.

Such a vision appears quite radical on the face of it. Yet I have to stress that my calls for decentralization and "alternative" technologies are, by themselves, insufficient to create a humane, ecological society. We should not delude ourselves into the belief that a mere change in demographics, logistics, design, or scale automatically yields a real change in social life or spiritual sensibility. Decentralization and a sophisticated alternative technology can help, of course. The kind of decentralized communities and eco-technologies that I've described here could help open up a new era of direct democracy by providing the free time and social comprehensibility that would make it possible for ordinary people to manage the affairs of society without the mediation of ruling classes, giant bureaucracies, or elitist professional political functionaries. However, a genuine ecological vision ultimately needs to directly answer such nagging questions as "who owns what?" and "who runs what?" The answers we give to these questions will have enormous power to shape our future.

I would argue that the best form of government in an ecological society would be direct democratic self-government; that the best form of ownership of productive enterprises and resources would be neither corporate nor state but communal at the municipal level; and that the best form of economic management would be community self-management. In such a vision, broad policies and concrete decisions that deal with community life, agriculture, and industrial production would be made, whenever possible, by active citizens in face-to-face assemblies. Among the many benefits of such a democratic, cooperative commonwealth is the fact that it would help encourage a non-hierarchical, non-domineering sensibility within the human community that would ultimately influence human society's view of its relationship with the rest of the natural world.

To be sure, moving from today's capitalist society—based on giant industrial and urban belts, a highly chemical agribusiness, centralized and bureaucratic power, a staggering armaments economy, massive pollution, and exploited labor—toward the ecological society that I have only begun to describe here will require a complex and difficult transition strategy. I have no pat formulas for making such a revolution. A few things seem clear, however. A new politics must be created that eschews the snares of co-optation within the system that is destroying social and ecological life. We need a social movement that can effectively resist and ultimately replace the nation-state and corporate capitalism; not one that limits its sights to "improving" the current system.

Direct nonviolent resistance is clearly an important element of this new politics. The marvelous genius of the anti-nuke alliances of the 1970s was that they intuitively sensed the need to break away from the "system" and form a strong independent opposition. To a large extent, to be sure, they adopted a direct-action strategy because earlier attempts to stop nuclear power plants by working within the system had failed. Endless months or years of litigation, hearings, the adoption of local ordinances, petitions, and letter-writing campaigns to congresspeople had all essentially failed to stop the construction of new nuclear power plants. Stronger measures were required in order to finally stop new construction. Yet I believe that an even more important feature of direct action is that it forms a decisive step toward recovering the personal power over social life that the centralized, overbearing bureaucracies have usurped from the people. It provides an experiential bridge to a possible future society based on direct grassroots democracy.

Similarly, community organizing is a key element of a radical new politics, particularly those forms of association where people meet face-to-face, identify their common problems, and solve them through mutual aid and volunteer community service. Such community organizations encourage social solidarity, community self-reliance, and individual initiative. Community gardens, block clubs, land trusts, housing cooperatives, parent-run daycare centers, barter networks, alternative schools, consumer and producer cooperatives, community theaters, study groups, neighborhood newspapers, public access television stations—all of these meet immediate and usually neglected community needs. But, they also serve, to greater or lesser degrees, as schools for democratic citizenship. Through participation in such efforts we can become more socially responsible and more skilled at democratically discussing and deciding important social questions.

However—and this may shock most conventional anarchists—I also think we need to explore the possibilities of grassroots electoral politics. While it cannot be denied that most ways of participating in the electoral arena only serve to legitimize the nation-state, with its standing bureaucracy and limited citizen involvement, I think it is important and possible for grassroots activists to intervene in local politics and create *new* kinds of local structures such as ballot initiatives, community assemblies, town meetings, and neighborhood councils that can increasingly take over direct democratic control of municipal governments.

The success of such a libertarian municipalist movement will depend on its ability, over time, to democratize one community after another and establish confederal regional relationships between these local communities. We will need such a geographical, political, and economic base if we are ever to seriously challenge the nation-state and multinational corporations. We will need to create such a *dual power* in order to wrest important and immediate concessions from the existing system and ultimately to supplant it. I see no other realistic alternative for creating a genuinely ecological society.

Such a revolution will obviously not happen all at once in some grand, spontaneous, and violent insurrection. The new politics I advocate has an almost cellular form of growth, a process that involves organic proliferation and differentiation like that of a fetus in a womb. While an ecological revolution will require confrontational struggles, now and in the future, it will also require patient, long-term local community organizing and imaginative grassroots political work.

This strategy is what I mean by green politics. The goal here is not simply to "represent" the growing citizens' movement by taking over the existing top–down political apparatus of the municipality, let alone the nation-state. The goal is to establish or restore town meetings, neighborhood assemblies, or even neighborhood councils of active citizens as the foundation of local control. Radical ecology candidates should run in local elections on a platform fundamentally oriented toward establishing such citizen assemblies and legally restructuring the governance structure of the city by placing a premium on political participation, face-to-face discussion of the public's business, and the complete accountability of citizens who are elected delegates to larger, confederal councils or who serve on purely administrative bodies.

These neighborhood assemblies can also be started before they are legally recognized. Indeed, unofficial citizen assemblies could establish a "shadow" or "parallel" city council that is made up of elected and recallable delegates from each neighborhood assembly. Such shadow city councils, while legally powerless in their initial phases, could exercise a very effective *moral* influence on an official city council until they acquire increasing legal power of their own. They could track the agenda and business of the official city councils in close detail, propose needed reforms, and challenge any legislative measures that they find incompatible with the public interest, thereby mobilizing the people into an increasingly effective political force.

As direct political democracy is being institutionalized, piecemeal steps can also be taken on many different levels to increase the municipalization of the economy. While not infringing on the proprietary rights of small retail outlets, service establishments, artisan shops, small farms, local manufacturing enterprises, and homeowners, this new kind of municipality could start to purchase larger economic enterprises, particularly those enterprises that are about to be closed and could be managed more efficiently by their own workers than by profit-oriented entrepreneurs or corporations. The use of land trusts as a means not only for providing good public housing but promoting small-scale artisanal production could occupy a high place on the agenda of a municipality's economic program. Cooperatives, community gardens, and farmers' markets could be fostered with municipal funds and placed under growing public oversight—a policy that might very well command greater consumer loyalty than we would expect to find toward profit-oriented corporate enterprises.

In such a political and economic context, the ecological restoration of the municipality and the surrounding countryside could begin to take firm root. Public lands could be expanded and restored. Farmers could be supported to make the transition to diversified, organic forms of agriculture to meet local and regional needs. Corporate farms could be increasingly restricted. Programs could be started to facilitate the reconstruction and repopulation of rural areas by interested city dwellers willing to create new communities of their own. Safe and effective birth-control methods could be made available free or at low cost. Recycling could become mandatory. Local business and residential codes could encourage significant energy conservation and promote a switch over to safe and renewable energy sources. The shift to ecologically sound production technologies could begin.

Finally, we cannot hope to realize this vision in only one neighborhood, town, or city. Ours needs to be a confederal society based on the coordination of all municipalities in a bottom–up system of administration as distinguished from the top–down rule of the nation-state. Be it on a county-wide or regional basis, our new municipalities should be united by confederal councils, each occupied by popularly chosen "deputies" who are easily recallable by the communities they serve. These confederal bodies should be strictly *administrative;* they would make no *policy* decisions but merely coordinate and administer decisions made by the municipal citizens' bodies that select them.

Confederation, which has a long though almost lost history of its own, should not be confused with the state, which has always conflicted with confederal structures presumably in the name of "efficiency" and, very typically, the "complexity" of our "modern" society. These claims are sheer hogwash. What troubles me today is that so many radicals accept the claptrap about the "complexities" of modern society and rarely recognize that when cities have eight, ten, or twelve million residents they are no longer even "cities" but shapeless disempowered urban blobs that are direly in need of decentralization—physically as well as institutionally.

Of course, all these ideas about a left libertarian municipal strategy are only the bare outlines of a *minimal* program for moving towards social and ecological harmony. This strategic approach, however, would help solve a number of immediate problems and point us in the direction of more fundamental social changes. It would begin to build up a popular dual power base from which to effectively challenge the corporations and the nation-state. Successful alliances can likely be built around every element of this minimal program because its goals are rooted in a *general* human interest that transcends the real but particularistic interests of class, nationality, ethnicity, and gender. Such genuinely populist goals can be formulated in ways that can unite a majority of people—men and women, people of different colors, poor folks, workers in industrial and service industries, and middle-class professionals as well as a few of our elitist opponents who just might have their consciences pricked. . . .

We need to consciously revive an older image of the "American Dream" that was communitarian, democratic, and utopian, however defective it was in other respects. While the current system is rotten at its core, it still retains vestiges of earlier, often more libertarian institutions that have been very uncomfortably incorporated into the present ones. Let's build on these institutions and traditions. To use a slogan I've coined in recent years, "We must democratize the republic and then radicalize the democracy."

[From] Environmental Blackmail in
Minority Communities

~~

Robert D. Bullard

ENVIRONMENTAL problems have become potent political issues, especially as they threaten public health. Social equity and distributive concerns, however, have not fared so well over the years. Many of the conflicts that have resulted among core environmentalists, the poor, and minorities can be traced to distributional equity questions. How are the benefits and burden of environmental reform distributed? Who gets what, where, and why? Do environmental reforms have regressive impacts? After nearly three decades of modern environmentalism, the equity issues have not been resolved.

~~

Environmentalism in the United States grew out of the progressive conservation movement that began in the 1890s. The modern environmental movement, however, has its roots in the civil rights and anti-war movements of the late 1960s.[1] The more radical student-activists splintered off from the civil rights and anti-war movement to form the core of the environmental movement in the early 1970s. The student environmental activists affected by the Earth Day enthusiasm in colleges and universities across the nation had hopes of bringing environmental reforms to the urban poor. They saw their role as environmental advocates for the poor, since the poor had not taken action on their own.[2] These advocates of the poor, however, were met with resistance and suspicion. Growing tension between the environmental movement and the social equity movement contributed to environmentalism being tagged an "elitist" movement.[3]

Morrison and Dunlap grouped environmental elitism into three types: (1) compositional elitism, i.e., environmentalists come from privileged class strata; (2) ideological elitism, i.e., environmental reforms are a subterfuge for distributing the benefits to environmentalists and costs to non-environmentalists; and (3) impact elitism, i.e., environmental reforms have regressive distributional impacts.[4]

Impact elitism has been the major sore point between environmentalists and the groups who see some reform proposals creating, exacerbating, and sustaining social inequities. The root of this conflict lies in the "jobs vs. environment" argument. Embedded in this argument are three competing advocacy groups: (1) environmental groups concerned about leisure and recreation, wildlife and wilderness preservation, resource conservation, pollution abatement, and industry regulation; (2) social justice advocates, whose major concerns include basic civil rights, social equity, expanded opportunity, economic mobility, and institutional discrimination; and (3) economic boosters, who have as their chief concerns maximizing profits, industrial expansion, economic stability, laissez faire operation, and deregulation.

Economic boosters were somewhat successful in convincing social justice advocates that environmental regulations had regressive distributive impacts. It was argued that acceptance of many reform proposals would result in plant closures, layoffs, and economic dislocation. Kazis and Grossman refer to this practice as "job blackmail."[5] The public is led to believe that there is no alternative to "business as usual" operation. If workers want to keep their jobs, they must work under conditions which may be hazardous to them, their families, and their community. Black workers are especially vulnerable to job blackmail because of high unemployment and their concentration in low-paying (high-risk) blue-collar occupations.

There is inherent conflict between the interests of capital and those of labor. Employers are empowered to move jobs (and sometimes hazards) in a political economic world-system. For example, firms may choose to move their operations from the Northeast and Midwest to the South and Sunbelt, or they may move the jobs to Third World countries where labor is cheaper and where there are fewer health and environmental regulations. Moreover, labor unions may feel it necessary to tone down their demands for improved worker safety conditions in a depressed economy for fear of layoffs, plant closings, and relocation of industries (e.g., moving to right-to-work states which proliferate in the South). The conflicts, fears, and anxieties that are manifested are usually built on the false assumption that environmental regulations are automatically linked to job loss. . . .

Who Benefits and Who Pays?

Poor and minority residents had the most to gain in the passage of environmental regulations such as the Clean Air Act since they lived closest to the worst sources of the pollution.[6] These communities, however, continue to be burdened with a disproportionately large share of industrial pollution problems, even after the passage of all the regulations. Uneven enforcement of environmental and land-use regulations is a contributor to this problem.

Zoning, deed restrictions, and other "protectionist" devices have failed to effectively segregate industrial uses from residential uses in many black and lower income communities. The various social classes, with or without land use controls, are "unequally able to protect their environmental interests."[7] Rich neighborhoods are able to leverage their economic and political clout into fending off unwanted uses (even public housing for the poor) while residents of poor neighborhoods have to put up with all kinds of unwanted neighbors, including noxious facilities.

Public opposition has been more vocal in middle and upper income groups on the issue of noxious facility siting. The Not in My Back Yard (NIMBY) syndrome has been the usual reaction in these communities. As affluent communities became more active in opposing a certain facility, the siting effort shifted toward a more powerless community.[8] Opposition groups often called for the facilities to be sited "somewhere else." "Somewhere Else, USA" often ends up being located in poor, powerless, minority communities. It is this unequal sharing of benefits and burden that has engendered feelings of unfair treatment among poor and minority communities.

Facility siting in the United States is largely reflective of the long pattern of disparate treatment of black communities. There is a "direct historical connection between the exploitation of the land and the exploitation of people, especially black people,"[9] Polluting industries have exploited the pro-growth and pro-jobs sentiment exhibited among the poor, working class, and minority communities. Industries such as paper mills, waste disposal and treatment facilities, heavy metals operations, and chemical plants, searching for operating space, found minority communities to be a logical choice for their expansion. These communities and their leaders were seen as having a Third World view of development. That is, "any development is better than no development at all." Moreover, many residents in these communities were suspicious of environmentalists, a sentiment that aligned them with the pro-growth advocates.

The sight and smell of paper mills, waste treatment and disposal facilities, incinerators, chemical plants, and other industrial operations were promoted as trade-offs for having jobs near "poverty pockets." For example, a paper mill spewing its stench in one of Alabama's poverty-ridden blackbelt counties led Governor George Wallace to declare: "Yeah, that's the smell of prosperity. Sho' does smell sweet, don't it?"[10] Similar views have been reported of residents and community leaders in West Virginia's, Louisiana's, and Texas's "chemical corridor."[11]

The 1980s have seen a shift in the way black communities react to the jobs–environment issue. This shift has revolved around the issue of equity. Blacks have begun to challenge the legitimacy of environmental blackmail and the notion of trade-offs. They are now asking: Are the costs borne by the black community imposed to spare the larger community? Can environmental inequities (resulting from industrial facility siting decisions) be compensated? What are "acceptable" risks? Concern about equity is at the heart of black people's reaction to industrial facility siting where there is an inherent imbalance between localized costs and dispersed benefits. Few residents want garbage dumps and landfills in their backyards. The price of siting noxious facilities has skyrocketed in recent years as a result of more stringent federal regulations and the growing militancy among the poor, working class, and minority communities. Compensation appears to hold little promise in mitigating locational conflict and environmental disputes in these communities.

Environmental disputes are likely to increase in the future as tighter federal regulations take effect. All states will soon be required to have the treatment and disposal capacity to handle the hazardous wastes generated within their borders. Currently, some industries ship their wastes across state lines. It is not yet known what type of siting pattern will emerge from the new federal mandate. States, however, will need to respond to the equity issue if they expect to have successful siting strategies.

Mobilizing Black Community Residents

A "new" form of environmentalism has taken root in America and in the black community. Since the late 1970s, a new grassroots social movement emerged around the toxics threat. Citizens mobilized arond the anti-waste theme. The movement has a number of distinguishing characteristics. It

1. focuses on equity;
2. challenges mainstream environmentalism for its tactics but not its goals;
3. emphasizes the needs of the community and workplace as primary agenda items;
4. uses its own self-taught "experts" and citizen lawsuits instead of relying on legislation and lobbying;
5. takes a "populist" stance on environmental issues relying on active members rather than dues-payers from mailing lists; and
6. embraces a democratic ideology akin to the civil rights and women's movement of the sixties.[12]

These social activists or "toxics warriors" acquired new skills in areas where they had little expertise or no prior experience. They soon became resident "experts" on the toxics issue. They did not limit their attacks to well-publicized toxic contamination issues, but sought remedial actions on problems like "housing, transportation, air quality, and even economic development—issues the traditional environmental agenda had largely ignored."[13]

There is no single agenda or integrated political philosophy in the hundreds of environmental organizations found in the nation. The types of issues that environmental organizations tackle can greatly influence the type of constituents they attract. The issues that are most likely to attract black community

Type of Environmental Groups and "Issue Characteristics" that Attract Black
Community Residents

| | Type of environmental group | | | |
Issue characteristic	Mainstream	Grassroots	Social action	Emergent coalition
Appeal to urban mobilized group	−[a]	+[b]	+	+
Concerned about inequality and distributional impacts	−/+[c]	−/+	+	+
Endorse the "politics of equity" and direct action	−/+	+	+	−/+
Focus on economic–environmental tradeoffs	−	−/+	+	+
Champion of the political and economic "underdog"	+	−/+	+	−/+

[a]−: Group is unlikely to have characteristic.
[b]+: Group is likely to have characteristic.
[c]−/+: Group in some cases may have characteristic.
Source: Adapted from Richard P. Gale, "The Environmental Movement and the Left:
Antagonists or Allies?" *Sociological Inquiry* 53 (Spring 1983): Table 1: 194.

residents are those that have been couched in an anti-environmental blackmail
framework (see the table). They include those that

1. focus on the inequality and distributional impacts;
2. endorse the "politics of equity" and direct action;
3. appeal to urban mobilized groups;
4. advocate safeguards against job loss and plant closure; and
5. are ideologically aligned with policies that favor social and political
   "underdogs."

Mainstream environmental organizations, including the "classic" and "mature" groups, have had a great deal of influence in shaping the nation's environmental policy. Classic environmentalists continue to have a heavy emphasis on
preservation and outdoor recreation, while mature environmentalists are busy in
the area of "tightening regulations, seeking adequate funding for agencies, occasionally focusing on compliance with existing statutes through court action, and
opposing corporate efforts to repeal environmental legislation or weaken standards."[14] These organizations, however, have not had a great deal of success in
attracting poor and working class persons, including the large urban black

underclass (that is burdened with both poverty and pollution) in the nation's central cities or the rural southern blackbelt. Many of these individuals do not see the mainstream environmental movement as a vehicle that is championing the causes of the "little man," the "underdog," or the "oppressed."

The emergence of grassroots environmental groups, some of which are affiliated with mainstream environmental organizations, have begun to bridge the class and ideological gap between core environmentalists and the various orbits around which the movement was built. In some cases, these groups mirror their larger counterparts at the national level in terms of problems and issues selected, membership, ideological alignment, and tactics used. Grassroots groups usually are organized around area-specific and single-issue problems. They are in many cases more inclusive than mainstream environmental organizations. Grassroots environmental organizations, however, may or may not choose to focus on equity, distributional impacts, and economic–environmental trade-off issues. These groups do appeal to some black community residents, especially those who have been active in other confrontational protest activities.

Environmental groups in the black community quite often emerge out of established social action organizations. For example, black leadership has deep roots in the black church and other voluntary associations. Morris contends that the black community "possesses (1) certain basic resources, (2) social activists with strong ties to mass-based indigenous institutions, and (3) tactics and strategies that can be effectively employed against a system of domination."[15] These indigenous institutions have led the opposition against social injustice and racial discrimination. Many black community residents have affiliation with civic clubs, neighborhood associations, community improvement groups, and an array of anti-poverty and anti-discrimination organizations. A protest infrastructure, thus, is already in place for the emergence of an environmental equity movement in the black community.

Social action groups that take on environmental issues as part of their agenda are often on the political left. They broaden their base of support and sphere of influence by incorporating environmental equity issues as agenda items that favor the disenfranchised and dispossessed. The push for equity is an extension of the civil rights movement, a movement where direct confrontation and the politics of protest were real weapons. In short, social action environmental organizations retain much of their civil rights flavor.

The fourth type of environmental group that has appealed to black community residents grew out of coalitions between environmentalists (mainstream and grassroots), social action advocates, and organized labor. These somewhat fragile coalitions operate from the position that social justice and environmental quality are compatible goals. Although these groups are beginning to formulate agendas for action, mistrust acts as a limiting factor. These coalitions have memberships that cut across racial, class, and geographic boundaries. Compositional factors may engender less group solidarity and sense of "control" among black members, compared to the indigenous social action or grassroots environmental groups where blacks are in the majority and make the decisions.

Thus, environmentalists have had a difficult task convincing blacks and the poor that they are on their side. Mistrust is engendered among economically and politically oppressed groups in this country when they see environmental reforms being used to direct social and economic resources away from problems of poor countries toward priorities of the affluent. For example, tighter government regulations and public opposition to disposal facility siting have opened up the Third World as the new dumping ground for this nation's toxic wastes.[16] Few of these poor countries have laws or the infrastructure to handle the wastes from the United States and other Western industrialized nations. Blacks and other ethnic minorities in this country also see their communities being inundated with all types of toxics.[17] This is especially the case in the southern United States (e.g., one of the most underdeveloped regions of the nation) where more than one-half of all blacks live. . . .

Toxic waste disposal has generated protests in many communities across the country. The first national environmental protest by blacks came in 1982 after the mostly black Warren County, North Carolina, was selected as the burial site for 32,000 cubic yards of soil contaminated with the highly toxic PCBs (polychlorinated biphenyls). The soil was illegally dumped along the roadways in fourteen North Carolina counties in 1978. Black civil rights activists, political leaders, and local residents marched in protest demonstrations against the construction of the PCB landfill in their community. Why was Warren County selected as the landfill site? The decision made more political sense than environmental sense.[18]

Although the protests were unsuccessful in halting the landfill construction, they marked the first time blacks mobilized a nationally broad-based group to protest environmental inequities. The protests prompted Congressman Walter E. Fauntroy (Representative from the District of Columbia), who had been active in the demonstrations, to initiate the U.S. General Accounting Office (1983) study of hazardous waste landfill siting in the South. The GAO study observed a strong relationship between the siting of offsite hazardous landfills and race of surrounding communities. Three of the four offsite hazardous waste landfills in EPA's Region IV were located in black communities, while blacks made up only 20 percent of the region's population.

Toward the Politics of Inclusion

Because exposure to environmental toxins varies across population groups, distributive politics have come to play an important role in explaining the vastly different action strategies employed by middle income white communities and lower income black communities. The middle class–dominated environmental movement of the 1960s and 1970s built an impressive political base for environmental reform and regulatory relief. Many environmental problems in the 1980s, however, had social impacts somewhat different from earlier ones. A disproportionate burden of pollution is carried by the urban poor and minority residents.

Few environmentalists realized the sociological implications of the NIMBY (Not in My Back Yard) phenomenon.[19] Given the political climate of the times, the hazardous wastes, garbage dumps, and polluting industries were likely to end up in somebody's backyard. But whose backyard? More often than not, these locally unwanted land uses (LULUs) ended up in poor, powerless, black communities rather than in affluent suburbs. This pattern has proven to be the rule, even though the benefits derived from industrial waste production are directly related to affluence. Public officials and private industry have, in many cases, responded to the NIMBY phenomenon using the "PIBBY" principle, "Place in Blacks' Back Yards."

Social justice movements have begun to move environmentalism to the left in an effort to address some of the distributional impact and equity issues. Documentation of civil rights violations has strengthened the move to make environmental quality a basic right of all individuals. Rising energy costs, a continued erosion of the economy's ability to provide jobs, and rising real incomes are factors that favor environmentalism of the left blending with the objectives of labor, minorities and other "underdog" groups, and middle class environmentalists.

Mainstream environmental organizations were late in broadening their base of support to include blacks and other minorities, the poor, and working class persons. The "energy crisis" in the 1970s was a major impetus that moved many environmentalists to embrace equity issues confronting the poor in this country and countries of the Third World. Environmentalism, over the years, has shifted from a "participatory" to a "power" strategy where the "core of active environmental movement is focused on litigation, political lobbying, and technical evaluation rather than on mass mobilization for protest marches."[20]

Institutional racism and discrimination continue to influence the quality of life in many of the nation's black communities. For example, the ability to exit a negative or health-threatening physical environment is directly associated with affluence. Federal policies, for example, were key elements in the development of spatially differentiated metropolitan areas where blacks and other visible minorities are segregated from whites and the poor from the more affluent citizens. Moreover, the federal government is the "proximate and essential cause of urban apartheid" in the United States.[21] The end result of the nation's apartheid-type policies on black households has meant limited mobility, reduced housing options and residential packages, and decreased environmental choices. For example, air pollution in inner-city neighborhoods can be found at levels up to five times greater than those found in suburban areas. Urban areas, in general, have "dirtier air and drinking water, more waste water and solid waste problems, and greater exposure to lead and other heavy metals than non-urban areas."[22] . . .

Conclusion

Black communities are beginning to incorporate environmental safeguards into their agendas for economic development. Although economically vulnerable (few business and employment centers are indigenous to the community), a growing segment within the black community has begun to demand an environment–development balance. Job blackmail seems to be losing ground mainly because the promise of jobs and a broadened tax base for local residents has been more promise than anything else. Many communities that host noxious facilities have been left to suffer from the tragedy of poverty, pollution, increased health risks, and lowered property values. Residents also must contend with the stigma of living in a "contaminated" community.

The solution to the current environmental dilemma does not reside in compensation. Proposals that call for those less fortunate to accept risks others can escape will only heighten environmental inequities between poor and affluent communities. Many poor and minority communities, because of economic necessity, would be forced to adapt to lower quality physical environments.

Institutionalized discrimination continues to affect public policy decisions related to the enforcement of environmental regulations. The politics of pollution have placed public officials squarely in the middle of environmental disputes and locally unwanted land uses as in the case of municipal garbage landfills and incinerators, hazardous waste storage and treatment facilities, and chemical plants.

Although the effects of pollution have no geographic boundaries, blacks and lower income groups are often "trapped" in polluted environments because of low incomes, housing discrimination and residential segregation, limited residential choices, discriminatory zoning regulations, and ineffective land use policies. Moreover, black communities are beginning to integrate environmental issues into traditional civil rights agendas and to develop viable action strategies to combat environmental degradation, discrimination, job blackmail, and public policy decisions that have disparate distributional impacts on black and poor communities.

The 1990s offer some challenging opportunities for the environmental movement to embrace social justice and other redistributive policies. Population shifts and demographic trends all point to a more diverse nation. It is time for the environmental movement to diversify and reach out to the "other" America.

Notes

1. C. R. Humphrey and F. R. Buttel, *Environment, Energy, and Society* (Belmont, Calif.: Wadsworth, 1982).

2. S. P. Hays, *Beauty, Health and Permanence: Environmental Politics in the United States, 1955–1985* (Cambridge: Cambridge University Press, 1987), 269.

3. See, for example, D. E. Morrison, "How and Why Environmental Consciousness Has Trickled Down," in *Distributional Conflict in Environmental Resource Policy*, ed. A. Schnaiberg, N. Watts, and K. Zimmerman (New York: St. Martin's Press, 1986), 187–220; D. E. Morrison and R. E. Dunlap, "Environmentalism and Elitism: A Conceptual and Empirical Analysis," *Environmental Management* 10 (1986): 981–89; and R. D. Bullard and B. H. Wright, "Blacks and the Environment," *Humbolt Journal of Social Relations* 14 (1987): 165–84, and "Environmentalism and the Politics of Equity: Emergent Trends in the Black Community," *Mid-America Review of Sociology* 12 (1987): 21–37.

4. Morrison and Dunlap, "Environmentalism and Elitism."

5. R. Kazis and R. Grossman, *Fear at Work: Job Blackmail, Labor, and the Environment* (New York: Pilgrim Press, 1983), 37.

6. Humphrey and Buttel, *Environment, Energy, and Society.*

7. J. R. Logan and H. Molotch, *Urban Futures: The Political Economy of Place* (Berkeley: University of California Press, 1987), 158.

8. M. R. Edelstein, *Contaminated Communities: The Social and Psychological Impacts of Residential Toxic Exposure* (Boulder, Colo.: Westview Press, 1987), 186–87.

9. D. R. Goldfield, *Promised Land: The South Since 1945* (Arlington Heights, Ill.: Harlan Davidson, 1987), 211–12.

10. Ibid., 197.

11. See, for example, B. A. Franklin, "In the Shadow of the Valley," *Sierra* 71 (1986): 38–43, and M. H. Brown, *The Toxic Cloud: The Poisoning of America's Air* (New York: Harper & Row, 1987).

12. R. Gottlieb and H. Ingram, "The New Environmentalists," *Progressive* 52 (1988): 14–15.

13. Ibid., 14.

14. R. P. Gale, "The Environmental Movement and the Left: Antagonists or Allies," *Sociological Inquiry* 53 (1983): 184.

15. A. D. Morris, *The Origins of the Civil Rights Movement: Black Communities Organizing for Change* (New York: Free Press, 1984), 282.

16. A. Porterfield and D. Weir, "The Export of Hazardous Waste," *Nation* 245 (October 1987): 340–44.

17. Commission for Racial Justice, *Toxic Wastes and Race: A National Report on the Racial and Socioeconomic Characteristics of Communities with Hazardous Wastes Sites* (New York: United Church of Christ, 1987).

18. K. Geiser and G. Waneck, "PCB and Warren County," *Science for the People* 15 (1983): 13–17.

19. Morrison, "How and Why Environmental Consciousness Has Trickled Down," 187–200.

20. A. Schnaiberg, *The Environment: From Surplus to Scarcity* (New York: Oxford University Press, 1980), 366–67.

21. J. A. Kushner, *Apartheid in America: An Historical and Legal Analysis of Contemporary Racial Segregation in the United States* (Arlington, Va.: Carrolton Press, 1980), 130.

22. Kazis and Grossman, *Fear at Work*, 48.

[From] Nature, Self, and Gender:
Feminism, Environmental Philosophy, and the
Critique of Rationalism

Val Plumwood

ENVIRONMENTAL philosophy has recently been criticized on a number of counts by feminist philosophers. I want to develop further some of this critique and to suggest that much of the issue turns on the failure of environmental philosophy to engage properly with the rationalist tradition, which has been inimical to both women and nature. Damaging assumptions from this tradition have been employed in attempting to formulate a new environmental philosophy that often makes use of or embeds itself within rationalist philosophical frameworks that are not only biased from a gender perspective, but have claimed a negative role for nature as well. . . .

Rationalism and the Ethical Approach

The ethical approach aims to center a new view of nature in ethics, especially universalizing ethics or in some extension of human ethics. This approach has been criticized from a feminist perspective by a number of recent authors. I partly agree with and partly disagree with these criticisms; that is, I think that the emphasis on ethics as the central part (or even the whole) of the problem is misplaced, and that although ethics (and especially the ethics of noninstrumental value) has a role, the particular ethical approaches that have been adopted are problematic and unsuitable. I shall illustrate this claim by a brief discussion of Paul Taylor's *Respect for Nature*.[1] . . .

Paul Taylor's book is a detailed working out of an ethical position that rejects the standard and widespread Western treatment of nature as instrumental to human interests and instead takes living things, as teleological centers of life, to be worthy of respect in their own right. Taylor aims to defend a biocentric (life-centered) ethical theory in which a person's true human self includes his or her biological nature, but he attempts to embed this within a Kantian ethical framework that makes strong use of the reason/emotion dichotomy[2]; thus we are assured that the attitude of respect is a moral one because it is universalizing and disinterested, "that is, each moral agent who sincerely has the attitude advocates its universal adoption by all other agents, regardless of whether they are so inclined and regardless of their fondness or lack of fondness for particular individuals."[3] The essential features of morality having been established as distance from emotion and "particular fondness," morality is then seen as the domain of reason and its touchstone, belief. Having carefully distinguished the "valuational, conative, practical and affective dimensions of the attitude of respect," Taylor goes on to pick out the essentially cognitive "valuational" aspect as central and basic to all the others: "It is *because* moral agents look at animals and plants in this way that they are disposed to pursue the aforementioned ends and purposes"[4] and, similarly, to have the relevant emotions and affective attitudes. The latter must be held at an appropriate distance and not allowed to get the upper hand at any point. Taylor claims that actions do not express moral respect unless they are done as a matter of moral principle conceived as ethically obligatory and pursued disinterestedly and not through inclination, solely or even primarily:

> If one seeks that end solely or primarily from inclination, the attitude being expressed is not moral respect but personal affection or love. . . . It is not that respect for nature *precludes* feelings of care and concern for living things. One may, as a matter of simple kindness, not want to harm them. But the fact that one is so motivated does not itself indicate the presence of a moral attitude of respect. Having the desire to preserve or protect the good of wild animals and plants for their sake is neither contrary to, nor evidence of, respect for nature. It is only if the person who has the desire understands that the actions fulfilling it would be obligatory even in the absence of the desire, that the person has genuine respect for nature.[5]

There is good reason to reject as self-indulgent the "kindness" approach that reduces respect and morality in the protection of animals to the satisfaction of the carer's own feelings. Respect for others involves treating them as worthy of consideration for their own sake and not just as an instrument for the carer's satisfaction, and there is a sense in which such "kindness" is not genuine care or respect for the other. But Taylor is doing much more than this—he is treating care, viewed as "inclination" or "desire," as irrelevant to morality. Respect for nature on this account becomes an essentially *cognitive* matter (that of a person believing something to have "inherent worth" and then acting from an understanding of ethical principles as universal).

The account draws on the familiar view of reason and emotion as sharply separated and opposed, and of "desire," caring, and love as merely "personal" and "particular" as opposed to the universality and impartiality of understanding and of "feminine" emotions as essentially unreliable, untrustworthy, and morally irrelevant, an inferior domain to be dominated by a superior, disinterested (and of course masculine) reason. This sort of rationalist account of the place of emotions has come in for a great deal of well-deserved criticism recently, both for its implicit gender bias and its philosophical inadequacy, especially its dualism and its construal of public reason as sharply differentiated from and controlling private emotion.[6]

A further major problem in its use in this context is the inconsistency of employing, in the service of constructing an allegedly biocentric ethical theory, a framework that has itself played such a major role in creating a dualistic account of the genuine human self as essentially rational and as sharply discontinuous from the merely emotional, the merely bodily, and the merely animal elements. For emotions and the private sphere with which they are associated have been treated as sharply differentiated and inferior as part of a pattern in which they are seen as linked to the sphere of nature, not the realm of reason.

And it is not only women but also the earth's wild living things that have been denied possession of a reason thus construed along masculine and oppositional lines and which contrasts not only with the "feminine" emotions but also with the physical and the animal. Much of the problem (both for women and nature) lies in rationalist or rationalist-derived conceptions of the self and of what is essential and valuable in the human makeup. It is in the name of such a reason that these other things—the feminine, the emotional, the merely bodily or the merely animal, and the natural world itself—have most often been denied their virtue and been accorded an inferior and merely instrumental position. Thomas Aquinas states this problematic position succinctly: "the intellectual nature is alone requisite for its own sake in the universe, and all others for its sake."[7] And it is precisely reason so construed that is usually taken to characterize the authentically human and to create the supposedly sharp separation, cleavage, or discontinuity between all humans and the nonhuman world, and the similar cleavage within the human self. The supremacy accorded an oppositionally construed reason is the key to the anthropocentrism of the Western tradition. The Kantian-rationalist framework, then, is hardly the area in which to search for a solution. Its use, in a way that perpetuates the supremacy of reason and its opposition to contrast areas, in the service of constructing a supposedly biocentric ethic is a matter for astonishment.

Ethical universalization and abstraction are both closely associated with accounts of the self in terms of rational egoism. Universalization is explicitly seen in both the Kantian and the Rawlsian framework as needed to hold in check natural self-interest; it is the moral complement to the account of the self as "disembodied and disembedded," as the autonomous self of liberal theory, the rational egoist of market theory, the falsely differentiated self of object-relations theory. In the same vein, the broadening of the scope of moral concern along with the according of rights to the natural world has been seen by influential environmental philosophers as the final step in a process of increasing moral abstraction and generalization, part of the move away from the merely particular—*my* self, *my* family, *my* tribe—the discarding of the merely personal and, by implication, the merely selfish. This is viewed as moral progress, increasingly civilized as it moves further away from primitive selfishness. Nature is the last area to be included in this march away from the unbridled natural egoism of the particular and its close ally, the emotional. Moral progress is marked by increasing adherence to moral rules and a movement away from the supposedly natural (in human nature), and the completion of its empire is, paradoxically, the extension of its domain of adherence to abstract moral rules to nature itself.

On such a view, the particular and the emotional are seen as the enemy of the rational, as corrupting, capricious, and self-interested. And if the "moral emotions" are set aside as irrelevant or suspect, as merely subjective or personal, we can only base morality on the rules of abstract reason, on the justice and rights of the impersonal public sphere.

This view of morality as based on a concept of reason as oppositional to the personal, the particular, and the emotional has been assumed in the framework of much recent environmental ethics. But as a number of feminist critics of the masculine model of moral life and of moral abstraction have pointed out, this increasing abstraction is not necessarily an improvement.[8] The opposition between the care and concern for particular others and generalized moral concern is associated with a sharp division between public (masculine) and private (feminine) realms. Thus it is part of the set of dualistic contrasts in which the problem of the Western treatment of nature is rooted. And the opposition between care for particular others and general moral concern is a false one. There *can* be opposition between particularity and generality of concern, as when concern for particular others is accompanied by *exclusion* of others from care or chauvinistic attitudes toward them, but this does not automatically happen, and emphasis on oppositional cases obscures the frequent cases where they work together—and in which care for particular others is essential to a more generalized morality. Special relationships, which are treated by universalizing positions as at best morally irrelevant and at worst a positive hindrance to the moral life, are thus mistreated. For as Blum stresses, special relationships form the basis for much of our moral life and concern, and it could hardly be otherwise.[9] With nature, as with the human sphere, the capacity to care, to experience sympathy, understanding, and sensitivity to the situation and fate of particular others, and to take responsibility for others is an index of our moral being. Special relationship with, care for, or empathy with particular aspects of nature as experiences rather than with nature as abstraction are essential to provide a depth and type of concern that is not otherwise possible. Care and responsibility for particular animals, trees, and rivers that are known well, loved, and appropriately connected to the self are an important basis for acquiring a wider, more generalized concern. (As we shall see, this failure to deal adequately with particularity is a problem for deep ecology as well.)

Concern for nature, then, should not be viewed as the completion of a process of (masculine) universalization, moral abstraction, and disconnection, discarding the self, emotions, and special ties (all, of course, associated with the private sphere and femininity). Environmental ethics has for the most part placed itself uncritically in such a framework, although it is one that is extended with particular difficulty to the natural world. Perhaps the kindest thing that can be said about the framework of ethical universalization is that it is seriously incomplete and fails to capture the most important elements of respect, which are not reducible to or based on duty or obligation any more than the most important elements of friendship are, but which are rather an expression of a certain kind of selfhood and a certain kind of relation between self and other. . . .

The Discontinuity Problem

The problem is not just one of restriction *in* ethics but also of restriction *to* ethics. Most mainstream environmental philosophers continue to view environmental philosophy as mainly concerned with ethics. For example, instrumentalism is generally viewed by mainstream environmental philosophers as a problem in ethics, and its solution is seen as setting up some sort of theory of intrinsic value. This neglects a key aspect of the overall problem that is concerned with the definition of the human self as separate from nature, the connection between this and the instrumental view of nature, and broader *political* aspects of the critique of instrumentalism.

One key aspect of the Western view of nature, which the ethical stance neglects completely, is the view of nature as sharply discontinuous or ontologically divided from the human sphere. This leads to a view of humans as apart from or "outside of" nature, usually as masters or external controllers of it. Attempts to reject this view often speak alternatively of humans as "part of nature" but rarely distinguish this position from the obvious claim that human fate is interconnected with that of the biosphere, that humans are subject to natural laws. But on the divided-self theory it is the essentially or authentically human part of the self, and in that sense the human realm proper, that is outside nature, not the human as a physical phenomenon. The view of humans as outside of and alien to nature seems to be especially strongly a Western one, although not confined to the West. There are many other cultures which do not hold it, which stress what connects us to nature as genuinely human virtues, which emphasize continuity and not dissimilarity.

As ecofeminism points out, Western thought has given us a strong human/ nature dualism that is part of the set of interrelated dualisms of mind/body, reason/nature, reason/emotion, masculine/feminine and has important inter-connected features with these other dualisms.[10] This dualism has been espe-cially stressed in the rationalist tradition. In this dualism what is characteristi-cally and authentically human is defined against or in opposition to what is taken to be natural, nature, or the physical or biological realm. This takes various forms. For example, the characterization of the genuinely, properly, characteristically, or authentically human, or of human virtue, in polarized terms to exclude what is taken to be characteristic of the natural is what John Rodman has called "the Differential Imperative" in which what is virtuous in the human is taken to be what maximizes distance from the merely natural.[11] The maintenance of sharp dichotomy and polarization is achieved by the rejection and denial of what links humans to the animal. What is taken to be authentically and characteristically human, defining of the human, as well as the ideal for which humans should strive is *not* to be found in what is shared with the natural and animal (e.g., the body, sexuality, reproduction, emo-tionality, the senses, agency) but in what is thought to separate and distin-guish them—especially reason and its offshoots. Hence humanity is defined not as part of nature (perhaps a special part) but as separate from and in opposition to it. Thus the relation of humans to nature is treated as an oppositional and value dualism.

The process closely parallels the formation of other dualisms, such as masculine/feminine, reason/emotion, and spirit/body criticized in feminist thought, but this parallel logic is not the only connection between human/ nature dualism and masculine/feminine dualism. Moreover, this exclusion of the natural from the concept of the properly human is not the only dualism involved, because what is involved in the construction of this dualistic concep-tion of the human is the rejection of those parts of the human character identified as feminine—also identified as less than fully human—giving the masculine conception of what it is to be human. Masculinity can be linked to this exclusionary and polarized conception of the human, via the desire to exclude and distance from the feminine and the nonhuman. The features that are taken as characteristic of humankind and as where its special virtues lie, are those such as rationality, freedom, and transcendence of nature (all tradition-ally viewed as masculine), which are viewed as not shared with nature. Human-ity is defined oppositionally to both nature and the feminine.

The upshot is a deeply entrenched view of the genuine or ideal human self as not including features shared with nature, and as defined *against* or in *opposi-tion to* the nonhuman realm, so that the human sphere and that of nature cannot significantly overlap. Nature is sharply divided off from the human, is alien and usually hostile and inferior. Furthermore, this kind of human self can only have certain kinds of accidental or contingent connections to the realm of nature. I shall call this the discontinuity problem or thesis and I argue later that it plays a key role with respect to other elements of the problem.

Rationalism and Deep Ecology

Although the discontinuity problem is generally neglected by the ethical stance, a significant exception to its neglect within environmental philosophy seems to be found in deep ecology, which is also critical of the location of the problem within ethics. Furthermore, deep ecology also seems initially to be more likely to be compatible with a feminist philosophical framework, emphasizing as it does connections with the self, connectedness, and merger. Nevertheless, there are severe tensions between deep ecology and a feminist perspective. Deep ecology has not satisfactorily identified the key elements in the traditional framework or observed their connections to rationalism. As a result, it fails to reject adequately rationalist assumptions and indeed often seems to provide its own versions of universalization, the discarding of particular connections, and rationalist accounts of self.

Deep ecology locates the key problem area in human–nature relations in the separation of humans and nature, and it provides a solution for this in terms of the "identification" of self with nature. "Identification" is usually left deliberately vague, and corresponding accounts of self are various and shifting and not always compatible. There seem to be at least three different accounts of self involved—indistinguishability, expansion of self, and transcendence of self—and practitioners appear to feel free to move among them at will. As I shall show, all are unsatisfactory from both a feminist perspective and from that of obtaining a satisfactory environmental philosophy, and the appeal of deep ecology rests largely on the failure to distinguish them.

The Indistinguishability Account

The indistinguishability account rejects boundaries between self and nature. Humans are said to be just one strand in the biotic web, not the source and ground of all value and the discontinuity thesis is, it seems, firmly rejected. Warwick Fox describes the central intuition of deep ecology as follows: "We can make no firm ontological divide in the field of existence . . . there is no bifurcation in reality between the human and nonhuman realms. . . . to the extent that we perceive boundaries, we fall short of deep ecological consciousness."[12] But much more is involved here than the rejection of discontinuity, for deep ecology goes on to replace the human-in-environment image by a holistic or gestalt view that "dissolves not only the human-in-environment concept, but every compact-thing-in-milieu concept"—except when talking at a superficial level of communication.

Deep ecology involves a cosmology of "unbroken wholeness which denies the classical idea of the analyzability of the world into separately and independently existing parts."[13] It is strongly attracted to a variety of mystical traditions and to the Perennial Philosophy, in which the self is merged with the other—"the other is none other than yourself." As John Seed puts it: "I am protecting the rain forest" develops into "I am part of the rain forest protecting myself. I am that part of the rain forest recently emerged into thinking."[14]

There are severe problems with these claims, arising not so much from the orientation to the concept of self (which seems to me important and correct) or from the mystical character of the insights themselves as from the indistinguishability metaphysics which is proposed as their basis. It is not merely that the identification process of which deep ecologists speak seems to stand in need of much more clarification, but that it does the wrong thing. The problem, in the sort of account I have given, is the discontinuity between humans and nature that emerges as part of the overall set of Western dualisms. Deep ecology proposes to heal this division by a "unifying process," a metaphysics that insists that everything is really part of and indistinguishable from everything else. This is not only to employ overly powerful tools but ones that do the wrong job, for the origins of the particular opposition involved in the human/nature dualism remain unaddressed and unanalyzed. The real basis of the discontinuity lies in the concept of an authentic human being, in what is taken to be valuable in human character, society, and culture, as what is distinct from what is taken to be natural. The sources of and remedies for this remain unaddressed in deep ecology. Deep ecology has confused dualism and atomism and then mistakenly taken indistinguishability to follow from the rejection of atomism. The confusion is clear in Fox, who proceeds immediately from the ambiguous claim that there is no "bifurcation in reality between the human and nonhuman realms" (which could be taken as a rejection of human discontinuity from nature) to the conclusion that what is needed is that we embrace an indistinguishability metaphysics of unbroken wholeness in the whole of reality. But the problem must be addressed in terms of this specific dualism and its connections. Instead deep ecology proposes the obliteration of all distinction.

Thus deep ecology's solution to removing this discontinuity by obliterating *all* division is far too powerful. In its overgenerality it fails to provide a genuine basis for an environmental ethics of the kind sought, for the view of humans as metaphysically unified with the cosmic whole will be equally true whatever relation humans stand in with nature—the situation of exploitation of nature exemplifies such unity equally as well as a conserver situation and the human self is just as indistinguishable from the bulldozer and Coca-Cola bottle as the rocks or the rain forest. What John Seed seems to have in mind here is that once one has realized that one is indistinguishable from the rain forest, its needs would become one's own. But there is nothing to guarantee this—one could equally well take one's own needs for its.

This points to a further problem with the distinguishability thesis, that we need to recognize not only our human continuity with the natural world but also its distinctness and independence from us and the distinctness of the needs of things in nature from ours. The indistinguishability account does not allow for this, although it is a very important part of respect for nature and of conservation strategy.

The dangers of accounts of the self that involve self-merger appear in feminist contexts as well, where they are sometimes appealed to as the alternative to masculine-defined autonomy as disconnection from others. As Jean Grimshaw writes of the related thesis of the indistinctness of persons (the acceptance of the loss of self-boundaries as a feminine ideal):

> It is important not merely because certain forms of symbiosis or "connection" with others can lead to damaging failures of personal development, but because care for others, understanding of them, are only possible if one can adequately distinguish oneself *from* others. If I see myself as "indistinct" from you, or you as not having your own being that is not merged with mine, then I cannot preserve a real sense of your well-being as opposed to mine. Care and understanding require the sort of distance that is needed in order not to see the other as a projection of self, or self as a continuation of the other.[15]

These points seem to me to apply to caring for other species and for the natural world as much as they do to caring for our own species. But just as dualism is confused with atomism, so holistic self-merger is taken to be the only alternative to egoistic accounts of the self as without essential connection to others or to nature. Fortunately, this is a false choice; as I argue below, nonholistic but relational accounts of the self, as developed in some feminist and social philosophy, enable a rejection of dualism, including human/nature dualism, without denying the independence or distinguishability of the other. To the extent that deep ecology is identified with the indistinguishability thesis, it does not provide an adequate basis for a philosophy of nature.

The Expanded Self

In fairness to deep ecology it should be noted that it tends to vacillate between mystical indistinguishability and the other accounts of self, between the holistic self and the expanded self. Vacillation occurs often by way of slipperiness as to what is meant by identification of self with the other, a key notion in deep ecology. This slipperiness reflects the confusion of dualism and atomism previously noted but also seems to reflect a desire to retain the mystical appeal of indistinguishability while avoiding its many difficulties. Where "identification" means not "identity" but something more like "empathy," identification with other beings can lead to an expanded self. According to Arne Naess, "The self is as comprehensive as the totality of our identifications. . . . Our Self is that with which we identify."[16] This larger self (or Self, to deep ecologists) is something for which we should strive "insofar as it is in our power to do so," and according to Fox we should also strive to make it as large as possible. But this expanded self is not the result of a critique of egoism; rather, it is an enlargement and an extension of egoism.[17] It does not question the structures of possessive egoism and self-interest; rather, it tries to allow for a wider set of interests by an expansion of self. The motivation for the expansion of self is to allow for a wider set of concerns while continuing to allow the self to operate on the fuel of self-interest (or Self-interest). This is apparent from the claim that "in this light . . . ecological resistance is simply another name for self defense."[18] Fox quotes with approval John Livingstone's statement: "When I say that the fate of the sea turtle or the tiger or the gibbon is mine, I mean it. All that is in my universe is not merely mine; it is *me*. And I shall defend myself. I shall defend myself not only against overt aggression but also against gratuitous insult."[19]

Deep ecology does not question the structures of rational egoism and continues to subscribe to two of the main tenets of the egoist framework—that human nature is egoistic and that the alternative to egoism is self-sacrifice. Given these assumptions about egoism, the obvious way to obtain some sort of human interest in defending nature is through the expanded Self operating in the interests of nature but also along the familiar lines of self-interest. The expanded-self strategy might initially seem to be just another pretentious and obscure way of saying that humans empathize with nature. But the strategy of transferring the structures of egoism is highly problematic, for the widening of interest is obtained at the expense of failing to recognize unambiguously the distinctness and independence of the other. Others are recognized morally only to the extent that they are incorporated into the self, and their difference denied. And the failure to critique egoism and the disembedded, nonrelational self means a failure to draw connections with other contemporary critiques.

The Transcended or Transpersonal Self

To the extent that the expanded Self requires that we detach from the particular concerns of the self (a relinquishment that despite its natural difficulty we should struggle to attain), expansion of self to Self also tends to lead into the third position, the transcendence or overcoming of self. Thus Fox urges us to strive for *impartial* identification with *all* particulars, the cosmos, discarding our identifications with our own particular concerns, personal emotions, and attachments. Fox presents here the deep ecology version of universalization, with the familiar emphasis on the personal and the particular as corrupting and self-interested—"the cause of possessiveness, war and ecological destruction."[20]

This treatment of particularity, the devaluation of an identity tied to particular parts of the natural world as opposed to an abstractly conceived whole, the cosmos, reflects the rationalistic preoccupation with the universal and its account of ethical life as oppositional to the particular. The analogy in human terms of impersonal love of the cosmos is the view of morality as based on universal principles or the impersonal and abstract "love of man." Thus Fox reiterates (as if it were unproblematic) the view of particular attachments as ethically suspect and as oppositional to genuine, impartial "identification," which necessarily falls short with all particulars.

Because this "transpersonal" identification is so indiscriminate and intent on denying particular meanings, it cannot allow for the deep and highly particularistic attachment to place that has motivated both the passion of many modern conservationists and the love of many indigenous peoples for their land (which deep ecology inconsistently tries to treat as a model). This is based not on a vague, bloodless, and abstract cosmological concern but on the formation of identity, social and personal, in relation to particular areas of land, yielding ties often as special and powerful as those to kin, and which are equally expressed in very specific and local responsibilities of care. This emerges clearly in the statements of many indigenous peoples, such as in the moving words of Cecilia Blacktooth explaining why her people would not surrender their land:

> You ask us to think what place we like next best to this place where we always lived. You see the graveyard there? There are our fathers and our grandfathers. You see that Eagle-nest mountain and that Rabbit-hole mountain? When God made them, He gave us this place. We have always been here. We do not care for any other place. . . . We have always lived here. We would rather die here. Our fathers did. We cannot leave them. Our children were born here— how can we go away? If you give us the best place in the world, it is not so good as this. . . . This is our home. . . . We cannot live any where else. We were born here and our fathers are buried here. . . . We want this place and no other. . . .[21]

In inferiorizing such particular, emotional, and kinship-based attachments, deep ecology gives us another variant on the superiority of reason and the inferiority of its contrasts, failing to grasp yet again the role of reason and incompletely critiquing its influence. To obtain a more adequate account than that offered by mainstream ethics and deep ecology it seems that we must move toward the sort of ethics feminist theory has suggested, which can allow for both continuity and difference and for ties to nature which are expressive of the rich, caring relationships of kinship and friendship rather than increasing abstraction and detachment from relationship.

The Problem in Terms of the Critique of Rationalism

I now show how the problem of the inferiorization of nature appears if it is viewed from the perspective of the critique of rationalism and seen as part of the general problem of revaluing and reintegrating what rationalist culture has split apart, denied, and devalued. Such an account shifts the focus away from the preoccupations of both mainstream ethical approaches and deep ecology, and although it does retain an emphasis on the account of the self as central, it gives a different account from that offered by deep ecology. I conclude by arguing that one of the effects of this shift in focus is to make connections with

other critiques, especially feminism, central rather than peripheral or accidental, as they are currently viewed by deep ecologists in particular.

First, what is missing from the accounts of both the ethical philosophers and
the deep ecologists is an understanding of the problem of discontinuity as
created by a dualism linked to a network of related dualisms. Here I believe a
good deal can be learned from the critique of dualism feminist philosophy has
developed and from the understanding of the mechanisms of dualisms ecofeminists have produced. A dualistically construed dichotomy typically polarizes
difference and minimizes shared characteristics, construes difference along
lines of superiority/inferiority, and views the inferior side as a means to the
higher ends of the superior side (the instrumental thesis). Because its nature is
defined oppositionally, the task of the superior side, that in which it realizes
itself and expresses its true nature, is to separate from, dominate, and control
the lower side. This has happened both with the human/nature division and
with other related dualisms such as masculine/feminine, reason/body, and
reason/emotion. Challenging these dualisms involves not just a reevaluation of
superiority/inferiority and a higher status for the underside of the dualisms (in
this case nature) but also a reexamination and reconceptualizing of the dualistically construed categories themselves. So in the case of the human/nature
dualism it is not just a question of improving the status of nature, moral or
otherwise, while everything else remains the same, but of reexamining and
reconceptualizing the concept of the human, and also the concept of the con-
trasting class of nature. For the concept of the human, of what it is to be fully
and authentically human, and of what is genuinely human in the set of characteristics typical humans possess, has been defined oppositionally, by *exclusion*
of what is associated with the inferior natural sphere in very much the way that
Lloyd, for example, has shown in the case of the categories of masculine and
feminine, and of reason and its contrasts.[22] Humans have both biological and
mental characteristics, but the mental rather than the biological have been
taken to be characteristic of the human and to give what is "fully and authentically" human. The term "human" is, of course, not merely descriptive here
but very much an evaluative term setting out an ideal: it is what is essential or
worthwhile in the human that excludes the natural. It is not necessarily denied
that humans have some material or animal component—rather, it is seen in this
framework as alien or inessential to them, not part of their fully or truly human
nature. The human essence is often seen as lying in maximizing control over
the natural sphere (both within and without) and in qualities such as rationality, freedom, and transcendence of the material sphere. These qualities are also
identified as masculine, and hence the *oppositional* model of the human coincides or converges with a masculine model, in which the characteristics attributed are those of the masculine ideal.

Part of a strategy for challenging this human/nature dualism, then, would
involve recognition of these excluded qualities—split off, denied, or construed

as alien, or comprehended as the sphere of supposedly *inferior* humans such as women and blacks—as equally and fully human. This would provide a basis for the recognition of *continuities* with the natural world. Thus reproductivity, sensuality, emotionality would be taken to be as fully and authentically human qualities as the capacity for abstract planning and calculation. This proceeds from the assumption that one basis for discontinuity and alienation from nature is alienation from those qualities which provide continuity with nature in ourselves.

This connection between the rationalist account of nature within and nature without has powerful repercussions. So part of what is involved is a challenge to the centrality and dominance of the rational in the account of the human self. Such a challenge would have far-reaching implications for what is valuable in human society and culture, and it connects with the challenge to the cultural legacy of rationalism made by other critiques of rationalism such as feminism, and by critiques of technocracy, bureaucracy, and instrumentalism.

What is involved here is a reconceptualization of the human side of the human/nature dualism, to free it from the legacy of rationalism. Also in need of reconceptualization is the underside of this dualism, the concept of nature, which is construed in polarized terms as bereft of qualities appropriated to the human side, as passive and lacking in agency and teleology, as pure materiality, pure body, or pure mechanism. So what is called for here is the development of alternatives to mechanistic ways of viewing the world, which are also part of the legacy of rationalism.

Instrumentalism and the Self

There are two parts to the restructuring of the human self in relation to nature—reconceptualizing the human and reconceptualizing the self, and especially its possibilities of relating to nature in other than instrumental ways. Here the critique of the egoistic self of liberal individualism by both feminist and social philosophers, as well as the critique of instrumental reason, offers a rich set of connections and insights on which to draw. In the case of both of these parts what is involved is the rejection of basically masculine models, that is, of humanity and of the self.

Instrumentalism has been identified as a major problem by the ethical approach in environmental philosophy but treated in a rather impoverished way, as simply the problem of establishing the inherent worth of nature. Connection has not been made to the broader account that draws on the critique of instrumental reason. This broader account reveals both its links with the discontinuity problem and its connection with the account of the self. A closer look at this further critique gives an indication of how we might develop an account that enables us to stress continuity without drowning in a sea of indistinguishability.

We might notice first the strong connections between discontinuity (the polarization condition of dualism) and instrumentalism—the view that the excluded sphere is appropriately treated as a means to the ends of the higher sphere or group, that its value lies in its usefulness to the privileged group that is, in contrast, worthwhile or significant in itself. Second, it is important to maintain a strong distinction and maximize distance between the sphere of means and that of ends to avoid breaking down the sharp boundaries required by hierarchy. Third, it helps if the sphere treated instrumentally is seen as lacking ends of its own (as in views of nature and women as passive), for then others can be imposed upon it without problem. There are also major connections that come through the account of the self which accompanies both views.

The self that complements the instrumental treatment of the other is one that stresses sharply defined ego boundaries, distinctness, autonomy, and separation from others—that is defined *against* others, and lacks essential connections to them. This corresponds to object-relations account of the masculine self associated with the work of Nancy Chodorow and also to the self-interested individual presupposed in market theory.[23] This self uses both other humans and the world generally as a means to its egoistic satisfaction, which is assumed to be the satisfaction of interests in which others play no essential role. If we try to specify these interests they would make no essential reference to the welfare of others, except to the extent that these are useful to serve predetermined ends. Others as means are interchangeable if they produce equivalent satisfactions—anything which conduces to that end is as valuable, other things being equal, as anything else which equally conduces to that end. The interests of such an individual, that of the individual of market theory and of the masculine self as theorized by Chodorow, are defined as essentially independent of or disconnected from those of other people, and his or her transactions with the world at large consist of various attempts to get satisfaction for these predetermined private interests. Others are a "resource," and the interests of others connect with the interests of such autonomous selves only accidentally or contingently. They are not valued for themselves but for their effects in producing gratification. This kind of instrumental picture, so obviously a misdescription in the case of relations to other humans, is precisely still the normal Western model of what our relations to nature should be.

Now this kind of instrumental, disembedded account of the relation of self to others has been extensively criticized in the area of political theory from a variety of quarters, including feminist theory, in the critique of liberalism, and in environmental philosophy. It has been objected that this account does not give an accurate picture of the human self—that humans are social and connected in a way such an account does not recognize. People do have interests that make *essential* and not merely accidental or contingent reference to those of others, for example, when a mother wishes for her child's recovery, the child's flourishing is an essential *part* of her flourishing, and similarly with close others and indeed for others more widely ("social others"). But, the objection continues, this gives a misleading picture of the world, one that omits or impoverishes a whole significant dimension of human experience, a dimension which provides important insight into gender difference, without which we cannot give an adequate picture of what it is to be human. Instead we must see human beings and their interests as *essentially* related and interdependent. As Karen Warren notes, "Relationships are not something extrinsic to who we are, not an 'add on' feature of human nature; they play an essential role in shaping what it is to be human."[24] That people's interests are relational does not imply a holistic view of them—that they are merged or indistinguishable. Although some of the mother's interests entail satisfaction of the child's interests, they are not identical or even necessarily similar. There is overlap, but the relation is one of intentional inclusion (her interest is *that* the child should thrive, that certain of the child's key interests are satisfied) rather than accidental overlap.

This view of self-in-relationship is, I think, a good candidate for the richer account of self deep ecologists have sought and for which they have mistaken holistic accounts. It is an account that avoids atomism but that enables a recognition of interdependence and relationship without falling into the problems of indistinguishability, that acknowledges both continuity and difference, and that breaks the culturally posed false dichotomy of egoism and altruism of interests; it bypasses both masculine "separation" and traditional-feminine "merger" accounts of the self. It can also provide an appropriate foundation for an ethic of connectedness and caring for others, as argued by Gilligan and Miller.[25]

Thus is it unnecessary to adopt any of the stratagems of deep ecology—the indistinguishable self, the expanded self, or the transpersonal self—in order to provide an alternative to anthropocentrism or human self-interest. This can be better done through the relational account of self, which clearly recognizes the distinctness of nature but also our relationship and continuity with it. On this relational account, respect for the other results neither from the containment of self nor from a transcendence of self, but is an *expression* of self in relationship, not egoistic self as merged with the other but self as embedded in a network of essential relationships with distinct others.

The relational account of self can usefully be applied to the case of human relations with nature and to place. The standard Western view of the relation of the self to the nonhuman is that it is always *accidentally* related, and hence the nonhuman can be used as a means to the self-contained ends of human beings. Pieces of land are real estate, readily interchangeable as equivalent means to the end of human satisfaction; no place is more than "a stage along life's way, a launching pad for higher flights and wider orbits than your own."[26] But, of course, we do not all think this way, and instances of contrary behavior would no doubt be more common if their possibility were not denied and distorted by both theoretical and social construction. But other cultures have recognized such essential connection of self to country clearly enough, and many indigenous voices from the past and present speak of the grief and pain in loss of their land, to which they are as essentially connected as to any human other. When Aboriginal people, for example, speak of the land as part of them, "like brother and mother," this is, I think, one of their meanings.[27] If instrumentalism is impoverishing and distorting as an account of our relations to other human beings, it is equally so as a guiding principle in our relations to nature and to place.

But to show that the self can be essentially related to nature is by no means to show that it normally would be, especially in modern Western culture. What is culturally viewed as alien and inferior, as not worthy of respect or respectful knowledge, is not something to which such essential connection can easily be made. Here the three parts of the problem—the conception of the human, the conception of the self, and the conception of nature—connect again. And normally such essential relation would involve particularity, through connection to and friendship for *particular* places, forests, animals, to which one is particularly strongly related or attached and toward which one has specific and meaningful, not merely abstract, responsibilities of care.

One of the effects of viewing the problem as arising especially in the context of rationalism is to provide a rich set of connections with other critiques; it makes the connection between the critique of anthropocentrism and various other critiques that also engage critically with rationalism, such as feminism and critical theory, much more important—indeed essential—to the understanding of each. The problem of the Western account of the human–nature relation is seen in the context of the other related sets of dualisms; they are linked through their definitions as the underside of the various contrasts of reason. Since much of the strength and persistence of these dualisms derives from their connections and their ability to mirror, confirm, and support one another, critiques of anthropocentrism that fail to take account of these connections have missed an essential and not merely additional feature.

Anthropocentrism and androcentrism in particular are linked by the rationalist conception of the human self as masculine and by the account of authentically human characteristics as centered around rationality and the exclusion of its contrasts (especially characteristics regarded as feminine, animal, or natural) as less human. This provides a different and richer account of the notion of anthropocentrism, now conceived by deep ecology in terms of the notion of equality, which is both excessively narrow and difficult to articulate in any precise or convincing way in a context where needs are so different. The perception of the connection as at best accidental is a feature of some recent critiques of ecofeminism, for example the discussion of Fox and Eckersley on the relation of feminism and environmental philosophy.[28] Fox misses entirely the main thrust of the ecofeminist account of environmental philosophy and the critique of deep ecology which results or which is advanced in the ecofeminist literature, which is that it has failed to observe the way in which anthropocentrism and androcentrism are linked. It is a consequence of my arguments here that this critique needs broadening—deep ecology has failed to observe (and often even goes out of its way to deny) connections with a number of other critiques, not just feminism, for example, but also socialism, especially in the forms that mount a critique of rationalism and of modernity. The failure to observe such connections is the result of an inadequate historical analysis and understanding of the way in which the inferiorization of both women and nature is grounded in rationalism, and the connections of both to the inferiorizing of the body, hierarchical concepts of labor, and disembedded and individualist accounts of the self.

Instead of addressing the real concerns of ecofeminism in terms of connection, Fox takes ecofeminism as aiming to replace concern with anthropocentrism by concern with androcentrism. This would have the effect of making ecofeminism a reductionist position which takes women's oppression as the basic form and attempts to reduce all other forms to it. This position is a straw woman; the effect of ecofeminism is not to absorb or sacrifice the critique of anthropocentrism, but to deepen and enrich it.[29]

Notes

The author would like to thank Jim Cheney and Karen Warren for comments on an earlier draft.

1. P. Taylor, *Respect for Nature* (Princeton, N.J.: Princeton University Press, 1986).
2. Ibid., 44.
3. Ibid., 41.
4. Ibid., 82.
5. Ibid., 85–86.
6. See, for example, S. Benhabib, "The Generalised and the Concrete Other," in *Women and Moral Theory,* ed. E. Kittay and D. Meyers (Totowa, N.J.: Rowman & Allenheld, 1987), 154–77; L. A. Blum, *Friendship, Altruism, and Morality* (Boston: Routledge & Kegan Paul, 1980); and C. Gilligan, *In a Different Voice* (Cambridge, Mass.: Harvard University Press, 1982).
7. T. Regan and P. Singer, eds., *Animal Rights and Human Obligations* (Englewood Cliffs, N.J.: Prentice-Hall, 1976), 56.
8. See, for example, L. Nicholson, "Women, Morality, and History," *Social Research* 50 (1983): 514–36.
9. Blum, *Friendship, Altruism, and Morality,* 78–83.
10. K. Warren, "Feminism and Ecology: Making Connections," *Environmental Ethics* 9 (1987): 3–20, and "The Power and Promise of Ecological Feminism," *Environmental Ethics* 12 (1990): 121–46.
11. J. Rodman, "Paradigm Change in Political Science," *American Behavioral Scientist* 24 (1980): 54–55.
12. W. Fox, "Deep Ecology: A New Philosophy for Our Time?" *Ecologist* 14 (1984): 196.
13. Ibid., 197.
14. J. Seed, J. Macy, et al., *Thinking Like a Mountain: Towards a Council of All Beings* (Philadelphia: New Society Publishers, 1988), 36.

15. J. Grimshaw, *Philosophy and Feminist Thinking* (Minneapolis: University of Minnesota Press, 1986), 182–83.

16. Quoted in W. Fox, "Approaching Deep Ecology: A Response to Richard Sylvan's Critique of Deep Ecology," in *Environmental Studies Paper* 20 (Hobart: University of Tasmania Centre for Environmental Studies, 1986), 54.

17. Ibid., 13–19.

18. Ibid., 60.

19. Ibid.

20. W. Fox, *Towards a Transpersonal Ecology: Developing New Foundations for Environmentalism* (Boston: Shambhala, 1990), 12.

21. T. C. McLuhan, ed., *Touch the Earth* (London: Abacus, 1973), 28.

22. G. Lloyd, *The Man of Reason* (London: Methuen, 1984).

23. N. Chodorow, *The Reproduction of Mothering* (Berkeley: University of California Press, 1979).

24. Warren, "Power and Promise of Ecological Feminism," 143.

25. Gilligan, *In a Different Voice;* J. B. Miller, *Toward a New Psychology of Women* (Boston: Beacon Press, 1976).

26. M. Berman, *All That Is Solid Melts into Air: The Experience of Modernity* (New York: Simon and Schuster, 1982), 327.

27. B. Neidjie, *Kakadu Man* (Canberra: Mybrood P/L, 1985), 41; B. Neidjie and K. Taylor, eds., *Story About Feeling* (Wyndham: Magabala Books, 1989), 4, 146.

28. Fox, *Towards a Transpersonal Ecology;* R. Eckersley, "Divining Evolution," *Environmental Ethics* 11 (1989): 99–116.

29. This reductionist position has a few representatives in the literature, but it cannot be taken as representative of the main body of ecofeminist work.

[From] Green Reason: Communicative Ethics
for the Biosphere

John Dryzek

Introduction

The fields of environmental ethics and politics are currently home to a variety of lively and radical challenges to established institutions, practices, and moralities. Although deep ecologists, animal rights activists, ecofeminists, social ecologists, Heideggerians, pantheists, sociobiologists, and others find much to disagree about, they are united by rejection of the narrowly anthropocentric and utilitarian world views of industrial society and liberal morality. Unfortunately, however, the nefarious aspects of this rejected status quo can creep back in quietly through the back door in the form of what may be termed the subversion of ethics by epistemology. This subversion can be anticipated to the extent that an environmental ethic fails to attend fully to issues of knowledge and rationality. While connections between ethics and epistemology are readily identified (at least at the level of metaethics), in practice (i.e., at the level of applied ethics . . .) epistemology is often ignored. This neglect may be safe enough in many fields of human endeavor, but when it comes to the environment the oversight is dangerous. In this paper, I seek to correct this oversight and so close the back door.

One may expect the undermining of ethics by epistemology to the extent that an environmental ethic consorts—whether by design, accident, or oversight—with exclusively instrumental notions of reason.[1] The association with instrumental rationality applies most obviously if the ethic in question is seen as providing only the ends for instrumental actions; however, absolute prohibitions and compulsions (concerning, for example, respect for the rights of natural environments) are not immune, for such directives operate and make sense only in an environment of instrumental action—if only as constraints upon this action.

I begin my argument by outlining the threat to both the environment and environmental ethics posed by the lingering grip of instrumental reason. The search for a solution usually begins with the popular nostrum of ecological spirituality. I argue for a different cure, one that expands rationality to encompass communicative practices. Even though contemporary proponents of communicative rationality proceed in exclusively anthropocentric terms, a recognition of agency in the natural world, which a number of recent scientific developments point to, can overcome this limitation and render communicative rationality fit to regulate human dealings with the environment.

The Rational Roots of Environmental Decay

It can be argued that instrumental rationality underlies our current environmental predicament. Instrumental rationality, on this account, invokes a Cartesian dichotomy between subject and object. The human mind is subject; all else—including the natural world, and other people—consists of objects, to be manipulated, therefore dominated, in the interests of the mind's desires. Instrumental rationality is therefore abstract, estranged from nature (and society) and estranging to the extent that we subscribe to it. The expansion of this kind of rationality is often associated with the Enlightenment's disenchantment of the world, which paves the way for the destruction of that world for the sake of utility and industrialization at the hands of an arrogant humanism.[2] Ecofeminists equate such practices with patriarchal and masculine epistemology, which predates the Enlightenment by several thousand years.

The upshot is that in using the technological powers in our hands to turn the world to our use, we are destroying that world. No longer able to devise correctives for the proliferating secondary and tertiary effects of our instrumental interventions, we find that nature takes its revenge upon us in the form of environmental crisis.

This critique of instrumental rationality can also be extended to abstractly rational argument in favor of *general* moral principles. In this context, feminists argue that most contemporary political theory, whether liberal, Marxist, or Frankfurt School, works from a model of *man* which is universal, uniform, ahistorical, and transcendent, excluding a model of *woman* which is contextual, relational, and particularistic.[3] Ecofeminists add that the traditional model of man is alienated from natural contexts too.

One goal of environmental ethics is, of course, to generate solutions to the problems associated with our estrangement from the natural world. To what extent, then, are existing schemes crippled by their vestigial ties to exclusively instrumental rationality? Consider, first of all, deep ecology, which is claimed to be the most radically anti-anthropocentric (its critics would say misanthropic) ethic. When it comes to implementing this program, Devall and Sessions can suggest little more than that "policies must be changed."[4] In other words, instrumentally rational actions (such as population control) are commended to the very agencies (governments and other organizations) whose rationality is elsewhere condemned for contributing to environmental decay. In their inattention to the side effects of their proposed strategies Devall and Sessions are likely to discover that their ends are subverted by their means.

Further examples of a lingering stress on instrumental reason are readily identifiable. In his classic argument for the rights of natural objects, Stone asks that these rights be embodied in law—a system of instrumental-analytic rationality *par excellence*.[5] Lemons suggests that we take ideas promulgated by natural science, such as homeostasis and diversity, as the basis for an environmental ethic—and, implicitly, as the end for instrumental manipulations.[6]

A subtle extension of the dialectic of Enlightenment may come into play here. According to Horkheimer and Adorno, the dialectic of Enlightenment tells us that the more successful we become in securing the material conditions for human freedom (in part through control of the natural world), the more repressed we become as human subjects, unable to partake of freedom.[7] To overstate my proposed extension: the more assiduously we cultivate the ethical principles for benign but still instrumental action toward the environment, the less likely it becomes that we shall be able to reconcile ourselves to that environment in productive fashion. That is, nature will become still more firmly the "other" from which we are estranged, even if our instrumental manipulations of it are well motivated.

The challenge here then is to locate an epistemology less prone to the subversion of environmental ethics than the exclusively instrumental fixation associated with dominant (post-Enlightenment) conceptions of rationality. Another way of stating the same point is that we shold seek what Habermas disparages as the "resurrection of nature."[8] On this account, nature was not simply disenchanted by the Enlightenment—it was killed. As a result, no longer could meanings and purposes be discerned in the nonhuman world. How then may they be retrieved?

Two Ways to Resurrect Nature

Although the idea that nature merits resurrection is indeed current in the field of environmental ethics, most of those who subscribe to this idea seek resurrection through spirituality, religion, feeling, and intuition. That is, they accept the dichotomy established by Enlightenment rationalists and seek a return to pre-Enlightenment—or even prehistoric—sensibilities.

The idea that spirit is ultimately preferable to rationality is perhaps held most strongly by deep ecologists, although a host of other writers—including some critics of deep ecology—is equally enamoured of spirit and suspicious of any kind of reason. It is an easy step from condemnations of rationality to arguments for more holistic, intuitive, emotional, spiritual, or experiential "oneness" to mediate our relations with the natural world (and one another). Franciscan Christianity, Taoism, Buddhism, pagan religions, feminist spirituality, and American Indian beliefs all have their adherents and admirers.[9]

An advocacy of a particular spiritual position can be rooted in rejection of another spirituality, rather than in opposition to rationality. For example, Lynn White argues that because the source of environmental crisis is one kind of religion—specifically, the Judeo-Christian tradition that places man above nature—the solution must lie in adoption of a different kind of religion. Gary Snyder makes a similar point in bemoaning the establishment of "male deities located off the planet."[10]

Nevertheless, even if a particular spirituality is the problem, it does not follow that a different spirituality has to be the solution. Nor does it follow that if a particular rationality is the problem, then spirituality is the solution. Although the right kind of spirituality may be one answer, I argue that the right kind of rationality is a better one. I draw on the rationality debates now cutting across a variety of disciplines to argue that a broadened notion of rationality can meet the concerns of ecological anti-rationalists. I contend that provided our notions of rationality are expanded in the right direction, human dealings with the environment are indeed best governed by rational standards and that a regressive emphasis on spirit is therefore unnecessary. To be sure, because the rationality debates have for the most part missed the ecological dimension, some specifically green correctives must be brought to bear upon them. Thus, the kind of reason I argue for here is not only expanded beyond instrumental conceptions, but is also avowedly ecological.

The Hazards of Spiritual Alternatives

Before turning to an examination of this kind of rationality, let me identify some of the shortcomings inherent in excessive reliance upon its spiritual alternatives. Clearly an ecologically sensitive spirituality is not automatically to be commended. For an extreme negative model, we need look no further than the Third Reich and Hitler's invitation to good Aryans to think with their blood rather than their brains. Along with Teutonic mythology, Naziism embodied a peculiar kind of reverence for (German) nature and father*land*. Today's German Greens are well aware of this history, and so avoid any association with ecological spirituality.

Even if Naziism is dismissed as an irrelevant possibility involving only perversion and abuse of ecological spirituality, one can discern political dangers in the schemes of some contemporary ecological philosophers. For example, Devall and Sessions prescribe the true realization of the "self" in a larger communal "Self" of "organic wholeness" as an antidote to liberal individualism.[11] Even though the "Self" of Devall and Sessions is benign, extending beyond humanity to the natural world, willing immersion in a larger "Self" is also surely the essence of totalitarianism.

Some advocates of an ecological spirituality are impressed by the functions of myth and ritual in preliterate societies; nevertheless, as Luke points out, myth and ritual in primal societies can also form the substance of attempts to control and manipulate nature and other persons—the very sins of which instrumental rationality is accused.[12]

Although there are important differences between an earth ceremony at a gathering of contemporary environmentalists and a Nuremburg rally, spirituality as such cannot speak to these differences and help us choose one over the other. Thus, ecological spirituality by itself provides no defence against authoritarianism. As Bookchin points out, ecological religious sensibilities have often coexisted with despotic social order (as in ancient Egypt).[13]

Even if one dismisses these authoritarian possibilities to embrace a more tolerant and pluralistic spirituality, there are two reasons why any such orientation remains inadequate. First, natural systems are complex; it is a familiar adage that "everything is connected to everything else" in ecosystems.[14] It is also the case that interventions in complex systems often have counterintuitive results, as actions ramify extensively through these systems. As a result, intuitions, good intentions, and sympathetic sensibilities are insufficient guides to action. Think, for example, of the well-intentioned fire-control policies long followed in the forests of the American West which interrupted the life cycles of species and the well-being of ecosystems that depend on periodic scorching.

To take another example, one might out of a reverence for all things living remove only deadwood from a forest for fuel, thereby undermining the key habitat dead trees provide.

Now it might be argued here that an appropriate spirituality could somehow be combined with a suitably tamed instrumental rationality to effectively cope with complexity. However, often ecological systems are *so* complex that they defy the efforts of instrumental rationalists to model them. In such cases, spirituality is not likely to be of much help either. I suggest below that a noninstrumental kind of reason can compensate for the deficiencies of instrumental rationality under complex conditions.

A second shortcoming of a spiritual approach is contingent on the conditions of our interactions with the natural world. One may assume that these conditions are in a state of some disequilibrium (otherwise, there would be little need to worry about environmental ethics, policies, and politics). Thus, even if a primarily spiritual orientation toward nature is adequate for maintaining an ecologically harmonious society, it contains no effective guidance about how to reach this happy state from our current plight (except perhaps through a massive exercise in spiritual empowerment). To put it crudely, there is no effective "theory of transition." Most of those who speak of ecological spirituality say little about this transition, let alone any practical political program.

Required here then is a noninstrumental capacity analogous to that of "resilience" in natural systems, which can be defined in terms of a capacity to return to stable operating range from a disequilibrium state. Natural systems can do this on their own without us. Moreover, if Lovelock is right about the ability of the planet's biota to sustain the physical conditions for all life—thereby constituting an entity he calls Gaia—these systems can also correct for many human excesses.[15] Nevertheless, larger stresses in systems with substantial human complicity require a human contribution to problem solving (as even Lovelock admits).

Communicative Reason

At this juncture we might seem in a bit of a quandary. On the one hand, instrumental rationality and abstract reasoning about values imply hierarchy and domination. On the other, spirituality is an inadequate alternative. Its inadequacy is implicitly confirmed by Spretnak, who qualifies her advocacy of green spirituality with a recognition that "holistic, or ecological, thinking is not a retreat from reason; it is an enlargement of it to more comprehensive and hence more efficient means of analysis."[16] Spretnak, of course, wishes to enlarge reason by incorporating spirituality, but, like other environmentalists who bemoan "dualistic thinking," she offers no hints as to how this might be done. In contrast, the alternative I propose is to expand reason in a different direction.

How then can an expanded, nonhierarchical conception of rationality point to what Whitebook calls a "non-regressive reconciliation with nature" that may allow us to escape from this impasse?[17] We may begin to chart this escape by noting that rationality is properly a property of community, and not just individuals, if for no other reason than that social isolates have no standards of judgment. As Dewey argues, "our intelligence is bound up . . . with the community of life of which we are a part."[18] We can describe a collective as *communicatively* rational to the extent that its interactions are egalitarian, uncoerced, competent, and free from delusion, deception, power, and strategy.[19] Communicative rationality is best thought of as a regulative ideal for human social practices, which can then be condemned to the extent of their violation of its precepts. No realizable blueprint is implied.

Most of those who recognize this kind of rationality believe it is embedded first and foremost in processes involving the creation of meaning—culture, socialization, friendship, and so forth. Nevertheless, communicative rationality may also be conducive to the resolution of complex problems, inasmuch as it promotes the free harmonization of actions by disparate individuals concerned with the different facets of such problems. Thus, communicative reason may rest more easily in a complex world than either spirituality or instrumental rationality.

One might argue that the ideal discursive community of communicative rationality is presupposed even in discussions about ecological spirituality, for if one accepts that some spiritualities have more benign ecological implications than others—and surely this is unarguable—then one needs some means of sorting them out. These means cannot themselves be spiritual, since spirituality is internal to the schemes one is sifting. Within the Catholic schema, Catholics are right by revelation; within the pagan schema, pagans are right by revelation. Arguments across the boundaries of spiritual schemes, however, have to be reasoned arguments—of exactly the kind that proponents of such schemes deploy in the literature on environmental ethics. In deploying arguments, moreover, one is implicitly accepting the constitutive principles of a discursively rational community (however much one violates these principles in practice). My point here echoes Apel's analysis of scientific communities.[20] Apel points out that the practice of science presupposes a measure of communicative rationality within these communities. Just as scientists cannot deny their humanity, those who proclaim spirituality cannot, in this age of lost innocence, deny their rationality.

Communicative rationality as generally stated (e.g., by Habermas) is not, however, conducive to harmonious relationships with the natural world. A first defect arises from its transcendent, ahistorical leanings. In practice, all ecological contexts are different, and individuals are likely to interpret and experience them in diverse ways. This problem can be overcome by the explicit recognition of the ineliminable plurality in human discourse. In this way, communicative rationality becomes simply a *procedural* standard for human interaction, dictating no *substantive* resolution of disputes.

A second defect cuts deeper. If communication is seen merely as a property of human dealings with each other, then its rationality may coexist easily with instrumental and dominating attitudes toward the nonhuman world. Indeed, Habermas proposes this coexistence as a *solution* to the problem posed by the dialectic of Enlightenment that will move critical theory beyond the impasse reached by the earlier work of Adorno and Horkheimer. Habermas tries to draw a clear line between the relationships we construct with the natural world and those we establish with one another. He avers that the only attitude toward the natural world which is fruitful in securing the material conditions for human existence is an instrumental one.[21] The domination of nature is a price that Habermas is willing to pay for fulfillment of the Enlightenment's promise of human emancipation: "the dignity of the subject . . . is attained at the price of denying all worth to nature."[22] To Habermas, there is ultimately no ontological distinction between inorganic and organic nature. A lump of iron and an ecosystem should be treated in the same terms, as objects for manipulation. Only in our relationships with other persons can instrumental rationality be overcome and communicative rationality flourish; Habermas's goal here is to "prevent social relations becoming like our relations with the natural world."[23]

Habermas believes that we can only truly know that which we have ourselves created—language—and that nature will always remain estranged and separate. We cannot truly *know* anything about nature; we can only observe the results of our interventions in it. Challenged on the potentially destructive environmental implications of this dichotomy, Habermas replies that one should not confuse ethics with epistemology.[24] Thus, he believes that an environmental ethic can be grafted onto our instrumental relations with the natural world—although, given that Habermas believes that the only entities that bear value are those which can participate in discourse, this ethic has to be anthropocentric. As a result, Habermas ends up just where the interesting problems in environmental ethics (and epistemology) begin. However, the best move here is not to reject communicative rationality, but to extend it.

From Communicative to Ecological Rationality

How may communicative rationality be extended to incorporate procedural standards which are not obviously intrinsic to human discourse, but which are essential to good order in human interactions with the natural world? One place to begin might be with the establishment of ecological principles—or ecosystem analogues—such as diversity, homeostasis, flexibility, and resilience as critical standards in human discourse. In so doing, we would not submit to nature's authority, in the manner advocates of biocentrism (the doctrine that value is created by and in natural systems) sometimes seem to demand. Nor would we merely apply nature's standards to human communities. . . . Rather, individual ecological principles would always be applied, debated, redeemed, or rejected. In this sense, these principles would supplement the familiar standards intrinsic to the idea of communicative rationality (equality, noncoercion, truthfulness, etc.).

If we take away the dressing of communicative rationality, this first proposal is a bit facile, reducing as it does to advocacy of ecological principles in human debates. As such, it severs ethics from epistemology once again, though it grafts environmental ethics onto communicative, rather than instrumental, rationality. For their part, critical communications theorists would probably object that such a move is tantamount to the coercive imposition of an external, substantive, and transcendent judgment upon human discourse. One might equally well impose economic efficiency, political stability, or social harmony as a standard, for none of these principles is intrinsic to the idea of rational discourse, and so cannot be grounded in it.

How might one go about establishing the special claims of ecology upon human communication? One could start by arguing that intersubjective discourse presupposes some ecological—and not just linguistic—standards. Although it is easy to forget, our communications with one another can proceed only in and through the media made available by the natural world (in addition to our own medium of language). It is not just brute matter we are taking advantage of here, for, if Lovelock is right, the atmosphere in which we live, talk, hear, write, read, smell, and touch is composed and regulated by the planet's biota acting in concert.[25] This biota makes possible and maintains a physical environment fit for itself—and for us, and our communications. With this awareness in mind, we can no longer speak of communicative acts in a vacuum. Because any such act is made possible by this ecological system, it can be called to account in accordance with ecological standards. If indeed nature is a silent participant in every conversation, then perhaps it deserves a measure of the respect that we accord to human participants. If critical communications theorists argue that only entities capable of entering into communication can be assigned value, then there is a sense in which Gaia passes their test.

Assuming that the Gaia hypothesis holds, then we live *in* a highly differentiated, self-regulating global system whose "intelligence," which though not *conscious,* is of a complexity equal to that of any group of humans. Thus, "the Gaia hypothesis implies that the stable state of our planet includes man as a part of, or partner in, a very democratic entity."[26] Any special capabilities we do have—perhaps even, as Lovelock himself suggests, as Gaia's "nervous system and a brain"[27]—do not set us apart, but emphasize our embeddedness.

Lovelock himself equivocates between two extremes on the implications of his hypothesis for the standing of Gaia's "intelligence." On the one hand, he develops a reductionist model sufficient to explain climatic stability in the face of wide fluctuations in the flow of solar radiation. This model is demonstrated in a hypothetical "Daisyworld" populated only by light and dark daisies whose relative numbers, and hence the planet's albedo, change in response to the intensity of radiation.[28] Somewhat surprisingly, in the same volume Lovelock endorses a mystical view which interprets Gaia in religious terms.[29]

If one eschews these two extremes, then the Gaia hypothesis indicates that there is agency (but not divinity) in the natural world. But let me stress that this hypothesis and its supporting evidence are not the only indications of such agency, which can also be found at lower levels of biological organization. For example, in her discussion of the work of the celebrated geneticist Barbara McLintock, Keller argues that the key to McLintock's success is her "feeling for the organism," or, more precisely, for "the prodigous capacity of organisms to devise means for guaranteeing their own survival."[30] Thus, to McLintock, "the objects of her study have become subjects in their own right; they claim from her a kind of attention that most of us experience only in relation to other persons."[31]

To the biologist Charles Birch, this extension of subjectivity to nonhuman entities is the essence of "postmodern biology."[32] He treats "human experience as a high-level exemplification of entities in general, be they cells or atoms or electrons. All are subjects."[33] He argues that we should recognize the "self-determination exercised by natural entities in response to possibilities of their future."[34] Such an approach is also found in the work of Jane Goodall on chimpanzees and Donald Griffin on animal thinking.[35] Goodall and Griffin practice an essentially hermeneutic biology involving imaginative attempts to reconstruct the actions-in-context of other thinking beings.

Obviously there is a large gap between an "intelligent" Gaia and thinking organisms. In the early twentieth century this gap would have been handled by interpreting ecosystems as teleological entities seeking ever higher stages of ecological succession, culminating in climax. Today this superorganismic view of ecosystems is out of fashion in academic ecology, which has become thoroughly reductionistic and stochastic. Whether this epistemological commitment has more to do with academic ecology's desire for permission to worship in the temple of science than with the intrinsic superiority of the reductionist view remains an open question.

Regardless of its source, any recognition of agency in nature clearly undercuts the Cartesian subject–object dualism that legitimates the domination of nature—just as a recognition of *human* agency undermines the instrumental manipulation that legimates authoritarian politics. Nevertheless, agency in the natural world also makes the restriction of communicative rationality to purely human communities appear arbitrary. This world is not silent and passive, but *already* full of "values, purposes, and meanings," irrespective of what we ascribe to it.[36] As Abram argues, human perception can be reinterpreted in terms of reception of communication from the natural world.

In this discussion of communicative possibilities encompassing human and natural systems I have taken for granted the communicative competence of humans and sought analogues in nature; nevertheless, this issue may also be approached from the opposite direction by contemplating what is natural in humans. Human nature is not just human; it is also nature. We can communicate not only because we are human, but also because we are natural. This precondition for communicative competence applies to humans, other primates, cetaceans, and insects alike. True, human communication mechanisms, language in particular, are more elaborate than those of most other species; however, greater continuity across human and nonhuman species is evident in nonlinguistic forms of communication, such as body movements or pheromones.

If the idea of communicative interaction can indeed encompass the natural world, then so too can standards of communicative rationality. These standards, nevertheless, will not be the same as those enumerated above for speech among humans. So what standards are appropriate, and in what rational processes could such standards be embodied?

Toward a Communicative Ecological Ethic

The specification of a communicative ethic for interactions encompassing the natural world is no small task, and what follows is intended to be suggestive rather than definitive. The task becomes somewhat easier upon noting that the objective here is a set of procedural criteria to regulate actions, rather than a full resolution of the content of actions.

Any attempt at substantive resolution here would involve flirting with instrumental rationality (which, when all is said and done, is often unavoidable). Such resolution may, however, be appropriate with reference to one universal principle: respect for the perceptual media furnished by nature. This principle in turn implies special respect for any "vital organs" that sustain these media (most especially, the life-sustaining composition of the atmosphere). According to Lovelock, these organs may well be the tropical forests, wetlands, and continental shelves (we would do well to find out if they are!).[37]

For the most part, though, substantive norms will have to be contingent on time, place, and particular human and ecological circumstances. It is also worth bearing in mind that perfection is impossible. Procedural criteria should function as critical standards from which some practices depart more than others.

An approach to the specification of such criteria can begin by noting the sense in which there can be equality in interactions with the natural world. Although equality in communicative competence of the sort that one can hypothesize within human communities is out of the question here, one can still postulate equality in the minimal terms of the very ability to communicate. This recognition rules out two extremes. The first is the idea that ecological processes should be engineered by human minds that essentially transcend the natural world. This first extreme finds its culmination in the notion that a "noosphere" could supplant the ecosphere.[38] The second extreme is based on the idea that "nature knows best,"[39] carrying with it implicit rejection of the idea that human problem-solving intelligence has any meaningful role to play in environmental affairs. To avoid these extremes we need a symbiotic intelligence in which both human minds and the self-organizing, self-regulating properties of natural systems play a part.

"Intelligence" in natural systems does not arise through the existence of any communications center; Gaia may have vital organs, but she has no brain. Rather, the feedback processes which organize, regulate, and maintain natural systems are of a diffuse and internal type—signals do not pass through any central thermostat analog. Bearing in mind the principle of rough equality in communicative capability, we should be wary of highly centralized decision mechanisms—national environmental bureaucracies, multinational mining or logging corporations, international resource management agencies, and so forth—which could dominate, ignore, or suppress local ecological signals. The principle of rough equality suggests instead that diffuse feedback processes in the natural world should be matched by diffuse decision processes in human societies. This contention obviously provides further support to a presumption that "small is beautiful" in social organization—and, in practical political terms, to bioregionalism.

Obviously, though, not all of nature's feedback processes are localized. They can also be regional, even global. Think, for example, of ozone depletion or the greenhouse effect. The principle of rough equality does not limit the size and scope of political institutions in such cases. However, their designers should be careful to limit the purview of any such regional or global institutions to issues and problems which are themselves regional or global. Given the tendency of large organizations toward aggrandisement, the benefit of any doubt should probably go to the small-scale level.

Economic institutions, for their part, cannot escape size limitations so easily. Corporations whose reach is limited could not extend their operations to "pollution havens" in which they have no other interest. Similarly, the World Bank has no business making decisions for particular development projects based on universalistic, contextually inappropriate criteria. Such decisions have already led to numerous social and ecological disasters in the Third World, for example, in connection with the construction of large dams.[40]

What can we say about decision processes beyond questions of appropriate scale? Obviously there is much we do not know—and cannot know—about the workings of the natural world (and, for that matter, the human world). Thus, some kind of experimental practice in better living with the world seems to be appropriate. Yet experimentation in the image of science—manipulative, analytic, piecemeal, controlled, seeking generalizations across contexts—clearly violates the canons of communicative ethics. A more appropriate experimental practice would interpret any particular interaction of human and natural systems in terms of a complex, nonreducible, and unique entity. This kind of "holistic experimentation" (sketched in a nonecological context by Mitroff and Blankenship) makes no attempt to control conditions and keep them constant, generalize results beyond the case at hand, or distinguish between experimenters and subjects.[41] Nor does it impose any restrictions on the kinds of knowledge and perceptions admissible in experimental design, evaluation, and redesign. The trick is, of course, to extend participation in such experimentation to nonhuman entities.

This requirement returns us to the question of the perception of things natural and its relationship to communication. If in fact we can equate perception with communication, then the contemporary gross failings in human perception can be called to account by standards of communicative reason. Perceptual failure pervades industrial societies, as people simply fail to recognize the effects of their actions on the natural world (not to mention other people). Although these effects are sometimes visible, even to urban dwellers, who cannot escape the effects of pollution, in other ways nature is easy to ignore, especially by people who have no idea where and how their food is grown, or what resources go into making the goods they buy. Communicative ethics suggests improved perception.

Improvement could be sought at the level of social institutions. It is clear that small-scale, autonomous societies really do have to pay a great deal of attention to signals from their local environment. This necessity helps to explain the ecological sensibilities found in many preliterate societies: those without such orientations soon expire. These perceptual considerations obviously reinforce the argument for appropriate scale in social institutions—and in holistic experimentation.

Perceptual capabilities can also be addressed at the level of individuals. Again, it is possible to extend some critical theory notions here. In his most recent attempts to ground his theoretical project, Habermas appeals to the "reconstructive science" associated with figures such as Noam Chomsky, Lawrence Kohlberg, and Jean Piaget.[42] The stages of individual moral and cognitive development identified by Kohlberg and Piaget do, according to Habermas, serve as a fixed and true model for social evolution. Higher levels of individual development are characterized by increasing linguistic competence, by sensitivity to links with other individuals, by awareness of the interests of others—and, he adds, unfortunately, by recognition of the qualitatively different status of human and nonhuman entities.[43] Again, though, Habermas has taken what are really just contingent empirical conjectures, generalized them into timeless and nonfalsifiable truths, and frozen their boundaries. Thus, he rules out the possibility that sensitivity to interconnections with the natural environment might also enter individual development.

Habermas's perspective may be limited by what bourgeois society currently allows and encourages in the way of individual development, which he mistakes for timeless truth. One can imagine moral development that proceeds further.

Conclusion

By now I hope I have demonstrated the promise of a communicative epistemology for environmental ethics which embraces the natural world in rational terms. There is no need here for mystical notions about spiritual communion with nature. Immersion in the world can be a thoroughly rational affair, provided we expand our notion of rationality in the appropriate directions. Reason too can be green. But clearly much remains to be done in the construction of a communicative ethics of rational interaction that embraces the natural world.

Notes

1. Instrumental rationality may be defined in terms of the capacity to devise, select, and effect good means to clarified ends.

2. D. Ehrenfeld, *The Arrogance of Humanism* (Oxford: Oxford University Press, 1978).

3. See S. T. Leonard, *Critical Theory in Political Practice* (Princeton, N.J.: Princeton University Press, 1990).

4. B. Devall and G. Sessions, *Deep Ecology: Living as if Nature Mattered* (Salt Lake City: Peregrine Smith, 1985), 70, 73.

5. C. D. Stone, "Should Trees Have Standing? Toward Legal Rights for Natural Objects," *Southern California Law Review* 45 (1972): 450–501.

6. J. Lemons, "Cooperation and Stability as a Basis for Environmental Ethics," *Environmental Ethics* 3 (1981): 219–30.

7. M. Horkheimer and T. Adorno, *Dialectic of Enlightenment* (New York: Herder & Herder, 1972).

8. J. Habermas, *Knowledge and Human Interests* (Boston: Beacon Press, 1971), 32–33. The reason Habermas disparages this resurrection is that he believes it could only occur in mystical form. Such romanticism may have been attractive to his Frankfurt School precursors, especially Adorno, Marcuse, and Horkheimer, but it has no place in Habermas's own rationalistic ambitions.

9. For suggestions, see L. White, Jr., "The Historical Roots of Our Ecologic Crisis," *Science* 155 (1967): 1203–17 [this volume, 5–14]; C. Spretnak, *The Spiritual Dimension of Green Politics* (Santa Fe: Bear, 1986); D. La Chapelle, *Earth Wisdom* (San Diego, Calif.: Guild of Tudors, 1978); Devall and Sessions, *Deep Ecology*, 8, 90–91, 100–101; W. Fox, "On Guiding Stars to Deep Ecology: A Reply to Naess," *Ecologist* 14 (1984): 203–4; and A. Naess, "A Defense of the Deep Ecology Movement," *Environmental Ethics* 6 (1984): 266. Clearly religions differ in their environmental implications and so constitute fit objects for comparative scrutiny in the light of ecological concerns. See, for example, E. C. Hargrove, ed., *Religion and Environmental Crisis* (Athens: University of Georgia Press, 1986).

10. Quoted in Spretnak, *Spiritual Dimension at Green Politics*, 33.

11. Devall and Sessions, *Deep Ecology*, 67.

12. T. Luke, "Deep Ecology and Distributive Justice" (Paper presented at the annual meeting of the Midwest Political Science Association, 1967), 17–18.

13. M. Bookchin, "Social Ecology Versus Deep Ecology: A Challenge for the Ecology Movement," *Green Perspectives* 4–5 (1987): 7–8.

14. B. Commoner, *The Closing Circle* (New York: Bantam, 1972).

15. J. E. Lovelock, *Gaia: A New Look at Life on Earth* (Oxford: Oxford University Press, 1979).

16. Spretnak, *Spiritual Dimension of Green Politics*, 29.

17. J. Whitebook, "The Problem of Nature in Habermas," *Telos* 40 (1979): 42.

18. J. Dewey, *Human Nature and Conduct* (New York: Modern Library, 1922), 314.

19. J. Habermas, *The Theory of Communicative Action*, vol. 1, *Reason and the Rationalization of Society* (Boston: Beacon Press, 1984).

20. Karl-Otto Apel, "The *A Priori* of Communication and the Foundation of the Humanities," *Man and World* 5 (1972): 3–37.

21. See, for example, J. Habermas, "A Reply to My Critics," in *Habermas: Critical Debates*, ed. J. B. Thompson and D. Held (Cambridge, Mass.: MIT Press, 1982), 243–45.

22. Whitebook, "Problem of Nature in Habermas," 53.

23. C. Alford, *Science and the Revenge of Nature* (Gainesville: University of Florida Press, 1985), 77.

24. Habermas, "Reply to My Critics," 241–42.

25. Lovelock, *Gaia*.

26. Ibid., 145.

27. Ibid., 147.

28. J. Lovelock, *The Ages of Gaia: A Biography of Our Living Earth* (New York: Norton, 1988), 45–61.

29. Ibid., 206.

30. E. F. Keller, *A Feeling for the Organism: The Life and Work of Barbara McLintock* (San Francisco: Freeman, 1983), 199.

31. Ibid., 200.

32. C. Birch, "The Postmodern Challenge to Biology," in *The Reenchantment of Science: Postmodern Perspectives*, ed. D. Griffin (Albany: State University of New York Press, 1988), 69–78. "Postmodern" used in this sense has no nihilistic or relativist connotations.

33. Ibid., 71.

34. Ibid., 75.

35. J. Goodall, *The Chimpanzees of Gombe: Patterns of Behavior* (Cambridge, Mass.: Harvard University Press, 1986); D. R. Griffin, *Animal Thinking* (Cambridge, Mass.: Harvard University Press, 1984).

36. D. Abram, "The Perceptual Implications of Gaia," *Ecologist* 15 (1985): 88.

37. Lovelock, *Gaia*, 129–41.

38. V. I. Vernadsky, "The Biosphere and the Noosphere," *American Scientist* 33 (1945): 1–12.

39. Commoner, *Closing Circle*.

40. E. Goldsmith and N. Hildyard, *The Social and Environmental Effects of Large Dams* (Camelford: Wadebridge Ecological Centre, 1985).

41. I. Mitroff and L. V. Blankenship, "On the Methodology of the Holistic Experiment: An Approach to the Conceptualization of Large-Scale Social Experiments," *Technological Forecasting and Social Change* 4 (1973): 339–53.

42. Habermas, *Theory of Communicative Action*.

43. Ibid., 68–69.

PART IV

$\sim$

Sustainable Development and
International Justice

THE MOST dramatic development in environmental consciousness in recent years has been the globalization of ecological concern. Although the seeds of a global consciousness can be found in the environmental rhetoric of the 1960s, it was such local concerns as air and water pollution that galvanized people into action on the first Earth Day in 1970. By Earth Day 1990, however, the problems of "global environmental change"—ozone depletion, climate change, and biodiversity loss—had come to the fore.

The recognition that environmental problems are global in scale has brought with it new concerns about poverty and underdevelopment. "Poverty is the worst polluter," it is sometimes said. Poor people degrade their environments in order to get by—cutting trees in order to cook and keep warm, abusing soils in order to scratch out a living here and now, poaching wildlife if that is the only way to earn an income.

Poverty is a creation of society rather than a brute fact of nature. From the mid-nineteenth century to present, global inequality has been increasing. According to the World Bank, there are now more than 1 billion people living in poverty. Yet in the decade of the 1980s, the poor countries transferred about $500 billion of their wealth to rich countries. In large part these transfers were payments on loans owed to commercial banks. In many cases, these payments have directly affected the standard of living of poor people in developing countries. Moreover, the search for hard currency to service these debts has led some governments to undertake large-scale, environmentally destructive projects in attempts to boost exports.

Even those who are not disposed to worry about poor people in faraway places have reason to be concerned about the developing world, for these countries have the potential to greatly affect the global environment. If India uses chloroflourocarbons in manufacturing refrigerators for food storage, then

175

ozone depletion will continue on a global scale. If China inefficiently uses its massive coal reserves in order to industrialize, then climate change may be inevitable. If Brazil further develops Amazonia in an effort to provide economic opportunity for its landless, unemployed people, then much of the world's biodiversity will be lost before it has even been described.

The idea that environmental problems are fundamentally global in scope is implicit in the Stockholm Declaration of 1972, the final statement of the first United Nations Conference on the Environment. However, from the beginning, the conference was plagued with tension and dissension. Environmental consciousness was dawning in the developed world, and the leaders of these countries wanted to open an international front in the battle to save the environment. But the leaders of some of the developing countries had a different agenda: they saw concern for the environment as a distraction from the problems of development, neocolonialism, and racism. They were also concerned that their national sovereignty and ability to develop would be hampered by international environmental regulation. Out of this conflict came a curious document. Its first clause links responsibilities to protect the environment with the need to end apartheid and colonialism. It goes on to declare that all nations have "the sovereign right to exploit their own resources pursuant to their own environmental policies."

Despite the weakness and perhaps incoherence of the Stockholm Declaration, it touched off two decades of United Nations activity on environmental issues. In the 1980s, the General Assembly created the World Commission on Environment and Development, composed of distinguished leaders from all regions of the world and chaired by the prime minister of Norway, Gro Harlem Brundtland. *Our Common Future*, the report of the Brundtland Commission, set the terms of the debate over environment and development for at least the next decade. The commission surveyed the problems faced by the world's people, emphasizing the "interlocking crises" of population, economics, and ecological destruction. The commission argued that we are all in it together (we have a "common future") and that the nations of the world must switch from development at any cost to "sustainable development."

The concept of sustainable development has been welcomed in most circles, although there is a lack of agreement about what it means. Some have wanted to emphasize the "sustainable" part, while others have emphasized "development." The environmentalist Wolfgang Sachs is among the minority who sees environment and development as fundamentally in conflict with each other. In his view, the concept of sustainable development paves the way for a new global "ecocracy" that will manage the planet's ecology in the same incompetent and self-interested way in which planners and experts have managed the global economy.

In June 1992, on the twentieth anniversary of the Stockholm meeting, the United Nations Conference on Environment and Development was convened. When the largest gathering of national leaders ever assembled met in Rio de Janeiro, Brazil, there were high hopes that these world leaders would take meaningful action on a range of global environmental problems and agree on an "Earth Charter" that would clearly and unambiguously define the human relationship to nature.

The meeting was fractious even before it began. Some developing countries objected to the very idea of an Earth Charter, arguing that the title of any such document should also make reference to development. Pressure from religious fundamentalists and some women's groups prevented any significant discussion of population problems. Malaysia and some other exporters of tropical woods refused to permit an agreement on forestry. The United States, in conjunction with the Arab oil producers, weakened the climate stabilization treaty. And the United States stood alone in refusing to sign the biodiversity treaty.

The Rio Declaration on Environment and Development, which was ultimately signed, is a surprisingly conservative document. Its first principle is that "human beings are at the centre of concerns for sustainable development," and, echoing Stockholm, it reiterates that states have the sovereign right to exploit their own resources pursuant to their own policies.

As the Rio conference illustrated, there is a great deal of conflict around the issues of environment and development. Many people in the developing nations believe that the world system is fundamentally unjust and that any attempt to address global environmental issues must consider questions of international justice. This perspective is largely shared by several European countries, but not by the United States. Both the Bush and Reagan administrations took the position that what the world needs is free markets and international trade; environmental quality would come as a result.

A similar perspective is articulated by economists Terry Anderson and Donald Leal in their critique of sustainable development. They believe that implementing sustainable-development policies would require large bureaucracies that would inevitably fail, as those established in the Communist societies of Eastern Europe for other purposes failed. They argue that free markets can produce innovative solutions to environmental problems if governments define and enforce property rights and then step out of the way.

A very different perspective is offered by the Commission on Developing Countries and Global Change, a group of scientists from the developing world. They argue that voices from the developing world have not been heard; if our global problems of environment and development are to be solved, there must be burden-sharing between the developed and developing countries. According to the commission, the nations of the North have sought to evade their responsibility by demanding repayment of economic debts while overlooking their own environmental debts; the environmental problems that are emphasized are those of most concern to the rich countries, while the environmental problems of the poor are ignored.

Finally, the Indian social scientist Rajni Kothari challenges us to think about the moral dimensions of sustainable development. He believes that we have exported our crisis of the spirit to future generations and to nature. If we are to

178 REFLECTING ON NATURE

survive these crises, we must develop a "sense of sanctity about the Earth" and a thirst for justice among all living things.

Developments in the science of "global change" have made it clear that the integrity of many of our planetary systems will stand or fall together; yet, as the selections that follow indicate, the human community is deeply divided on how to respond to what the Brundtland Commission called our "interlocking crises." Because these divisions underlie many responses to the environmental problems that we face, they will continue to be a focus of environmental thought and action as we move into the twenty-first century.

Further Reading

Afshar, Haleh, ed. *Women, Development and Survival in the Third World*. London: Longman, 1991.

These case studies explore the interplay between historical perceptions and myths about women and the realities that shape their roles in development.

Attfield, Robin, and Barry Wilkins, eds. *International Justice and the Third World*. London: Routledge, 1992.

Based on the premise that global justice is both necessary and possible, this collection explores various ethical and conceptual issues regarding development.

Brown, Lester R., et al. *State of the World 1993*. New York: Norton, 1993.

A survey of such issues as the gender gap in development, supporting indigenous peoples, and reconciling trade and environment.

Cooper, David E., and Joy A. Palmer, eds. *The Environment in Question*. London: Routledge, 1992.

This broad collection of essays on global environmental problems represents a diversity of perspectives and disciplines.

de la Court, T. *Beyond Brundtland*. New York: New Horizons Press, 1990.

A critique of the Brundtland Commission report and a sketch of green development for the 1990s.

Sen, Gita, and Caren Grown. *Development, Crises, and Alternative Visions*. New York: Monthly Review Press, 1987.

The result of collective efforts among women activists and researchers from the developing world, this brief book examines the effects of orthodox development policies and presents alternative strategies.

Shiva, Vandana, in association with J. Bandyopadhyay et al. *Ecology and the Politics of Survival: Conflicts over Natural Resources in India*. Tokyo: United Nations University Press, 1991.

This collection of case studies examines conflicts over the environment and development in India.

Declaration of Principles

───────◆───────

United Nations Conference on the Environment, Stockholm, 1972

1. MAN HAS the fundamental right to freedom, equality and adequate conditions of life, in an environment of a quality which permits a life of dignity and well-being, and bears a solemn responsibility to protect and improve the environment for present and future generations. In this respect, policies promoting or perpetuating apartheid, racial segregation, discrimination, colonial and other forms of oppression and foreign domination stand condemned and must be eliminated.

2. The natural resources of the earth including the air, water, land, flora and fauna and especially representative samples of natural ecosystems must be safeguarded for the benefit of present and future generations through careful planning or management as appropriate.

3. The capacity of the earth to produce vital renewable resources must be maintained and wherever practicable restored and improved.

4. Man has a special responsibility to safeguard and wisely manage the heritage of wildlife and its habitat which are now gravely imperiled by a combination of adverse factors. Nature conservation including wildlife must therefore receive importance in planning for economic developments.

5. The nonrenewable resources of the earth must be employed in such a way as to guard against the danger of their future exhaustion and to insure that benefits from such employment are shared by all mankind.

6. The discharge of toxic substances or of other substances and the release of heat, in such quantities or concentrations as to exceed the capacity of the environment to render them harmless, must be halted in order to insure that serious or irreversible damage is not inflicted upon ecosystems. The just struggle of the peoples of all countries against pollution should be supported.

7. States shall take all possible steps to prevent pollution of the seas by substances that are liable to create hazards to human health, to harm living

179

resources and marine life, to damage amenities or to interfere with other legitimate uses of the sea.

8. Economic and social development is essential for insuring a favorable living and working environment for man and for creating conditions on earth that are necessary for the improvement of the quality of life.

9. Environmental deficiencies generated by the conditions of underdevelopment and the natural disasters pose grave problems and can be remedied by accelerated development through the transfer of substantial assistance as a supplement to the domestic effort of the developing countries and such timely assistance as may be required.

10. For the developing countries, stability of prices and adequate earnings for primary commodities and raw materials are essential to environment management since economic factors as well as ecological processes must be taken into account.

11. The environmental policies of all states should enhance and not adversely affect the present or future development potential of developing countries, nor should they hamper the attainment of better living conditions for all, and appropriate steps should be taken by states and international organizations with a view to reaching agreement on meeting the possible national and international economic consequences resulting from the application of environmental measures.

12. Resources should be made available to preserve and improve the environment, taking into account the circumstances and particular requirements of developing countries and any costs which may emanate from their incorporating environmental safeguards into their development planning and the need for making available to them, upon their request, additional international technical and financial assistance for this purpose.

13. In order to achieve a more rational management of resources and thus to improve the environment, states should adopt an integrated and coordinated approach to their development planning so as to insure that development is compatible with the need to protect and improve the human environment for the benefit of their population.

14. Rational planning constitutes an essential tool for reconciling any conflict between the needs of development and the need to protect and improve the environment.

15. Planning must be applied to human settlements and urbanization with a view to avoiding adverse effects on the environment and obtaining maximum social, economic and environmental benefits for all. In this respect projects which are designed for colonialist and racist domination must be abandoned.

16. Demographic policies which are without prejudice to basic human rights, and which are deemed appropriate by governments concerned, should be applied in those regions where the rate of population growth or excessive population concentrations are likely to have adverse effects in the environment

or development, or where low population density may prevent improvement of the human environment and impede development.

17. Appropriate national institutions must be entrusted with the task of planning, managing or controlling the environmental resources of states with the view to enhancing environmental quality.

18. Science and technology, as part of their contribution to economic and social development, must be applied to the identification, avoidance and control of environmental risks and the solution of environmental problems and for the common good of mankind.

19. Education in environmental matters, for the younger generation as well as adults, giving due consideration to the underprivileged, is essential in order to broaden the basis for an enlightened opinion and responsible conduct by individuals, enterprises and communities in protecting and improving the environment in its full human dimension. It is essential that mass media of communications avoid contributing to the deterioration of the environment, but, on the contrary, disseminate information of an educational nature on the need to protect and improve the environment in order to enable man to develop in every respect.

20. Scientific research and development in the context of environmental problems, both national and multinational, must be promoted in all countries, especially the developing countries. In this connection, the free flow of up-to-date scientific information and experience must be supported and assisted, to facilitate the solution of environmental problems: environmental technologies should be made available to developing countries on terms which would encourage their wide dissemination without constituting an economic burden on the developing countries.

21. States have, in accordance with the Charter of the United Nations and the principles of international law, the sovereign right to exploit their own resources pursuant to their own environmental policies, and the responsibility to insure that activities within their jurisdiction or control do not cause damage to the environment of other states or of areas beyond the limits of national jurisdiction.

22. States shall cooperate to develop further the international law regarding liability and compensation for the victim of pollution and other environmental damage caused by activities within the jurisdiction or control of such states to areas beyond their jurisdiction.

23. Without prejudice to such general principles as may be agreed upon by the international community, or to the criteria and minimum levels which will have to be determined nationally, it will be essential in all classes to consider the systems of values prevailing in each country, and the extent of the applicability of standards which are valid for the most advanced countries but which may be inappropriate and of unwarranted social cost for the developing countries.

24. International matters concerning the protection and improvement of the environment should be handled in a cooperative spirit by all countries, big or small, on an equal footing. Cooperation through multilateral or bilateral arrangements or other appropriate means is essential to prevent, eliminate or reduce and effectively control adverse environmental effects resulting from activities conducted in all spheres, in such a way that due account is taken of the sovereignty and interests of all states.

25. States shall insure that international organizations play a coordinated, efficient and dynamic role for the protection and improvement of the environment.

26. Man and his environment must be spared the effects of nuclear weapons and all other means of mass destruction. States must strive to reach prompt agreement, in the relevant international organs, on the elimination and complete destruction of such weapons.

[From] *Our Common Future*

World Commission on Environment and Development

IN THE MIDDLE of the twentieth century, we saw our planet from space for the first time. Historians may eventually find that this vision had a greater impact on thought than did the Copernican revolution of the sixteenth century, which upset the human self-image by revealing that the Earth is not the centre of the universe. From space, we see a small and fragile ball dominated not by human activity and edifice but by a pattern of clouds, oceans, greenery, and soils. Humanity's inability to fit its doings into that pattern is changing planetary systems, fundamentally. Many such changes are accompanied by life-threatening hazards. This new reality, from which there is no escape, must be recognized—and managed.

Fortunately, this new reality coincides with more positive developments new to this century. We can move information and goods faster around the globe than ever before; we can produce more food and more goods with less investment of resources; our technology and science gives us at least the potential to look deeper into and better understand natural systems. From space, we can see and study the Earth as an organism whose health depends on the health of all its parts. We have the power to reconcile human affairs with natural laws and to thrive in the process. In this our cultural and spiritual heritages can reinforce our economic interests and survival imperatives.

This Commission believes that people can build a future that is more prosperous, more just, and more secure. Our report, *Our Common Future,* is not a prediction of ever increasing environmental decay, poverty, and hardship in an ever more polluted world among ever decreasing resources. We see instead the possibility for a new era of economic growth, one that must be based on policies that sustain and expand the environmental resource base. And we believe such growth to be absolutely essential to relieve the great poverty that is deepening in much of the developing world.

But the Commission's hope for the future is conditional on decisive political action now to begin managing environmental resources to ensure both sustainable human progress and human survival. We are not forecasting a future; we are serving a notice—an urgent notice based on the latest and best scientific evidence—that the time has come to take the decisions needed to secure the resources to sustain this and coming generations. We do not offer a detailed blueprint for action, but instead a pathway by which the peoples of the world may enlarge their spheres of co-operation.

The Global Challenge

Successes and Failures

Those looking for success and signs of hope can find many: Infant mortality is falling; human life expectancy is increasing; the proportion of the world's adults who can read and write is climbing; the proportion of children starting school is rising; and global food production increases faster than the population grows.

But the same processes that have produced these gains have given rise to trends that the planet and its people cannot long bear. These have traditionally been divided into failures of 'development' and failures in the management of our human environment. On the development side, in terms of absolute numbers there are more hungry people in the world than ever before, and their numbers are increasing. So are the numbers who cannot read and write, the numbers without safe water or safe and sound homes, and the numbers short of woodfuel with which to cook and warm themselves. The gap between rich and poor nations is widening—not shrinking—and there is little prospect, given present trends and institutional arrangements, that this process will be reversed.

There are also environmental trends that threaten to radically alter the planet, that threaten the lives of many species upon it, including the human species. Each year another 6 million hectares of productive dryland turns into worthless desert. Over three decades, this would amount to an area roughly as large as Saudi Arabia. More than 11 million hectares of forests are destroyed

The World Commission on Environment and Development first met in
October 1984, and published its report 900 days later, in April 1987.
Over those few days:

- The drought-triggered, environment-development crisis in Africa
  peaked, putting 35 million people at risk, killing perhaps a million.
- A leak from a pesticides factory in Bhopal, India, killed more
  than 2,000 people and blinded and injured over 200,000 more.
- Liquid gas tanks exploded in Mexico City, killing 1,000 and leaving thousands more homeless.
- The Chernobyl nuclear reactor explosion sent nuclear fallout
  across Europe, increasing the risks of future human cancers.
- Agricultural chemicals, solvents, and mercury flowed into the
  Rhine River during a warehouse fire in Switzerland, killing millions of fish and threatening drinking water in the Federal Republic of Germany and the Netherlands.
- An estimated 60 million people died of diarrhoeal diseases related
  to unsafe drinking water and malnutrition; most of the victims
  were children.

yearly, and this, over three decades, would equal an area about the size of
India. Much of this forest is converted to low-grade farmland unable to support the farmers who settle it. In Europe, acid precipitation kills forests and
lakes and damages the artistic and architectural heritage of nations; it may have
acidified vast tracts of soil beyond reasonable hope of repair. The burning of
fossil fuels puts into the atmosphere carbon dioxide, which is causing gradual
global warming. This 'greenhouse effect' may by early next century have
increased average global temperatures enough to shift agricultural production
areas, raise sea levels to flood coastal cities, and disrupt national economies.
Other industrial gases threaten to deplete the planet's protective ozone shield
to such an extent that the number of human and animal cancers would rise
sharply and the oceans' food chain would be disrupted. Industry and agriculture put toxic substances into the human food chain and into underground
water tables beyond reach of cleansing.

There has been a growing realization in national governments and multilateral institutions that it is impossible to separate economic development issues
from environment issues; many forms of development erode the environmental
resources upon which they must be based, and environmental degradation can
undermine economic development. Poverty is a major cause and effect of

global environmental problems. It is therefore futile to attempt to deal with environmental problems without a broader perspective that encompasses the factors underlying world poverty and international inequality.

These concerns were behind the establishment in 1983 of the World Commission on Environment and Development by the UN General Assembly. The Commission is an independent body, linked to but outside the control of governments and the UN system. The Commission's mandate gave it three objectives: to re-examine the critical environment and development issues and to formulate realistic proposals for dealing with them; to propose new forms of international co-operation on these issues that will influence policies and events in the direction of needed changes; and to raise the levels of understanding and commitment to action of individuals, voluntary organizations, businesses, institutes, and governments.

Through our deliberations and the testimony of people at the public hearings we held on five continents, all the commissioners came to focus on one central theme: many present development trends leave increasing numbers of people poor and vulnerable, while at the same time degrading the environment. How can such development serve next century's world of twice as many people relying on the same environment? This realization broadened our view of development. We came to see it not in its restricted context of economic growth in developing countries. We came to see that a new development path was required, one that sustained human progress not just in a few places for a few years, but for the entire planet into the distant future. Thus 'sustainable development' becomes a goal not just for the 'developing' nations, but for industrial ones as well.

The Interlocking Crises

Until recently, the planet was a large world in which human activities and their effects were neatly compartmentalized within nations, within sectors (energy, agriculture, trade), and within broad areas of concern (environmental, economic, social). These compartments have begun to dissolve. This applies in particular to the various global 'crises' that have seized public concern, particularly over the past decade. These are not separate crises: an environmental crisis, a development crisis, an energy crisis. They are all one.

The planet is passing through a period of dramatic growth and fundamental change. Our human world of 5 billion must make room in a finite environment for another human world. The population could stabilize at between 8 billion and 14 billion sometime next century, according to UN projections. More than 90 per cent of the increase will occur in the poorest countries, and 90 per cent of that growth in already bursting cities.

Economic activity has multiplied to create a $13 trillion world economy, and this could grow five- or tenfold in the coming half-century. Industrial production has grown more than fiftyfold over the past century, four-fifths of this growth since 1950. Such figures reflect and presage profound impacts upon the biosphere, as the world invests in houses, transport, farms, and industries. Much of the economic growth pulls raw material from forests, soils, seas, and waterways.

A mainspring of economic growth is new technology, and while this technology offers the potential for slowing the dangerously rapid consumption of finite resources, it also entails high risks, including new forms of pollution and the introduction to the planet of new variations of life forms that could change evolutionary pathways. Meanwhile, the industries most heavily reliant on environmental resources and most heavily polluting are growing most rapidly in the developing world, where there is both more urgency for growth and less capacity to minimize damaging side effects.

These related changes have locked the global economy and global ecology together in new ways. We have in the past been concerned about the impacts of economic growth upon the environment. We are now forced to concern ourselves with the impacts of ecological stress—degradation of soils, water regimes, atmosphere, and forests—upon our economic prospects. We have in the more recent past been forced to face up to a sharp increase in economic interdependence among nations. We are now forced to accustom ourselves to an accelerating ecological interdependence among nations. Ecology and economy are becoming ever more interwoven—locally, regionally, nationally, and globally—into a seamless net of causes and effects.

Impoverishing the local resource base can impoverish wider areas: deforestation by highland farmers causes flooding on lowland farms; factory pollution robs local fishermen of their catch. Such grim local cycles now operate nationally and regionally. Dryland degradation sends environmental refugees in their millions across national borders. Deforestation in Latin America and Asia is causing more floods, and more destructive floods, in downhill, downstream nations. Acid precipitation and nuclear fallout have spread across the borders of Europe. Similar phenomena are emerging on a global scale, such as global warming and loss of ozone. Internationally traded hazardous chemicals entering foods are themselves internationally traded. In the next century, the environmental pressure causing population movements may increase sharply, while barriers to that movement may be even firmer than they are now.

Over the past few decades, life-threatening environmental concerns have surfaced in the developing world. Countrysides are coming under pressure from increasing numbers of farmers and the landless. Cities are filling with people, cars, and factories. Yet at the same time these developing countries must operate in a world in which the resources gap between most developing and industrial nations is widening, in which the industrial world dominates in the rule-making of some key international bodies, and in which the industrial world has already used much of the planet's ecological capital. This inequality is the planet's main 'environmental' problem; it is also its main 'development' problem.

International economic relationships pose a particular problem for environmental management in many developing countries. Agriculture, forestry, energy production, and mining generate at least half the gross national product of many developing countries and account for even larger shares of livelihoods and employment. Exports of natural resources remain a large factor in their economies, especially for the least developed. Most of these countries face enormous economic pressures, both international and domestic, to overexploit their environmental resource base.

The recent crisis in Africa best and most tragically illustrates the ways in which economics and ecology can interact destructively and trip into disaster. Triggered by drought, its real causes lie deeper. They are to be found in part in national policies that gave too little attention, too late, to the needs of smallholder agriculture and to the threats posed by rapidly rising populations. Their roots extend also to a global economic system that takes more out of a poor continent than it puts in. Debts that they cannot pay force African nations relying on commodity sales to overuse their fragile soils, thus turning good land to desert. Trade barriers in the wealthy nations—and in many developing ones—make it hard for Africans to sell their goods for reasonable returns, putting yet more pressure on ecological systems. Aid from donor nations has not only been inadequate in scale, but too often has reflected the priorities of the nations giving the aid, rather than the needs of the recipients. The production base of other developing world areas suffers similarly both from local failures and from the workings of international economic systems. As a consequence of the 'debt crisis' of Latin America, that region's natural resources are now being used not for development but to meet financial obligations to creditors abroad. This approach to the debt problem is short-sighted from several standpoints: economic, political, and environmental. It requires relatively poor countries simultaneously to accept growing poverty while exporting growing amounts of scarce resources.

A majority of developing countries now have lower per capita incomes than when the decade began. Rising poverty and unemployment have increased pressure on environmental resources as more people have been forced to rely more directly upon them. Many governments have cut back efforts to protect the environment and to bring ecological considerations into development planning.

The deepening and widening environmental crisis presents a threat to national security—and even survival—that may be greater than well-armed, ill-disposed neighbours and unfriendly alliances. Already in parts of Latin America, Asia, the Middle East, and Africa, environmental decline is becoming a source of political unrest and international tension. The recent destruction of much of Africa's dryland agricultural production was more severe than if an invading army had pursued a scorched-earth policy. Yet most of the affected governments still spend far more to protect their people from invading armies than from the invading desert.

Globally, military expenditures total about $1 trillion a year and continue to grow. In many countries, military spending consumes such a high proportion of gross national product that it itself does great damage to these societies' development efforts. Governments tend to base their approaches to 'security' on traditional definitions. This is most obvious in the attempts to achieve security through the development of potentially planet-destroying nuclear weapons systems. Studies suggest that the cold and dark nuclear winter following even a limited nuclear war could destroy plant and animal ecosystems and leave any human survivors occupying a devastated planet very different from the one they inherited.

The arms race—in all parts of the world—pre-empts resources that might be used more productively to diminish the security threats created by environmental conflict and the resentments that are fuelled by widespread poverty.

Many present efforts to guard and maintain human progress, to meet human needs, and to realize human ambitions are simply unsustainable—in both the rich and poor nations. They draw too heavily, too quickly, on already overdrawn environmental resource accounts to be affordable far into the future without bankrupting those accounts. They may show profits on the balance sheets of our generation, but our children will inherit the losses. We borrow environmental capital from future generations with no intention or prospect of repaying. They may damn us for our spendthrift ways, but they can never collect on our debt to them. We act as we do because we can get away with it: future generations do not vote; they have no political or financial power; they cannot challenge our decisions.

But the results of the present profligacy are rapidly closing the options for future generations. Most of today's decision makers will be dead before the planet feels the heavier effects of acid precipitation, global warming, ozone depletion, or widespread desertification and species loss. Most of the young voters of today will still be alive. In the Commission's hearings it was the young, those who have the most to lose, who were the harshest critics of the planet's present management.

Sustainable Development

Humanity has the ability to make development sustainable—to ensure that it meets the needs of the present without compromising the ability of future generations to meet their own needs. The concept of sustainable development does imply limits—not absolute limits but limitations imposed by the present state of technology and social organization on environmental resources and by the ability of the biosphere to absorb the effects of human activities. But technology and social organization can be both managed and improved to make way for a new era of economic growth. The Commission believes that widespread poverty is no longer inevitable. Poverty is not only an evil in itself, but sustainable development requires meeting the basic needs of all and extending to all the opportunity to fulfil their aspirations for a better life. A world in which poverty is endemic will always be prone to ecological and other catastrophes.

Meeting essential needs requires not only a new era of economic growth for nations in which the majority are poor, but an assurance that those poor get their fair share of the resources required to sustain that growth. Such equity would be aided by political systems that secure effective citizen participation in decision making and by greater democracy in international decision making.

Sustainable global development requires that those who are more affluent adopt life-styles within the planet's ecological means—in their use of energy, for example. Further, rapidly growing populations can increase the pressure on resources and slow any rise in living standards; thus sustainable development can only be pursued if population size and growth are in harmony with the changing productive potential of the ecosystem.

Yet in the end, sustainable development is not a fixed state of harmony, but rather a process of change in which the exploitation of resources, the direction of investments, the orientation of technological development, and institutional change are made consistent with future as well as present needs. We do not pretend that the process is easy or straightforward. Painful choices have to be made. Thus, in the final analysis, sustainable development must rest on political will.

The Institutional Gaps

The objective of sustainable development and the integrated nature of the global environment/development challenges pose problems for institutions, national and international, that were established on the basis of narrow preoccupations and compartmentalized concerns. Governments' general response to the speed and scale of global changes has been a reluctance to recognize sufficiently the need to change themselves. The challenges are both interdependent and integrated, requiring comprehensive approaches and popular participation.

Yet most of the institutions facing those challenges tend to be independent, fragmented, working to relatively narrow mandates with closed decision processes. Those responsible for managing natural resources and protecting the environment are institutionally separated from those responsible for managing the economy. The real world of interlocked economic and ecological systems will not change; the policies and institutions concerned must.

There is a growing need for effective international co-operation to manage ecological and economic interdependence. Yet at the same time, confidence in international organizations is diminishing and support for them dwindling.

The other great institutional flaw in coping with environment/development challenges is governments' failure to make the bodies whose policy actions degrade the environment responsible for ensuring that their policies prevent that degradation. Environmental concern arose from damage caused by the rapid economic growth following the Second World War. Governments, pressured by their citizens, saw a need to clean up the mess, and they established environmental ministries and agencies to do this. Many had great success—within the limits of their mandates—in improving air and water quality and enhancing other resources. But much of their work has of necessity been after-the-fact repair of damage: reforestation, reclaiming desert lands, rebuilding urban environments, restoring natural habitats, and rehabilitating wild lands.

The existence of such agencies gave many governments and their citizens the false impression that these bodies were by themselves able to protect and enhance the environmental resource base. Yet many industrialized and most developing countries carry huge economic burdens from inherited problems such as air and water pollution, depletion of ground-water, and the proliferation of toxic chemicals and hazardous wastes. These have been joined by more recent problems—erosion, desertification, acidification, new chemicals, and new forms of waste—that are directly related to agricultural, industrial, energy, forestry, and transportation policies and practices.

The mandates of the central economic and sectoral ministries are also often too narrow, too concerned with quantities of production or growth. The mandates of ministries of industry include production targets, while the accompanying pollution is left to ministries of environment. Electricity boards produce power, while the acid pollution they also produce is left to other bodies to clean up. The present challenge is to give the central economic and sectoral ministries the responsibility for the quality of those parts of the human environment affected by their decisions, and to give the environmental agencies more power to cope with the effects of unsustainable development.

The same need for change holds for international agencies concerned with development lending, trade regulation, agricultural development, and so on. These have been slow to take the environmental effects of their work into account, although some are trying to do so.

The ability to anticipate and prevent environmental damage requires that the ecological dimensions of policy be considered at the same time as the economic, trade, energy, agricultural, and other dimensions. They should be considered on the same agendas and in the same national and international institutions.

This reorientation is one of the chief institutional challenges of the 1990s and beyond. Meeting it will require major institutional development and reform. Many countries that are too poor or small or that have limited managerial capacity will find it difficult to do this unaided. They will need financial and technical assistance and training. But the changes required involve all countries, large and small, rich and poor.

The Policy Directions

The Commission has focused its attention in the areas of population, food security, the loss of species and genetic resources, energy, industry, and human settlements—realizing that all of these are connected and cannot be treated in isolation one from another. This section contains only a few of the Commission's many recommendations.

Population and Human Resources

In many parts of the world, the population is growing at rates that cannot be sustained by available environmental resources, at rates that are outstripping any reasonable expectations of improvements in housing, health care, food security, or energy supplies.

The issue is not just numbers of people, but how those numbers relate to available resources. Thus the 'population problem' must be dealt with in part by efforts to eliminate mass poverty, in order to assure more equitable access to resources, and by education to improve human potential to manage those resources.

Urgent steps are needed to limit extreme rates of population growth. Choices made now will influence the level at which the population stabilizes next century within a range of 6 billion people. But this is not just a demographic issue; providing people with facilities and education that allow them to choose the size of their families is a way of assuring—especially for women—the basic human right of self-determination.

Governments that need to do so should develop long-term, multifaceted population policies and a campaign to pursue broad demographic goals: to strengthen social, cultural, and economic motivations for family planning; and to provide to all who want them the education, contraceptives, and services required.

Human resource development is a crucial requirement not only to build up technical knowledge and capabilities, but also to create new values to help individuals and nations cope with rapidly changing social, environmental, and development realities. Knowledge shared globally would assure greater mutual understanding and create greater willingness to share global resources equitably.

Tribal and indigenous peoples will need special attention as the forces of economic development disrupt their traditional life-styles—life-styles that can offer modern societies many lessons in the management of resources in complex forest, mountain, and dryland ecosystems. Some are threatened with virtual extinction by insensitive development over which they have no control. Their traditional rights should be recognized and they should be given a decisive voice in formulating policies about resource development in their areas.

Food Security: Sustaining the Potential

Growth in world cereal production has steadily outstripped world population growth. Yet each year there are more people in the world who do not get enough food. Global agriculture has the potential to grow enough food for all, but food is often not available where it is needed.

Production in industrialized countries has usually been highly subsidized and protected from international competition. These subsidies have encouraged the overuse of soil and chemicals, the pollution of both water resources and foods with these chemicals, and the degradation of the countryside. Much of this effort has produced surpluses and their associated financial burdens. And some of this surplus has been sent at concessional rates to the developing world, where it has undermined the farming policies of recipient nations. There is, however, growing awareness in some countries of the environmental and economic consequences of such paths, and the emphasis of agricultural policies is to encourage conservation.

Many developing countries, on the other hand, have suffered the opposite problem: farmers are not sufficiently supported. In some, improved technology allied to price incentives and government services has produced a major breakthrough in food production. But elsewhere, the food-growing small farmers have been neglected. Coping with often inadequate technology and few economic incentives, many are pushed onto marginal land: too dry, too steep, lacking in nutrients. Forests are cleared and productive drylands rendered barren.

Most developing nations need more effective incentive systems to encourage production, especially of food crops. In short, the 'terms of trade' need to be turned in favour of the small farmer. Most industrialized nations, on the other hand, must alter present systems in order to cut surpluses, to reduce unfair competition with nations that may have real comparative advantages, and to promote ecologically sound farming practices.

Food security requires attention to questions of distribution, since hunger often arises from lack of purchasing power rather than lack of available food. It can be furthered by land reforms, and by policies to protect vulnerable subsistence farmers, pastoralists, and the landless—groups who by the year 2000 will include 220 million households. Their greater prosperity will depend on integrated rural development that increases work opportunities both inside and outside agriculture.

Species and Ecosystems: Resources for Development

The planet's species are under stress. There is a growing scientific consensus that species are disappearing at rates never before witnessed on the planet, although there is also controversy over those rates and the risks they entail. Yet there is still time to halt this process.

The diversity of species is necessary for the normal functioning of ecosystems and the biosphere as a whole. The genetic material in wild species contributes billions of dollars yearly to the world economy in the form of improved crop species, new drugs and medicines, and raw materials for industry. But utility aside, there are also moral, ethical, cultural, aesthetic, and purely scientific reasons for conserving wild beings.

A first priority is to establish the problem of disappearing species and threatened ecosystems on political agendas as a major economic and resource issue.

Governments can stem the destruction of tropical forests and other reservoirs of biological diversity while developing them economically. Reforming forest revenue systems and concession terms could raise billions of dollars of additional revenues, promote more efficient, long-term forest resource use, and curtail deforestation.

The network of protected areas that the world will need in the future must include much larger areas brought under some degree of protection. Therefore, the cost of conservation will rise—directly and in terms of opportunities for development forgone. But over the long term the opportunities for development will be enhanced. International development agencies should therefore give comprehensive and systematic attention to the problems and opportunities of species conservation.

Governments should investigate the prospect of agreeing to a 'Species Convention', similar in spirit and scope to other international conventions reflecting principles of 'universal resources'. They should also consider international financial arrangements to support the implementation of such a convention.

Energy: Choices for Environment and Development

A safe and sustainable energy pathway is crucial to sustainable development; we have not yet found it. Rates of increase in energy use have been declining. However, the industrialization, agricultural development, and rapidly growing populations of developing nations will need much more energy. Today, the average person in an industrial market economy uses more than 80 times as much energy as someone in sub-Saharan Africa. Thus any realistic global energy scenario must provide for substantially increased primary energy use by developing countries.

To bring developing countries' energy use up to industrialized country levels by the year 2025 would require increasing present global energy use by a factor of five. The planetary ecosystem could not stand this, especially if the increases were based on non-renewable fossil fules. Threats of global warming and acidification of the environment most probably rule out even a doubling of energy use based on present mixes of primary sources.

Any new era of economic growth must therefore be less energy-intensive than growth in the past. Energy efficiency policies must be the cutting edge of national energy strategies for sustainable development, and there is much scope for improvement in this direction. Modern appliances can be redesigned to deliver the same amounts of energy-services with only two-thirds or even one-half of the primary energy inputs needed to run traditional equipment. And energy efficiency solutions are often cost-effective.

After almost four decades of immense technological effort, nuclear energy has become widely used. During this period, however, the nature of its costs, risks, and benefits have become more evident and the subject of sharp controversy. Different countries world-wide take up different positions on the use of nuclear energy. The discussion in the Commission also reflected these different views and positions. Yet all agreed that the generation of nuclear power is only justifiable if there are solid solutions to the unsolved problems to which it gives rise. The highest priority should be accorded to research and development on environmentally sound and ecologically viable alternatives, as well as on means of increasing the safety of nuclear energy.

Energy efficiency can only buy time for the world to develop 'low-energy paths' based on renewable sources, which should form the foundation of the global energy structure during the twenty-first century. Most of these sources are currently problematic, but given innovative development, they could supply the same amount of primary energy the planet now consumes. However, achieving these use levels will require a programme of coordinated research, development, and demonstration projects commanding funding necessary to ensure the rapid development of renewable energy. Developing countries will require assistance to change their energy use patterns in this direction.

Millions of people in the developing world are short of fuelwood, the main domestic energy of half of humanity, and their numbers are growing. The wood-poor nations must organize their agricultural sectors to produce large amounts of wood and other plant fuels.

The substantial changes required in the present global energy mix will not be achieved by market pressures alone, given the dominant role of governments as producers of energy and their importance as consumers. If the recent momentum behind annual gains in energy efficiency is to be maintained and extended, governments need to make it an explicit goal of their policies for energy pricing to consumers. Prices needed to encourage the adoption of energy-saving measures may be achieved through several means. Although the Commission expresses no preference, 'conservation pricing' requires that governments take a long-term view in weighing the costs and benefits of the various measures. Given the importance of oil prices on international energy policy, new mechanisms for encouraging dialogue between consumers and producers should be explored.

A safe, environmentally sound, and economically viable energy pathway that will sustain human progress into the distant future is clearly imperative. It is also possible. But it will require new dimensions of political will and institutional co-operation to achieve it.

Industry: Producing More with Less

The world manufactures seven times more goods today than it did as recently as 1950. Given population growth rates, a five- to tenfold increase in manufacturing output will be needed just to raise developing-world consumption of manufactured goods to industrialized world levels by the time population growth rates level off next century.

Experience in the industrialized nations has proved that anti-pollution technology has been cost-effective in terms of health, property, and environmental damage avoided, and that it has made many industries more profitable by making them more resource-efficient. While economic growth has continued, the consumption of raw materials has held steady or even declined, and new technologies offer further efficiencies.

Nations have to bear the costs of any inappropriate industrialization, and many developing countries are realizing that they have neither the resources nor—given rapid technological change—the time to damage their environments now and clean up later. But they also need assistance and information from industrialized nations to make the best use of technology. Transnational corporations have a special responsibility to smooth the path of industrialization in the nations in which they operate.

Emerging technologies offer the promise of higher productivity, increased efficiency, and decreased pollution, but many bring risks of new toxic chemicals and wastes and of major accidents of a type and scale beyond present coping mechanisms. There is an urgent need for tighter controls over the export of hazardous industrial and agricultural chemicals. Present controls over the dumping of hazardous wastes should be tightened.

Many essential human needs can be met only through goods and services provided by industry, and the shift to sustainable development must be powered by a continuing flow of wealth from industry.

The Urban Challenge

By the turn of the century, almost half of humanity will live in urban centres; the world of the twenty-first century will be a largely urban world. Over only 65 years, the developing world's urban population has increased tenfold, from around 100 million in 1920 to 1 billion today. In 1940, one person in 100 lived in a city of 1 million or more inhabitants; by 1980, one in 10 lived in such a city. Between 1985 and the year 2000, Third World cities could grow by another three-quarters of a billion people. This suggests that the developing world must, over the next few years, increase by 65 per cent its capacity to produce and manage its urban infrastructure, services, and shelter merely to maintain today's often extremely inadequate conditions.

Few city governments in the developing world have the power, resources, and trained personnel to provide their rapidly growing populations with the land, services, and facilities needed for an adequate human life: clean water, sanitation, schools, and transport. The result is mushrooming illegal settlements with primitive facilities, increased overcrowding, and rampant disease linked to an unhealthy environment. Many cities in industrial countries also face problems—deteriorating infrastructure, environmental degradation, inner-city de-

cay, and neighbourhood collapse. But with the means and resources to tackle
this decline, the issue for most industrial countries is ultimately one of political
and social choice. Developing countries are not in the same situation. They have
a major urban crisis on their hands.

Governments will need to develop explicit settlements strategies to guide the
process of urbanization, taking the pressure off the largest urban centres and
building up smaller towns and cities, more closely integrating them with their
rural hinterlands. This will mean examining and changing other policies—
taxation, food pricing, transportation, health, industrialization—that work
against the goals of settlements strategies.

Good city management requires decentralization—of funds, political power,
and personnel—to local authorities, which are best placed to appreciate and
manage local needs. But the sustainable development of cities will depend on
closer work with the majorities of urban poor who are the true city builders,
tapping the skills, energies, and resources of neighbourhood groups and those
in the 'informal sector'. Much can be achieved by 'site and service' schemes
that provide households with basic services and help them to get on with
building sounder houses around these.

International Co-operation and Institutional Reform

The Role of the International Economy

Two conditions must be satisfied before international economic exchanges can
become beneficial for all involved. The sustainability of ecosystems on which
the global economy depends must be guaranteed. And the economic partners
must be satisfied that the basis of exchange is equitable. For many developing
countries, neither condition is met.

Growth in many developing countries is being stifled by depressed commodity prices, protectionism, intolerable debt burdens, and declining flows of
development finance. If living standards are to grow so as to alleviate poverty,
these trends must be reversed.

A particular responsibility falls to the World Bank and the International
Development Association as the main conduit for multilateral finance to developing countries. In the context of consistently increased financial flows, the
World Bank can support environmentally sound projects and policies. In financing structural adjustment, the International Monetary Fund should support wider and longer term development objectives than at present: growth,
social goals, and environmental impacts.

The present level of debt service of many countries, especially in Africa and
Latin America, is not consistent with sustainable development. Debtors are
being required to use trade surpluses to service debts, and are drawing heavily
on non-renewable resources to do so. Urgent action is necessary to alleviate

debt burdens in ways that represent a fairer sharing between both debtors and lenders of the responsibilities and burdens.

Current arrangements for commodities could be significantly improved: more compensatory financing to offset economic shocks would encourage producers to take a long-term view, and not to overproduce commodities; and more assistance could be given from diversification programmes. Commodity-specific arrangements can build on the model of the International Tropical Timber Agreement, one of the few that specifically includes ecological concerns.

Multinational companies can play an important role in sustainable development, especially as developing countries come to rely more on foreign equity capital. But if these companies are to have a positive influence on development, the negotiating capacity of developing countries vis-à-vis transnationals must be strengthened so they can secure terms that respect their environmental concerns.

However, these specific measures must be located in a wider context of effective co-operation to produce an international economic system geared to growth and the elimination of world poverty.

Managing the Commons

Traditional forms of national sovereignty raise particular problems in managing the 'global commons' and their shared ecosystems—the oceans, outer space, and Antarctica. Some progress has been made in all three areas; much remains to be done.

The UN Conference on the Law of the Sea was the most ambitious attempt ever to provide an internationally agreed regime for the management of the oceans. All nations should ratify the Law of the Sea Treaty as soon as possible. Fisheries agreements should be strengthened to prevent current overexploitation, as should conventions to control and regulate the dumping of hazardous wastes at sea.

There are growing concerns about the management of orbital space, centring on using satellite technology for monitoring planetary systems, on making the most effective use of the limited capacities of geosynchronous orbit for communications satellites, and on limiting space debris. The orbiting and testing of weapons in space would greatly increase this debris. The international community should seek to design and implement a space regime to ensure that space remains a peaceful environment for the benefit of all.

Antarctica is managed under the 1959 Antarctic Treaty. However, many nations outside of that pact view the Treaty System as too limited, both in participation and in the scope of its conservation measures. The Commission's recommendations deal with the safe-guarding of present achievements, the incorporation of any minerals development into a management regime, and various options for the future.

Peace, Security, Development, and the Environment

Among the dangers facing the environment, the possibility of nuclear war is undoubtedly the gravest. Certain aspects of the issues of peace and security bear directly upon the concept of sustainable development. The whole notion of security as traditionally understood—in terms of political and military threats to national sovereignty—must be expanded to include the growing impacts of environmental stress—locally, nationally, regionally, and globally. There are no military solutions to 'environmental insecurity'.

Governments and international agencies should assess the cost-effectiveness, in terms of achieving security, of money spent on armaments compared with money spent on reducing poverty or restoring a ravaged environment.

But the greatest need is to achieve improved relations among those major powers capable of deploying weapons of mass destruction. This is needed to achieve agreement on tighter control over the proliferation and testing of various types of weapons of mass destruction—nuclear and non-nuclear—including those that have environmental implications.

Institutional and Legal Change

The report that follows contains throughout many specific recommendations for institutional and legal change. These cannot be adequately summarized here. However, the Commission's main proposals are embodied in six priority areas.

Getting at the Sources   Governments must begin now to make the key national, economic, and sectoral agencies directly responsible and accountable for ensuring that their policies, programmes, and budgets support development that is economically and ecologically sustainable.

By the same token, the various regional organizations need to do more to integrate environment fully in their goals and activities. New regional arrangements will especially be needed among developing countries to deal with transboundary environmental issues.

All major international bodies and agencies should ensure that their programmes encourage and support sustainable development, and they should greatly improve their coordination and co-operation. The Secretary-General of the United Nations Organization should provide a high-level centre of leadership for the UN system to assess, advise, assist, and report on progress made towards this goal.

Dealing with the Effects   Governments should also reinforce the roles and capacities of environmental protection and resource management agencies. This is needed in many industrialized countries, but most urgently in developing countries, which will need assistance in strengthening their institutions. The UN Environment Programme (UNEP) should be strengthened as the principal source on environmental data, assessment, and reporting and as the principal advocate and agent for change and international co-operation on critical environment and natural resource protection issues.

Assessing Global Risks   The capacity to identify, assess, and report on risks of irreversible damage to natural systems and threats to the survival, security, and well-being of the world community must be rapidly reinforced and extended. Governments, individually and collectively, have the principal responsibility to do this. UNEP's Earthwatch programme should be the centre of leadership in the UN system on risk assessment.

However, given the politically sensitive nature of many of the most critical risks, there is also a need for an independent but complementary capacity to assess and report on critical global risks. A new international programme for co-operation among largely non-governmental organizations, scientific bodies, and industry groups should therefore be established for this purpose.

Making Informed Choices   Making the difficult choices involved in achieving sustainable development will depend on the widespread support and involvement of an informed public and of non-governmental organizations, the scientific community, and industry. Their rights, roles, and participation in development planning, decision making, and project implementation should be expanded.

Providing the Legal Means   National and international law is being rapidly outdistanced by the accelerating pace and expanding scale of impacts on the ecological basis of development. Governments now need to fill major gaps in existing national and international law related to the environment, to find ways to recognize and protect the rights of present and future generations to an environment adequate for their health and well-being, to prepare under UN auspices a universal Declaration on environmental protection and sustainable development and a subsequent Convention, and to strengthen procedures for avoiding or resolving disputes on environment and resource management issues.

Investing in Our Future   Over the past decade, the overall cost-effectiveness of investments in halting pollution has been demonstrated. The escalating economic and ecological damage costs of not investing in environmental protection and improvement have also been repeatedly demonstrated—often in grim tolls of flood and famine. But there are large financial implications: for renewable energy development, pollution control, and achieving less resource-intensive forms of agriculture.

Multilateral financial institutions have a crucial role to play. The World Bank is presently reorienting its programmes towards greater environmental concerns. This should be accompanied by a fundamental commitment to sustainable development by the Bank. It is also essential that the regional Development Banks and the International Monetary Fund incorporate similar objectives in their policies and programmes. A new priority and focus is also needed in bilateral aid agencies.

Given the limitations on increasing present flows of international aid, proposals for securing additional revenue from the use of international commons and natural resources should now be seriously considered by governments.

A Call for Action

Over the course of this century, the relationship between the human world and the planet that sustains it has undergone a profound change.

When the century began, neither human numbers nor technology had the power radically to alter planetary systems. As the century closes, not only do vastly increased human numbers and their activities have that power, but major, unintended changes are occurring in the atmosphere, in soils, in waters, among plants and animals, and in the relationships among all of these. The rate of change is outstripping the ability of scientific disciplines and our current capabilities to assess and advise. It is frustrating the attempts of political and economic institutions, which evolved in a different, more fragmented world, to adapt and cope. It deeply worries many people who are seeking ways to place those concerns on the political agendas.

The onus lies with no one group of nations. Developing countries face the obvious life-threatening challenges of desertification, deforestation, and pollution, and endure most of the poverty associated with environmental degradation. The entire human family of nations would suffer from the disappearance of rain forests in the tropics, the loss of plant and animal species, and changes in rainfall patterns. Industrial nations face the life-threatening challenges of toxic chemicals, toxic wastes, and acidification. All nations may suffer from the releases by industrialized countries of carbon dioxide and of gases that react with the ozone layer, and from any future war fought with the nuclear arsenals controlled by those nations. All nations will have a role to play in changing trends, and in righting an international economic system that increases rather than decreases inequality, that increases rather than decreases numbers of poor and hungry.

The next few decades are crucial. The time has come to break out of past patterns. Attempts to maintain social and ecological stability through old approaches to development and environmental protection will increase instability. Security must be sought through change. The Commission has noted a number of actions that must be taken to reduce risks to survival and to put future development on paths that are sustainable. Yet we are aware that such a reorientation on a continuing basis is simply beyond the reach of present decision-making structures and institutional arrangements, both national and international.

This Commission has been careful to base our recommendations on the realities of present institutions, on what can and must be accomplished today. But to keep options open for future generations, the present generation must begin now, and begin together.

To achieve the needed changes, we believe that an active follow-up of this report is imperative. It is with this in mind that we call for the UN General Assembly, upon due consideration, to transform this report into a UN Programme on Sustainable Development. Special follow-up conferences could be initiated at the regional level. Within an appropriate period after the presentation of this report to the General Assembly, an international conference could be convened to review progress made, and to promote follow-up arrangements that will be needed to set benchmarks and to maintain human progress.

First and foremost, this Commission has been concerned with people—of all countries and all walks of life. And it is to people that we address our report. The changes in human attitudes that we call for depend on a vast campaign of education, debate, and public participation. This campaign must start now if sustainable human progress is to be achieved.

The members of the World Commission on Environment and Development came from 21 very different nations. In our discussions, we disagreed often on details and priorities. But despite our widely differing backgrounds and varying national and international responsibilities, we were able to agree to the lines along which change must be drawn.

We are unanimous in our conviction that the security, well-being, and very survival of the planet depend on such changes, now.

[From] Environment and Development: The Story of a Dangerous Liaison

Wolfgang Sachs

NEIL ARMSTRONG'S journey to the moon brought us under the spell of a new image—not of the moon but of the Earth. Looking back from the *Apollo* spaceship, Armstrong shot those pictures which now adorn the covers of so many reports about the future of the planet: a small and fragile ball, shining blue against the dark of outer space, delicately covered by clouds, oceans, greenery, and soils. Never before had the planet in its entirety been visible to the human eye; space photography imparted a new reality to the planet. In its beauty and vulnerability, the floating globe arouses wonder and awe. For the first time it has become possible to speak of *our* planet.

But the possessive noun reveals a deep ambivalence. On the one hand, "our" can imply participation and highlight humanity's dependence on an encompassing reality. On the other hand, it can imply ownership and emphasize humanity's supposed vocation to master and to manage this common property. Consequently, the image of "our" planet conveys a contradictory message; it can either call for moderation or for megalomania.

The same ambivalence characterizes the career of the concept "environment." While it was originally advanced to put development politics under indictment, it is now raised like a banner to announce a new era of development. Indeed, after "ignorance" and "poverty" in previous decades, "survival of the planet" is likely to become the emergency of the 1990s, in the name of which a new frenzy of development will be unleashed. Significantly, the report of the World Commission on Environment and Development (the Brundtland Report), after having evoked the image of the planet floating in space, concludes its opening paragraph by stating: "This new reality, from which there is no escape, must be recognized—*and managed.*"

The Emergence of Global Issues

For better or worse, the vicissitudes of the international development discussion follow closely the rise and fall of political sensibilities within the Northern countries. Unfettered enthusiasm for economic growth in 1945 reflected the West's desire to restart the economic machine after a devastating war, the emphasis on manpower planning echoed American fears after the shock of *Sputnik* in 1957, the discovery of basic needs was stimulated by Johnson's domestic war on poverty in the 1960s. What development means depends on how the rich nations feel. "Environment" is no exception to this rule.

The UN Conference on the Human Environment held in Stockholm in June 1972, the occasion on which "environment" arrived on the international agenda, was first proposed by Sweden, which was worried about acid rain, pollution in the Baltic and the levels of pesticides and heavy metals in fish and birds. Countries discovered that they were not self-contained units but contingent on actions taken by others. Thus a new category of problems, the "global issues," emerged. The Stockholm Conference was the prelude to a series of large UN meetings throughout the 1970s (on population, food, human settlements, water, desertification, science and technology, and renewable energy) that set out to alter the post-war perception of an open global space where many nations can individually strive to maximize economic growth. Instead a different view began to be promoted: the concept of an interrelated world system operating under a number of common constraints.

The cognitive furniture for this shift was provided by a particular school of thought that had gained prominence in interpreting the significance of pollution and non-natural disasters. In the United States during the 1960s, environmental issues forced their way into public consciousness: due to Los Angeles smog and the slow death of Lake Erie, oil spills and the planned flooding of the Grand Canyon, the number of articles on the environment in the *New York Times* skyrocketed from about 150 in 1960 to about 1,700 in 1970. Local incidents, which were increasingly seen as adding up to a larger picture, were put into a global perspective by scientists who borrowed their conceptual framework from ecosystems theory in order to interpret the predicament of a world rushing towards industrialization. Infinite growth, they maintained, is based on self-delusion, because the world is a closed space, finite and of limited carrying capacity. Perceiving global space as a system whose stability rests on the equilibrium of its components, like population, technology, resources (including food) and environment, they foresaw—echoing Malthus' early challenge to the assumption of inevitable progress—an imminent disruption of the balance between population growth (exacerbated by technology) on the one hand, and resources and environment on the other. Paul Ehrlich's *Population Bomb*, *The Ecologist*'s "Blueprint for Survival," and, especially, the Club of Rome's *Limits to Growth* made it seem natural to imagine the future of the globe as being decided by the interaction of quantitative growth curves.

The global ecosystems approach was not without competitors; but both the biocentric and the humanist perspective were foreign to the perception of the international development elite. Attributing absolute value to nature for its own sake, as environmentalists in the tradition of Thoreau, Emerson and Muir did, would have barred the way to continuing, albeit in a more sophisticated and flexible manner, the exploitation of nature. And recognizing the offences against nature as just another sign of the supremacy of technological expansion over people and their lives, as humanist authors like Mumford or Schumacher suggested, would go against the grain of development aspirations and could hardly please the guardians of the growth machine. In fact, only an interpretation which magnified rather than undermined their managerial responsibilities could raise their hopes in the face of a troubled future. The global ecosystems approach perfectly suited their vantage point from the heights of international organizations for it proposed global society as the unit of analysis and put the Third World, by denouncing population growth, at the centre of attention. Moreover, the model simplified and rendered intelligible an otherwise complicated and confusing situation by disembedding resource conflicts from any particular local or political context. The language of aggregate data series suggests a clear-cut picture, abstract figures lend themselves to playing with scenarios, and a presumed mechanical causality between the various components creates the illusion that global strategies can be effective. And even if the ideal of growth crumbled, there was, for those who felt in charge of running the world, still some objective to fall comfortably back to: stability.

The Marriage Between Environment
and Development

However, there was still a long way to go until, in 1987, the Brundtland Report could finally announce the marriage between craving for development and concern for the environment. As the adamant rejection of all "no-growth" positions, in particular by Third World governments at the Stockholm Conference demonstrated, the compulsion to drive up the GNP had turned many into cheerful enemies of nature. It was only in the course of the 1970s, under the additional impact of the oil crisis, that it began to dawn on governments that continued growth not only depended upon capital formation and a skilled workforce but also on the long-term availability of natural resources. Concerns about the conservation of inputs to future growth, led to development planners gradually adopting a strand of thought which goes back to the introduction of forest management in Germany around 1800: that—in the words of Gifford Pinchot, the steward of Theodore Roosevelt's conservation programme—"conservation means the greatest good for the greatest number for the longest time." Tomorrow's growth was seen to be under the threat of nature's revenge. Consequently, it was time to extend the attention span of planning and to call for the "efficient management of natural resources" as part of the development package: "We have in the past been concerned about the impacts of economic growth upon the environment. We are now forced," concludes the Brundtland Report, "to concern ourselves with the impacts of ecological stress—degradation of soils, water regimes, atmosphere, and forests—upon our economic prospects."

Another roadblock on the way to wedding "environment" to "development" has been an ossified vision of growth. The decades of smoke-stack industrialization had left the impression that growth was invariably linked to squandering ever more resources. Under the influence of the appropriate technology movement, however, this notion of development began to crumble and give way to an awareness of the availability of technological choices. It was, after all, in Stockholm that NGOs had gathered for the first time to stage a counter-conference which called for alternative paths in development. Later, initiatives like the Declaration of Cocoyoc and the Dag Hammarskjöld Foundation's "What Now?" helped—perhaps unwittingly—to challenge the assumption of an invariable technological process and to pluralize the road to growth. Out of this awareness of technological flexibility grew, towards the end of the 1970s, a new perception of the ecological predicament: the "limits to growth" are no longer seen as an insurmountable barrier blocking the surge of growth, but as discrete obstacles forcing the flow to take a different route. "Soft-path" studies in areas from energy to health care proliferated and charted new beds for the misdirected river.

Finally, environmentalism was regarded as inimical to the alleviation of poverty throughout the 1970s. The claim to be able to abolish poverty has been—and still is—the single most important pretension of the development ideology, in particular after its enthronement as the official priority goal after the speech at Nairobi by the then World Bank President, Robert McNamara, in 1973. Poverty had long been regarded as unrelated to environmental degradation, which was attributed to the impact of industrialization; the poor entered the equation only as future claimants to an industrial life style. But with spreading deforestation and desertification, the poor were quickly identified as agents of destruction and became the targets of campaigns to promote "environmental consciousness." Once blaming the victim had entered the professional consensus, the old recipe could be offered for meeting the new disaster: since growth was supposed to remove poverty, the environment could only be protected through a new era of growth. As it says in the Brundtland Report: "Poverty reduces people's capacity to use resources in a sustainable manner; it intensifies pressure on the environment. . . . A necessary but not sufficient condition for the elimination of absolute poverty is a relatively rapid rise in per capita incomes in the Third World." The way was thus cleared for the marriage between "environment" and "development"; the newcomer could be welcomed to the old family.

The Rejuvenation of Development

"No development without sustainability; no sustainability without development" is the formula which establishes the newly formed bond. "Development" emerges rejuvenated from this liaison, the ailing concept gaining another lease on life. This is nothing less than the repeat of a proven ruse: every time in the last 30 years that the destructive effects of development were recognized, the concept was extended in such a way as to include both injury and therapy. For example, when it became obvious, around 1970, that the pursuit of development actually intensified poverty, the notion of "equitable development" was invented to as to reconcile the irreconcilable: the creation of poverty with the abolition of poverty. In the same vein, the Brundtland Report incorporated concern for the environment into the concept of development by erecting "sustainable development" as the conceptual roof for both violating and healing the environment.

Certainly, the new era requires development experts to widen their attention span and to monitor water and soils, air and energy use. But development remains what it has always been, an array of interventions for boosting GNP: "Given expected population growth, a five- to tenfold increase in world industrial output can be anticipated by the time world population stabilizes sometime in the next century." Brundtland thus ends up suggesting further growth, but no longer, as in the old days of development, in order to achieve the happiness of the greatest number, but to contain the disaster for the generations to come. The threat to the planet's survival looms large. Has there ever been a better excuse for intrusion? New areas of intervention open up, nature becomes a domain of politics, and a new breed of technocrats feels the vocation to steer growth along the edge of the abyss. . . .

Towards a Global Ecocracy?

In the 1990s, concern about depleting resources and worldwide pollution has reached the commanding heights of international politics. Multilateral agencies distribute biomass converters and design forestry programmes. Economic summits quarrel about carbon dioxide emissions and scientists launch satellites to check on the planet's health. But the discourse which is rising to prominence has taken on a fundamentally biased orientation: it calls for extended management, but disregards intelligent self-limitation. As the dangers mount, new products, procedures and programmes are invented to stave off the threatening effects of industrialism and to keep the system afloat. Capital, bureaucracy and science—the venerable trinity of Western modernization—declare themselves indispensable in the new crisis and promise to prevent the worst through better engineering, integrated planning and more sophisticated models. However, fuel-efficient machines, environmental risk assessments and the close monitoring of natural processes, well-intended as they may be, have two assumptions in common: first, that society will always be driven to test the limits of nature, and second, that the exploitation of nature should neither be maximized nor minimized, but ought to be optimized. As the 1987 report of the World Resources Institute states on its first page: "The human race relies on the environment and therefore must manage it wisely." Clearly, the "therefore" is the crux of the matter; it is relevant only if the competitive dynamic of the industrial system is taken for granted. Otherwise, the environment would not be in danger and could be left without management. Calls for securing the survival of the planet are often, upon closer inspection, nothing less than calls for the survival of the industrial system.

Capital, bureaucracy and science-intensive solutions to environmental decline, however, are not without social costs. The Promethean task of keeping the global industrial machine running at an ever-increasing speed while at the same time safeguarding the biosphere will require a quantum leap in surveillance and regulation. How else should the myriad decisions, from the individual to the national and the global levels, be made? In this regard, it is of secondary importance whether the streamlining of industrialism will be achieved, if at all, through market incentives, strict legislation, remedial programmes, sophisticated spying or outright prohibitions. What matters is that all these strategies call for more centralism, in particular for a stronger state. Since ecocrats rarely call into question the industrial model of living in order to reduce the burden on nature, they are left with the necessity of synchronizing the innumerable activities of society with all the skill, foresight and technological tools they can muster—a prospect which could have inspired Orwell to another novel. The real historical challenge, therefore, must be addressed in something other than ecocratic terms: how is it possible to build ecological societies with less government and less professional dominance?

The ecocratic discourse which is set to unfold in the 1990s starts with the conceptual marriage of "environment" and "development," finds its cognitive base in ecosystems theory, and aims at new levels of administrative monitoring and control. Unwilling to reconsider the logic of competitive productivism which is at the root of the planet's ecological plight, it reduces ecology to a set of managerial strategies aimed at resource efficiency and risk management. It treats as a technical problem what in fact amounts to no less than a civilizational impasse—namely, that the level of productive performance already achieved turns out to be not viable in the North, let alone for the rest of the globe. With the rise of ecocracy, however, the fundamental debate that is needed on issues of public morality—like how society should live, or what, how much and in what way it should produce and consume—falls into oblivion. Instead, Western aspirations are implicitly taken for granted, not only in the West but worldwide, and societies which choose not to put all their energy into production and deliberately accept a lower throughput of commodities become unthinkable. What falls by the wayside are efforts to elucidate the much broader range of futures open to societies which limit their levels of material output in order to cherish whatever ideals emerge from their heritages. The ecocratic perception remains blind to diversity outside the economic society of the West.

The Rio Declaration on Environment and Development

Preamble

The United Nations Conference on Environment and Development,

Having met at Rio de Janeiro from 3 to 14 June 1992,

Reaffirming the Declaration of the United Nations Conference on the Human Environment, adopted at Stockholm on 16 June 1972, and seeking to build upon it,

With the goal of establishing a new and equitable global partnership through the creation of new levels of cooperation among States, key sectors of societies and people,

Working towards international agreements which respect the interests of all and protect the integrity of the global environmental and developmental system,

Recognizing the integral and interdependent nature of the Earth, our home,

Proclaims that:

Principle 1   Human beings are at the centre of concerns for sustainable development. They are entitled to a healthy and productive life in harmony with nature.

Principle 2   States have, in accordance with the Charter of the United Nations and the principles of international law, the sovereign right to exploit their own resources pursuant to their own environmental and developmental policies, and the responsibility to ensure that activities within their jurisdiction or control do not cause damage to the environment of other States or of areas beyond the limits of national jurisdiction.

Principle 3   The right to development must be fulfilled so as to equitably meet developmental and environmental needs of present and future generations.

Principle 4   In order to achieve sustainable development, environmental protection shall consitute an integral part of the development process and cannot be considered in isolation from it.

Principle 5   All States and all people shall cooperate in the essential task of eradicating poverty as an indispensable requirement for sustainable development, in order to decrease the disparities in standards of living and better meet the needs of the majority of the people of the world.

Principle 6   The special situation and needs of developing countries, particularly the least developed and those most environmentally vulnerable, shall be given special priority. International actions in the field of environment and development should also address the interests and needs of all countries.

Principle 7   States shall cooperate in a spirit of global partnership to conserve, protect and restore the health and integrity of the Earth's ecosystem. In view of the different contributions to global environmental degradation, States have common but differentiated responsibilities. The developed countries acknowledge the responsibility that they bear in the international pursuit of sustainable development in view of the pressures their societies place on the global environment and of the technologies and financial resources they command.

Principle 8   To achieve sustainable development and a higher quality of life for all people, States should reduce and eliminate unsustainable patterns of production and consumption and promote appropriate demographic policies.

Principle 9   States should cooperate to strengthen endogenous capacity-building for sustainable development by improving scientific understanding through exchanges of scientific and technological knowledge, and by enhancing the development, adaptation, diffusion and transfer of technologies, including new and innovative technologies.

Principle 10   Environmental issues are best handled with the participation of all concerned citizens, at the relevant level. At the national level, each individual shall have appropriate access to information concerning the environment that is held by public authorities, including information on hazardous materials and activities in their communities, and the opportunity to participate in decision-making processes. States shall facilitate and encourage public awareness and participation by making information widely available. Effective access to judicial and administrative proceedings, including redress and remedy, shall be provided.

Principle 11   States shall enact effective environmental legislation. Environmental standards, management objectives and priorities should reflect the environmental and developmental context to which they apply. Standards applied by some countries may be inappropriate and of unwarranted economic and social cost to other countries, in particular developing countries.

Principle 12   States should cooperate to promote a supportive and open international economic system that would lead to economic growth and sustainable development in all countries, to better address the problems of environmental degradation. Trade policy measures for environmental purposes should not constitute a means of arbitrary or unjustifiable discrimination or a disguised restriction on international trade. Unilateral actions to deal with environmental challenges outside the jurisdiction of the importing country should be avoided. Environmental measures addressing transboundary or global environmental problems should, as far as possible, be based on an international consensus.

Principle 13   States shall develop national law regarding liability and compensation for the victims of pollution and other environmental damage. States shall also cooperate in an expeditious and more determined manner to develop further international law regarding liability and compensation for adverse effects of environmental damage caused by activities within their jurisdiction or control to areas beyond their jurisdiction.

Principle 14   States should effectively cooperate to discourage or prevent the relocation and transfer to other States of any activities and substances that cause severe environmental degradation or are found to be harmful to human health.

Principle 15   In order to protect the environment, the precautionary approach shall be widely applied by States according to their capabilities.

Where there are threats of serious or irreversible damage, lack of full scientific certainty shall not be used as a reason for postponing cost-effective measures to prevent environmental degradation.

Principle 16   National authorities should endeavour to promote the internalization of environmental costs and the use of economic instruments, taking into account the approach that the polluter should, in principle, bear the cost of pollution, with due regard to the public interest and without distorting international trade and investment.

Principle 17   Environmental impact assessment, as a national instrument, shall be undertaken for proposed activities that are likely to have a significant adverse impact on the environment and are subject to a decision of a competent national authority.

Principle 18   States shall immediately notify other States of any natural disasters or other emergencies that are likely to produce sudden harmful effects on the environment of those States. Every effort shall be made by the international community to help States so afflicted.

Principle 19   States shall provide prior and timely notification and relevant information to potentially affected States on activities that may have a significant adverse transboundary environmental effect and shall consult with those States at an early stage and in good faith.

Principle 20   Women have a vital role in environmental management and development. Their full participation is therefore essential to achieve sustainable development.

Principle 21   The creativity, ideals and courage of the youth of the world should be mobilized to forge a global partnership in order to achieve sustainable development and ensure a better future for all.

Principle 22   Indigenous people and their communities, and other local communities, have a vital role in environmental management and development because of their knowledge and traditional practices. States should recognize and duly support their identity, culture and interests and enable their effective participation in the achievement of sustainable development.

Principle 23   The environment and natural resources of people under oppression, domination and occupation shall be protected.

Principle 24   Warfare is inherently destructive of sustainable development. States shall therefore respect international law providing protection for the environment in times of armed conflict and cooperate in its further development, as necessary.

Principle 25   Peace, development and environmental protection are interdependent and indivisible.

Principle 26   States shall resolve all their environmental disputes peacefully and by appropriate means in accordance with the Charter of the United Nations.

Principle 27   States and people shall cooperate in good faith and in a spirit of partnership in the fulfilment of the principles embodied in this Declaration and in the further development of international law in the field of sustainable development.

[From] *Free Market Environmentalism*

———————— ◦❧◦ ————————

Terry L. Anderson and Donald R. Leal

ALTHOUGH THERE ARE different interpretations of sustainability, advocates generally

- perceive that the biosphere imposes limits on economic growth,
- express a lack of faith in either science or technology as leading to human betterment,
- are extremely averse to environmental risks,
- support redistributive justice and egalitarian ethics,
- profess concern over population growth and have faith in the wisdom of human capital development [education], and
- have survival of species and protection of the environment and of minority cultures, rather than economic growth per se, as goals.[1]

Sustainable development, as advocated by today's ecological economists, is a holdover from the 1960s and 1970s when economists were struggling with steady-state and zero-growth economic models. Again using intuitive concepts like the "Economics of the Coming Spaceship Earth," political controls are required to carefully balance product consumption, energy use, and wastes to maintain a "steady-state economy."[2] During the 1970s, the demands for strict political control of resource consumption were driven by a concern that energy resources were being exhausted. Although all indications tell us that price deregulation solved the energy crisis, the steady-state theories formed the basis for many regulations, from climate control in buildings to lower speed limits to fuel efficiency standards, and ultimately to a new bureaucracy, the Department of Energy. Today, the same regulatory zeal under the guise of sustainable development is being driven by fears of global warming.

Unfortunately, the politics of regulation at the global level are likely to dwarf problems that are inherent in national pollution regulations. At the national level, there are governmental institutions that can implement regulations, and in democracies there is some hope of controlling the regulators. Global regulation, however, would require international treaties or organizations to specify and implement the regulations. But this raises important and complex questions of who will come to the bargaining table and who will negotiate with whom. If agreement is reached, who will do the enforcing? If fines or taxes are to be imposed, who will collect them and who will receive the proceeds? . . .

Sustainable Development
Versus Free Market Environmentalism

Innovative solutions to atmospheric pollution should focus on ways that government can define and enforce property rights, thus reducing the costs of bargaining toward an optimal level of pollution. Instead, believers in the apocalyptic predictions of global warming call for regulatory approaches under the banner of sustainable development. Unfortunately, the rhetorical appeal of sustainable development and "its beguiling simplicity and apparently self-evident meaning have obscured its inherent ambiguity."[3] Hence, the concept has become everything to all people.

One version of sustainability (which is not inconsistent with neoclassical economics) calls for "maximizing-subject-to-constraints." According to this version, all ecological principles and environmental ethics must be taken into account by the institutional framework that governs development. Such values can be incorporated through markets, with the private provision of recreational and environmental amenities. The key difference is that free market environmentalism incorporates these values through voluntary exchanges while sustainable development seeks solution-oriented technologies and the "right prices" to internalize third-party effects.

A more extreme version requires "maintenance of resources," meaning that no resource stocks should be diminished. This goal is impossible to achieve, however, if there is to be any present consumption of nonrenewable resources. With a copper mine, for example, none of the mineral could be taken from the Earth and converted into valuable capital goods because the stock of copper available for future generations would be diminished. The maintenance of resources ignores the possibility that consumption of some nonrenewable resource may reduce the consumption of other resources that are far more important to human life or the ecosystem. For example, by consuming petroleum, which is in finite but unknown supply, we can produce medical supplies that improve and extend human life. Does it make sense to save oil for future generations simply to guarantee them the same oil supply to which we have access? As economists Barnett and Morse concluded in their seminal study of resource scarcity, "By devoting itself to improving the lot of the living . . . each generation . . . transmits a more productive world to those who follow."[4] Strict adherence to sustainability precludes this investment.

In short, the seemingly simple concept of sustainable development gets considerably more complex when we recognize opportunity costs and attempt to implement policy. If ecological principles and environmental ethics are to be factored into development policy, we still must ask who will do the factoring. Again, there is diversity of opinion among sustainable development advocates, but generally it is acknowledged that some "institutional modifications" will be necessary. A leading natural resources textbook summarizes these modifications:

1. an institution for stabilizing population,
2. an institution for stabilizing the stock of physical wealth and throughput, and
3. an institution to ensure that the stocks and flows are allocated fairly among the population.[5]

When these institutional modifications are dissected, the "beguiling simplicity and apparent self-evident meaning" of sustainable development are replaced with the reality of political controls to discipline the citizens.

Fundamentally, "sustainable development" is a notion of discipline . . . disciplining our current consumption. This sense of "intergenerational responsibility" is a new political principle, a virtue that must now guide economic growth. The industrial world has already used so much of the planet's ecological capital that the sustainability of future life is in doubt. That can't continue.[6]

The method of discipline is the primary distinguishing factor between sustainable development and free market environmentalism. Market prices discipline consumers to allocate their scarce budgets among competing demands, and they discipline producers to conserve on scarcer, higher-priced resources by finding substitutes that are less scarce. This discipline works well as long as consumers and producers are faced with the full costs of their actions. It breaks down, however, when third-party effects or externalities allow costs to be imposed on others without their consent. Emission of global-warming gases lacks the discipline of markets precisely because there are no markets for the atmosphere. Sustainable development and free market environmentalism come together on the point that environmental problems arise when this discipline is lacking.

Sustainable development, however, stands in sharp contrast to free market environmentalism when it comes to the appropriate mechanism for discipline.

Sustainable development policies require political regulation to discipline consumers and producers and limit economic growth. In the absence of growth, those at the bottom of the economic ladder can only improve their lot by taking from those at the top, so population must be controlled, consumption must be curtailed, risks must be limited, new environmental ethics must be developed, and wealth must be redistributed.

The disciplinary mechanism required for sustainable development also contrasts with free market environmentalism in that it depends on omniscient, benevolent experts who can model ecosystems and determine solutions. In order to attain the "appropriate technology," the "correct level of population growth," or the "proper environmental ethic," political managers must have the necessary information, knowledge, and ethics to manage for sustainability. They must possess technical knowledge about quantities and qualities of resources, both human and physical, and they must have knowledge about what constitutes the material needs of both present and future generations. Furthermore, they must set aside any self-interest to manage for the benefit of present and future generations.

Because this form of scientific management is inimical to ecological notions of process and evolution, some advocates of sustainable development urge "societal adaptation as the appropriate response to new ecological awareness, rather than more sophisticated, expert dominated management."[7] How this "societal adaptation" will come about is often unclear, but the following Green Party manifesto emphasizes the role of government: "A Green Government would replace the false gods [of markets, greed, consumption, and growth] with cooperation, self-sufficiency, sharing and thrift."[8] This personification of a "Green Government" as the ecologically sensitive decision maker assumes that "the government," whether democratic or authoritarian, will be omniscient, benevolent, and ecologically sensitive.

Both the scientific management approach and the societal adaptation approach to sustainable development violate basic principles of ecology. It is impossible to concentrate knowledge about all of the possible variations in an ecosystem, especially if the ecosystem is taken to mean the global environment. There is so much disagreement about whether and why there is global warming simply because there are so many variables that are difficult to predict or model. It is difficult enough to manage Yellowstone National Park as an ecosystem, let alone the entire Earth.[9] Furthermore, to assume that the experts will do what is "right" rather than what is politically expedient is naive. There is simply too much evidence that politicians and bureaucrats act in their own self-interest much more frequently than they act for the "public good." Accepting that "Green Government" will take over the responsibility of guaranteeing ecologically sensitive development assumes that a political process is in place to channel the self-interest of voters and politicians toward that end.

Finally, sustainable development violates ecological principles by seeking static solutions to dynamic problems. Proponents of sustainability advocate specific limits on energy consumption (especially fossil fuel), emissions, deforestation, and population as if there is an ultimate solution to the global-warming problem. These static regulations are not designed to respond to changing information. Advocates of sustainability might argue that democratic processes will ensure the change, but there is little theory or evidence to support such an argument.

In contrast, free market environmentalism is an approach to environmental problems that is consistent with principles of ecology. Free market environmentalism accepts that individuals are unlikely to set aside self-interest and asks how institutions can harness this survival trait to solve problems. It recognizes that information about the environment is so diffuse that a small group of experts cannot manage the planet as an ecosystem. Individuals must be relied upon to process time- and place-specific information and to discover niches, just as other species in the ecosystem do.

Free market environmentalism also emphasizes that economic growth and environmental quality are not incompatible. In fact, higher incomes allow us to afford more environmental quality in addition to material goods. It is no accident that less developed countries have more pollution, lower health standards, and more environmental hazards. The simple fact is that dynamic, growing economies, like dynamic ecosystems, are more resilient in coping with unanticipated environmental problems. Ecologist William Clark has pointed out that resilience is the essence of a healthy ecosystem: "the decreased frequency of variation in the system [is] accompanied by increased vulnerability to and cost of variation. . . . "[10] Aaron Wildavsky contrasted anticipation with resilience, stressing that we are better off avoiding the obvious, high-probability dangers and developing the resilience to deal with harms as they arise.[11]

Advocates of sustainable development argue that human betterment should be measured in terms of health, education, improved living standards for the most disadvantaged, and a cleaner environment. These conditions are precisely the results of economic growth. Countries with higher per capita incomes have better education, lower mortality rates, longer lives, and better living standards for the poor. If sustainable development is taken to mean no or even slower growth, the Third World countries not only will be deprived of higher material living standards, they also will be deprived of the other measures of well-being, including health, safety, and education.

Many may believe that free market environmentalism falls short of expectations because it cannot provide a specific solution to a dynamic problem. And it is true that this approach offers no guarantees. But all environmental policy would be better conceived if we recognized that the dynamic nature of ecosystems imposes this constraint; there are no guarantees in nature. Free market environmentalism can no more dictate the optimal solution than ecologists can tell us what is the right way for an ecosystem to evolve.

Instead, free market environmentalism emphasizes the importance of human institutions that facilitate rather than discourage the evolution of individual rights. Even if regulatory solutions can improve environmental quality, these benefits must be traded off against negative impacts on material wealth and health and against the costs to individual freedom and liberty. Shed of its beguiling simplicity, sustainable development is a guise for political control reminiscent of the governments being rejected in eastern Europe. Not only has that form of political control despoiled the environment and deprived people of higher living standards, it has oppressed individuals. In contrast to regulatory solutions to environmental problems that require heroic assumptions about omniscient and benevolent experts wielding the coercive powers of government, free market environmentalism decentralizes power and harnesses self-interest through market incentives. Market processes with consumer and producer sovereignty have a demonstrated record for improving the quantity and quality of goods and services produced. Expanding these processes to include natural resources and environmental amenities offers the only possibility for improving environmental quality, raising living standards, and, perhaps most important, expanding individual liberty.

Notes

1. S. Batie, "Sustainable Development: Challenges to the Profession of Agricultural Economics," *American Journal of Agricultural Economics* 71 (1989): 1085.

2. K. Boulding, "The Economics of the Coming Spaceship Earth," in *Environmental Quality in a Growing Economy,* ed. H. Jarret (Baltimore: Johns Hopkins University Press, 1966); H. Daly, *Steady-State Economics* (San Francisco: Freeman, 1977).

3. T. J. O'Riordan, "The Politics of Sustainability," in *Sustainable Environmental Management,* ed. R. K. Turner (Boulder, Colo.: Westview Press, 1988).

4. H. Barnett and C. Morse, *Scarcity and Growth: The Economics of Natural Resource Availability* (Baltimore: Johns Hopkins University Press, 1963), 249.

5. T. Tietenberg, *Environmental and Natural Resource Economics* (Glenview, Ill.: Scott, Foresman, 1984), 437.

6. G. H. Brundtland, "From the Cold War to a Warm Atmosphere," *New Perspectives Quarterly* 6 (1989): 5.

7. G. Francis, "Great Lakes Governance and the Ecosystem Approach: Where Next?" *Alternatives* 3 (1986): 66.

8. "Green Economics," *Economist,* 24 June 1989, 48.

9. J. Bagen and D. Leal, eds., *The Yellowstone Primer: Land and Resource Management in the Greater Yellowstone Ecosystem* (San Francisco: Pacific Research Institute for Public Policy, 1990).

10. W. C. Clark, "Witches, Floods, and Wonder Drugs: Historical Perspectives on Risk Management?" in *Societal Risk Assessment: How Safe Is Safe Enough?* ed. R. C. Schwing and W. A. Albers, Jr. (New York: Plenum, 1988), chap. 4.

11. A. Wildavsky, *Searching for Safety* (New Brunswick, N.J.: Transaction Books, 1988), chap. 3.

[From] *For Earth's Sake: A Report from the Commission on Developing Countries and Global Change*

Commission on Developing Countries and Global Change

Understanding the Environment/Development Crisis: Back to Basics

The world today is characterized by unacceptably sharp differences between the poor and the opulent, the hungry and the overfed, the powerful and the powerless. The twentieth century saw an unprecedented increase in overall economic output: however, simultaneously, it also saw extreme social and economic human inequality. The world's population has more than tripled since 1900. At the same time, the gross world product has increased 21 times, the consumption of fossil fuels 30 times, and industrial production 50 times. This enormous increase in wealth has not benefited all people equitably. The average income of the richest one billion people is 20 times larger than that of the poorest billion.

Most parts of the Third World are facing a severe economic and social crisis. Notwithstanding the apparent promise of development, throughout the 1980s, the increasing severity of socioeconomic conditions was undeniable. Not only did existing development problems continue, but also the poor countries faced declining rates of expansion in production (see Box 1). Asymmetries between the South and the North have become even more pronounced. In some regions and countries, per capita incomes have declined to the level of 20 or 30 years ago. Poverty, along with its social, environmental, and human implications, has increased.

At the same time, the environment worldwide is in crisis. At local, regional, and global levels, key features and processes of the natural world are being damaged or obliterated. Even though human societies have, since their earliest origins, affected many kinds of environmental transformation in the course of development, nothing compares to the changes that have been wrought in recent decades. Consequent awareness of critical environmental issues—

BOX 1

Failing Hopes: Examples of Reduced Growth and Increased Dependency in the South

In sub-Saharan Africa, per capita income declined by 12 percent from 1980 to 1989. However, this average conceals even greater declines in many countries. In Uganda for instance, per capita income declined 28 percent; in Niger, 24 percent; and in Zambia, 20 percent. Some of the most adversely affected countries are also among the poorest countries.

In Latin America and the Caribbean, per capita gross national product (GNP) declined by 9.6 percent from 1981 to 1990. In Central America, the decline in per capita GNP reached 17.2 percent. In this period, Latin America and the Caribbean sent net transfers of 212 billion United States dollars to creditors. The fact that the payments were to creditors from the First World eloquently expresses a critical dimension of the relationships of deepening dependency. Meanwhile, the number of poor in Latin America increased by 40 million, representing 43 percent of the population in 1986; in 1980, this figure was 41 percent. More integral measurements indicate that by 1990, poverty affected 62 percent of the population of Latin America and the Caribbean.

atmospheric change, water pollution, unsustainable exploitation of renewable resources, deforestation, erosion, degraded carrying capacity, loss of biological diversity—has now extended well beyond academic circles into the central arena of public debate.

In many cases, the socioeconomic crisis is the result of development styles that destroy both human potentials and the environment. In fact, the two phenomena—the global environmental crisis and socioeconomic decline in the South—are the result of unsustainable systems of production and consumption in the North, inappropriate development models in the South, and a fundamentally inequitable world order. South–North relations are based on gross overexploitation of, and underpayment for, Southern resources and human labour. The competitive forces that make economic growth a necessity, operating within this imbalanced global political economy, have led to uneven, distorted development and levels of resource and environmental degradation that threaten life and the future of humanity itself. Within many countries of the South, these same kinds of relationships between environmental degradation and extreme poverty hold. In sum, through inappropriate production processes and technologies, the Earth's resources are being exhausted and polluted at an accelerating rate. An ever-increasing volume of goods and services are being produced, the majority of which are channeled toward filling the consumption demands of a minority, leaving the basic human needs of the poorer majority unmet.

From a Third World perspective, the development crisis and the environmental crisis in fact constitute a single social–ecological crisis—the most pressing challenge of our times. If current trends are not reversed, there will be ever-scarcer resources to meet the demands of current and future generations of humanity, productive capacities will diminish, and the poverty levels of the peoples of the South will worsen.

An Evolutionary Overview

The state of the biophysical environment and the natural resource base in any particular region is the result of complex interactions between local ecosystems and human activities. The latter is conditioned by economic systems and conditions, social and cultural processes, the political order, legal and administrative systems, and the kinds of technologies in use.

No society's relationship with nature is static. Interactions change over time, and major shifts mark new historical phases. But historically, through an ongoing and gradual process of learning and adjustment, many cultures have adopted modes of self-reproduction and ways of interacting with nature that were sustainable. Over generations, new practices were selected and adopted; those that could not be sustained were abandoned. Such cultures coded the "dos" and "don'ts" into patterns of everyday life, forming a powerful body of indigenous knowledge that was evident in many forms of ecologically sound production in agriculture, fisheries, water management, and other sectors. These indigenous mechanisms were often disrupted by unforseen natural catastrophes and invasions by foreign cultures. In some cases, populations moved to unfamiliar natural environments, disrupting systems of social organization that had evolved to a particular natural environment. In general, however, lifestyles, values, demographic pressures, and levels of technology were such that environmental burdens were minimized.

It was not until modern-day colonialism that there were ruptures on a global scale to the sociocultural mechanisms behind sustainable livelihoods. Traditional knowledge and resource-management systems were disregarded by the new rulers. The colonial powers wanted to acquire the wealth generated by the careful management of local environments or appropriate the land for production of goods for European markets. They did not, however, understand these environments or the rationale for, and systems of, traditional management (see Box 2).

The natural resources of the colonized territories were exploited and exported as raw materials, while imported products began to flood their markets. The local populations steadily losing control over their resource base, became

BOX 2

The Economic–Ecological System of Traditional India

Farmers living in India's semi-arid lands, recognizing the risks of settled agriculture in an area with heavy weather fluctuations, traditionally adopted sustainable and risk-minimizing techniques. Indian villagers transformed their environment into a complex ecosystem of croplands, grasslands, and forests—an interactive, multipurpose biological system that responded to the seasonal rhythms of the area and minimized the social and economic impact of rainfall variation. Farmlands produced grains to feed people, and the crop residues fed farm animals; livestock provided not only milk but also manure and draught power; grasslands provided green fodder during the wet season; forests and trees provided firewood and leaf fodder during the dry season. Because the land was parched for most of the year, many water-storage devices were developed across the country. Indians thus became some of the world's greatest water harvesters—when the British landed, there were already hundreds of thousands of water tanks across India.

This system of production was supported by an elaborate arrangement of property rights and religious practices. Not only the cow but also the grazing lands were sacred. Many forests were also set aside as sacred groves, while the ponds themselves and their catchments also had religious significance.

The wealth generated in villages, through self-reliance and careful management of the local natural resource base, supported a range of skilled artisans producing a great variety of renowned and widely traded goods. Major cities sprang up along the Ganges River and elsewhere. Even the desert supported wealthy cities. Thus, before the British came, India was one of the wealthiest and most urbanized countries in the world, nearly totally literate. But the British failed to understand the Indian concept of community property management. As the community lands yielded to the state, the colonizing British disregarded their functions within the local village ecosystems and considered them wastelands. They became state property managed by a bureaucracy; the ensuing process was tantamount to systematic, state-sponsored destruction.

The entire economic–ecological system of India was turned on its head to produce goods for the metropolitan markets in the colonizing nation. Old Indian cities along the Ganges and elsewhere, dependent on the evolved urban–rural links, were pauperized; cities became steadily deurbanized; artisans went bankrupt and were pushed into the countryside; and the incidence of illiteracy, poverty, and famine grew greatly. Even today, most of the old Indian cities remain extremely poor. Within

> the hierarchy of urban systems, their place of primacy has been usurped by coastal metropolises like Bombay, Calcutta, and Madras, which did not even exist two centuries ago. These cities emerged and prospered as the Indian hinterland and its resources became linked to, and drained by, an external economy. Indian society and environment imploded under this colossal impact.

increasingly alienated. What were once community-managed commons steadily turned into state resources, whose purpose was mainly to benefit commercial interests.

As a general trend, environmental degradation became widespread with increasingly intense commercialization of the economy. As forests disappeared in parts of Africa and India, for example, firewood became scarce. As the availability of fodder declined, grasslands were severely overstocked and their productivity began to collapse. As erosion increased, once-fertile land became wasteland. The scarcity of biomass engendered an acute human crisis. Women suffered the most, as the daily tasks of collecting fodder, wood, and water became more and more onerous. Children, especially girls, were increasingly required to work alongside their mothers to support the family.

In Africa and Asia, where independence was achieved in relatively recent history, a class of peoples educated by the colonizers, and no longer understanding or appreciating traditional ways, became leaders of the nations of the Third World. The result has been a deepening of the Westernization process. In the end, the colonization of the resource base appears easier to reverse than the colonization of the mind.

Similarly, in Latin America, where independence was won earlier than in Africa and Asia, the end of colonialism did not at first involve major changes. Production processes remained much the same as those that existed during the colonial period. The production of raw materials for export continued, with control now concentrated in a new elite who had become owners of the land. However, important changes in modes of production did occur with the agrarian reform—the result of armed revolution in Mexico—and other agrarian transformations in Latin America. In most countries, national constitutions incorporated the demands of the poorest, and access to land was recovered by indigenous and campesino communities. To a large degree, the traditional knowledge of these communities was again applied. Ultimately, however, the lack of consistency in agrarian policy, the lack of real participation by rural people, and changes in the international order after the Second World War have resulted in the subservience of rural policies to industrialization.

Accordingly, colonial trade patterns—involving export of cheap raw materials and import of industrial products—have dominated the economies of most

Southern nations since the Second World War. In addition and throughout this period, multilateral financial, technical, and aid agencies have promoted the replacement of local production practices in the South with technologies that are often environmentally damaging.

Recent decades have seen a further shift of resource control from local communities to centralized, commercial institutions. Community management and discipline in the use of natural resources declined further. Government loans and support have promoted further changes in rural production toward satisfying urban demands. As the monoculture of the Green Revolution began to take over, the genetic diversity on farms declined rapidly. Forests were sacrificed to meet urban and industrial needs. Unplanned and indiscriminate industrialization resulted in the proliferation of slums, pollution, and health hazards. The highly capital- and resource-intensive urbanization systems of the industrial powers, transplanted into impoverished economies, produced further disparities and inequalities. The gulf between the "haves" and "have-nots" widened and, as the "haves" captured increasing quantities of natural resources, environmental destruction wreaked further havoc on the "have-nots." Thus, a dual society has flourished in almost all countries of the South, with the gap between rich and poor growing simultaneously with environmental destruction and the erosion of community rights over the resource base.

In response to the social injustice associated with environmental destruction, protests began to emerge in the Third World during the 1970s and 1980s. These protests—for example, the Chipko Movement (the famous hug-the-tree movement) in the Garhwal Himalaya of India and the Set Setal urban youth movement in Senegal—signal the beginning of a rise in consciousness in the South.

Differing Perspectives on Key Issues

To date, the South has had little influence in defining the key issues in the global environmental debate. As a result, issues of world poverty and inequity have become isolated from, and overshadowed by, global environmental concerns. Thus, although the environmental crisis has begun to force some changes in production and consumption, the bearing of these changes on critical socioeconomic and political conditions has been largely incidental and, at times, negative (see Box 3).

A new context is needed for the global environment/development debate. It must define basic concepts, such as sustainability and the "global" environment, and basic issues, such as burden sharing and population. . . .

Approaching Sustainability: Choosing Priorities   To date, Northern concerns have directed the global environmental debate. These concerns reflect a definition of sustainability in which the physical environment is the primary focus and long-term intergenerational issues are key. Thus, primary moral

BOX 3
Costs of Dealing with the Costs of Pollution: An Example of Socioeconomic Fallout from Environmental Action

As one example of the often subtle socioeconomic implications of adaptations made to accommodate environmental concerns, to the extent that price adjustments to reflect environmental costs are being made by the North, the unintended effect is to contribute even further to North–South disparities. Because their economic base lies mainly in industrial production, environmental costs of production in many Northern countries are primarily associated with pollution. These costs are being steadily integrated into the price of goods as a result of public policies to control pollution; the costs being determined by the price of the control technologies.

Integrating the costs of land and resource degradation, the forms of degradation more commonly associated with the primary production economy of the South, is a much more complex matter. Firstly, the costs of rectifying these problems are more difficult to determine. Secondly, the prices of many Southern commodities are largely determined by monopolistic, transnational corporations. Thus, the Southern producers are "price-takers" and have to date been unable to collaborate in rationalizing supplies. Many Southern commodities also face stiff competition from substitutes.

The North is increasingly building into the price of its products—including the products it sells to the South—the expenditures it makes to control environmental degradation associated with pollution. However, there is nothing being built into the price of commodities shipped by the South to the North that reflects the associated costs of environmental degradation. Indeed, the terms of trade of several of these commodities have been consistently declining. The need to consider how the treatment of externalities can be equalized in internationally traded goods is but one small example of the kinds of factors that must be introduced to environmental decision-making.

obligations have to do with maintaining the options and interests of future generations. A critical message from virtually all quarters of the South is that social concerns, economic issues, and intragenerational equity—the very obvious "here and now" disparities in wealth and opportunities—are the keys to resolving the environment/development crisis. Behind this message lies the notion of people-centred development. It is hardly surprising that the South is skeptical of the primacy given to issues such as atmospheric change within the "global" agenda. In the South, even the basic needs of a large proportion of the population are not being met, and economic and environmental priorities are largely ignored.

For example, the Global Environment Fund (GEF), sponsored by the United Nations Development Programme (UNDP), the United Nations Environment Programme (UNEP), and the World Bank, finances projects that aim to prevent global warming, preserve biodiversity, reduce threats to the ozone layer, and control the pollution of international waters. These issues were selected by donor governments; they do not reflect the most pressing environmental problems of the Southern, recipient countries. Southern priority problems such as desertification and lack of clean drinking water could, for instance, have been included in the GEF. In comparison to funding for GEF projects, UNEP's anti-desertification fund has received almost no financial support, although it was set up in the late 1970s.

Moreover, given the Northern focus on the biophysical dimension of environmental change, analysis is done primarily within the natural sciences, and the topics that dominate the international agenda and dictate funding priorities are constrained by narrowly scientific perspectives. In comparison, key social dimensions of change are given relatively little attention.

Perhaps most disturbing is the sense that neither equity nor the environment itself are the concerns that underlie the recent Northern interest in "sustainable development." Rather, primary concerns continue to lie in sustaining Northern consumption levels and maintaining the conditions necessary for economic growth. Notwithstanding growing skepticism about the adequacy of the "techno-fix" approach, the associated position is that ecological problems can be technologically controlled in a market system, provided only that some adjustments are made to ensure that prices include environmental externalities. Even the depletion of natural resources is not viewed as a fundamental problem—it is assumed that new technologies will allow for continuous substitution (although there are fears that the growing Southern population and its increasing resource demands will mean less for the North and for future generations).

In contrast, the environmental priorities of the South are underpinned by grim and undeniable human realities. In many countries of the South, environmental issues are issues of life and death. And, conversely, where poverty is widespread, lack of development may be a greater barrier to a reasonable quality of life than would the enviromental impacts associated with current forms of development.

It is critical to any meaningful approach to "sustainable development" that environmental issues be integrated with issues of equity, social justice, human rights, and development. Fundamentally, the main cause of the environment/ development crisis is unsustainable forms and levels of production and consumption in the North and their export to the South. It follows that, to resolve the crisis, more than technological approaches are required. Unsustainable output and expenditure levels in the North must be reduced, and socially and environmentally inappropriate development systems in the South must be reformed. A more equitable international order must therefore accompany the shift to more ecological and equitable national development. At the same time, constant attention must be given to the development implications of environmental decisions.

The Nature of "Global"   Selective and sectoral environmental issues now dominate the international environmental debate. It is clear that many players in this debate do not give "global" status to critical environmental problems that represent massive impediments to national and regional development and environmental quality in the South. These players, including many Northern governments, wish to separate out from the global agenda those environmental problems that manifest themselves locally and regionally, thus limiting responsibility for these problems to the national level. As a result, the current international agenda sidesteps the systemic international causes of environmental degradation. There is an apparent desire, at least at the official level, to avoid any serious discussion of the restructuring of international economic relations. The ethic of caring and sharing is far from prominent in the arena of international environmental debate.

Concretely, key Northern concerns focus primarily on long-term impacts involving selected, planetary-level, geophysical variables (ozone depletion, climate change). In the South, the most immediate and pressing environmental problems relate to the depletion and degradation of the biomass base, on which the majority of the population continues to be directly dependent. Indeed, as a large proportion of industrial output from the South is biomass based, economic activity in all sectors is threatened. An additional priority is the pollution, contamination, and resulting health impacts associated with inadequately controlled industrial development and misapplications of chemical technologies.

The land, resource, and health issues that preoccupy the South are as global in nature as those espoused by the North. The South's priorities must be reflected in the international agenda as global issues. The roots of many ecological problems, regardless of the scale at which they manifest themselves, can be traced not only to local and national factors but also to the global system within which nations operate. Thus, the definition of "global" in the context of environmental problems must include the following elements:

- problems that are geographically widespread in effect;
- problems whose causes may be local or national, but whose effects are transboundary;
- problems that are local or national in scale, but recur within many regions; and

• problems that reflect international economic and political dynamics
(for instance, policies and practices of international agencies and
transnational corporations).

Defining the Global Commons   The North tends to frame many of its
environmental concerns within the context of the "global commons." Until
recently, the concept of global commons has been primarily reserved for those
regions or resources over which no individual or state ownership could be
claimed: in particular, the atmosphere, the open oceans, Antarctica, and outer
space. In the absence of such ownership, the overuse and abuse of the area or
resource is deemed to be inevitable (see Box 4). Indeed, these global commons
all currently suffer to varying degrees the negative effects of exploitation,
pollution, and mismanagement by various nations, and all have been the subject of proposed treaties or international agreements for cooperative management. In some cases, treaties have been set forth to allocate ownership and
distribution of resources.

Now, however, other environmental regions and features are being increasingly perceived as global resources, even though ownership, or at least potential control over ownership, is vested in particular nation states. Regions that
are, in some quarters, being newly proclaimed as global commons include
tropical rain forests. Their status as a global resource is supported by claims to
the effect that they are "the lungs of the world" and repositories of a significant
proportion of the planet's biological richness.

Indeed, many of the planet's richest sources of biodiversity are found in
some of the world's poorest nations. Given current rates of species extinction,
there is increasing pressure from the North (most particularly, agribusiness
and pharmaceutical interests) to have Third World genetic resources designated a universal heritage—a sort of nonterritorial global commons. Ironi-
cally, the loss of biodiversity in many of these areas has often come at the
hands of technologies (such as the Green Revolution) and forms of exploitation promoted by the North, at the expense of indigenous practices that
helped sustain genetic diversity.

We cannot deny the local and global importance of biodiversity. However,
efforts to extend the concept of global commons to nationally based resources
are a threat to Southern sovereignty over Southern resources and, consequently, to the rights of the Third World to benefit economically from endemic
resources. Given that Northern countries are unlikely to consider their natural
resources in this light, the message from the North reads "What's mine is
mine, and what's yours is ours."

Burden Sharing   Although the economic debt of the Third World has
received abundant attention, the environmental debt of the North has been
greatly underplayed. Conversely, the substantial contributions of many peoples
of the Third World, and of the poor in general, in conserving their environ-

---

BOX 4

The Commons: Collective Ownership or "No-Man's-Land"?

In Western tradition, "the commons" are areas or resources for which no formal and exclusive ownership exists. An alternative perspective, common to many indigenous societies worldwide, is to view the commons as subject to a form of collective ownership, in which members of the collective share both benefits and responsibilities. In other words, the commons are managed through equality in access and community discipline. The implications of this latter approach are very different from the "overuse and abuse" implications of the Western commons. Many forms of traditional collective land ownership—for example, the *bona* of Iran, the *zanjera* of the Philippines, the *acadia* of West Africa, and the common pastures of England—are managed and maintained to the good of the entire community and future generations. Social traditions, rather than legal arrangements, are usually key to communal maintenance of the quality and carrying capacity of the land. Given the prevailing balance of political and economic power, the danger is that the Western perception of common property will largely determine current debate on management of the global commons.

---

ment are seldom acknowledged in the international arena. For example, the work of north Indian and Nepalese farmers in terracing mountains to conserve soil is an enormous labour investment in environmental sustainability that has rarely been acknowledged.

The North bears primary responsibility for many of the problems currently on the agenda of the global environmental debate. It is the South, however, that is likely to experience greater hardships as a result of these problems. Moreover, just as poor countries have borne the brunt of the global economic crisis, the perception is that sacrifices believed to be necessary in the pursuit of sustainable development will also fall unfairly on the poor countries. There is a fear that development efforts will be made more costly by environmental measures imposed by international regulations. Indeed, current perceptions about the causes of, and solutions to, environmental degradation may, intentionally or not, foster international actions and decisions whose effect is to arrest development in the South. This would lead to a hardening of current global inequalities. As well, in addition to the fact that many resources taken from Third World countries are given little economic value, many natural resources (in particular, genetic resources) taken from the South are altered and sold back to Third World countries at high prices.

The issue of how the burden of adjustment will be distributed is critical to any meaningful global environmental negotiations. . . . While the South would like to fully participate in global environmental management, a fair system of global environmental governance, built on the principle of equal human rights, is essential. We must be watchful for political biases in interpreting relative responsibility for environmental problems. Such interpretations are based on what is depicted as hard scientific fact; in fact, the data are often inadequate and open to various and frequently contradictory interpretations.

Environment, Technology, and Ethics

Rajni Kothari

TWENTY, even ten, years ago one had still to establish the 'case' for the environment. To this end, beginning with the Stockholm conference, a major intellectual and political effort was mounted, an effort that has proved successful. Unfortunately, this very success has been co-opted by the status quo, with the result that while everyone talks of the environment, the destruction of nature goes on apace, indeed at an increasing pace. The environment is proving to be a classic case of 'doublespeak', a lot of sophistry, and not a little deliberate duplicity and cunning.

A decade ago, there was reluctance on the part of national governments and international agencies to include the environmental dimension in their strategies of development. This reluctance has given way to acceptance, and 'sustainable development' has become a universal slogan. Yet nothing much seems to have changed in mainstream development policy. There is no genuine striving towards an alternative perspective on development, no ethical shift that makes sustainable development a reality. 'Sustainability' has been adopted as rhetoric, not as an ethical principle which restructures our relationship with the Earth and its creatures in the realm of knowledge and in arenas of action.

In the absence of an ethical imperative, environmentalism has been reduced to a technological fix, and as with all technological fixes, solutions are seen to lie once more in the hands of manager technocrats. Economic growth, propelled by intensive technology and fuelled by an excessive exploitation of nature, was once viewed as a major factor in environmental degradation; it has suddenly been given the central role in solving the environmental crisis. The market economy is given an even more significant role in organizing nature and society. The environmentalist label and the sustainability slogan have become deceptive jargons that are used as convenient covers for conducting business as usual. This is particularly the case with the world's privileged groups, whose privileges are tied to the status quo, and who will therefore hold on to those privileges as long as they can.

But there are other voices which give a different meaning to sustainability, one which is rooted in ethics, not in monetary policy, and which goes hand in hand with the striving towards an alternative mode of development. Without such striving, 'sustainability' is an empty term, because the current model of development destroys nature's wealth and hence is non-sustainable. And it is ecologically destructive *because* it is ethically vacuous—not impelled by basic values, and not anchored in concepts of rights and responsibilities. Thinking and acting ecologically is basically a matter of ethics, of respecting the rights of other beings, both human and non-human.

[First I] will address these two opposing meanings of 'sustainability' and their respective development paradigms. [I] will differentiate between sustainability as a narrow economic ideal and sustainability as an ethical ideal, between sustainability of privileges and sustainability of life on Earth. Once the conflict was between 'environment' and 'development'. I now see a conflict between the two meanings of 'sustainable development', because sustainability has become everyone's catchword, even though it means entirely different things to different people.

Later I shall lay out the profile of an alternative design for development, one which is environmentally and ethically sound, and at the same time economically, socially, and politically just. But before I do, it is necessary to provide an analysis of the reasons why the present mode of development which once held out such promise and gave rise to the vision of 'continuous progress for all' has come to grief. In what follows, I shall provide such an analysis in the context of the fast-changing processes of history, their philosophical underpinning, and their consequences for the politics of development. We shall see that it is more from the striving of ordinary folk as they face the modern trauma that new possibilities might emerge than from the doings of counter-elites spawned by social movements, though the catalytic role of the latter should not be underestimated. The issue is less whose efforts should succeed than which interventions are likely to endure because they are ethically grounded.

The Crisis in World Order

We may begin with some fundamentals. The most fundamental point to grasp is that we live in a period of profound transformation which is engulfing and interlocking diverse regions, cultures, and ecosystems into a common enterprise, and in the process giving rise to new conflicts waged on a scale unheard of in earlier times. Whereas thinkers from time immemorial have defined the human predicament as the need to overcome conflict through some kind of a social order, most of them thought in terms of a single society, or of conflicts between two or more societies. *For the first time we are realizing that the human predicament is on a world scale.* And all actors in it, and perhaps most of all the weakest and the most deprived among them, need to think in terms that cover all persons and societies. The end of colonialism, the unprecedented increase in population, the urgency of the economic problem, the sudden sense of the bounties of nature drying up, and a feeling of scarcity of basic resources in place of a feeling of continuous progress—all point, on the one hand, to a scenario of growing conflict that will become worldwide in scope, and on the other hand, to the need to work out new solutions based on a new structure of human cooperation.

It is only by thinking in terms of a new concept of ordering the world as a whole that there can be any salvation for a humanity that has lost its moorings. This will require new ways of attending to human problems; but it is not impossible to do this once the problems become clear, and we are able to move out of the old grooves in which we habitually think.

It is necessary to grasp this point. For it is only at times of deep crisis that major changes become possible, for better or for worse, and human beings are capable of both. It is a time when we can either seize the opportunity by deciding to control our future and usher in a new era, or we may miss the opportunity and be pushed into a downward course by forces beyond our control, after which it may be difficult to retrieve lost ground. That we are caught in such a historic moment should be clear to anyone who reflects on the concrete realities of the world we live in and the developments taking place in different parts of this world—in economics, in politics, in the availability and distribution of resources, in the relationship between food and population, in patterns of trade and control of technology, and in the strategic and power relations in which the different nations and regions find themselves confronting each other.

The Causes of World Crisis

Now while it is recognized that the contemporary human condition is one of a deepening crisis, perception as to the nature of the crisis and its causes has changed over the last two decades. For a long time—and this view still persists—the crisis was perceived in terms of an ideological struggle between different ways of life and systems of belief, not infrequently associated with a struggle for power between rival blocs of countries. A very large part of human energy and world resources was devoted to this conflict, which is by no means over and which in no small way accounts for the terrible arms race that enveloped the world and still persists. Later, attention focused on something more

immediate and very pressing, but which had somehow escaped human sensitivity for so long: the great economic schism that is dividing the world into
extremes of affluence and deprivation, with concentrations of poverty, scarcity,
and unemployment in one vast section, and over-abundance, over-production,
and over-consumption in another and much smaller section. Furthermore,
both these are in a relationship in which resources from the poorer regions have
for long been drained, and continue to be drained, through new instruments of
appropriation. The last few years have witnessed an increasing concern with
this single problem of poverty and inequity on a global scale, though it must be
admitted that very little has been done systematically to solve it; indeed, it has
been getting worse.

All these perceptions of the nature of the human crisis are still relevant. But
perhaps one needs to think beyond single dimensions and look to more fundamental causes. After all, the fact that a century of unprecedented material
progress has also been one of sprawling misery and increasing domination of
the world by just a few powers suggests that there is something basically wrong
with our world and the global structures that have permeated it. Indeed, there
is something basically wrong with the way modern humanity has gone about
constructing its world.

Industrialization was supposed to be an end to the condition of scarcity for
humankind as a whole; in fact, it has made even ordinary decent existence
more scarce and inaccessible for an increasing number of human beings. Modern education was supposed to lead to continuous progress and enlightenment
for all, and with that a greater equality among men and women; in fact, it has
produced a world dominated by experts, bureaucrats, and technocrats, one in
which the ordinary human being feels increasingly powerless. Similarly, modern communication and transportation were supposed to produce a 'small
world' in which the fruits of knowledge and development in one part of the
globe could become available to all the others; in fact, modern communication
and transportation have produced a world in which a few metropolitan centres
are sucking in a large part of world resources and depriving the other regions of
whatever comforts, skills, and local resources they once used to enjoy. Surely
then there is something more deeply wrong with the structure of this world
than the mere production of nuclear weapons or the economic handicap of the
poorer countries. The world in which we live is indeed very badly divided, but
the divisions are more fundamental than those of ideology, or of military or
economic power. Perhaps there is something wrong with the *basic model of life*
humankind has created in the modern age.

Colonizing the Future

That this might indeed be the case is indicated by the rupture that has occurred
for the first time in world history between the present and the future, the

future including both the very young among us and the yet-unborn generations. While rational anticipation and prudence in preparing oneself against the
future were inherent in all earlier thought, the future consequences of present
action were never as morally relevant and urgent as they are today.

This is a result of the basic way of life we have created in the modern age,
especially our creation of modern technology. Technology has a powerful impact on beings that have no voice in decisions regarding how technology is to be
used. As the growing economic, energy, and environmental crises are now
showing us, decisions taken at one point in time have the power to affect future
generations in ways that are by and large irreversible. The consequences of
what our parents and the older generation among us did—the ravaging of
nature, the depletion of resources, the pattern of investment, the stockpiling of
armaments, the building of highly centralized economic and political structures that are difficult to change (except by long struggle and violence)—are
being felt by the younger generation of today. How is one to assure that the
interest of the younger generation and the yet-to-be-born generations of the
future are somehow represented in the present? They have no voice in the
decision-making processes of modern society, least of all in representative
systems of government of which only the old (whom we prefer to call 'adults')
have a monopoly. It was once an assumption of planning and of prudence
generally that one must sacrifice or postpone gratification in the present so that
the future generations can live a better life. In fact, modern civilization does
just the opposite. We are so involved in our own gratification in the present,
stimulated by the mass media and advertisement agencies, that we are sacrificing the life chances of future generations.

Thus, just as decisions made in the metropolitan centres of the world and
their ever-rising consumption of finite resources are adversely affecting millions of people in far-off places, decisions made by the present generation are
affecting and will continue to affect the future of the young and the yet-unborn
generations. These are serious questions to which the present models of politics and economics provide no answer. They call for a different kind of consciousness, one which takes a total view of existence; empathizes with the
weak, the distant, the unborn, and the inarticulate; and intervenes in legislative and administrative processes at various levels of the world without, however, degenerating into some kind of brahminical class that arrogates to itself
all knowledge and wisdom. As yet such consciousness (which no doubt exists
here and there) is still very dim and, at any rate, not very influential in the
decision-making processes of business and government. But the need for someone to represent the future—the 'last child', the 'seventh generation'—in the
decisions made in the present cannot be overemphasized.[1]

Sustainability cannot be real if the future itself is colonized. Sustainability
therefore cannot be realized by those who have only learned how to act in the
short term. For real lessons in sustainability we need to turn to peoples and

cultures that have acted on behalf of future generations. Women, particularly Third World women, who produce sustenance for their children are intimately in touch with the future through their nurturance. It is little wonder that ecology movements, like Chipko in India, spring from these cultural pockets which have conserved the qualities of caring—caring for the 'last man' as Gandhi asked his countrymen to do, or the 'last child' as I would like to put it.[2] The Native Americans, who also have a special commitment to the future as part of their understanding of nature's ways, have conceptualized it in an even more telling way: to use and protect nature's creation 'so that seven generations from this day our children will enjoy the same things we have now'. Oren Lyons, spokesman for the traditional circles of elders, has been carrying this message into the contemporary world, pleading:

> Take care how you place your moccasins upon the earth, step with care, for the faces of the future generations are looking up from earth waiting their turn for life.
>
> Today belongs to us, tomorrow we'll give it to the children, but today is ours. You have the mandate, you have the responsibility. Take care of your people—not yourselves, your people.[3]

Colonizing Nature

That our basic model of life is wrong is also indicated by what we have done to other species and forms of life as well as to inanimate nature. We increasingly destroy other animal species, vegetation, the chemical sources of life, and the seabeds and rocky lands whose bounty has been the source of so much imagination, wonder, joy, and creativity. Springing from the unending acquisitiveness of our technological way of life and a concomitant decline in our sensitivity to other humans, we have been on a rampage that threatens our common organic bond with the whole of creation—and thus both our own survival and that of other species.

Modern humanity, and in particular Western technological humanity, has accumulated wealth by denying the rights of others to share in nature's bounty. These 'others' include marginal communities (tribes and small villages), future generations, and other species. Inequality, non-sustainability, and ecological instability all arise from the selfish and arrogant notion that nature's gifts are for private exploitation, not for sharing. In contrast to this rapaciousness, many cultures of the world have based their relationship with nature on the assumption that human beings are members of the Earth family, and must respect the rights of other members of the family. In traditional India, human beings were believed to be part of the cosmic family—*Vasudhevkutamkam*. The belief that trees and plants, rivers and mountains have intrinsic value created ethical constraints on human use of the environment. Hunters and gatherers have always apologized to nature before killing plants and animals. Rural women in India offer leaves to the tree goddess, *Patnadevi*, before collecting fodder from the forest.

The living Earth has a right to life, and that right is the primary moral argument for sustainable life. As Aldo Leopold has pointed out, ethics is the recognition of constraints put on an individual as a member of a community, and the ecological ethic simply enlarges the boundaries of the community to include soils, waters, plants, and animals, or collectively, the land.[4] The modern West is slowly rediscovering the ethics of nature's rights as the basis for conservation and ecological recovery. The Earth is no longer just a bundle of resources. As James Lovelock has suggested, she is *Gaia*, a living being.[5] Animals are not just resources and game for human consumption. Peter Singer has argued for animal liberation as a component of human liberation.[6] And Christopher Stone has raised the issue of whether trees have rights.[7] The women of Gharwal, the backbone of the Chipko movement, who risked their lives to save their trees, clearly believe that trees have rights, and that the rights of trees are of a higher order than those of human beings because trees provide the *conditions* for life on Earth.

Sustainability ultimately rests on the democracy of all life, on the recognition that human beings are not masters but members of the Earth family.

Human Capacities for a New World Order

None of these issues—the rampage of technology, the divisions of global society, the sacrifice of the life chances of future generations, or the destruction of other species and other sources of life and sustenance—were adequately raised in earlier philosophical discussions about the human predicament. The predicament that faces humankind today includes all these issues; and the salvation that we must work out for ourselves and for the whole of nature must address itself to all these issues. In this sense, the crisis that we face is far more total than ever before.

And yet, human beings throughout history have shown an almost infinite capacity for identifying their own immediate purposes with larger purposes. We have come a long way from the primeval stage when we identified with just a few of our kind and cared little for others. Today we are able to identify not only with our own national or regional collectivity but with the whole of the human species, and even with non-human species. Our capacity to symbolize and identify with abstract entities enables us to think in cosmic terms and embrace entities and identities that range from the ephemeral to the eternal.

Nor is this entirely new. At many times in history humanity has shown a striking empathy for the whole of creation. The intellectual and religious movements that led to a deep sense of regard for life in all forms and an abhorrence of violence in all forms, including violence to other forms of life, had their mainsprings in this innate human power to symbolize and identify with creation and to revolt against human excesses. This is what powerful movements like Buddhism and Jainism represented in my own land. Similar movements took place in other regions. It is true that often, as in India, this kind of feeling for life produced a rather quiescent attitude toward life's purposes and even a metaphysic that undermined humanity's self-confidence. It will be necessary to guard against this kind of defeatist religiosity. But such an attitude is by no means inherent in developing a larger identity with creation.

The conclusion I draw is that if there is to be a moral imperative for sustainable development, there needs to be a sense of sanctity about the Earth. Concern for the environment has to emanate from the basic human capacity to experience the sacred, the capacity to wonder at the blessings that are still with us, to seek after the mysteries of the cosmic order, and a corresponding modesty of the self and its claims on that order. Respect for life has to be a fundamentally spiritual notion, based on faith in the inalienable rights of all living beings. The basic sanctions behind them are not contractual but transcendental. They are not primarily claims bestowed by law but are inherent in the very nature of life.

Humanity, then, does have the capacity to create a new world order. Indeed, of all the species only humanity has the capacity to transform its history on a global scale. Human beings are the abstracting animals, the historical animals, the aesthetic animals, the animal that through language, memory, empathy, and will—including the will to transcend the temptations of the moment—can integrate sense perceptions with intricate systems of knowledge, awareness, and morality, as well as with the as yet unknown and unravelled realms of mystery and wonder. Indeed, it is out of these unique capacities that our ultimate salvation must emerge. The predicaments that we face, however, are immediate; we need to move quickly beyond all the structures we have created—political, socioeconomic, and technological—and evolve new criteria for human effort and cooperation.

It is not that humanity must sacrifice all its activities, knowledge, and institutional structures, or surrender all its achievements and start all over again in a clean, new state. Evolution does not take such form. It is rather that our view of which values and purposes should inform our actions and institutions must be consciously re-viewed; and, wherever choices are called for, these should be exercised. We have the capacity to exercise such choices. Maybe some small technological 'breakthrough' in one field or another will again lull us to sleep. But we now know that all such breakthroughs are temporary and cannot take the place of a fundamental restructuring of society. Gadgets may temporarily overpower the mind, but ultimately the mind must come into its own and address itself to the moral questions of life.

The point is that every few hundred years a new challenge presents itself. And each time, it calls for new understanding and a new paradigm of action. Ours is one such moment in the history of humankind and the universe.

The Ethics of Sustainable Development

Contemporary concern for sustainable development is an authentic moral concern to the degree that it poses an alternative to the dominant model of modern development. Its moral significance lies not in the specialized concerns of experts and counter-experts (whether they be professional ethicists, scientists, or technicians), but in a vision of a new way of life that is at once comprehensible and accessible to all human beings.

One can identify four primary criteria for sustainable development when it is conceived as an ethical ideal: a holistic view of development; equity based on the autonomy and self-reliance of diverse entities instead of on a structure of dependence founded on aid and transfer of technology with a view to 'catching up'; an emphasis on participation; and an accent on the importance of local conditions and the value of diversity. To these we must add two still more basic concerns, or rather two broad considerations that should inform all our concerns. One is a fundamentally normative perspective on the future, particularly from the viewpoint of the coming generations for whom we are responsible. The other is a cosmic view of life as sacred.

The report of the World Commission on Environment and Development, *Our Common Future*,[8] is misleading if it suggests that the so-called 'underdeveloped' countries can experience the life they see on Western television programmes without further degradation of the global environment. 'Our common future' cannot lie in an affluence that is ecologically suicidal, and socially and economically exclusive. It can, and must, lie in a curtailment of wants, as Gandhi constantly reminded his countrymen and others.[9] We have more than enough empirical evidence that the destruction of the biosphere lies first and foremost in the wasteful lifestyles of the world's privileged groups, and that the problem of poverty emanates from this same source. Consumption, as an end in itself, excludes the rights of others, both because it makes heavy demands on resources, but also because, in self-gratification, it is blind to others' needs.

The moral approach to development suggested here also involves a certain understanding of how we can most authentically know and relate to the rest of nature. The presumption that the role of science and technology was to develop nature in the service of humankind has turned out to be an illusion. It was based on a view of science itself as an instrument of human power over nature, other men and women, other forms of life, and all the qualities of being that constitute the cosmic order. This must give place to the original purpose of science, namely, seeking to understand the mysteries of nature with a deep sense of humility and wonder. True science is practised by persons with a fundamental philosophical scepticism about the scope and limits of human knowledge, who never for a moment assume that all is knowable and that secular knowledge provides the key to "mastering" the universe. Such a moral vision will make for a partnership between science and nature, and—equally vital—between scientists and all peoples whose lives are rooted in the wisdom of their ancestors. There is a vast area of research and development that lies ahead in this field. The scientist will have to take on a more modest role as a participant in a total system of relationships. As was stressed earlier, one of the basic postulates of an alternative philosophy of development is to treat life as a whole and not in fragments. This calls for a perspective on science that is oriental rather than occidental, feminist rather than *macho*, rural rather than urban, one that draws on the accumulated wisdom of centuries (each succeeding century and generation refining the inherited pool) rather than one that rejects all that is past and traditional.

The shift to sustainable development is primarily an ethical shift. It is not a technological fix, nor a matter of new financial investment. It is a shift in values such that nature is valued in itself and for its life support functions, not merely for how it can be converted into resources and commodities to feed the engine of economic growth. Respect for nature's diversity, and the responsibility to conserve that diversity, define sustainable development as an ethical ideal. Out of an ethics of respect for nature's diversity flows a respect for the diversity of cultures and livelihoods, the basis not only of sustainability, but also of justice and equity. The ecological crisis is in large part a matter of treating nature's diversity as dispensable, a process that has gone hand in hand with the view that a large portion of the human species is dispensable as well. To reverse the ecological decline we require an ethical shift that treats all life as indispensable.

Notes

1. R. Kothari, *Transformation and Survival: In Search of a Humane World Order* (New Delhi: Ajanta, 1988).
2. S. Bahuguna, ed., *Chipko Message* (Chipko Information Centre, Parvatiya Navjivan Mandal, P.O. Silyara, Tehri Gharwal, 1984); Core Group of the United Nations University's Major Project on Peace and Global Transformation, *The Last Child* (Delhi: Lokvani, 1990).
3. O. Lyons, "An Iroquois Perspective," in *American Indian Environments: Ecological Issues in Native American History*, ed. C. Vecsey and R. W. Venables (Syracuse, N.Y.: Syracuse University Press, 1980).
4. A. Leopold, *A Sand County Almanac, and Sketches Here and There* (New York: Oxford University Press, 1949).
5. J. Lovelock, *Gaia: A New Look at Life on Earth* (Oxford: Oxford University Press, 1979).
6. P. Singer, *Animal Liberation*, 2nd ed. (New York: Random House, 1990).
7. C. D. Stone, *Should Trees Have Standing? Toward Legal Rights for Natural Objects* (Los Altos, Calif.: William Kaufmann, 1974).
8. World Commission on Environment and Development, *Our Common Future* (Oxford: Oxford University Press, 1987).
9. J. D. Sethi, *Gandhi Today* (New Delhi: Vikas, 1978).

PART V

――――― ∽ ―――――

Contemporary Issues and Controversies

―― *Wilderness Preservation* ――

FOR MOST American environmentalists, wilderness preservation is of the utmost importance. Not only is wilderness a sanctuary for diverse forms of nonhuman life, but it has the potential to transform our lives and provide experiences that are often described as sacred or sublime. But despite the respect for wilderness acknowledged by most environmentalists, there are serious problems translating the value of wilderness into specific action. As environmental concern has become global in scope, one of the greatest difficulties that has emerged is that of achieving cross-cultural agreement on how environmental values should be put into practice. Wilderness values are rooted in specific cultural traditions that are not always shared by other people across the globe.

Ramachandra Guha, an environmental scientist from India, agrees that wilderness preservation is an important value, but argues that American environmentalists are obsessed with wilderness and that this obsession has detrimental consequences for people in the developing world. The focus on wilderness preservation, Guha suggests, shifts attention away from more important issues that affect a majority of the world's population on a daily basis—problems such as soil erosion, air and water pollution, food security, and fuel shortages. For most people in the developing world, environmental concern is not about protecting ideals such as wilderness or enhancing quality of life, but is a matter of basic survival.

J. Baird Callicott takes up Guha's critique and suggests that American conservationist philosophy is committed to a wilderness idea that is both conceptually flawed and practically unworkable. The idea of wilderness, as defined in the Wilderness Act of 1964, encapsulates the idea that Callicott believes is flawed: "A wilderness, in contrast with those areas where man and his works dominate the landscape, is hereby recognized as an area where the earth and its community of life are untrammeled by man, where man himself is a visitor who does not remain." According to Callicott, this received idea is "dualistic,

239

ethnocentric, and static." It is dualistic in that it separates human culture from wild nature; he argues that humans are a part of nature, like elephants and kudzu, for better or worse. In his view, the wilderness idea is ethnocentric because it overlooks the fact that many areas now considered wilderness were inhabited by aboriginal people; to pretend that these areas were untouched by humans is to say, in effect, that indigenous people don't count as participants in human culture. Finally, Callicott believes that the wilderness idea is static in that it fails to recognize that change is inherent in any natural system.

Holmes Rolston III defends the wilderness idea, maintaining that there are critical differences between nature and culture, as evidenced by the fact that cultural beings can organize to save or destroy nature, while natural beings cannot. The key difference, according to Rolston, is that culture permits great versatility and spontaneity in behavior; thus humans, as cultural beings, can overcome the pressure of natural selection. Rolston criticizes Callicott for blurring these distinctions and worries that such conceptual confusion may lead to the destruction of wilderness. By preserving wilderness, we are preserving important values that allow us to understand ourselves and our morality: "We never get our values straight until we value wilderness appropriately."

As the essays in this section show, the concept of wilderness is more complex than it may at first seem. Despite these difficulties, one thing is clear: wild areas are fast disappearing, and whatever wilderness remains will have to coexist with an expanding human population that demands ever higher standards of living. Preserving wilderness while guaranteeing that all humans have lives worth living is one of the greatest challenges of the next few decades.

Further Reading

Nash, Roderick. *Wilderness and the American Mind,* 3rd ed. New Haven, Conn.: Yale University Press, 1982.

The classic study of American attitudes toward wilderness.

Oelschlaeger, Max, ed. *The Wilderness Condition: Essays on Environment and Civilization.* San Francisco: Sierra Club Books, 1992.

A series of diverse contributions on the status and meaning of wilderness.

Shepard, Paul. *Nature and Madness.* San Francisco: Sierra Club Books, 1982.

A psychohistorical study of the human relationship to nature.

Radical American Environmentalism and Wilderness Preservation: A Third World Critique

$\sim$

Ramachandra Guha

Introduction

The respected radical journalist Kirkpatrick Sale recently celebrated "the passion of a new and growing movement that has become disenchanted with the environmental establishment and has in recent years mounted a serious and sweeping attack on it—style, substance, systems, sensibilities and all."[1] The vision of those whom Sale calls the "New Ecologists"—and what I refer to in this article as deep ecology—is a compelling one. Decrying the narrowly economic goals of mainstream environmentalism, this new movement aims at nothing less than a philosophical and cultural revolution in human attitudes toward nature. In contrast to the conventional lobbying efforts of environmental professionals based in Washington, it proposes a militant defence of "Mother Earth," an unflinching opposition to human attacks on undisturbed wilderness. With their goals ranging from the spiritual to the political, the adherents of deep ecology span a wide spectrum of the American environmental movement. As Sale correctly notes, this emerging strand has in a matter of a few years made its presence felt in a number of fields: from academic philosophy (as in the journal *Environmental Ethics*) to popular environmentalism (e.g., the group Earth First!).

In this article I develop a critique of deep ecology from the perspective of a sympathetic outsider. I critique deep ecology not as a general (or even a foot soldier) in the continuing struggle between the ghosts of Gifford Pinchot and John Muir over control of the U.S. environmental movement, but as an outsider to these battles. I speak admittedly as a partisan, but of the environmental movement in India, a country with an ecological diversity comparable to [that of] the United States, but with a radically dissimilar cultural and social history.

My treatment of deep ecology is primarily historical and sociological, rather than philosophical, in nature. Specifically, I examine the cultural rootedness of a philosophy that likes to present itself in universalistic terms. I make two main arguments: first, that deep ecology is uniquely American, and despite superficial similarities in rhetorical style, the social and political goals of radical environmentalism in other cultural contexts (e.g., West Germany and India) are quite different; second, that the social consequences of putting deep ecology into practice on a worldwide basis (what its practitioners are aiming for) are very grave indeed.

The Tenets of Deep Ecology

While I am aware that the term *deep ecology* was coined by the Norwegian philosopher Arne Naess, this article refers specifically to the American variant. Adherents of the deep ecological perspective in this country, while arguing intensely among themselves over its political and philosophical implications, share some fundamental premises about human–nature interactions. As I see it, the defining characteristics of deep ecology are fourfold.

First, deep ecology argues that the environmental movement must shift from an "anthropocentric" to a "biocentric" perspective. In many respects, an acceptance of the primacy of this distinction constitutes the litmus test of deep ecology. A considerable effort is expended by deep ecologists in showing that the dominant motif in Western philosophy has been anthropocentric—the belief that man and his works are the center of the universe—and conversely, in identifying those lonely thinkers (Leopold, Thoreau, Muir, Aldous Huxley, Santayana, etc.) who, in assigning man a more humble place in the natural order, anticipated deep ecological thinking. In the political realm, meanwhile, establishment environmentalism (shallow ecology) is chided for casting its arguments in human-centered terms. Preserving nature, the deep ecologists say, has an intrinsic worth quite apart from any benefits preservation may convey to future human generations. The anthropocentric–biocentric distinction is accepted as axiomatic by deep ecologists, it structures their discourse, and much of the present discussion remains mired within it.

The second characteristic of deep ecology is its focus on the preservation of unspoilt wilderness and the restoration of degraded areas to a more pristine condition—to the relative (and sometimes absolute) neglect of other issues on the environmental agenda. I later identify the cultural roots and portentous consequences of this obsession with wilderness. For the moment, let me indicate three distinct sources from which it springs. Historically, it represents a playing out of the preservationist (read *radical*) and utilitarian (read *reformist*) dichotomy that has plagued American environmentalism since the turn of the century. Morally, it is an imperative that follows from the biocentric perspective; other species of plants and animals, and nature itself, have an intrinsic right to exist. And finally, the preservation of wilderness also turns on a scientific argument—viz., the value of biological diversity in stabilizing ecological regimes and in retaining a gene pool for future generations. Truly radical policy proposals have been put forward by deep ecologists on the basis of these arguments. The influential poet Gary Snyder, for example, would like to see a 90 percent reduction in human populations to allow a restoration of pristine environments, while others have argued forcefully that a large portion of the globe must be immediately cordoned off from human beings.[2]

Third, there is a widespread invocation of Eastern spiritual traditions as forerunners of deep ecology. Deep ecology, it is suggested, was practiced both by major religious traditions and at a more popular level by "primal" peoples in non-Western settings. This complements the search for an authentic lineage in Western thought. At one level, the task is to recover those dissenting voices within the Judeo-Christian tradition; at another, to suggest that religious traditions in other cultures are, in contrast, dominantly if not exclusively "biocentric" in their orientation. This coupling of (ancient) Eastern and (modern) ecological wisdom seemingly helps consolidate the claim that deep ecology is a philosophy of universal significance.

Fourth, deep ecologists, whatever their internal differences, share the belief that they are the "leading edge" of the environmental movement. As the polarity of the shallow–deep and anthropocentric–biocentric distinctions makes clear, they see themselves as the spiritual, philosophical, and political vanguard of American and world environmentalism.

Toward a Critique

Although I analyze each of these tenets independently, it is important to recognize, as deep ecologists are fond of remarking in reference to nature, the interconnectedness and unity of these individual themes.

1. Insofar as it has begun to act as a check on man's arrogance and ecological hubris, the transition from an anthropocentric (human-centered) to a biocentric (humans as only one element in the ecosystem) view in both religious and scientific traditions is only to be welcomed. What is unacceptable are the radical conclusions drawn by deep ecology, in particular, that intervention in nature should be guided primarily by the need to preserve biotic integrity rather than by the needs of humans. The latter for deep ecologists is anthropocentric, the former biocentric. This dichotomy is, however, of very little use in understanding the dynamics of environmental degradation. The two fundamental ecological problems facing the globe are (i) overconsumption by the industrialized world and by urban elites in the Third World and (ii) growing militarization, both in a short-term sense (i.e., ongoing regional wars) and in a long-term sense (i.e., the arms race and the prospect of nuclear annihilation). Neither of these problems has any tangible connection to the anthropocentric–biocentric distinction. Indeed, the agents of these processes would barely comprehend

this philosophical dichotomy. The proximate causes of the ecologically waste-ful characteristics of industrial society and of militarization are far more mun-dane: at an aggregate level, the dialectic of economic and political structures, and at a micro-level, the life style choices of individuals. These causes cannot be reduced, whatever the level of analysis, to a deeper anthropocentric attitude toward nature; on the contrary, by constituting a grave threat to human sur-vival, the ecological degradation they cause does not even serve the best inter-ests of human beings! If my identification of the major dangers to the integrity of the natural world is correct, invoking the bogy of anthropocentricism is at best irrelevant and at worst a dangerous obfuscation.

2. If the above dichotomy is irrelevant, the emphasis on wilderness is posi-tively harmful when applied to the Third World. If in the United States the preservationist–utilitarian division is seen as mirroring the conflict between "people" and "interests," in countries such as India the situation is very nearly the reverse. Because India is a long settled and densely populated country in which agrarian populations have a finely balanced relationship with nature, the setting aside of wilderness areas has resulted in a direct transfer of resources from the poor to the rich. Thus, Project Tiger, a network of parks hailed by the international conservation community as an outstanding success, sharply pos-its the interests of the tiger against those of poor peasants living in and around the reserve. The designation of tiger reserves was made possible only by the physical displacement of existing villages and their inhabitants; their manage-ment requires the continuing exclusion of peasants and livestock. The initial impetus for setting up parks for the tiger and other large mammals such as the rhinoceros and elephant came from two social groups, first, a class of ex-hunters turned conservationists belonging mostly to the declining Indian feu-dal elite and second, representatives of international agencies, such as the World Wildlife Fund (WWF) and the International Union for the Conservation of Nature and Natural Resources (IUCN), seeking to transplant the American system of national parks onto Indian soil. In no case have the needs of the local population been taken into account, and as in many parts of Africa, the desig-nated wildlands are managed primarily for the benefit of rich tourists. Until very recently, wildlands preservation has been identified with environmental-ism by the state and the conservation elite; in consequence, environmental problems that impinge far more directly on the lives of the poor—e.g., fuel, fodder, water shortages, soil erosion, and air and water pollution—have not been adequately addressed.[3]

Deep ecology provides, perhaps unwittingly, a justification for the continua-tion of such narrow and inequitable conservation practices under a newly acquired radical guise. Increasingly, the international conservation elite is us-ing the philosophical, moral, and scientific arguments used by deep ecologists in advancing their wilderness crusade. A striking but by no means atypical example is the recent plea by a prominent American biologist for the takeover of large portions of the globe by the author and his scientific colleagues. Writing in a prestigious scientific forum, the *Annual Review of Ecology and Systematics*, Daniel Janzen argues that only biologists have the competence to decide how the tropical landscape should be used. As "the representatives of the natural world," biologists are "in charge of the future of tropical ecology," and only they have the expertise and mandate to "determine whether the tropical agroscape is to be populated only by humans, their mutualists, commensals, and parasites, or whether it will also contain some islands of the greater nature—the nature that spawned humans, yet has been vanquished by them." Janzen exhorts his colleagues to advance their territorial claims on the tropical world more forcefully, warning that the very existence of these areas is at stake: "if biologists want a tropics in which to biologize, they are going to have to buy it with care, energy, effort, strategy, tactics, time, and cash."[4]

This frankly imperialist manifesto highlights the multiple dangers of the preoccupation with wilderness preservation that is characteristic of deep ecology. As I have suggested, it seriously compounds the neglect by the American movement of far more pressing environmental problems within the Third World. But perhaps more importantly, and in a more insidious fashion, it also provides an impetus to the imperialist yearning of Western biologists and their financial sponsors, organizations such as the WWF and IUCN. The wholesale transfer of a movement culturally rooted in American conservation history can only result in the social uprooting of human populations in other parts of the globe.

3. I come now to the persistent invocation of Eastern philosophies as antecedent in point of time but convergent in their structure with deep ecology. Complex and internally differentiated religious traditions—Hinduism, Buddhism, and Taoism—are lumped together as holding a view of nature believed to be quintessentially biocentric. Individual philosophers such as the Taoist Lao Tzu are identified as being forerunners of deep ecology. Even an intensely political, pragmatic, and Christian-influenced thinker such as Gandhi has been accorded a wholly undeserved place in the deep ecological pantheon. Thus the Zen teacher Robert Aitken Roshi makes the strange claim that Gandhi's thought was not human-centered and that he practiced an embryonic form of deep ecology which is "traditionally Eastern and is found with differing emphasis in Hinduism, Taoism and in Theravada and Mahayana Buddhism."[5] Moving away from the realm of high philosophy and scriptural religion, deep ecologists make the further claim that at the level of material and spiritual practice "primal" peoples subordinated themselves to the integrity of the biotic universe they inhabited.

I have indicated that this appropriation of Eastern traditions is in part dictated by the need to construct an authentic lineage and in part a desire to present deep ecology as a universalistic philosophy. Indeed, in his substantial and quixotic biography of John Muir, Michael Cohen goes so far as to suggest that Muir was the "Taoist of the [American] West."⁶ This reading of Eastern traditions is selective and does not bother to differentiate between alternate (and changing) religious and cultural traditions; as it stands, it does considerable violence to the historical record. Throughout most recorded history the characteristic form of human activity in the "East" has been a finely tuned but nonetheless conscious and dynamic manipulation of nature. Although mystics such as Lao Tzu did reflect on the spiritual essence of human relations with nature, it must be recognized that such ascetics and their reflections were supported by a society of cultivators whose relationship with nature was a far more *active* one. Many agricultural communities do have a sophisticated knowledge of the natural environment that may equal (and sometimes surpass) codified "scientific" knowledge; yet, the elaboration of such traditional ecological knowledge (in both material and spiritual contexts) can hardly be said to rest on a mystical affinity with nature of a deep ecological kind. Nor is such knowledge infallible; as the archaeological record powerfully suggests, modern Western man has no monopoly on ecological disasters.

In a brilliant article, the Chicago historian Ronald Inden points out that this romantic and essentially positive view of the East is a mirror image of the scientific and essentially pejorative view normally upheld by Western scholars of the Orient. In either case, the East constitutes the Other, a body wholly separate and alien from the West; it is defined by a uniquely spiritual and nonrational "essence," even if this essence is valorized quite differently by the two schools. Eastern man exhibits a spiritual dependence with respect to nature—on the one hand, this is symptomatic of his prescientific and backward self, on the other, of his ecological wisdom and deep ecological consciousness. Both views are monolithic, simplistic, and have the characteristic effect—intended in one case, perhaps unintended in the other—of denying agency and reason to the East and making it the privileged orbit of Western thinkers.

The two apparently opposed perspectives have then a common underlying structure of discourse in which the East merely serves as a vehicle for Western projections. Varying images of the East are raw material for political and cultural battles being played out in the West; they tell us far more about the Western commentator and his desires than about the "East." Inden's remarks apply not merely to Western scholarship on India, but to Orientalist constructions of China and Japan as well:

> Although these two views appear to be strongly opposed, they often combine together. Both have a similar interest in sustaining the Otherness of India. The holders of the dominant view, best exemplified in the past in imperial administrative discourse (and today probably by that of "development economics"), would place a traditional, superstition-ridden India in a position of perpetual tutelage to a modern, rational West. The adherents of the romantic view, best exemplified academically in the discourses of Christian liberalism and analytic

psychology, concede the realm of the public and impersonal to the positivist. Taking their succour not from governments and big business, but from a plethora of religious foundations and self-help institutes, and from allies in the "consciousness industry," not to mention the important industry of tourism, the romantics insist that India embodies a private realm of the imagination and the religious which modern, western man lacks but needs. They, therefore, like the positivists, but for just the opposite reason, have a vested interest in seeing that the Orientalist view of India as "spiritual," "mysterious," and "exotic" is perpetuated.[7]

4. How radical, finally, are the deep ecologists? Notwithstanding their self-image and strident rhetoric (in which the label "shallow ecology" has an opprobrium similar to that reserved for "social democratic" by Marxist-Leninists), even within the American context their radicalism is limited and it manifests itself quite differently elsewhere.

To my mind, deep ecology is best viewed as a radical trend within the wilderness preservation movement. Although advancing philosophical rather than aesthetic arguments and encouraging political militancy rather than negotiation, its practical emphasis—viz., preservation of unspoilt nature—is virtually identical. For the mainstream movement, the function of wilderness is to provide a temporary antidote to modern civilization. As a special institution within an industrialized society, the national park "provides an opportunity for respite, contrast, contemplation, and affirmation of values for those who live most of their lives in the workaday world."[8] Indeed, the rapid increase in visitations to the national parks in postwar America is a direct consequence of economic expansion. The emergence of a popular interest in wilderness sites, the historian Samuel Hays points out, was "not a throwback to the primitive, but an integral part of the modern standard of living as people sought to add new 'amenity' and 'aesthetic' goals and desires to their earlier preoccupation with necessities and conveniences."[9]

Here, the enjoyment of nature is an integral part of the consumer society. The private automobile (and the life style it has spawned) is in many respects the ultimate ecological villain, and an untouched wilderness the prototype of ecological harmony; yet, for most Americans it is perfectly consistent to drive a thousand miles to spend a holiday in a national park. They possess a vast, beautiful, and sparsely populated continent and are also able to draw upon the natural resources of large portions of the globe by virtue of their economic and political dominance. In consequence, America can simultaneously enjoy the material benefits of an expanding economy and the aesthetic benefits of unspoilt nature. The two poles of "wilderness" and "civilization" mutually coexist in an internally coherent whole, and philosophers of both poles are assigned a prominent place in this culture. Paradoxically as it may seem, it is no accident that Star Wars technology and deep ecology both find their fullest expression in that leading sector of Western civilization, California.

Deep ecology runs parallel to the consumer society without seriously questioning its ecological and socio-political basis. In its celebration of American
wilderness, it also displays an uncomfortable convergence with the prevailing
climate of nationalism in the American wilderness movement. For spokesmen
such as the historian Roderick Nash, the national park system is America's
distinctive cultural contribution to the world, reflective not merely of its economic but of its philosophical and ecological maturity as well. In what Walter
Lippmann called the American century, the "American invention of national
parks" must be exported worldwide. Betraying an economic determinism that
would make even a Marxist shudder, Nash believes that environmental preservation is a "full stomach" phenomenon that is confined to the rich, urban, and
sophisticated. Nonetheless, he hopes that "the less developed nations may
eventually evolve economically and intellectually to the point where nature
preservation is more than a business."[10]

The error which Nash makes (and which deep ecology in some respects
encourages) is to equate environmental protection with the protection of wilderness. This is a distinctively American notion, borne out of a unique social and
environmental history. The archetypal concerns of radical environmentalists in
other cultural contexts are in fact quite different. The German Greens, for
example, have elaborated a devastating critique of industrial society which
turns on the acceptance of environmental limits to growth. Pointing to the
intimate links between industrialization, militarization, and conquest, the
Greens argue that economic growth in the West has historically rested on the
economic and ecological exploitation of the Third World. Rudolf Bahro is
characteristically blunt:

> The working class here [in the West] is the richest lower class in the world.
> And if I look at the problem from the point of view of the whole of humanity,
> not just from that of Europe, then I must say that the metropolitan working
> class is the worst exploiting class in history. . . . What made poverty bearable
> in eighteenth- or nineteenth-century Europe was the prospect of escaping it
> through exploitation of the periphery. But this is no longer a possibility, and
> continued industrialism in the Third World will mean poverty for whole gen-
> erations and hunger for millions.[11]

Here the roots of global ecological problems lie in the disproportionate share
of resources consumed by the industrialized countries as a whole *and* the urban
elite within the Third World. Since it is impossible to reproduce an industrial
monoculture worldwide, the ecological movement in the West must begin by
cleaning up its own act. The Greens advocate the creation of a "no growth"
economy, to be achieved by scaling down current (and clearly unsustainable)
consumption levels. This radical shift in consumption and production patterns
requires the creation of alternate economic and political structures—smaller in
scale and more amenable to social participation—but it rests equally on a shift

in cultural values. The expansionist character of modern Western man will have to give way to an ethic of renunciation and self-limitation, in which spiritual and communal values play an increasing role in sustaining social life. This revolution in cultural values, however, has as its point of departure an understanding of environmental processes quite different from deep ecology.

Many elements of the Green program find a strong resonance in countries such as India, where a history of Western colonialism and industrial develop- ment has benefited only a tiny elite while exacting tremendous social and environmental costs. The ecological battles presently being fought in India have as their epicenter the conflict over nature between the subsistence and largely rural sector and the vastly more powerful commercial-industrial sector. Perhaps the most celebrated of these battles concerns the Chipko (Hug the Tree) movement, a peasant movement against deforestation in the Himalayan foothills. Chipko is only one of several movements that have sharply ques- tioned the nonsustainable demand being placed on the land and vegetative base by urban centers and industry. These include opposition to large dams by displaced peasants, the conflict between small artisan fishing and large-scale trawler fishing for export, the countrywide movements against commercial forest operations, and opposition to industrial pollution among downstream agricultural and fishing communities.[12]

Two features distinguish these environmental movements from their Western counterparts. First, for the sections of society most critically affected by environ- mental degradation—poor and landless peasants, women, and tribals—it is a question of sheer survival, not of enhancing the quality of life. Second, and as a consequence, the environmental solutions they articulate deeply involve ques- tions of equity as well as economic and political redistribution. Highlighting these differences, a leading Indian environmentalist stresses that "environmen- tal protection per se is of least concern to most of these groups. Their main concern is about the use of the environment and who should benefit from it."[13] They seek to wrest control of nature away from the state and the industrial sector and place it in the hands of rural communities who live within that environment but are increasingly denied access to it. These communities have far more basic needs, their demands on the environment are far less intense, and they can draw upon a reservoir of cooperative social institutions and local ecological knowledge in managing the "commons"—forests, grasslands, and the waters—on a sustain- able basis. If colonial and capitalist expansion has both accentuated social in- equalities and signaled a precipitous fall in ecological wisdom, an alternate ecology must rest on an alternate society and polity as well.

This brief overview of German and Indian environmentalism has some major implications for deep ecology. Both German and Indian environmental tradi- tions allow for a greater integration of ecological concerns with livelihood and work. They also place a greater emphasis on equity and social justice (both within individual countries and on a global scale) on the grounds that in the absence of social regeneration environmental regeneration has very little chance of succeeding. Finally, and perhaps most significantly, they have escaped the preoccupation with wilderness perservation so characteristic of American cultural and environmental history.

A Homily

In 1958, the economist J. K. Galbraith referred to overconsumption as the unasked question of the American conservation movement. There is a marked selectivity, he wrote, "in the conservationists approach to materials consumption. If we are concerned about our great appetite for materials, it is plausible to seek to increase the supply, to decrease waste, to make better use of the stocks available, and to develop substitutes. But what of the appetite itself? Surely this is the ultimate source of the problem. If it continues its geometric course, will it not one day have to be restrained? Yet in the literature of the resource problem this is the forbidden question. Over it hangs a nearly total silence."[14]

The consumer economy and society have expanded tremendously in the three decades since Galbraith penned these words; yet his criticisms are nearly as valid today. I have said "nearly," for there are some hopeful signs. Within the environmental movement several dispersed groups are working to develop ecologically benign technologies and to encourage less wasteful life styles. Moreover, outside the self-defined boundaries of American environmentalism, opposition to the permanent war economy is being carried on by a peace movement that has a distinguished history and impeccable moral and political credentials.

It is precisely these (to my mind, most hopeful) components of the American social scene that are missing from deep ecology. In their widely noticed book, Bill Devall and George Sessions make no mention of militarization or the movements for peace, while activists whose practical focus is on developing ecologically responsible life styles (e.g., Wendell Berry) are derided as "falling short of deep ecological awareness."[15] A truly radical ecology in the American context ought to work toward a synthesis of the appropriate technology, alternate life style, and peace movements. By making the (largely spurious) anthropocentric–biocentric distinction central to the debate, deep ecologists may have appropriated the moral high ground, but they are at the same time doing a serious disservice to American and global environmentalism.[16]

Notes

I am grateful to Mike Bell, Tom Birch, Bill Burch, Bill Cronon, Diane Mayerfeld, David Rothenberg, Kirkpatrick Sale, Joel Seton, Tim Weiskel, and Don Worster for helpful comments.

1. K. Sale, "The Forest for the Trees: Can Today's Environmentalists Tell the Difference," *Mother Jones* 11 (November 1986): 26.

2. Quoted in ibid., 32.

3. See Centre for Science and Environment, *India: The State of the Environment 1982: A Citizens Report* (New Delhi: Centre for Science and Environment, 1982), and R. Sukumar, "Elephant–Man Conflict in Karnataka," in *The State of Karnataka's Environment*, ed. C. Saldanha (Bangalore: Centre for Taxonomic Studies, 1985). For Africa, see the brilliant analysis by H. Kjekshus, *Ecology Control and Economic Development in East African History* (Berkeley: University of California Press, 1977).

4. D. Janzen, "The Future of Tropical Ecology," *Annual Review of Ecology and Systematics* 17 (1986): 305–6.

5. R. A. Roshi, "Gandhi, Dogen, and Deep Ecology," reprinted as appendix C in B. Devall and G. Sessions, *Deep Ecology: Living as if Nature Mattered* (Salt Lake City: Peregrine Smith, 1985). For Gandhi's own views on social reconstruction, see the excellent three-volume collection edited by R. Iyer, *The Moral and Political Writings of Mahatma Gandhi* (Oxford: Clarendon Press, 1986–1987).

6. M. Cohen, *The Pathless Way* (Madison: University of Wisconsin Press, 1984), 120.

7. R. Inden, "Orientalist Constructions of India," *Modern Asian Studies* 20 (1986): 442. Inden draws inspiration from E. Said's forceful polemic, *Orientalism* (New York: Basic Books, 1980). It must be noted, however, that there is a salient difference between Western perceptions of Middle Eastern and Far Eastern cultures, respectively. Due perhaps to the long history of Christian conflict with Islam, Middle Eastern cultures (as Said documents) are consistently presented in pejorative terms. The juxtaposition of hostile and worshipping attitudes that Inden talks of applies only to Western attitudes toward Buddhist and Hindu societies.

8. J. Sax, *Mountains Without Handrails: Reflections on the National Parks* (Ann Arbor: University of Michigan Press, 1980), 42.

9. S. P. Hays, "From Conservation to Environment: Environmental Politics in the United States since World War Two," *Environmental Review* 6 (1982): 21. See also S. P. Hays, *Beauty, Health, and Permanence: Environmental Politics in the United States, 1955–1985* (Cambridge: Cambridge University Press, 1987).

10. R. Nash, *Wilderness and the American Mind*, 3rd ed. (New Haven, Conn.: Yale University Press, 1982).

11. R. Bahro, *From Red to Green* (London: Verso Books, 1984).

12. For an excellent review, see A. Agarwal and S. Narain, eds., *India: The State of the Environment, 1984–1985: A Citizens Report* (New Delhi: Centre for Science and Environment, 1985). See also R. Guha, *The Unquiet Woods: Ecological Change and Peasant Resistance in the Indian Himalaya* (Berkeley: University of California Press, 1990).

13. A. Agarwal, "Human–Nature Interactions in a Third World Country," *Environmentalist* 6 (1986): 167.

14. J. K. Galbraith, "How Much Should a Country Consume?" in *Perspectives on Conservation*, ed. Henry Jarrett (Baltimore: Johns Hopkins University Press, 1958), 91–92.

15. Devall and Sessions, *Deep Ecology*, 122. For Wendell Berry's own assessment of deep ecology, see his "Amplications: Preserving Wildness," *Wilderness* 50 (1987): 39–40, 50–54.

16. In this sense, my critique of deep ecology, although that of an outsider, may facilitate the reassertion of those elements in the American environmental tradition for

which there is a profound sympathy in other parts of the globe. A global perspective may also lead to a critical reassessment of figures such as Aldo Leopold and John Muir, the two patron saints of deep ecology. As Donald Worster has pointed out, the message of Muir (and, I would argue, of Leopold as well) makes sense only in an American context; he has very little to say to other cultures. See Worster's review of Stephen Fox's *John Muir and His Legacy,* in *Environmental Ethics* 5 (1983): 277–81.

[From] The Wilderness Idea Revisited: The Sustainable Development Alternative

J. Baird Callicott

. . . [T]HE DIALECTICAL HISTORY of American conservation philosophy has fostered a . . . recent popular wilderness fallacy. That fallacy has two closely connected formulations. The first is that the New World was, when Christopher Columbus stumbled upon it, in a totally "wilderness condition"—as Nash famously characterizes it.[1] The second is that any human alteration of pristine nature degrades it, and therefore biological conservation is served best by wilderness preservation; that is, the best way to conserve nature is to protect it from human inhabitation and utilization.

Here I briefly review the history of American conservation philosophy and the role that the wilderness idea has played in it. Then I argue that wilderness preservation, as a conservation stratagem, needs to be . . . not replaced, certainly, since nature reserves now fill and will continue to fill a vital niche in a more broadly conceived struggle to conserve biodiversity, but . . . refined, and augmented by a complementary approach. Having said what I am revisiting critically, let me set out as clearly and explicitly as I can a few caveats and qualifications.

First, I am as ardent an advocate of those patches of the planet called "wilderness areas" as any other environmentalist. My discomfort is with an idea, the received concept of wilderness, not with the ecosystems, so called.

Second, to suggest that something is amiss with the concept of wilderness is to suggest, at the same time, that something is amiss with its antithesis, the concept of civilization. Implicit in the most passionate pleas for wilderness preservation is a complacency about what passes for civilization. If all that we can feature is the present adolescent state of civilization and its mechanical motif continuing indefinitely into the future, then naturally the only way we can conceive of conserving nature is to protect bits of it from destructive development. A harmony-of-man-and-nature conservation philosophy such as Leopold espoused implies re-envisioning civilization as well as critically revisiting the wilderness idea.

Therefore, third, I do not advocate what is euphemistically called "multiple use" for all landscapes. I do not suggest we attempt to mix strip-mining, clear-cutting, stock-grazing, four-wheeling, downhill-skiing, and motor-camping with biological conservation. By suggesting that we try to shift the burden of conservation from wilderness preservation to sustainable development, I mean to suggest that we try to think up economic strategies that are compatible with ecosystem health and that are limited strictly by ecological exigencies. There is precious little designated wilderness as things stand. Such areas serve the cause of biological conservation most importantly as refugia for species not tolerant of or tolerated by people. Personally, I would like to see more wild lands designated as wilderness with this purpose in view, but given a global human population approaching 6 billion persons, the greatest part of the best land will be put to economic use whether we conservationists like it or not. We conservationists, however, may hope realistically that in the future, ecological, as well as technological, feasibility may be taken into account in designing new and redesigning old ways of human living with the land.

The Wilderness Idea in Historic American Conservation Philosophy

Ralph Waldo Emerson and Henry David Thoreau were the first notable American thinkers to insist, a century and a half ago, that wild nature might serve "higher" human spiritual values, as well as supply raw materials for meeting our more mundane physical needs. Nature can be a temple, Emerson enthused, in which to draw near to and commune with God. Too much civilized refinement, Thoreau argued, can over-ripen the human spirit; just as too little can coarsen it. "In wildness," he wrote, "is the preservation of the world."[2]

Building on the nature philosophies of Emerson and Thoreau, John Muir spearheaded a national, morally charged campaign for public appreciation and preservation of wilderness.[3] People's going to forest groves, mountain scenery, and meandering streams for religious transcendence, aesthetic contemplation, and healing rest and relaxation puts these resources to a higher and better use, in Muir's opinion, than did the lumber jacks, miners, shepherds, and cowboys who went to the same places in pursuit of the Almighty Dollar, and who were inspired only by the Main Chance.

Critics today, as formerly, may find an undemocratic and un-American presumption lurking in the Romantic-Transcendental conservation philosophies of Emerson, Thoreau, and Muir. To suggest that some of the human satisfactions that nature affords are morally superior to others may reflect only aristocratic biases and class privilege. Let me hasten to say that personally, I agree with Muir et al. Birdwatching, for example, is, in my opinion, morally superior to dirtbiking. But there is a contingent of powerful and influential professionals who do not agree. An axiom of neoclassical economics is that all human preferences concerning "resource" use are morally equal and should be weighed one against the other in the marketplace.

At the turn of the century, Gifford Pinchot, a younger contemporary of John Muir, formulated a novel conservation philosophy that reflected the general tenets of the Progressive era in American history. Notoriously, the country's vast biological capital has been plundered and squandered for the benefit, not of all its citizens, but for the profit of a few. Pinchot crystalized a populist, democratic conservation ethic in a credo—"the greatest good of the greatest number for the longest time"—that echoed John Stuart Mill's famous Utilitarian maxim, "the greatest happiness for the greatest number."[4] He bluntly reduced Emerson's "Nature" (with a capital "N") to "natural resources." Indeed, Pinchot insisted, "There are just two things on this material earth—people and natural resources."[5] He even equated conservation with the systematic exploitation of natural resources. "The first great fact about conservation," Pinchot noted, "is that it stands for development"—with the proviso that resource development be scientific and thus efficient. For those who might take the term "conservation" at face value and suppose that it meant saving natural resources for future use, Pinchot was quick to point out their error: "There has been a fundamental misconception," he wrote, "that conservation means nothing but the husbanding of resources for future generations. There could be no more serious mistake."[6] And it was none other than Pinchot who first characterized the Muirian contingent of nature lovers as aiming to "lock up" resources in the national parks and other wilderness reserves.[7]

The infamous schism in the traditional American conservation movement thus was rent. Muir and Pinchot, once friends and allies, quarreled, and each followed his separate path. Pinchot appropriated the term "conservation" for his utilitarian philosophy of scientific resource development, and Muir and his exponents came to be called "preservationists."

The third giant in twentieth-century American conservation philosophy is, of course, Aldo Leopold. At the Yale Forest School, founded with the help of the Pinchot family fortune, Leopold was steeped in what Hays called "the gospel of efficiency"—the scientific exploitation of natural resources, for the satisfaction of the broadest possible spectrum of human interests, over the longest time.[8] Moreover, for fifteen years Leopold worked for the Forest Service, whose first chief was Pinchot himself. Leopold's ultimately successful struggle for a system of wilderness reserves in the national forests was molded consciously to the doctrine of highest use, and his new science of game management essentially amounted to the direct transference of the principles of forestry from a standing crop of large plants to a standing crop of large animals.[9] However, Leopold gradually came to the conclusion that Pinchot's utilitarian conservation philosophy was inadequate, because it was not well informed by the new kid on the scientific block, ecology. As Leopold put it:

> Ecology is a new fusion point for all the sciences. . . . The emergence of ecology has placed the economic biologist in a peculiar dilemma: with one hand he points out the accumulated findings of his search for utility, or lack of utility, in this or that species; with the other he lifts the veil from a biota so complex, so conditioned by interwoven cooperations and competitions, that no man can say where utility begins or ends.[10]

Conservation, Leopold came to realize, must aim at something larger and more comprehensive than a maximum sustained flow of desirable products (like lumber and game) and experiences (like sport hunting and fishing, wilderness travel, and solitude) garnered from an impassive nature. It must take care to ensure the continued function of ecological processes and the integrity of ecosystems. For it is upon them, ultimately, that human resources and human well-being depend, for the present generation as well as for those to come. Indeed, Leopold quietly transformed the concept of conservation from its pre-ecological to its present deep ecological sense—from conservation understood as the wise use of natural resources to conservation understood as the maintenance of biological diversity and ecological health.

The word "preserve" in the summary moral maxim of Leopold's famous land ethic ("A thing is right when it tends to preserve the integrity, stability, and beauty of the biotic community. It is wrong when it tends otherwise"[11]) is unfortunate, because it seems to ally Leopold with the Preservationists in the familiar Preservation *vs.* Conservation feud. We tend to think of Leopold as having begun his career in the Conservationist camp and then gradually to have come over, armed with new ecological arguments, to the Preservationist camp. Leopold appears to be a mid-twentieth-century conservation prophet emerging from the woods wearing the hat of Gifford Pinchot and speaking with the voice of John Muir. His historical association with the wilderness movement cements this impression.

While still with the Forest Service, Leopold had campaigned hard to preserve a few relics of the American frontier in which he and like-minded sportsmen might play at being pioneers. After becoming a professor of wildlife management, he suggested that the designated wilderness areas he had helped to create might serve threatened species as biotic refugia. In the last decade of his life, he suggested that representative undeveloped biomes might serve science as a "base datum of land health."

While I would be the first to agree that designated and de facto wilderness areas are important as "land laboratories" and vitally important as biotic refugia, Leopold's unfortunate—and unintended—legacy for the American conservation policy debate has been to intensify the familiar alternative: either efficiently exploit the remaining and dwindling wild lands or lock them up and preserve them forever as wildernesses. But a review of his unpublished papers and published, but long-forgotten, articles (now conveniently collected in the new book of his essays) confirms Flader's opinion that Leopold was concerned primarily, in theory as well as on the ground, with integrating an optimal mix of wilderness with human habitation and economic utilization of land.[12]. . . .

Like Pinchot, Leopold attempted to distill his philosophy of conservation into a quotable definition. Indeed, it is often quoted, but little analyzed or appreciated: "Conservation is a state of harmony between men and land."[13] This definition represents a genuine third alternative to Pinchot's brazenly anthropocentric, utilitarian definition of conservation as efficient exploitation of "resources" and Muir's anti-anthropocentric definition of conservation as saving innocent "Nature" from inherently destructive human economic development.

Can we generalize Leopold's vision of an ecologically well-integrated family farm to an ecologically well-integrated technological society? Can we reconcile and integrate human economic activities with biological conservation? Can we achieve "win-win" rather than "zero-sum" solutions to development–environment conflicts? Can we design "sustainable economies," rather than zone the planet into ever-expanding sectors of conventional, destructive development and ever-shrinking wilderness sanctuaries? Can we succeed as a global technological society in enriching the environment as we enrich ourselves?

A Third World Critique of Conservation
Via Wilderness Preservation

I think we can. More to the point, I think we have to. The pressure of growing human numbers and rapid development, especially in the Third World, bodes ill for a global conservation strategy focused primarily on "wilderness" preservation and the establishment of nature sanctuaries. Such a strategy represents a holding action at best and a losing proposition at [worst].

. . . The United Nations biosphere reserve concept . . . specifically requires planners to take account of and to integrate local peoples culturally and economically into reserve designs. However, faced with the harsh realities of the coming century, the wilderness idea—even become the biosphere reserve concept—is, by itself, too little too late, and it is too defensive to save the planet and all of us, its people, from ecological collapse. We need to integrate wildlife sanctuaries into a broader philosophy of conservation that generalizes Leopold's vision of a mutually beneficial and mutually enhancing integration of the human economy with the economy of nature.

Here let me be both clear and emphatic, I am not suggesting that we open the remaining wild remnants to development, but that we begin to reconceive economic development in the light of ecology. Human economic activities should at least be compatible with the ecological health of the environments in which they occur, and, ideally, they should enhance it. In Leopold's agrarian idyll of conservation, not only does the ecological farm family actively manage its wild lands, but it also reforms its farming practices on the fields so that the two, the wild culture and the domestic culture, might coexist better. "Clean farming" was a frequent target of Leopold's pointed criticisms and wry wit; he may have been the first environmentalist clearly to recognize and lament the "industrialization" of agriculture during the twentieth century and the conversion of the classic, relatively benign and sustainable farm, into an environmentally destructive and unsustainable "food-factory."

. . . We who enjoy the benefits of modern industrial civilization with all its environmental costs can salve our consciences by pointing to the few odds and ends of arid, rough, scenic, or remote country that we have set aside, first for our own recreational, aesthetic, and spiritual needs, and second as ecologic refugia—little places where our fellow denizens of planet Earth can live and blossom. In so doing, we can avoid facing up to the fact that the ways and means of industrial civilization lie at the root of the current global environmental crisis. To Ramachandra Guha, the new voice for Third World environmental ethics, conservation via wilderness preservation "runs parallel to the consumer society without seriously questioning its ecological and sociopolitical basis."[14]

Without such questioning, the call of wilderness advocates for the recrudescence of big wilderness is quixotic. Wilderness is one pole of a dualism. To want more of it is to oppose the forces of conventional industrial development, certainly, but not to challenge the conventional conception of economic development. And since it pits—as a one-or-the-other-but-not-both choice—human economic interests against the interests of nature, it has little political appeal, and thus little chance of success.

In the Third World, on the other hand, industrial development often has resulted in human tragedy as well as environmental disaster. The green revolution, for example, has dispossessed small land holders and actually increased chronic hunger as prices fall, costs increase, and crops are exported to First World consumers. Industrial forestry similarly has disrupted traditional patterns of sustainable forest use, as well as played havoc with forest ecosystems. By contrast, according to Guha, Third World peasants have far more basic needs.

> Their demands on the environment are far less intense, and they can draw on a reservoir of cooperative social institutions and local ecological knowledge in managing the "commons"—forests, grasslands, and waters—on a sustainable basis.

Concerned to articulate a distinctive Third World environmental philosophy, Guha may have conceded too readily that conservation principally via wilderness preservation is even practicable in the United States. The violent confrontations of the Redwood Summer of 1990 in California and the ongoing, increasingly acrimonious Old Growth/Spotted Owl impasse in the Pacific Northwest make me wonder if Guha were not perpetuating uncritically a Third World myth when he describes North America as a "vast," superabundant, and "sparsely populated continent."

The late-twentieth-century crescendo of cut/graze/plow/pave or preserve conflicts here and abroad lead me to undertake a generalization of Guha's "Third World critique" of the wilderness idea. I wish to strike deeper than he and suggest that the popular wilderness idea is as inherently flawed as its counterpart, the conventional development idea. Most conservation biologists today recognize the paradoxical necessity of managing (and hence artificializing?) wilderness areas in order for them to continue to play their vital part in biological conservation. Just as paradoxically, refugia for species that require lots of living space may be compromised by wilderness recreation for which purpose such areas originally were set aside pursuant to the popular concept of wildernesses as areas where man is a visitor who does not remain.[15]

A Three-Point Critique
of the Received Concept of Wilderness

Upon close scrutiny, the simple, popular wilderness idea dissolves before one's gaze. First, the concept perpetuates the pre-Darwinian Western metaphysical dichotomy between "man" and nature, albeit with an opposite spin. (Fully aware that it is gender-biased, I use the term "man" both deliberately and apologetically to refer globally and collectively to the species *Homo sapiens*, because no other term carries the same connotation and flavor, a connotation and flavor that I wish to evoke in the course of this critique, including its decided sexism.) In fact, one of the principle psycho-spiritual benefits of wilderness experience is said to be contact with the radical "other," and wilderness preservation the letting be of the nonhuman other in its full otherness.[16]

Second, the wilderness idea is woefully ethnocentric. It ignores the historic presence and effects on practically all the world's ecosystems of aboriginal peoples.

Third, it ignores the fourth dimension of nature, time. In a recent discussion, Cordell and Reed say flatly, "Preservation implies cessation of change."[17] In ecosystems, however, change is as natural as it is inevitable; consequently, trying to preserve in perpetuity—trying to "freeze-frame"—the ecological status quo ante is as unnatural as it is impossible. A more sophisticated and refined concept of wilderness preservation among contemporary conservationists aims, rather, to perpetuate the integrity of evolutionary and ecological processes, instead of existing "natural" structures. Cordell and Reed, in fact, understand wilderness preservation not as an effort to halt change, but to slow "accelerating rates of change" and to preserve the "dynamic operation of natural processes . . . fire, drought, disease, predation, and geological change." However, even such a dynamic, process-sensitive notion of wilderness preservation is incomplete if it ignores the role that *Homo sapiens* has played historically practically everywhere and if it would deny *Homo sapiens* the opportunity to reestablish a positive symbiotic relationship with other species and a positive role in the unfolding of evolutionary processes.

The Wilderness Act of 1964 beautifully reflects the conventional understanding of wilderness. It reads: "A wilderness, in contrast with those areas where man and his works dominate the landscape, is hereby recognized as an area where the earth and its community of life are untrammeled by man, where man himself is a visitor who does not remain."[18]

This definition assumes, indeed it enshrines, a bifurcation of man and nature. That the man–nature dichotomy insidiously infects even our well-intentioned and noble efforts to limit our own grasp should not be surprising. A major theme both in Western philosophy, going back to the ancient Greeks, and in Western religion, going back to the ancient Hebrews, is how man is unique and set apart from the rest of nature.

In the Judeo-Christian religious tradition, man alone among all the other creatures is created in the image of God. In the Greco-Roman philosophical tradition, among all the other animals, man is uniquely rational. Subsequently, philosophers as different from one another as Thomas Aquinas, the perennial philosopher of the Catholic church, and René Descartes, the father of modern philosophy, variously synthesized these two strands of Western thought, Thomas in the Middle Ages and Descartes at the dawn of the Scientific Revolution. The classical Western segregation of man from nature thus became ever more ingrained, a veritable cachet of Western ideology, both religious and scientific. Moreover, all the wonderful works of man—from the pyramids of Egypt to the Gothic cathedrals of France, to say nothing of all the marvels of modern technology—seemed to confirm the radical metaphysical rift between us and the brute creation.

Now that man's technological dominion over the Earth is virtually absolute, and its community of life will survive only if we permit, a rising chorus of voices is crying, if not in the wilderness, at least for it—for man to show a little mercy, to allow a little untrammeled, unconquered nature to exist here and there. Until recently, man seemed the up-and-coming hero armed with Promethean science in the struggle with Titanic nature. Now, as the twentieth century winds to a close, victorious man seems to be a tyrant, his conquest a spoils, and nature the victim. For many ardent wilderness advocates, the roles of hero and villain are reversed, but the underlying dichotomy goes unchallenged.

Since Darwin's *Origin of Species* and *Descent of Man*, however, we have known that man is a part of nature. We are only a species among species, one among 20 or 30 million natural kinds. The natural works of other species, everyone seems to agree, can help as well as harm the biotic communities of which they are a part. Pursuing their own economic interests, bees assist the reproduction of flowering plants and thus perform an invaluable community service. Hundreds of other similar examples—from nitrogen-fixing bacteria to scavenging turkey vultures—could be cited. Elephants, on the other hand, pursuing their own economic interests, can be very destructive members of their biotic communities. So can deer. Hundreds of similar examples—from cow birds to kudzu—could be cited.

If man is a natural, a wild, an evolving species not essentially different in this respect from all the others, as Snyder reminds us, then the works of man, however precocious, are as natural as those of beavers, or termites, or any of the other species that dramatically modify their habitats. And if entirely natural, then the works of man, like those of bees and beavers, in principle may be, even if now they usually are not, beneficial—judged by the same objective ecological norms—to the biotic communities which we inhabit.

In one important (and relevant) respect, we are different from other species. The pollinating services performed by bees and the decomposition of dead wood and soil treatment provided by termites are instinctive behaviors. The migration routes of birds, the hunting techniques of predators, and many other animal behaviors that are learned might be regarded as "cultural," or at least "protocultural," rather than strictly hereditary or "instinctive." However, the cultural component in human behavior is so greatly developed as to have become more a difference of kind than of degree. To suggest that the works of man are not natural is not to suggest that they are supernatural or preternatural, but that they are products of culture, not instinct. Still, the cultural works of man are evolutionary phenomena no less than are other massive structures created by living things like, say, coral reefs. They are, one and all, natural in that sense of the word. Therefore, it is logically possible that they may be well attuned and symbiotically integrated with other contemporaneous evolutionary phenomena, with coral reefs and tropical forests, as well as the opposite.

Precisely because the works of man are largely cultural, they are capable of being reformed rapidly. Other animals cannot change what they do in and to their biotic communities, at least not very rapidly, and perhaps not ever consciously and deliberately. We can, since our economic behaviors are determined more by our cultures than by our genes. Whether to trammel nature totally—to "develop" every acre—or here and there to forbear is not the only question man should put to himself. How to work our works in ways that are at once humanly, socially, and ecologically benign rather than malignant—that's the more important, and problematic, question.

Now on to my second point, that the popular wilderness idea is ethnocentric. More than anyone else, Nash has molded the popular idea of wilderness in the contemporary American mind. He acknowledges, but skates rapidly over, American Indian complaints that the very concept of wilderness is a racist idea, and he expresses no doubt that the first European settlers of North America encountered a "wilderness condition." In the recent (and excellent) *Wilderness Idea* film by Hott and Garey, Nash is even more emphatic.[19] He says that the pilgrims literally stepped off the *Mayflower* into a wilderness of continental dimensions.

Upon the eve of European landfall, most of temperate North America was not, pace Nash, in a wilderness condition—not undominated by the works of man—unless one is prepared to ignore the existence of its aboriginal inhabitants and their works or to insinuate that they were not "man," i.e., not fully human human beings. In 1492, Antarctica was the only true wilderness land mass on the planet. (And by now, even a good bit of it has come under the iron heel of industrial man.)

Until rather recently, it was possible for environmental historians to minimize the ecological importance of the original human inhabitants of the New World, because the decimating effects of Old World diseases had not been taken into account in estimating their Pre-Columbian numbers. Kroeber calculated a hemispheric total of 8.5 million souls at contact and placed the population of the lands now comprised of the 48 (geographically) United States, Canada, Greenland, and Alaska at fewer than 1 million.[20] Dobyns, adding the impact of Old World diseases on the immunologically innocent New World aborigines to his demographic equations, proposed to increase Kroeber's estimates by, roughly, a factor of ten.[21] Tragically, only one Indian in ten seems to have survived the epidemics of small- and chicken-pox, diphtheria, measles, scarlet fever, and other infections that swept through North America from east to west during the fifteenth and sixteenth centuries—often passed from Indian to Indian before the leading edge of the pale-face tide arrived. As Witthoft described this inverse decimation, "Great epidemics and pandemics of these diseases are believed to have destroyed whole communities, depopulated whole regions, and vastly decreased the native population everywhere in the yet unexplored interior of the continent."[22]

In the spring of 1492, North America (not including Mexico) may not have been densely populated, but it was largely inhabited by some 10 million people. Nor were the Indians passive denizens of the continent's forests, prairies, swamps, deserts, and tundra, simply taking—like foraging Mandrill baboons—what usable plants and animals they happened to stumble upon. Most of temperate North America was managed actively by its aboriginal human inhabitants. In addition to domesticating and cultivating an extraordinarily wide range of food and medicine plants, native North Americans managed the continent's forest and savannah communities, principally with fire. Their pyrotechnology helped to determine the mix of species and reset succession in the various plant associations in which they lived. The European immigrants, in fact, found a man-made landscape, but they thought it was a wilderness because it didn't look like the man-made landscape that they had left behind.

It is important to note, however, that the same kind of country that now is designated or de facto wilderness in the United States also was frequented and utilized less by the American aborigines. The 2 percent of the 48 (geographically) United States presently devoted to wilderness is mostly in high, rough, or arid lands—and often all three. A good argument, therefore, could be made that an expansion of the present system of wilderness reserves to mirror ancient human land use patterns on this continent is consistent with long-established Nearctic evolutionary and ecological regimes.

The incredible abundance of wildlife encountered in the western hemisphere by the first European intruders was not, however, a concomitant of a universal wilderness condition, that is, not due to the absence of inherently destructive *Homo sapiens* in significant numbers everywhere. Rather, the biological wealth of North America on the eve of European landfall is more attributable to the bioregional management programs of the indigenous human population than to low numbers. Further, the ubiquity of grizzly bears throughout the west and big cats and wolves throughout the continent indicates a mutual tolerance of these species with *Homo sapiens americana* that was, apparently, disrupted when *Homo sapiens europi* began to persecute them as varmints.

I now take up my third point: Wilderness preservation, as the popular conservation alternative to destructive land use and development, suggests that, untrammeled by man, a wilderness will remain "stable," in a steady state. However, nature is inherently dynamic; it is constantly changing and ultimately evolving. Today, most of the pitifully small fenced-off patches of designated wilderness areas of temperate North America lack major components of their Holocene ecological complement—notably their large predators. Not only that, a fence, or the policy equivalent thereof, will not exclude all the exotic species that have accompanied or followed the migration of *Homo sapiens europi* to North America. Designated wilderness areas, paradoxically, must be restored and managed actively if they are to remain fit habitat for native species, but the necessity of means raises a question of ends, of values. Is maintaining "vignettes of primitive America" the most important and defensible goal of biological conservation? (Here, again, let me be clear. I am excluding from consideration biologically destructive economic desiderata such as hydroelectric impoundment.) Since we must manage nature actively and invasively to preserve the ecological status quo ante, the possibility of managing nature for more direct, less incidental conservation goals arises.

The whole notion of preserved wilderness areas—even were we to restore the wolf and the grizzly to representative spots in their original ranges, simulate the effects, where they existed, of *Homo sapiens americana*'s hunting and burning, and maintain a constant vigil against invasion by exotics—defies the fourth dimension of nature, time. In the course of time, ecological succession is reset continually by one or another natural disturbance. Paleo-ecological stud-ies reveal, moreover, that species composition within successional seres—the structure, in other words, of biotic communities—has changed over time. Fluctuations in climate drive migrations of glaciers, forests, deserts, and grass-lands. Exotic species, with or without human help, invade new environments, and in the course of time, become naturalized citizens. Indeed, the concepts of exotic/native species are "relative, scale dependent (temporally and spatially), and about as ambiguous as any in our conservation lexicon."[23] Are the feral mustangs roaming the American west, for example, natives or exotics? Soulé speculatively envisions lions, cheetahs, camels, elephants, saiga antelope, yaks, and spectacled bears joining horses in the name of "the restoration to the Nearctic of the great paleomammalian megafauna" which disappeared from this continent "only moments ago in evolutionary time."[24]

The wilderness idea has not only made conservation convenient—if Guha is correct to argue that it has served American conservationists as a subterfuge, allowing us to enjoy the benefits of industrial development and over consump-tion, while salving our consciences by setting aside a few undeveloped rem-nants for nature—but it also has made conservation philosophy simple and easy. If we conceive of wilderness as a static benchmark of pristine nature in reference to which all human modifications may be judged to be more or less degradations, then we can duck the hard intellectual job of specifying criteria for land health in four-dimensional, inherently dynamic landscapes long inhab-ited by *Homo sapiens* as well as by other species. The idea of healthy land maintaining itself is more sensitive to the dynamic quality of ecosystems than is the conventional idea of preserving vignettes of primitive America. Moreover, if the concept of land health replaces the popular, conventional idea of wilder-ness as a standard of conservation, then we might begin to envision ways of creatively reintegrating man and nature.

Conservation biologists just now are coming to grips with the problem of setting out objective criteria of ecological health in dynamic, long-humanized landscapes. Recent efforts to do so have been made by Costanza, Westman, and Ulanowicz.[25] While insisting upon the naturalness of change, the impor-tance of rate and scale of change for land health cannot be overemphasized. Cordell and Reed suggest that "'bad' change" is the result of "accelerating rates of environmental change" and Botkin again and again warns that, while change per se always has characterized the living earth, the current changes imposed upon nature by global industrial civilization are unprecedentedly rapid and radical and therefore, albeit natural, not normal.[26]. . .

. . . Can we envision and work to create an eminently livable, systemic, postindustrial technological society well adapted to, and at peace and in har-mony with, its organic environment? If illiterate, unscientific peoples can do it, can't a civilized, technological society also live, not merely in peaceful coexis-tence, but in benevolent symbiosis with nature? Is our current industrial civilization the only one imaginable? Aren't there more appropriate, alternative technologies? Can't we be good citizens of the biotic community, like the birds and the bees, drawing an honest living from nature and giving back as much or more than we take?

Notes

I thank Eugene C. Hargrove for providing an opportunity to broach the central ideas contained in this paper to the faculty of environmental ethics at the University of Georgia's Institute of Ecology. I have benefited from discussion of the role of wilderness in Aldo Leopold's philosophy of conservation with Susan L. Flader, Curt Meine, and Bryan Norton. John Lemons and an anonymous referee for *The Environmental Professional* generously and critically commented on an earlier draft of this paper and rescued it from more errors of fact and doctrine than those that remain.

1. R. Nash, *Wilderness and the American Mind* (New Haven, Conn.: Yale University Press, 1967).

2. H. D. Thoreau, *Excursions* (New York: Corinth, 1962), 185. For Emerson, see *Nature* (Boston: Beacon Press, 1989).

3. J. Muir, *Our National Parks* (Boston: Houghton Mifflin, 1901).

4. G. Pinchot, *Breaking New Ground* (New York: Harcourt, Brace, 1947), 325–26.

5. Ibid., 326.

6. Ibid., xix.

7. Ibid., 263.

8. S. P. Hays, *Conservation and the Gospel of Efficiency: The Progressive Conservation Movement* (Boston: Harvard University Press, 1959).

9. A. Leopold, "Forestry and Game Conservation," *Journal of Forestry* 19 (1918): 404–11, and "Wilderness and Its Place in Forest Recreation," *Journal of Forestry* 19 (1921): 718–21.

10. A. Leopold, "A Biotic View of Land," *Journal of Forestry* 37 (1939): 727.

11. A. Leopold, *A Sand County Almanac, and Sketches Here and There* (New York: Oxford University Press, 1949), 224–25.

12. S. Flader, *Thinking Like a Mountain: Aldo Leopold and the Evolution of an Ecological Attitude toward Deer, Wolves, and Forests* (Columbia: University of Missouri Press, 1974).

13. Leopold, *Sand County Almanac*, 207.

14. R. Guha, "Radical American Environmentalism and Wilderness Preservation: A Third World Critique," *Environmental Ethics* 12 (1989): 71–83.

15. See, for example, P. Reed, ed., *Preparing to Manage Wilderness in the 21st Century: Proceedings of the Conference* (Asheville, N.C.: Department of Agriculture, Forest Service, Southeastern Forest Experimentation Station, 1990).

16. T. Birch, "The Incarceration of Wilderness: Wilderness Areas as Prisons," *Environmental Ethics* 12 (1990): 3–26.

17. H. K. Cordell and P. Reed, "Untrammeled by Man: Preserving Diversity through Wilderness," in *Preparing to Manage Wilderness in the 21st Century*, ed. Reed, 31.

18. Quoted in Nash, *Wilderness and the American Mind*, 5.

19. L. Hott and D. Garey, *The Wilderness Idea: John Muir, Gifford Pinchot, and the First Great Battle for Wilderness* (Haydenville, Mass.: Florintine Films, 1989).

20. A. L. Kroeber, *Cultural and Natural Areas of Native North America* (Berkeley: University of California Press, 1939).

21. H. F. Dobyns, "Estimating Aboriginal American Population: An Appraisal of Techniques with a New Hemispheric Estimate," *Current Anthropology* 7 (1966): 395–412.

22. J. Witthoft, *Indian Prehistory of Pennsylvania* (Harrisburg: Pennsylvania Historical and Museum Commission, 1965), 28.

23. R. F. Noss, "Can We Maintain Our Biological and Ecological Integrity?" *Conservation Biology* 4 (1990): 242.

24. M. E. Soulé, "The Onslaught of Alien Species, and Other Challenges in the Coming Decades," *Conservation Biology* 4 (1990): 234–35.

25. See, for example, R. Constanza, "Toward an Operational Definition of Ecosystem Health," and R. Ulanowicz, "Ecosystem Health in Terms of Trophic Flow Networks" (Papers presented at the annual meeting of the AAAS, Washington, D.C., February 15, 1991); W. E. Westman, "Restoration Projects: Measuring Their Performance," *Environmental Professional* 13 (1991): 207–15.

26. Cordell and Reed, "Untrammeled by Man," 30–31; D. Botkin, *Discordant Harmonies: A New Ecology for the Twenty-First Century* (New York: Oxford University Press, 1990).

[From] The Wilderness Idea Reaffirmed

$\sim$

Holmes Rolston III

Introduction

Revisiting the wilderness, Callicott is a doubtful guide; indeed he has gotten himself lost. That is a pity, because . . . I readily endorse his positive arguments for developing a culture more harmonious with nature. But these give no cause for being negative about wilderness.

The wilderness concept, we are told, is "inherently flawed," triply so. It metaphysically and unscientifically dichotomizes man and nature. It is ethnocentric, because it does not realize that practically all the world's ecosystems were modified by aboriginal peoples. It is static, ignoring change through time. In the flawed idea and ideal, wilderness respects wild communities where man is a visitor who does not remain. In the revisited idea, also Leopold's ideal, humans, themselves entirely natural, reside in and can and ought to improve wild nature.

Human Culture and Wild Nature

Wilderness valued without humans perpetuates a false dichotomy, Callicott maintains. Going back to Cartesian and Greek philosophy and Christian theology, such a contrast between humans and wild nature is a metaphysical confusion that leads us astray and also is unscientific. But this is not so. One hardly needs metaphysics or theology to realize that there are critical differences between wild nature and human culture. Humans now superimpose cultures on the wild nature out of which they once emerged. There is nothing unscientific or non-Darwinian about the claim that innovations in human culture make it radically different from wild nature.

Information in wild nature travels intergenerationally on genes; information in culture travels neurally as persons are educated into transmissible cultures. In nature, the coping skills are coded on chromosomes. In culture, the skills are coded in craftsman's traditions, religious rituals, or technology manuals. Information acquired during an organism's lifetime is not transmitted genetically; the essence of culture is acquired information transmitted to the next generation. Information transfer in culture can be several orders of magnitude faster and overleap genetic lines. I have but two children; copies of my books and my former students number in the thousands. A human being develops typically in some one of ten thousand cultures, each heritage historically conditioned, perpetuated by language, conventionally established, using symbols with locally effective meanings. Animals are what they are genetically, instinctively, environmentally, without any options at all. Humans have myriad lifestyle options, evidenced by their cultures; and each human makes daily decisions that affect his or her character. Little or nothing in wild nature approaches this.

The novelty is not simply that humans are more versatile in their spontaneous natural environments. Deliberately rebuilt environments replace spontaneous wild ones. Humans can therefore inhabit environments altogether different from the African savannas in which they once evolved. They insulate themselves from environmental extremes by their rebuilt habitations, with central heat from fossil fuel or by importing fresh groceries from a thousand miles away. In that sense, animals have freedom within ecosystems, but humans have freedom from ecosystems. Animals are adapted to their niches; humans adapt their ecosystems to their needs. The determinants of animal and plant behavior, much less the determinants of climate or nutrient recycling, are never anthropological, political, economic, technological, scientific, philosophical, ethical, or religious. Natural selection pressures are relaxed in culture; humans help each other out compassionately with medicine, charity, affirmative action, or Head Start programs.

Humans act using large numbers of tools and things made with tools, extrasomatic artifacts. In all but the most primitive cultures, humans teach each other how to make clothes, thresh wheat, make fires, bake bread. Animals do not hold elections and plan their environmental affairs; they do not make bulldozers to cut down tropical rainforests. They do not fund development projects through the World Bank or contribute to funds to save the whales. They do not teach their religion to their children. They do not write articles revisiting and reaffirming the idea of wilderness. They do not get confused about whether their actions are natural or argue about whether they can improve nature.

If there is any metaphysical confusion in this debate, we locate it in the claim that "man is a natural, a wild, an evolving species, not essentially different in this respect from all the others."[1] Poets like Gary Snyder perhaps are entitled to poetic license. But philosophers are not, especially when analyzing the concept of wildness. They cannot say that "the works of man, however precocious, are as natural as those of beavers," being "entirely natural," and then, hardly taking a breath, say that "the cultural component in human behavior is so greatly developed as to have become more a difference of kind than of degree." If this were only poetic philosophy it might be harmless, but proposed as policy, environmental professionals who operate with such contradictory philosophy will fail tragically.

"Anthropogenic changes imposed upon ecosystems are as natural as any other."[2] Not so. Wilderness advocates know better; they do not gloss over these differences. They appreciate and criticize human affairs, with insight into their radically different character. Accordingly, they insist that there are intrinsic wild values that are not human values. These ought to be preserved for whatever they can contribute to human values, and because they are valuable on their own, in and of themselves. Just because the human presence is so radically different, humans ought to draw back and let nature be. Humans can and should see outside their own sector, their species self-interest, and affirm nonanthropogenic, noncultural values. Only humans have conscience enough to do this. That is not confused metaphysical dichotomy; it is axiological truth. To think that human culture is nothing but a natural system is not discriminating enough. It risks reductionism and primitivism.

These contrasts between nature and culture were not always as bold as they now are. Once upon a time, culture evolved out of nature. The early hunter-gatherers had transmissible cultures but, sometimes, were not much different in their ecological effects from the wild predators and omnivores among whom they moved. In such cases, this was as much through lack of power to do otherwise as from conscious decision. A few such aboriginal peoples may remain.

But we Americans do not and cannot live in such a twilight society. Any society that we envision must be scientifically sophisticated, technologically advanced, globally oriented, as well as (we hope) just and charitable, caring for universal human rights and for biospheric values. This society will try to fit itself in intelligently with the ecosystemic processes on which it is superposed. It will, we plead, respect wildness. But none of these decisions shaping society are the processes of wild nature. There is no inherent flaw in our logic when we are discriminating about these radical discontinuities between culture and nature. The dichotomy charge is a half-truth, and, taken for the whole, becomes an untruth.

Humans Improving Wild Nature

Might a mature, humane civilization improve wild nature? Callicott thinks that it is a "fallacy" to think that "the best way to conserve nature is to protect it from human habitation and utilization." But, continuing the analysis, surely the fallacy is to think that a nature allegedly improved by humans is anymore real nature at all. The values intrinsic to wilderness cannot, on pain of both logical and empirical contradiction, be "improved" by deliberate human management, because deliberation is the antithesis of wildness. That is the sense in which civilization is the "antithesis" of wilderness, but there is nothing "amiss" in seeing an essential difference here. Animals take nature ready to hand, adapted to it by natural selection, fitted into their niches; humans rebuild their world through artifact and heritage, agriculture and culture, political and religious decisions.

On the meaning of "natural" at issue here, that of nature proceeding by evolutionary and ecological processes, any deliberated human agency, however well intended, is intention nevertheless and interrupts these spontaneous processes and is inevitably artificial, unnatural. The architectures of nature and of culture are different, and when culture seeks to improve nature, the management intent spoils the wildness. Wilderness management, in that sense, is a contradiction in terms—whatever may be added by way of management of humans who visit the wilderness, or of restorative practices, or monitoring, or other activities that environmental professionals must sometimes consider. A scientifically managed wilderness is conceptually as impossible as wildlife in a zoo.

To recommend that *Homo sapiens* "reestablish a positive symbiotic relationship with other species and a positive role in the unfolding of evolutionary processes" is, so far as wilderness preservation is involved, not just bad advice, it is impossible advice. The cultural processes by their very "nature" interrupt the evolutionary process; there is no symbiosis, there is antithesis. Culture is a post-evolutionary phase of our planetary history; it must be superposed on the nature it presupposes. To recommend, however, that we should build sustainable cultures that fit in with the continuing ecological processes is a first principle of intelligent action, and no wilderness advocate thinks otherwise.

If there are inherent conceptual flaws dogging this debate, we have located another: Callicott's allegedly "improved" nature. In such modified nature, the different historical genesis brings a radical change in value type. Every wilderness enthusiast knows the difference between a pine plantation in the Southeast and an old-growth grove in the Pacific Northwest. Even if the "improvement" is more or less harmonious with the ecosystem, it is fundamentally of a different order. Asian ring-tailed pheasants are rather well naturalized on the contemporary Iowa landscape. But they are there by human introduction, and they remain because farmers plow the fields, plant corn, and leave shelter in the fencerows. They are really as much like pets as like native wild species, because they are not really on their own. . . .

Wilderness and Change

Another alleged flaw in the concept of wilderness is that its advocates do not know the fourth dimension, time. That is a strange charge; my experience has been just the opposite. In wilderness, the day changes from dawn to dusk, the seasons pass, plants grow, animals are born, grow up, and age. Rivers flow, winds blow, even the rocks erode; change is pervasive. Indeed, wilderness is that environment in which one is most likely to experience geological time. Try a raft trip through the Grand Canyon.

On the scale of deep time, some processes continue on and on, so that the perennial givens—wind and rain, soil and photosynthesis, life and death and life renewed—can seem almost forever. Species survive for millions of years; individuals are ephemeral. Life persists in the midst of its perpetual perishing. Mountains are reliably there generation after generation. The water cycles back, always moving. In wilderness, time mixes with eternity; that is one reason we value it so highly.

Callicott writes as if wilderness advocates had studied ecology and never heard of evolution. But they know that evolution is the control of development by ecology, and what they value is precisely natural history. They do not object to natural changes. They may not even object to artificial changes in rural landscapes. But, since they know the difference between nature and culture, they know that cultural changes may be quite out of kilter with natural changes. Leopold uses the word "stability" when he is writing in the time frame of land-use planning. On that scale, nature typically does have a reliable stability, and farmers do well to figure in the perennial givens.

In an evolutionary time frame, Leopold knows that relative stability mixes with change. "Paleontology offers abundant evidence that wilderness maintained itself for immensely long periods; that its component species were rarely lost, and neither did they get out of hand; that weather and water built soil as fast or faster than it was carried away." That is why "wilderness . . . assumes unexpected importance as a laboratory for the study of land health."[3] Wilderness is the original sustainable development.

With natural processes, "protect" is perhaps a better word than either "preserve" or "conserve." Wilderness advocates do not seek to prevent natural change. There is nothing illusory, however, about appreciating today in wilderness processes that have a primeval character. There, the natural processes of 1992 do not differ much from those of 1492, half a millennium earlier. We may enjoy that perennial character, constancy in change, in contrast with the rapid pace of cultural changes, seldom as dramatic as those on the American landscape of the last few centuries.

A management program in the U.S. Forest Service seeks to evaluate the "limits of acceptable change." This emphasis worries about the rapid pace of cultural change as this contrasts with the natural pace on landscapes. Cordell and Reed are trying to decide the limits of acceptable humanly introduced changes, artificial changes, since these are of such radically different kind and pace that they disrupt the processes of wilderness.[4] They do not oppose natural changes. At this point, we have an example of how and why environmental professionals will make disastrous decisions, if confused by what is and is not natural. Callicott warns them that they do have to worry about "accelerating rates of environmental change." But no one can begin to understand these accelerating rates of changes if the changes are thought of as being introduced by a species that is "entirely natural."

When we designate a desert wilderness in Nevada, there really isn't any problem deciding that mustangs are feral animals in contrast with desert bighorns, which are indigenous. There might have been ancestral horses in Paleolithic times in the American West, but they went extinct naturally. The present mustangs came from animals that the Europeans brought over in ships, originally from the plains of Siberia. Bighorns are what they are where they are by natural selection. Mustangs are not so. There is nothing conceptually problematic about that—unless one has never gotten clearly in mind the difference between nature and culture in the first place.

Aboriginal Peoples and Wilderness

What of the argument that we cannot have any wilderness, because there is none to be had? This is a much stronger claim than that there is no real wilderness left on the American landscape after the European cultural invasion. Even the aboriginals had already extinguished wilderness. Now we have a somewhat different account of the human presence from that earlier advocated. The claim is no longer that the Indians were just another wild species, "entirely natural," but that they actively managed the landscape, so dramatically altering it that there was no wilderness even when Columbus arrived in 1492. It is ethnocentric to think otherwise. This is because we Caucasians exaggerate our own power to modify the landscape and diminish their power. This is a judgment based on prejudice, not on facts.

How much did the American Indians modify the landscape? That is an empirical question in anthropology and ecology. We do not disagree that where there was Indian culture, this altered the locales in which they resided, so that these locales were not wilderness in the pure sense. In that respect, Indian culture is not different in kind from the white man's culture. What we need to know is the degree. Had the Indians, when the white man arrived, already transformed the pre-Indian wilderness beyond the range of its spontaneous self-restoration?

Callicott concedes, rightly, that most of what has been presently designated as wilderness was infrequently used by the aborigines, since it is high, rough, or arid. We have no reason to think that in such areas the aboriginal modifications are irreversible. Were the more temperate regions modified so extensively and irreversibly that so little naturalness remains as to make wilderness designation an illusion? Callicott has "no doubt that most New World ecosystems were in robust health." That suggests that they were not past self-regeneration.

The American Indians on forested lands had little agriculture; what agriculture they had tended to reset succession, and, when agriculture ceases, the subsequent forest regeneration will not be particularly unnatural. The Indian technology for larger landscape modification was bow and arrow, spear, and fire. The only one that extensively modifies landscapes is fire. Fire is—we have learned well by now—also quite natural. Fire suppression is unnatural, but no one argues that the Indians used that as a management tool, nor did they have much capacity for fire suppression. The argument is that they deliberately set fires. Does this make their fires radically different from natural fires? It does in terms of the source of ignition; the one is a result of environmental policy deliberation, the other of a lightning bolt.

But every student of fire behavior knows that on the scale of regional forest ecosystems, the source of ignition is not a particularly critical factor. The question is whether the forest is ready to burn, whether there is sufficient ground fuel to sustain the fire, whether the trees are diseased, how much duff there is, and so on. If conditions are not right, it will be difficult to get the fire going and it will burn out soon. If conditions are right, a human can start a regional fire this year. If some human does not, lightning will start it next year, or the year after that. On a typical summer day, the states of Arizona and New Mexico are each hit by several thousand bolts of lightning, mostly in the higher, forested regions. Doubtless the Indians started some fires too, but it is hard to think that their fires so dramatically and irreversibly altered the natural fire regime in the Southwest that meaningful wilderness designation is impossible today.

We do not want to be ethnocentric, but neither do we want to be naïve about the technological prowess of the American Indian cultures. They had no motors, indeed no wheels, no domestic animals, no horses (before the Spanish came), no beasts of burden. The Indians had a hard time getting so simple a thing as hot water. They had to heat stones and drop them in skins or tightly woven baskets. They lived on the landscape with foot and muscle, and in that sense, though they had complex cultures, they had culture with very reduced alterative power. Even in European cultures, in recent centuries the power of civilization to redo the world has accelerated logarithmically.

In Third World nations, perhaps areas that seem "natural" now are often the result of millennia of human modifications through fire, hunting, shifting cultivation, and selective planting and removal of species. This will have to be examined on a case-by-case basis, and we cannot prejudge the answers. We do not know yet how intensively the vast Brazilian rainforests were managed and whether no wilderness designation there is ecologically practicable, even if we desired it. Nor do wilderness enthusiasts advocate that such peoples be removed to accomplish this, were it is possible. What is protested is modern forms of development. Extractive reserves may be an answer, but extractive reserves for latex sold in world markets and manufactured into rubber products can hardly be considered aboriginal wisdom.

Sometimes we will have to make do with what wildness remains in the nooks and crannies of civilization. Meanwhile, where wilderness designation is possible and where there is an exploding population, what should we do? No one objects to trying to direct that explosion into more harmonious forms of human–nature encounter. But constraining an explosion takes some strong measures. One of these ought to be the designation of wilderness.

Perhaps the American Indians did not have enough contrast between their culture and the nature that surrounded them to produce the wilderness idea. It was not an idea that, within their limited power to remake nature, could occur to them. If you have only foot, muscle, bows, arrows, and fire, you do not think much about wilderness conservation. But we, in the twentieth century, do have the wilderness idea; it has crystallized with the possibility, indeed the impending threat, of destroying the last acre of primeval wilderness. It also has crystallized with our deepening scientific knowledge of how wild nature operates, of DNA, genes, and natural selection, and how dramatically different in kind, pace, and power the processes of culture can be. The Indians knew little of this; they lived still in an animistic, enchanted world.

And we need the wilderness idea desperately. When you have bulldozers that already have blacktopped more acreage than remains pristine, you can and ought to begin to think about wilderness. Such an idea, when it comes, is primitive in one sense: it preserves primeval nature, as much as it can. But it is morally advanced in another sense: it sees the intrinsic value of nature, apart from humans.

Ought implies can; the Indians could not, so they never thought much about the ought. We in the twentieth century can, and we must think about the ought. When we designate wilderness, we are not lapsing into some romantic atavism, reactionary and nostalgic to escape culture. We are breaking through culture to discover, nonanthropocentrically, that fauna and flora can count in their own right (an idea that Indians also might have shared). We realize that ecosystems sometimes can be so respected that humans only visit and do not remain (an idea that the Indians did not need or achieve). A "can" has appeared that has generated a new "ought."

Even some modern American Indians concur. In western Montana, the Salish and Kootenai tribes have set aside 93,000 acres of their reservation as the Mission Mountains Tribal Wilderness; in addition, they have designated the South Fork of the Jocko Primitive Area. In both areas, the Indian too is "a visitor who does not remain"; they want these areas "to be affected primarily by the forces of nature with the imprint of man's work substantially unnoticeable."[5] Indeed, in deference to the grizzly bears, in the summer season, the Indians do not permit any humans at all to visit 10,000 acres that are prime grizzly habitat. In both areas, they can claim even more restrictive environmental regulation on what people can do there than in the white man's wilderness. What, when, and how they hunt is an example.

Not a word of the above discussion disparages aboriginal Indian culture. To the contrary, that they survived with the bare skills they had is a credit to their endurance, courage, resolution, and wisdom. A wilderness enthusiast, if he or she has spent much time in the woods armed with only muscle and a few belongings in a backpack, is in an excellent position to appreciate the aboriginal skills.

Farmers, Sustainable Development, and Wilderness

Finding out how to remake civilization so that nature is conserved in the midst of sustainable development is indeed a more difficult and important task than saving wild remnants. Little wilderness can be safe unless the sustainable development problem is solved also. I can only endorse Callicott's desire to conserve nature in the midst of human culture. "Human economic activities should at least be compatible with the ecological health of the environments in which they occur." No party to the debate contests that. But this does not mean that wilderness ought not to be saved for what it is in itself.

"The farmer as a conservationist" is quite a good thing, and Leopold does well to hope that "land does well for its owner, and the owner does well by his land"; perhaps where a farmer begins, as did Leopold, with lands long abused, "both end up better by reason of their partnership." In that context, "conservation is a state of harmony between men and land." But none of that asks whether there also should be wilderness. Leopold tells us what he thinks about that after his trip to Germany. There was "something lacking. . . . I did not hope to find in Germany anything resembling the great 'wilderness areas' which we dream about and talk about." That was too much to hope; he could dream that only in America. But he did hope to find "a certain quality [—wildness—] which should be, but is not found" in the rural landscape, and, alas, not even that was there. "In Europe, where wilderness now has retreated to the Carpathians and Siberia, every thinking conservationist bemoans its loss."[6] That loss would not be restored if every farmer were a restoration ecologist. All that Leopold says about sustainable development is true, but there is no implication that wilderness cannot or ought not to be saved. Affirming sustainable development is not to deny wilderness.

Monastic Wilderness and Civilized Complacency

Nor is affirming wilderness to deny sustainable development. Callicott alleges, "Implicit in the most passionate pleas for wilderness preservation is a complacency about what passes for civilization." Not so. I cannot name a single wilderness advocate who cherishes wilderness "as an alibi for the lack of private reform," any who "salve their consciences" by pointing to "the few odds and ends" of wilderness and thus "avoid facing up to the fact that the ways and means of industrial civilization lie at the root of the current global environmental crisis." The charge is flamboyant; the content runs hollow. Wilderness advocates want wilderness and they also want, passionately, to "re-envision civilization" so that it is in harmony with the nature that humans do modify and inhabit. There is no tension between these ideas in Leopold, nor in any of the other passionate advocates of wilderness that Callicott cites, nor in any with whom I am familiar.

The contrast of monastic sanctuaries with the wicked everyday world risks a flawed analogy. Unless we are careful, we will make a category mistake, because both monastery and lay world are in the domain of culture, while wilderness is a radically different domain. Monastery sets an ideal unattainable in the real civil world (if we must think of it that way), but both worlds are human, both moral. We are judging human behavior in both places, concerned with how far it can be godly. By contrast, the wilderness world is neither moral nor human; the values protected there are of a different order. We are judging evolutionary achievements and ecological stability, integrity, beauty—not censuring or praising human behavior.

Confusion about nature and culture is getting us into trouble again. We are only going to get confused if we think that the issue of whether there should be monasteries is conceptually parallel to the issue of whether there should be wilderness. The conservation of value in the one is by the cultural transmission of a social heritage, including a moral and religious heritage, to which the monastery was devoted. The conservation of value in the other is genetic, in genes subject to natural selection for survival value and adapted fit. There is something godly in the wilderness too, or at least a creativity that is religiously valuable, but the contrast between the righteous and the wicked is not helpful here. The sanctuary we want is a world untrammelled by man, a world left to its own autonomous creativity, not an island of saintliness in the midst of sinners.

We do not want the whole Earth without civilization, for we believe that humans belong on Earth; Earth is not whole without humans and their civilization, without the political animal building his *polis* (Socrates), without peoples inheriting their promised lands (as the Hebrews envisioned). Civilization is a broken affair, and in the long struggle to make and keep life human, moral, even godly, perhaps there should be islands, sanctuaries, of moral goodness within a civilization often sordid enough. But that is a different issue from whether, when we build our civilizations for better or worse, we also want to protect where and as we can those nonhuman values in wild nature that preceded and yet surround us. An Earth civilized on every acre would not be whole either, for a whole domain of value—wild spontaneous nature—would have vanished from this majestic home planet.

Intrinsic Wilderness Values

I fear that we are seeing in Callicott's revisiting wilderness the outplay of a philosophy that does not think, fundamentally, that nature is of value in itself. Such a philosophy, though it may protest to the contrary, really cannot value nature for itself. All value in nature is by human projection; it is anthropogenic, generated by humans, though sometimes not anthropocentric, centered on humans. Callicott has made it clear that all so-called intrinsic value in nature is "grounded in human feelings" and "projected" onto the natural object that "excites" the value. "Intrinsic value ultimately depends upon human valuers." "Value depends upon human sentiments."[7]

He explains, "The source of all value is human consciousness, but it by no means follows that the locus of all value is consciousness itself. . . . An intrinsically valuable thing on this reading is valuable for its own sake, for itself, but it is not valuable in itself, i.e., completely independently of any consciousness, since no value can in principle . . . be altogether independent of a valuing consciousness. . . . Value is, as it were, projected onto natural objects or events by the subjective feelings of observers. If all consciousness were annihilated at a stroke, there would be no good and evil, no beauty and ugliness, no right and wrong; only impassive phenomena would remain." This, Callicott says, is a "truncated sense" of value where "'intrinsic value' retains only half its traditional meaning."[8]

Talk about dichotomies! Only humans produce value; wild nature is valueless without humans. All it has without humans is the potential to be evaluated by humans, who, if and when they appear, may incline, sometimes, to value nature in noninstrumental ways. "Nonhuman species . . . may not be valuable in themselves, but they may certainly be valued for themselves. . . . Value is, to be sure, humanly conferred, but not necessary homocentric."[9] The language of valuing nature for itself may be used, but it is misleading; value is always and only relational, with humans one of the relata. Nature in itself (a wilderness, for example) is without value. There is no genesis of wild value by nature on its own. Such a philosophy can value nature only in association with human habitation. But that—not some elitist wilderness conservation for spiritual meditation—is the view that many of us want to reject as "aristocratic bias and class privilege."

Sustainable development is, let's face it, irremediably anthropocentric. That is what we must have most places, and humans too have their worthy values. But must we have it everywhere? Must we have more of it and less wilderness? Maybe the value theory here is where the arrogance lies, not in some alleged ethnocentrism or misunderstood doctrine of the dominion of man.

A truncated value theory is giving us a truncated account of biodiversity. Callicott hardly wants wilderness as "sanctuaries," only as "refugia." A refugia is a seedbed from which other areas get restocked. That is one good reason for wilderness conservation, but we do not want wilderness simply as a place from which the game on our rural lands can be restocked, or even, if we have a more ample vision of wildlife recreation, from which the wildlife that yet persists on the domesticated landscape can be resupplied steadily. Wildernesses are not hatcheries for rural or urban wildlife. Nor are they just "laboratories" for baseline data for sound scientific management. Nor are they raw materials on which we can work our symbiotic enhancements. Nor are they places that can excite us into projecting truncated values onto them. Some of these are sometimes good reasons for conserving wilderness. Leopold sums them up as "the cultural value of wilderness."[10] But they are not the best reasons.

Leopold and Wilderness

Leopold pleads in the "Upshot," in his last book in the penultimate essay, entitled "Wilderness": "Wilderness was an adversary to the pioneer. But to the laborer in repose, able for the moment to cast a philosophical eye on his world, that same raw stuff is something to be loved and cherished, because it gives definition and meaning to his life."[11] He does not mean that wilderness is only a resource for personal development, though it is that. He means that we never know who we are or where we are until we know and respect our wild origins and our wild neighbors on this home planet. We never get our values straight until we value wilderness appropriately. The definition of the human kinds of values is incomplete until we have this larger vision of natural values.

Concluding his appeal for "raw wilderness," Leopold turns to the "Land Ethic," "The land ethic simply enlarges the boundaries of the community to include soils, waters, plants, and animals, or collectively: the land. . . . A land ethic of course cannot prevent the alteration, management, and use of these 'resources,' but it does affirm their right to continued existence, and, at least in spots, their continued existence in a natural state."[12] We may certainly assert that the founder of the Wilderness Society believed that wilderness conservation is essential in this right to continued existence in a natural state.

"I am asserting that those who love the wilderness should not be wholly deprived of it, that while the reduction of wilderness has been a good thing, its extermination would be a very bad one, and that the conservation of wilderness is the most urgent and difficult of all the tasks that confront us."[13] We must take it as anomalous (else it would be amusing or even tragic) to see Leopold's principal philosophical interpreter, himself a foremost environmental philosopher who elsewhere has said many wise things, now trying to revisit the wilderness idea and deemphasize it in Leopold.

Just before Leopold plunges into his passionate plea for the land ethic, he calls for "wilderness-minded men scattered through all the conservation bureaus." "A militant minority of wilderness-minded citizens must be on watch throughout the nation, and available for action in a pinch."[14] Alas! His trumpet call is replaced by an uncertain sound. Robert Marshall saluted Leopold as "The Commanding General of the Wilderness Battle."[15] How dismayed he would be by this dissension within his ranks.

On Earth, man is not a visitor who does not remain; this is our home planet and we belong here. Leopold speaks of man as both "plain citizen" and as "king." Humans too have an ecology, and we are permitted interference with, and rearrangement of, nature's spontaneous course; otherwise there is no culture. When we do this there ought to be some rational showing that the alteration is enriching, that natural values are sacrificed for greater cultural ones. We ought to make such development sustainable. But there are, and should be, places on Earth where the nonhuman community of life is untrammeled by man, where we only visit and spontaneous nature remains. If Callicott has his way, revisiting wilderness, there soon will be less and less wilderness to visit at all.

Notes

1. All unreferenced quotations are from J. B. Callicott, "The Wilderness Idea Revisited: The Sustainable Development Alternative," *Environmental Professional* 13 (1991): 236–45 [this volume, 262–65].

2. J. B. Callicott, "Standards of Conservation: Then and Now," *Conservation Biology* 4 (1990): 229–32.

3. A. Leopold, *A Sand County Almanac, and Sketches Here and There* (New York: Oxford University Press, 1949), 196.

4. H. K. Cordell and P. Reed, "Untrammeled by Man: Preserving Diversity through Wilderness," in *Preparing to Manage Wilderness in the 21st Century: Proceedings of the Conference,* ed. P. Reed (Asheville, N.C.: Department of Agriculture, Forest Service, Southeastern Forest Experimentation Station, 1990).

5. *Tribal Wilderness Ordinance of the Governing Body of the Confederated Salish and Kootenai Tribes,* 1982.

6. Leopold, *Sand County Almanac,* 200.

7. J. B. Callicott, "Non-anthropocentric Value Theory and Environmental Ethics," *American Philosophical Quarterly* 21 (1984): 305.

8. J. B. Callicott, "On the Intrinsic Value of Nonhuman Species," in *The Preservation of Species,* ed. B. Norton (Princeton, N.J.: Princeton University Press, 1986), 142–43, 156, 143.

9. Ibid., 160.

10. Leopold, *Sand County Almanac,* 200.

11. Ibid., 188.

12. Ibid., 201–4.

13. Leopold, quoted in C. Meine, *Aldo Leopold: His Life and Work* (Madison: University of Wisconsin Press, 1988), 245.

14. Leopold, *Sand County Almanac,* 200.

15. Leopold, quoted in Meine, *Aldo Leopold,* 248.

— *Animals* —

NOT LONG AGO it seemed unquestionable that cows belonged on plates, rats in laboratories, chimpanzees in zoos, and minks on the backs of the fashionably dressed. But since the publication of Peter Singer's landmark work, *Animal Liberation* (1975), all these practices have been called into question. It has gotten to the point, in many parts of America, that one had better think twice before walking down a crowded street wearing a fur coat.

Since the publication of *Animal Liberation*, there has been an explosion of writing by philosophers on the moral status of animals. Not surprisingly, since philosophers are a contentious lot, there has been much theoretical disagreement. What is surprising, however, is the extent of agreement on practice. As philosopher Lori Gruen shows, the case for changing our relationships with nonhuman animals has been articulated from a number of different moral perspectives. Rights theorists, utilitarians, and sympathy theorists have all argued that factory farming is wrong, that many uses of animals in laboratories cannot be defended, and that wearing fur is a moral offense. Of course, not all philosophers agree with these conclusions, but a substantial enough case has been made to put the defenders of the status quo on the defensive.

On the issue of zoos, concerns about animal welfare and the environment seem to conflict. The old reason for having zoos is that they provide entertainment for humans; these days, however, few zoo professionals endorse this reason. Increasingly, the case for zoos is made on the basis of their role in environmental education and in species preservation. American philosopher Dale Jamieson calls both of these supposed justifications into question. He argues that just as in the case of humans, there is a presumption in favor of liberty for animals. In his view, there is little evidence that zoos are successful enough in their education and preservation efforts to overcome this presumption. But even if zoos could succeed in saving endangered animals from extinction, Jamieson asks whether it is better "to confine a few hapless Mountain Gorillas in a zoo than to permit the species to become extinct."

Animal advocates have clashed with aboriginal peoples as well as with environmentalists. The Canadian anthropologist and geographer George Wenzel describes the conflict between some animal advocates and the Inuit people on the question of seal hunting. Wenzel argues that environmentalists and animal advocates who are *Quallunaat* (an Inuit word for people of European origin) often systematically appropriate aboriginal cultural images and oral traditions while denying native peoples their cultural autonomy. In this respect, environmentalists and animal advocates are no better than the missionaries who preceded them. Against claims that Inuit seal hunting is no longer part of a traditional culture—since it is pursued with snowmobiles and rifles—Wenzel argues that modern technology may change a practice without changing a culture; and at any rate, it is up to the Inuit to define their own traditional culture. This case, and others like it, present profound conflicts between universal moral values and the particular claims of local cultures.

As our thinking about animals and the environment matures, we will increasingly face hard choices among goods we wish to protect: the welfare of individual animals, species, indigenous cultures, and so on. From an evolutionary point of view, animals are our next of kin, yet their interests are barely represented in our political and legal systems. Perhaps more than in any other area of environmental concern, our treatment of nonhuman animals presents each of us with personal choices and conflicts. For how we choose to eat, clothe, and entertain ourselves has a direct effect on their well-being. The fate of a great many animals—whether they live or die, suffer or not—is up to us.

Further Reading

Hargrove, Eugene C., ed. *The Animal Rights/Environmental Ethics Debate*. Albany: State University of New York Press, 1992.

A collection of essays exploring the tensions between environmental philosophers and animal liberationists.

Midgley, Mary. *Animals and Why They Matter*. Athens: University of Georgia Press, 1983.

A subtle discussion of the roots of speciesism, and a reevaluation of the moral relations between humans and animals.

Singer, Peter. *Animal Liberation*, 2nd ed. New York: Random House, 1990.

The classic argument for a new ethic in our treatment of animals.

[From] Animals

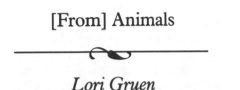

Lori Gruen

IN ORDER to satisfy the human taste for flesh, over 5 billion animals are slaughtered every year in the United States alone. Most chickens, pigs and calves raised for food never see the light of day. These animals are often so intensively confined that they are rarely able to turn around or spread a wing. An estimated 200 million animals are used routinely in laboratory experiments around the world annually. A large portion of the research causes the animals pain and discomfort while providing absolutely no benefit to human beings. An estimated 250 million wild animals are shot and killed each year by hunters in the United States. Over 650 different species of animals now threatened may be extinct by the turn of the century. These realities have caused many people to question our relationship to non-human animals.

The conditions under which animals are kept and the ways in which they are used by factory-farmers, experimenters, furriers, commercial developers and others tend to disregard the fact that animals are living, feeling creatures. Peter Singer's 1975 publication, *Animal Liberation,* challenged the attitude that animals are ours to use in whatever way we see fit and offered a 'new ethics for our treatment of animals'. This book also provided the moral foundation for a budding and boisterous animal liberation movement, and at the same time forced philosophers to begin addressing the moral status of animals. The ensuing discussion led to a general agreement that animals are not mere automata, that they are capable of suffering, and are due some moral consideration. The burden of proof shifted from those who want to protect animals from harm to those who believe that animals do not matter at all. The latter are now forced to defend their view against the widely accepted position that, at least, gratuitous animal suffering and death is not morally acceptable.

A few defences have been attempted. In his book, *The Case for Animal Experimentation,* Canadian philosopher Michael A. Fox set out to prove that animals are not members of the moral community and therefore humans have no moral obligation to them. He argued that 'a moral community is a social group composed of interacting autonomous beings where moral concepts and precepts can evolve and be understood. It is also a social group in which the mutual recognition of autonomy and personhood exist'.[1] An autonomous person, according to Fox, is one who is critically self-aware, able to manipulate complex concepts, capable of using sophisticated language, and has the capacity to plan, choose, and accept responsibility for actions. Members of the moral community as described are morally superior. Animals, not having valuable lives of their own to lead, cannot function as members of the moral community. He concludes that 'full members of the moral community may use less valuable species, which lack some or all of these traits, as means to their ends for the simple reason that they have no obligation not to do so'.[2]

Picking out one or more characteristics that are thought to differentiate non-humans from humans has been a constant theme in discussions regarding our relationship to animals. In the Christian tradition the line was drawn at possession of a soul: only creatures who had a soul mattered. When leaps of faith became unacceptable grounds for argument, the focus shifted to other 'measurable' differences such as tool use or brain size, but these did not prove particularly helpful in maintaining the desired distinction. The line-drawing concepts that Fox relied on, i.e., language use and autonomy, are more commonly used.

Some philosophers, most notably Donald Davidson in *Inquiries into Truth and Interpretation* and R. G. Frey in *Interests and Rights,* have argued that beings cannot have thoughts unless they can understand the speech of another.[3] Language, according to this view, is necessarily linked to propositional attitudes, such as 'desires', 'beliefs', or 'intentions'. A being cannot be excited or disappointed without language. While a being's ability to conceptualize and thus be aware of its role in directing the course of its life may indeed grant that being different moral status, the desired exclusion of all animals and no humans by virtue of their alleged lack of these abilities fails. It would be nonsensical to hold a lion morally responsible for the death of a gnu. As far as we know, lions aren't the sort of creatures that can engage in deliberations about the morality of such behaviour. Similarly, however, an infant cannot be held responsible for destroying an original sculpture, or a child held culpable for accidentally shooting her sister. Animals are not moral agents. While they may have choices, their choices are not the sort we would call value choices—choices which underlie ethical decisions. Infants, young children, developmentally impaired people, those in comas, victims of Alzheimer's disease, and other disabled human beings are also incapable of making moral decisions. All of these beings cannot be considered members of the moral community, as Fox would have it. Therefore, according to Fox's own logic, animals are not the only beings whom moral community members can use as we wish: the 'marginal' humans are also fair game.

Recognizing this problem, Fox attempts to bring humans, of whatever capability, into the protective moral community by arguing that their condition could very well have been our own. I might have been born without a brain, autistic or otherwise mentally impaired and if I had been, I would not want to be treated as if my suffering did not matter. Thus, 'charity, benevolence, humaneness, and prudence require' that we extend the moral community to include 'under-developed, deficient or seriously impaired human beings'.[4] One could argue, however, that I can no more imagine what it would be like to be autistic than I could imagine what it would be like to be an aardvark. Simply being part of the same species doesn't grant me a particularly special insight into another human's perspective, especially one who has a severe disability: my autonomous awareness doesn't necessarily provide me with a sensitivity toward deficient humans that I don't also have, or could not cultivate, towards animals. Fox's readiness to include the former but not the latter is arbitrary.

Recognizing this, and other mistakes in his work, Fox radically changed his views.[5] Less than a year after his book was published, Fox rejected the main thesis of his book, stating: 'I eventually came to believe that our basic moral obligations to avoid causing harm to other people should be extended to animals, and since I could not see any justification for our benefiting from harm caused other humans, I inferred that it would likewise be wrong for us to benefit from the suffering of animals.' Yet there is another conclusion that could have been drawn after recognizing that one couldn't find a moral basis for drawing the line around the human species while excluding non-humans. This is a position that is maintained by R. G. Frey. Frey recognizes that animals and 'marginal' humans deserve certain moral considerations and includes them within the moral community because they are beings who can suffer. However, he believes that their lives are not of comparable value to those of normal adult human beings, beings who are autonomous persons. Because he bases his argument on quality of life and assumes that the quality of life of a normal adult human is always greater than that of an animal or a deficient human, he concludes that one cannot invariably use animals in preference to 'marginal' humans. He writes, 'the only way we could justifiably do this is if we could cite something that always, no matter what, cedes human life greater value than animal life. I know of no such things'.[6]

Others have tried to argue that species membership is enough. Animals are not ethical beings and since they are not we owe them no moral considerations. They insist that this cannot be refuted by the argument for marginal humans because marginal humans are still humans and our obligations to them are derived from the essential nature of human beings, not from borderline cases. Frey, himself a proponent of a limited use of both animals and 'marginal' humans, has a compelling response to those who hold this human supremacist view. 'I cannot see that species membership is a ground for holding that we stand in a special moral relationship to our fellow humans . . . how, through merely being born, does one come to stand in a special moral relationship to humans generally?'[7]

Frey's position also has its problems. One might question his claim that normal adult humans necessarily have lives more worth living than normal adult animals. Yet Frey's evolving position, unlike those attempts to maintain a total rejection of the claim that animals matter, has benefitted tremendously from the arguments presented by the defenders of animals, arguments to which I will now turn. While there are a number of them, I will discuss two of the most common ethical positions, the rights argument and utilitarianism. I will point out some of the problems with these views and attempt to clarify common misunderstandings. I will then propose a less common way of looking at the question and suggest that this alternative may be worthy of further exploration.

Rights

The view that animals deserve moral consideration is often labelled with the words 'animal rights'. Journalists and activists alike have taken this slogan to refer to a wide range of positions. While 'animal rights' serves as a catchy way to draw attention to the plight of animals, much the way 'women's rights' did a couple of decades ago, it really refers to a very specific philosophical position. The view that animals have rights was most eloquently articulated by Tom Regan in *The Case for Animal Rights*.

Regan's view, greatly abbreviated, goes like this: only beings with inherent value have rights. Inherent value is the value that individuals have independent of their goodness or usefulness to others and rights are the things that protect this value. Only subjects-of-a-life have inherent value. Only self-conscious beings, capable of having beliefs and desires, only deliberate actors who can conceive of the future and entertain goals, are subjects-of-a-life. Regan believes that basically all mentally normal mammals of a year or more are subjects-of-a-life and thus have inherent value which allows them to have rights.

The rights which all subjects-of-a-life hold are moral rights, not to be confused with legal rights. Legal rights are the products of laws, which can vary from society to society. Moral rights, on the other hand, are said to belong to all subjects-of-a-life regardless of their colour, nationality, sex, and as Regan argues, species. When people speak of animal rights, then, they are not speaking of a cow's right to vote, a guinea pig's right to a fair trial, or a cat's right to religious freedom (three examples of legal rights that adults have in the United States), but about the right an animal has to be treated with respect as an individual with inherent value.

According to Regan, all beings who have inherent value have it equally. Inherent value cannot be gained by acting virtuously or lost by acting evilly. Florence Nightingale and Adolf Hitler, by virtue of the fact that they were subjects-of-a-life, and that fact alone, had equal inherent value. Inherent value is not something that can grow or diminish based on fads or fashion, popularity or privilege.

While this position is egalitarian and respects the value of individuals, it does not provide any guiding principle for action in cases where values conflict. Consider the following example, which Regan mentions: 'Imagine five survivors are on a lifeboat. Because of limits of size, the boat can only support four. All weigh approximately the same and would take up approximately the same amount of space. Four of the five are normal adult human beings. The fifth is a dog. One must be thrown overboard or else all will perish. Whom should it be?[8] Regan argues that we should kill the dog, because he says 'no reasonable person would deny that the death of any of the four humans would be a greater *prima facie* loss, and thus a greater *prima facie* harm, than would be true in the case of the dog. Death for the dog, in short, though a harm, is not comparable to the harm that death would be for any of the humans. To throw any one of the humans overboard, to face certain death, would be to make that individual worse-off (i.e., would cause *that* individual a greater harm) than the harm that would be done to the dog if the animal was thrown overboard.' He goes further and suggests that this would be true if the choice had to be made between the four humans and any number of dogs. He writes 'the rights view still implies that, special considerations apart, the million dogs should be thrown overboard and the four humans saved.'[9]

Regan argues that a human being is made worse off by being killed than a dog is, no matter who the dog or the human is. While it is true that humans can aspire to things that animals can't, such as finding a cure for AIDS or retarding the greenhouse effect, it is not obvious that the value of these aspirations plays any morally significant part in determining the severity of the harm that death is. For example, if I am thrown overboard before I get home to write the play I so often dream of writing or a dog is killed before he gets to go for one more run by the river, we both are having our desires thwarted and thwarted to the same degree—totally. One can only say that I am worse off because one thinks writing a play is more important than running by the river. But it surely isn't more important to the dog. The desire that a person has to accomplish their goals is presumably just as great for a dog, even if the goals are very different. As Dale Jamieson has put it, 'Death is the great equalizer. . . . Black or white, male or female, rich or poor, human or animal, death reduces us all to nothing.'[10]

Regan's rights view does have problems. It is a view that must either leave one paralysed when making tough decisions or force one to contradict oneself by maintaining that all are equal but in certain cases some beings are more equal than others. His view is one that tries to preserve the value of the individual apart from any consideration of that individual's worthiness or usefulness to others. However, in his attempt to minimize the impact on the individual of claims to promote 'the greater good' or 'welfare', Regan fails to provide a consistent prescription for action.

Utilitarianism

A utilitarian position does not focus on the equal value of all beings and therefore does not leave one unable to choose in conflict situations. Utilitarianism is, nonetheless, an egalitarian position. A utilitarian holds that in any situation the equal interests of all beings affected by an action must be considered equally. The equality that is important for this view is not the equal treatment of individuals, per se, but the equal consideration of their abilities to experience the world, most fundamental of which is the ability to suffer.

Like the rights view, a utilitarian position is one which does not allow arbitrary or prejudicial attitudes to influence moral judgements. All like interests are counted, regardless of the skin colour, sex, or species of the interest holder. As Peter Singer has stated, 'If a being suffers, there can be no moral justification for refusing to take that suffering into consideration. No matter what the nature of the being, the principle of equality requires that its suffering be counted equally with the like suffering—in so far as rough comparisons can be made—of any other being.'[11]

The utilitarian position works very well when the moral issue at hand involves making a decision that will cause pain or bring about pleasure. If an evil tyrant forces you to decide whether to slap your mother or have your cat's eye put out, a utilitarian would slap her mother and thus bring about the least amount of suffering, all else being equal. It should be pointed out that the principle of minimizing pain and maximizing pleasure does not apply only to physical suffering, but should also be looked to when psychological pain or pleasure is at stake, although, admittedly, that is harder to determine. But the utilitarian does run into problems when killing is involved. Let's return to Regan's lifeboat, only this time let's fill it with utilitarians and see what happens.

For a utilitarian, the lifeboat case becomes very complex. Because decisions must be based on a range of considerations, the example must be clarified before proceeding. Throwing any one of the passengers overboard may have effects on others who are not immediately present, such as their families and friends. Since a utilitarian must take into account the pain or suffering of everyone affected, not just those immediately present, we will have to assume that the survivors on the lifeboat lost all of their friends and family in the catastrophe which brought them to their current situation. This way, the only being affected by the act is the being who gets thrown overboard. We will also have to assume that whoever is thrown overboard will be painlessly killed by a lethal injection before being dumped in the ocean. No being's death will be longer, or more painful, than any other.

For a classical utilitarian, the answer is now fairly straightforward. The being who should be thrown overboard is that being who is the least happy now and is not likely to be particularly happy throughout his life. Since dogs are generally easily satisfied, this could mean that one of the humans should be thrown overboard. What matters to the utilitarian is not the species of those beings capable of contributing to the overall happiness of the moral universe, but the amount they contribute. In this situation, one is forced to reduce the total pleasure in the universe by removing one of the passengers in the lifeboat.

In order to minimize the overall loss of happiness, the being who is the most likely to lead an unhappy life will be the one to go.

Most people, even those who consider themselves utilitarians, can't easily swallow this decision. Indeed, it is exactly this sort of analysis that has spawned such theories as that held by Regan. Singer, however, defends a more sophisticated version of utilitarianism, namely preference utilitarianism, which attempts to sidestep this unsavoury conclusion. Singer argues that self-conscious, rational human beings are capable of having a specific preference for continued existence. Killing the humans on the lifeboat would clearly be in direct conflict with this preference. It is not clear that dogs have distinct preferences for continued existence, although they may have other preferences which would require continued existence in order to be satisfied. The conclusion that an 'enlightened' utilitarian might reach is similar to that reached by Regan, but the reasons are very different.

This agreement in practice is not uncommon. Those who agree with the rights argument as well as those who adhere to utilitarianism will not eat animals, but for different reasons. The former will be vegetarians, and perhaps vegans (those who avoid all animal products, including milk and eggs), because to use animals in such a way is not consistent with treating them as beings with inherent worth. To a person who holds the rights view, using an animal as a means to an end, in this case as food for the dinner table, is a violation of that being's right to be treated with respect. A utilitarian will abstain from eating animal products as long as the process that is used to raise them involves a net balance of suffering. If the animals live happy, stress-free, natural lives before they are painlessly killed, the utilitarian may not object to their use as food.

In the case of using animals in experimentation, the conclusions reached again differ more sharply in theory than in practice. According to Regan, 'the rights view is categorically abolitionist. . . . This is just as true when they [animals] are used in trivial, duplicative, unnecessary or unwise research as it is when they are used in studies that hold out real promise of human benefits. . . . The best we can do when it comes to using animals in science is—not to use them.'[12] Singer's position is very different. He would not advocate abolitionism in theory because 'in extreme circumstances, absolutist answers always break down . . . if a single experiment could cure a major disease, that experiment would be justifiable. But in actual life the benefits are always much, much more remote, and more often than not they are nonexistent . . . an experiment cannot be justifiable unless the experiment is so important that the use of a [brain-damaged] human being would also be justifiable.'[13]

Singer is not advocating that brain-damaged humans be used in experimentation, although some have accused him of holding this view. The point being made is that it is wrong to decide to experiment on animals rather than on humans with similar abilities to comprehend their situation if the readiness to experiment is based only on the fact that the animal is a different species. This bias in favour of one's own species has been called 'speciesism' and is considered morally on par with sexism and racism.

As the animal liberation issue has become more popular, species-based discrimination has become synonymous with bigotry. This is a dangerous simplification. Discrimination is not always unjust, and in fact, in some cases it may be crucial. As Mary Midgley has pointed out, 'It is never true that, in order to know how to treat a human being, you must first find out what race he belongs to. . . . But with an animal, to know the species is absolutely essential.'[14] The difference between an African and a cheetah is not the same as the difference between an African and an Eskimo. We do animals a great disservice if by including them in our sphere of moral concern we overlook their vast, marvellous differences from us, some of which may be relevant in moral deliberations.

Sympathy

Regan and Singer argue that giving greater weight to the interests of members of one's own species is indefensible. They suggest that animals and humans share the same morally relevant characteristics which provide each with equal claims. In a very simple world, this suggestion would not be problematic. But animals are not just animals—they are Lassie the dog and the family's companion cat; bald eagles and bunnies; snakes and skunks. Similarly, humans are not just humans—they are friends and lovers, family and foe. Kinship or closeness is a very important element in thinking about virtually every feature of our daily lives. To deny the reality of the influence this factor has on our decision-making in favour of some abstraction, like absolute equality, may be considered saintly, but probably is not possible for most mortals faced with complex decisions.

This focus on abstraction is not unique in moral theorizing. Philosophers long before Regan and Singer postulated that in order for a decision to be ethical it must go beyond our own preferences or partiality. Ethics, it has been said, must be universal, and universality can only be accomplished through abstract reasoning. If one values the life of a being who can enjoy life, then one must value every life of like beings in the same way. As Regan says, 'We know that many—literally, billions and billions—of these animals are subjects-of-a-life in the sense explained and so have inherent value if we do. And since, in order to arrive at the best theory of our duties to one another, we must recognize our equal inherent value as individuals, reason—not sentiment, not emotion—reason compels us to recognize the equal inherent value of these animals and, with this, their equal right to be treated with respect.'[15]

In the preface to *Animal Liberation*, Singer describes the justification of opposition to the Nazi experiments and animal experiments as 'an appeal to basic moral principles which we all accept, and the application of these principles to the victims of both kinds of experiments is demanded by reason, not emotion'. Obviously, reason has played a tremendous role in discussions of morality in general and particularly in discussions pertaining to the way moral principles apply to animals. If reason were the sole motivator of ethical behaviour, one might wonder why there are people who are familiar with the reasoning of Singer's work, for example, but who nonetheless continue to eat animals. While many have suggested that to act rationally entails acting morally, reason is only one element in decision making. Emotion, though often dismissed, plays a crucial role as well. Feelings of outrage or revulsion, sympathy or compassion are important to the development of complete moral sensibilities. As Mary Midgley has said, 'Real scruples, and eventually moral principles, are developed out of this kind of raw material. They would not exist without it.'[16]

Recognizing that appeals to sympathy are avoided by other proponents of animal liberation, John Fisher suggests that the very project of including animals in the moral community may be undermined by neglecting the powerful role sympathy plays. He argues that sympathy is fundamental to moral theory because it helps to determine who the proper recipients of moral concern are. Fisher suggests that those beings with whom we can sympathize must be morally considered. Presumably, how we treat those beings would be a function of our ability to sympathize with them.[17]

By arguing for the inclusion of animals in the moral sphere on the basis of reason, not emotion, philosophers are perpetuating an unnecessary dichotomy between the two. Certainly it is possible that a decision based on emotion alone may be morally indefensible, but it is also possible that a decision based on reason alone may be objectionable as well. One way to overcome the false dualism between reason and emotion is by moving out of the realm of abstraction and getting closer to the effects of our everyday actions. Much of the problem with the attitude many have towards animals stems from a removal from them. Our responsibility for our own actions has been mediated. Who are these animals who suffer and die so that I can eat pot roast? I do not deprive them of movement and comfort; I do not take their young from them; I do not have to look into their eyes as I cut their throats. Most people are shielded from the consequences of their actions. Factory-farms and laboratories are not places where many people go. The sympathy that people might naturally feel towards a being who is suffering, coupled with reasoned moral principles, would probably cause most to object to these institutions. While it is not possible for everyone directly to experience the effect of each and every one of their actions, that is no reason not to try. As feminist theorist Marti Kheel suggests, 'in our complex, modern society we may never be able to fully experience the impact of our moral decisions, we can, nonetheless, attempt as far as possible to experience emotionally the knowledge of this fact.'[18]

❧

While there are different philosophical principles that may help in deciding how we ought to treat animals, one strand runs through all those that withstand critical scrutiny: we ought not to treat animals the way we, as a society, are treating them now. We are very rarely faced with lifeboat decisions; our moral choices are not usually ones that exist in extremes. It simply isn't the case that I will suffer great harm without a fur coat or a leg of lamb. The choice between our baby and our dog is one that virtually none of us will be forced to make. The hypothetical realm is one where we can clarify and refine our moral intuitions and principles, but our choices and the suffering of billions of animals are not hypothetical. However the lines are drawn, there are no defensible grounds for treating animals in any way other than as beings worthy of moral consideration.

Notes

1. M. A. Fox, *The Case for Animal Experimentation* (Berkeley: University of California Press, 1986), 50.

2. Ibid., 88.

3. D. Davidson, *Inquiries into Truth and Interpretation* (Oxford: Oxford University Press, 1984); R. G. Frey, *Interests and Rights: The Case Against Animals* (Oxford: Clarendon Press, 1980).

4. Fox, *Case for Animal Experimentation*, 61–63.

5. M. A. Fox, letter in the *Scientist*, 15 December 1986, and "Animal Experimentation: A Philosopher's Changing Views," *Between the Species* 3 (1987): 55–60.

6. R. G. Frey, "Moral Standing, the Value of Lives, and Speciesism," *Between the Species* 4 (1988): 197.

7. Frey, *Interests and Rights*, 199.

8. T. Regan, *The Case for Animal Rights* (Berkeley: University of California Press, 1983), 285.

9. Ibid., 324–25.

10. D. Jamieson, "Two Problems with Regan's Theory of Rights" (Paper presented at the meeting of the Pacific Division, American Philosophical Association, 1985).

11. P. Singer, *Practical Ethics*, 2nd ed. (New York: Cambridge University Press, 1993), 57 [this volume, 54].

12. T. Regan, "The Case for Animal Rights," in *In Defense of Animals*, ed. P. Singer (Oxford: Basil Blackwell, 1985), 24.

13. P. Singer, *Animal Liberation*, 2nd ed. (New York: Random House, 1990), 85.

14. M. Midgley, *Animals and Why They Matter* (Athens: University of Georgia Press, 1983), 98.

15. Regan, "Case for Animal Rights," 23–24.

16. Midgley, *Animals and Why They Matter*, 43.

17. J. Fisher, "Taking Sympathy Seriously," *Environmental Ethics* 9 (1987): 197–215.

18. M. Kheel, "The Liberation of Nature: A Circular Affair," *Environmental Ethics* 7 (1985): 135–49.

Against Zoos

Dale Jamieson

Zoos and Their History

We can start with a rough-and-ready definition of zoos: they are public parks which display animals, primarily for the purposes of recreation or education. Although large collections of animals were maintained in antiquity, they were not zoos in this sense. Typically these ancient collections were not exhibited in public parks, or they were maintained for purposes other than recreation or education.

The Romans, for example, kept animals in order to have living fodder for the games. Their enthusiasm for the games was so great that even the first tigers brought to Rome, gifts to Caesar Augustus from an Indian ruler, wound up in the arena. The emperor Trajan staged 123 consecutive days of games in order to celebrate his conquest of Dacia. Eleven thousand animals were slaughtered, including lions, tigers, elephants, rhinoceroses, hippopotami, giraffes, bulls, stags, crocodiles and serpents. The games were popular in all parts of the Empire. Nearly every city had an arena and a collection of animals to stock it. In fifth-century France there were twenty-six such arenas, and they continued to thrive until at least the eighth century.

In antiquity rulers also kept large collections of animals as a sign of their power, which they would demonstrate on occasion by destroying their entire collections. This happened as late as 1719 when Elector Augustus II of Dresden personally slaughtered his entire menagerie, which included tigers, lions, bulls, bears and boars.

The first modern zoos were founded in Vienna, Madrid and Paris in the eighteenth century and in London and Berlin in the nineteenth. The first American zoos were established in Philadelphia and Cincinnati in the 1870s. Today in the United States alone there are hundreds of zoos, and they are visited by millions of people every year. They range from roadside menageries run by hucksters, to elaborate zoological parks staffed by trained scientists.

The Roman games no longer exist, though bullfights and rodeos follow in their tradition. Nowadays the power of our leaders is amply demonstrated by their command of nuclear weapons. Yet we still have zoos. Why?

Animals and Liberty

Before we consider the reasons that are usually given for the survival of zoos, we should see that there is a moral presumption against keeping wild animals in captivity. What this involves, after all, is taking animals out of their native habitats, transporting them great distances and keeping them in alien environments in which their liberty is severely restricted. It is surely true that in being taken from the wild and confined in zoos, animals are deprived of a great many goods. For the most part they are prevented from gathering their own food, developing their own social orders and generally behaving in ways that are natural to them. These activities all require significantly more liberty than most animals are permitted in zoos. If we are justified in keeping animals in zoos, it must be because there are some important benefits that can be obtained only by doing so.

This conclusion is not the property of some particular moral theory; it follows from most reasonable moral theories. Either we have duties to animals or we do not. If we do have duties to animals, surely they include respecting those interests which are most important to them, so long as this does not conflict with other, more stringent duties that we may have. Since an interest in not being taken from the wild and kept confined is very important for most animals, it follows that if everything else is equal, we should respect this interest.

Suppose, on the other hand, that we do not have duties to animals. There are two further possibilities: either we have duties to people that sometimes concern animals, or what we do to animals is utterly without moral import. The latter view is quite implausible, and I shall not consider it further. People who have held the former view, that we have duties to people that concern animals, have sometimes thought that such duties arise because we can 'judge the heart of a man by his treatment of animals', as Kant remarked in 'Duties to Animals'. It is for this reason that he condemns the man who shoots a faithful dog who has become too old to serve. If we accept Kant's premise, it is surely plausible to say that someone who, for no good reason, removes wild animals from their natural habitats and denies them liberty is someone whose heart deserves to be judged harshly. If this is so, then even if we believe that we do not have duties to animals but only duties concerning them, we may still hold that there is a presumption against keeping wild animals in captivity. If this presumption is to be overcome, it must be shown that there are important benefits that can be obtained only by keeping animals in zoos.

Arguments for Zoos

What might some of these important benefits be? Four are commonly cited: amusement, education, opportunities for scientific research and help in preserving species.

Amusement was certainly an important reason for the establishment of the early zoos, and it remains an important function of contemporary zoos as well. Most people visit zoos in order to be entertained, and any zoo that wishes to remain financially sound must cater to this desire. Even highly regarded zoos, like the San Diego Zoo, have their share of dancing bears and trained birds of prey. But although providing amusement for people is viewed by the general public as a very important function of zoos, it is hard to see how providing such amusement could possibly justify keeping wild animals in captivity.

Most curators and administrators reject the idea that the primary purpose of zoos is to provide entertainment. Indeed, many agree that the pleasure we take in viewing wild animals is not in itself a good enough reason to keep them in captivity. Some curators see baby elephant walks, for example, as a necessary evil, or defend such amusements because of their role in educating people, especially children, about animals. It is sometimes said that people must be interested in what they are seeing if they are to be educated about it, and entertainments keep people interested, thus making education possible.

This brings us to a second reason for having zoos: their role in education. This reason has been cited as long as zoos have existed. For example, in 1898 the New York Zoological Society resolved to take 'measures to inform the public of the great decrease in animal life, to stimulate sentiment in favor of better protection, and to cooperate with other scientific bodies . . . [in] efforts calculated to secure the perpetual preservation of our higher vertebrates'. Despite the pious platitudes that are often uttered about the educational efforts of zoos, however, there is little evidence that zoos are very successful in educating people about animals. Stephen Kellert's paper 'Zoological Parks in American Society', delivered at the annual meeting of the American Association of Zoological Parks and Aquariums in 1979, indicates that zoo-goers are much less knowledgeable about animals than backpackers, hunters, fishermen and others who claim an interest in animals, and only slightly more knowledgeable than those who claim no interest in animals at all. Even more disturbing, zoo-goers express the usual prejudices about animals; 73 per cent say they dislike rattle-snakes, 52 per cent vultures and only 4 per cent elephants. One reason why some zoos have not done a better job in educating people is that many of them make no real effort at education. In the case of others the problem is an apathetic and unappreciative public.

Edward G. Ludwig's study of the zoo in Buffalo, New York, in the *International Journal for the Study of Animal Problems* for 1981, revealed a surprising amount of dissatisfaction on the part of young, scientifically inclined zoo employees. Much of this dissatisfaction stemmed from the almost complete indifference of the public to the zoo's educational efforts. Ludwig's study indicated that most animals are viewed only briefly as people move quickly past cages. The typical zoo-goer stops only to watch baby animals or those who are begging, feeding or making sounds. Ludwig reported that the most common expressions used to describe animals are 'cute', 'funny-looking', 'lazy', 'dirty', 'weird' and 'strange'.

Of course, it is undeniable that some education occurs in some zoos. But this very fact raises other issues. What is it that we want people to learn from visiting zoos? Facts about the physiology and behaviour of various animals? Attitudes towards the survival of endangered species? Compassion for the fate of all animals? To what degree does education require keeping wild animals in captivity? Couldn't most of the educational benefits of zoos be obtained by presenting films, slides, lectures and so forth? Indeed, couldn't most of the important educational objectives better be achieved by exhibiting empty cages with explanations of why they are empty?

A third reason for having zoos is that they support scientific research. This, too, is a benefit that was pointed out long ago. Sir Humphrey Davy, one of the founders of the Zoological Society of London, wrote in 1825: 'It would become Britain to offer another, and a very different series of exhibitions to the population of her metropolis; namely, animals brought from every part of the globe to be applied either to some useful purpose, or as objects of scientific research—not of vulgar admiration!' Zoos support scientific research in at least three ways: they fund field research by scientists not affiliated with zoos; they employ other scientists as members of zoo staffs; and they make otherwise inaccessible animals available for study.

The first point we should note is that very few zoos support any real scientific research. Fewer still have staff scientists with full-time research appointments. Among those that do, it is common for their scientists to study animals in the wild rather than those in zoo collections. Much of this research, as well as other field research that is supported by zoos, could just as well be funded in a different way—say, by a government agency. The question of whether there should be zoos does not turn on the funding for field research which zoos currently provide. The significance of the research that is actually conducted in zoos is a more important consideration.

Research that is conducted in zoos can be divided into two categories: studies in behaviour and studies in anatomy and pathology.

Behavioural research conducted on zoo animals is very controversial. Some have argued that nothing can be learned by studying animals that are kept in the unnatural conditions that obtain in most zoos. Others have argued that captive animals are more interesting research subjects than are wild animals: since captive animals are free from predation, they exhibit a wider range of physical and behavioural traits than animals in the wild, thus permitting researchers to view the full range of their genetic possibilities. Both of these positions are surely extreme. Conditions in some zoos are natural enough to permit some interesting research possibilities. But the claim that captive animals are more interesting research subjects than those in the wild is not very plausible. Environments trigger behaviours. No doubt a predation-free environment triggers behaviours different from those of an animal's natural habitat, but there is no reason to believe that better, fuller or more accurate data can be obtained in predation-free environments than in natural habitats.

Studies in anatomy and pathology are the most common forms of zoo research. Such research has three main purposes: to improve zoo conditions so that captive animals will live longer, be happier and breed more frequently; to contribute to human health by providing animal models for human ailments; and to increase our knowledge of wild animals for its own sake.

The first of these aims is surely laudable, if we concede that there should be zoos in the first place. But the fact that zoo research contributes to improving conditions in zoos is not a reason for having them. If there were no zoos, there would be no need to improve them.

The second aim, to contribute to human health by providing animal models for human ailments, appears to justify zoos to some extent, but in practice this consideration is not as important as one might think. There are very severe constraints on the experiments that may be conducted on zoo animals. In an article entitled 'A Search for Animal Models at Zoos', published in *ILAR News* in 1982, Richard Montali and Mitchell Bush drew the following conclusion:

> Despite the great potential of a zoo as a resource for models, there are many limitations and, of necessity, some restrictions for use. There is little opportunity to conduct overly manipulative or invasive research procedures—probably less than would be allowed in clinical research trials involving human beings. Many of the species are difficult to work with or are difficult to breed, so that the numbers of animals available for study are limited. In fact, it is safe to say that over the past years, humans have served more as 'animal models' for zoo species than is true of the reverse.

Whether for this reason or others, much of what has been done in using zoo animals as models for humans seems redundant or trivial. For example, the article cited above reports that zoo animals provide good models for studying lead toxicity in humans, since it is common for zoo animals to develop lead poisoning from chewing paint and inhaling polluted city air. There are available for study plenty of humans who suffer from lead poisoning for the same reasons. That zoos make available some additional non-human subjects for this kind of research seems at best unimportant and at worst deplorable.

Finally, there is the goal of obtaining knowledge about animals for its own sake. Knowledge is certainly something which is good and, everything being equal, we should encourage people to seek it for its own sake. But everything is not equal in this case. There is a moral presumption against keeping animals in captivity. This presumption can be overcome only by demonstrating that there are important benefits that must be obtained in this way if they are to be obtained at all. It is clear that this is not the case with knowledge for its own sake. There are other channels for our intellectual curiosity, ones that do not exact such a high moral price. Although our quest for knowledge for its own sake is important, it is not important enough to overcome the moral presumption against keeping animals in captivity.

In assessing the significance of research as a reason for having zoos, it is important to remember that very few zoos do any research at all. Whatever benefits result from zoo research could just as well be obtained by having a few zoos instead of the hundreds which now exist. The most this argument could establish is that we are justified in having a few very good zoos. It does not provide a defence of the vast majority of zoos which now exist.

A fourth reason for having zoos is that they preserve species that would otherwise become extinct. As the destruction of habitat accelerates and as breeding programmes become increasingly successful, this rationale for zoos gains in popularity. There is some reason for questioning the commitment of zoos to preservation: it can be argued that they continue to remove more animals from the wild than they return. Still, zoo breeding programmes have had some notable successes: without them the Père David Deer, the Mongolian Wild Horse and the European Bison would all now be extinct. Recently, however, some problems have begun to be noticed.

A 1979 study by Katherine Ralls, Kristin Brugger and Jonathan Ballou, which was reported in *Science*, convincingly argues that lack of genetic diversity among captive animals is a serious problem for zoo breeding programmes. In some species the infant mortality rate among inbred animals is six or seven times that among non-inbred animals. In other species the infant mortality rate among inbred animals is 100 per cent. What is most disturbing is that zoo curators have been largely unaware of the problems caused by inbreeding because adequate breeding and health records have not been kept. It is hard to believe that zoos are serious about their role in preserving endangered species when all too often they do not take even this minimal step.

In addition to these problems, the lack of genetic diversity among captive animals also means that surviving members of endangered species have traits very different from their conspecifics in the wild. This should make us wonder what is really being preserved in zoos. Are captive Mongolian Wild Horses really Mongolian Wild Horses in any but the thinnest biological sense?

There is another problem with zoo breeding programmes: they create many unwanted animals. In some species (lions, tigers and zebras, for example) a few males can service an entire herd. Extra males are unnecessary to the programme and are a financial burden. Some of these animals are sold and wind up in the hands of individuals and institutions which lack proper facilities. Others are shot and killed by Great White Hunters in private hunting camps. In order to avoid these problems, some zoos have been considering proposals to 'recycle' excess animals: a euphemism for killing them and feeding their bodies to other zoo animals. Many people are surprised when they hear of zoos killing animals. They should not be. Zoos have limited capacities. They want to maintain diverse collections. This can be done only by careful management of their 'stock'.

Even if breeding programmes were run in the best possible way, there are limits to what can be done to save endangered species. For many large mammals a breeding herd of at least a hundred animals, half of them born in captivity, is required if they are to survive in zoos. As of 1971 only eight mammal species satisfied these conditions. Paul and Anne Ehrlich estimate in their book *Extinction* that under the best possible conditions American zoos could preserve only about a hundred species of mammals—and only at a very high price: maintaining a breeding herd of herbivores costs between $75,000 and $250,000 per year.

There are further questions one might ask about preserving endangered species in zoos. Is it really better to confine a few hapless Mountain Gorillas in a zoo than to permit the species to become extinct? To most environmentalists the answer is obvious: the species must be preserved at all costs. But this smacks of sacrificing the lower-case gorilla for the upper-case Gorilla. In doing this, aren't we using animals as mere vehicles for their genes? Aren't we preserving genetic material at the expense of the animals themselves? If it is true that we are inevitably moving towards a world in which Mountain Gorillas can survive only in zoos, then we must ask whether it is really better for them to live in artificial environments of our design than not to be born at all.

Even if all of these difficulties are overlooked, the importance of preserving endangered species does not provide much support for the existing system of zoos. Most zoos do very little breeding or breed only species which are not endangered. Many of the major breeding programmes are run in special facilities which have been established for that purpose. They are often located in remote places, far from the attention of zoo-goers. (For example, the Bronx Zoo operates its Rare Animal Survival Center on St Catherine's Island off the coast of Georgia, and the National Zoo runs its Conservation and Research Center in the Shenandoah Valley of Virginia.) If our main concern is to do what we can to preserve endangered species, we should support such large-scale breeding centres rather than conventional zoos, most of which have neither the staff nor the facilities to run successful breeding programmes.

~

The four reasons for having zoos which I have surveyed carry some weight. But different reasons provide support for different kinds of zoo. Preservation and perhaps research are better carried out in large-scale animal preserves, but these provide few opportunities for amusement and education. Amusement and perhaps education are better provided in urban zoos, but they offer few opportunities for research and preservation. Moreover, whatever benefits are obtained from any kind of zoo must confront the moral presumption against keeping wild animals in captivity. Which way do the scales tip? There are two further considerations which, in my view, tip the scales against zoos.

First, captivity does not just deny animals liberty but is often detrimental to them in other respects as well. The history of chimpanzees in the zoos of Europe and America is a good example.

Chimpanzees first entered the zoo world in about 1640 when a Dutch prince, Frederick Henry of Nassau, obtained one for his castle menagerie. The chimpanzee didn't last very long. In 1835 the London Zoo obtained its first chimpanzee; he died immediately. Another was obtained in 1845; she lived six months. All through the nineteenth and early twentieth centuries zoos obtained chimpanzees who promptly died within nine months. It wasn't until the 1930s that it was discovered that chimpanzees are extremely vulnerable to human respiratory diseases, and that special steps must be taken to protect them. But for nearly a century zoos removed them from the wild and subjected them to almost certain death. Problems remain today. When chimpanzees are taken from the wild the usual procedure is to shoot the mother and kidnap the child. The rule of thumb among trappers is that ten chimpanzees die for every one that is delivered alive to the United States or Europe. On arrival many of these animals are confined under abysmal conditions.

Chimpanzees are not the only animals to suffer in zoos. In 1974 Peter Batten, former director of the San Jose Zoological Gardens, undertook an exhaustive study of two hundred American zoos. In his book *Living Trophies* he documented large numbers of neurotic, overweight animals kept in cramped, cold cells and fed unpalatable synthetic food. Many had deformed feet and appendages caused by unsuitable floor surfaces. Almost every zoo studied had excessive mortality rates, resulting from preventable factors ranging from vandalism to inadequate husbandry practices. Battan's conclusion was: 'The majority of American zoos are badly run, their direction incompetent, and animal husbandry inept and in some cases nonexistent.'

Many of these same conditions and others are documented in *Pathology of Zoo Animals*, a review of necropsies conducted by Lynn Griner over the last fourteen years at the San Diego Zoo. This zoo may well be the best in the country, and its staff is clearly well-trained and well-intentioned. Yet this study documents widespread malnutrition among zoo animals; high mortality rates from the use of anaesthetics and tranquillizers; serious injuries and deaths sustained in transport; and frequent occurrences of cannibalism, infanticide and fighting almost certainly caused by overcrowded conditions. Although the zoo has learned from its mistakes, it is still unable to keep many wild animals in captivity without killing or injuring them, directly or indirectly. If this is true of the San Diego Zoo, it is certainly true, to an even greater extent, at most other zoos.

The second consideration is more difficult to articulate but is, to my mind, even more important. Zoos teach us a false sense of our place in the natural order. The means of confinement mark a difference between humans and animals. They are there at our pleasure, to be used for our purposes. Morality and perhaps our very survival require that we learn to live as one species among many rather than as one species over many. To do this, we must forget what we learn at zoos. Because what zoos teach us is false and dangerous, both humans and animals will be better off when they are abolished.

[From] *Animal Rights, Human Rights: Ecology, Economy and Ideology in the Canadian Arctic*

George Wenzel

Introduction

Millions of people living in the United States, the United Kingdom, and Western Europe now hold as an article of faith that the preservation of seals in Canadian waters, and hence the cessation of Canadian seal hunting, is a moral test of the relationship between human beings and the other animals on this planet. A perception of this test as critical has been built by three decades of strident argument, invective, and protest. Canada has been the focus of the campaign against seal hunting because it is the only industrialized nation carrying on widespread commercial sealing activities. For many Americans and Europeans, the Canadian seal controversy comprises everything they know about seals, animal rights, and environmentalism. The place and importance of seals in Inuit culture is certainly far less well known.

The nature of this debate is encapsulated in two photographs that appeared in a direct-mail pamphlet opposed to Canadian sealing. The first picture shows a newborn, or whitecoat, harp seal. The pup's coal-black eyes stare serenely into those of the viewer. Except for those calm eyes, the animal is almost pure white and behind it is pristine and glittering ice. The second photo is of a terrified pup facing a roughly clothed man who looms over it. In his hands is a spiked club poised to strike. The background is no longer unsullied ice; rather the whole surface is mottled with pools of blood that stretch into the far distance. The front cover of this brochure thoughtfully warns that its contents may be disturbing.

Until a few years ago, these two photographs offered a powerful statement about economic reality for generations of Canadian fishermen. Each spring, for some two hundred years, the men of Newfoundland and the Gulf of St. Law-

rence turned to harp sealing as a source of income. Without sealskins, loans
were unavailable for fishing.

Today these pictures carry an entirely different meaning. They draw a battle
line between the harmony and stability of nature and the wanton disregard of
man toward our planet; nature is benevolent, man is cruel. The harp seal pup
has become a symbol for environmental awareness and for a social philosophy
that has come to be generally known as the animal rights movement. These
photographs also present the clash between Inuit and animal rightists because
the movement perceives Inuit use of seals in the same terms.

Although animal rights appears to be a product of the last thirty years, its
roots run considerably deeper. Where it differs from its historical antecedents,
both philosophically and ethically, is that, while the ethos of respect and rights
for animals has long been a matter of individual conscience, the modern animal
rights movement seeks militant economic and political solutions to end what it
refers to as speciesism, the dominance of all other animals by man.

It has become alarmingly commonplace to paint a whole spectrum of opinion
and viewpoint, and hence organizations, as 'animal rights advocates'. As a general label, the animal rights appelation is misleading. In fact, it has, at times,
been placed on groups as different in philosophy and intent as the Wilderness
Society and the RSPCA, the radical ecologists, anti-vivisectionists, as well as
self-proclaimed animal rightists. The *mélange* is often contradictory. (In similar
fashion, 'the fur industry' has become a catch-all for animal activists that includes within its sweep the Hudson's Bay Company, designers of fur fashions,
mink ranchers, Inuit and Indian hunter-trappers, and even wearers of fur.)

Confused and loose application of the animal rights label can, at times, also
be related to the way the movement has attempted to portray itself. For instance, some animal rightists have selected a patchwork of ideas from orthodox
ecology, conservation, and wildlife management theory. Ideas have been 'borrowed' from the works of naturalists like Leopold and Muir, often free from
any original context, to legitimize the protectionist perspective. In the process,
the separation between conservationist and animal rights points of view has
become blurred. In a similar manner, the seal protest brought together a
mixture of radical and mainstream ecological thought to serve its specific needs
and objectives.

The other side of this coin is the willingness of pro-sealing forces, the 'fur
industry', to respond to virtually all criticism of its position by labelling
critics as 'animal rightist'. In the end, both sides' rhetoric reflects hardening
attitudes. . . .

The Animal Rights Situation

The animal rights movement, for all the success achieved through the seal
protest and European sealskin ban, presently also occupies a stance that is, at

least, uncomfortable to maintain vis-à-vis Inuit. During the movement's early days (pre-1985), animal rightists publicly portrayed themselves as being in fundamental sympathy with Native Peoples caught up in the seal protest. At the same time . . . the movement tried to maintain this sympathetic public face while dismissing further dialogue with Inuit over seals as dwelling on past history.

The expansion of the seal protest into a much wider anti-wild fur/trapping campaign intensified, rather than relieved, the pressure the movement came to receive from Canadian aboriginal people. Indeed, the effect of this criticism about organizations' views of Native hunter-trappers led to the withdrawal of some seal protest members, notably Greenpeace International and Greenpeace Canada, from the fur campaign.

The fur campaign, which encompassed within its scope not just Inuit but all northern Natives, seems to have, in fact, galvanized a hardening of attitude among the protest groups that chose to persist.

. . . [T]he anomalous relationship that had punctuated Inuit–seal protest dialogue became clarified as a simple case of two political bodies openly in opposition to each other. Native People ceased to represent a moral counter-point to the animal rights view, but rather have become 'a political problem'. The movement then began to 'test' arguments for offsetting Inuit critiques of their protest, so as at least to reduce it to a manageable political level.

These political counter-efforts, as they have been internally developed, have followed the same kind of selective perception process Hunter has described with regard to the early stages of the seal protest.[1] In the seal campaign this included not only the strong anthropomorphization of individual seals, but also the creating of an image of sealers as an anonymous, emotionless entity. A powerful contrast was thus manufactured between a viewer's felt preference for baby seals and the 'abnormal' behavior, in terms of the general experience of the seal campaign's audience, of Euro-Canadian sealers.

Since 1985, it appears that a similar selective perception strategy has been adopted with regard to the political problem Inuit and other aboriginal peoples pose to animal rights objectives. For instance, the term 'Natives' has been adopted by animal advocates to categorize the whole spectrum of aboriginal opposition to their program(s) and is applied to aboriginal critics whether they represent Indigenous Survival International or an ethnically identifiable ab-original group. . . .

From 1985 onward, the movement has increasingly oriented its rhetoric toward the 'demythologizing' of such concepts as tradition or subsistence with regard to contemporary Inuit and Indian culture. Livingston has labelled the continued application of these terms to modern aboriginal consumptive activi-ties like Inuit seal hunting and Cree trapping as the product of 'neo-traditionalism.'[2] Likewise, Greanville and O'Sullivan have conceptually linked present-day Inuit and Indian use of wildlife to the efforts of these Peoples to reach agreement with Canada on the issue of Native land claims.[3] In so doing, animal rightists have interpreted Native subsistence activities to be mainly a tactic for exacting financial compensation from government and, in so doing, have lost sight of the larger issue—aboriginal political, social, and economic self-determination—which the term 'land claims' so poorly conveys.

Inuit and other Canadian Native Peoples have argued that the animal rights movement, by refusing to acknowledge the particular cultural, ecological, economic, and historical circumstances of aboriginal life and interaction with wildlife, has acted with little difference from earlier generations of southern imperialists. In essence, that it has acted with same ethnocentric raison d'être that has characterized all but perhaps the earliest moments of Inuit contact with Western culture.

To a large extent, that is the conclusion reached here, especially about the movement's behavior and attitude toward Inuit since the early 1980s. Like earlier missionaries, religious and secular, who have 'visited' themselves upon Inuit, the movement's advocates have followed a course of action based on the enlightened perspective from which *Qallunaat* culture has proceeded in its relations with Inuit.

Many feel, however, that the animal rightists, having been rebuffed, have accepted Inuit criticism with less grace than many of the southerners who preceded them. As the gap between Inuit and the movement has widened, it has become not uncommon to find Inuit seal hunting easily compared in some circles with East African ivory poaching. Moreover, this feat is accomplished with little, if any, reflection about the cultural and historical circumstances that might offer insight into the activities of Inuit or the African peoples whom we categorize as poachers.[4] The breadth of such generalization, in fact, makes it important to ask how it is achieved.

The link that permits such comparison is the way the movement defines wildlife and, especially, the lives of individual animals as an inherent 'Good'. While this perspective is, perhaps, a valid one within a strictly Western cultural context, its application to non-Western societies, without regard to either the specifics of culture or history, raises serious question about the way the movement substitutes action for responsibility as it pursues its objective. This is especially the case in the Inuit sealing controversy because the matter is not clouded by endangered species concerns or First versus Third World hostility as it is in many other areas of the world. (Indeed, the latter dynamic is so far absent in the North that some animal rightists have sanguinely declared that Inuit are, in reality, part of Euro-Canadian culture.)

The animal rights movement has long argued that it is free of cultural constraint precisely because there can be no 'Good' equal in moral weight to the one it has accepted. If this is true, then Watson is correct in pursuing the universal establishment of animal rights as a general social philosophy.[5] The fact, however, that the movement has taken upon itself the special task of 'demythologizing' Native culture(s) suggests that it feels the sting of the cultural imperialism accusation which Inuit have levelled at it and that the public upon whom it depends is aware of this.

Another important question which arises directly from the Inuit sealing situation concerns the appropriateness of the animal rights movement's attempts to reinterpret Inuit, Cree, or other Native cultures' traditions for its followers and the general public. This process, which includes not only demythologizing but also the appropriating of aspects of these traditions, has played an important role in the animal rights campaign regarding Native People. . . .

While the appropriation of Native clothing and artifacts has long been the pleasure of hobbyists, the kinds of systematic appropriation of aboriginal cultural image and oral tradition, while rejecting any acknowledgement of Native cultural reality, has become a mark of the conflict dynamic between the movement and Native People. The only secure defense against the perpetuation of this kind of ethnocentrism in the northern sealing conflict is to allow Inuit the right to their own culture, history and traditions.

This, in turn, must necessarily be accompanied by *Qallunaat* allowing Inuit the means to express their chief contribution to this history, the practice of their culture. The animal rights movement has, to date, been at best grudging in this regard. Instead, it has chosen to apply labels, like neo-traditional and speciesist, not analysis, to those practices which it finds not to its liking. At least until the time comes when animal rights advocates establish a valid, non-ethnocentric basis for their application of these labels to Native society, it must be recognized that the interest Inuit hold in this debate is deeply rooted in their traditional culture.

As the situation exists today, animal rightists seek to impose upon Inuit an atomistic form of anthropomorphism, in which animals are individually idealized as each having inherent moral worth. This view is in contradistinction to that of Inuit for whom animals, through their meat and pelts, offer the means by which individual humans contribute to the collective security of the social group. The movement, however, summarily rejects the proposition that Inuit perception and behavior toward animals can be rooted in anything more complex than a desire to obtain the imported goods that sealskins can provide.

In adopting this stance toward what is, in fact, a well-considered ecosystemic cultural adaptation, the movement rejects not only the practices by which Inuit sustain themselves, but also the right of Inuit to any course of action which it does not validate. Recently, this view appears to provide a license through which all aspects of contemporary Inuit culture, from seal harvesting to the settlement of aboriginal title to traditional land and resources, can be placed in a negative perspective.

The Inuit seal controversy is far from over despite the renewal of the European sealskin ban. This is because, first, Inuit, despite protest denials to the contrary, must adapt to a unique phase in their experience with southern society. It is the 'animal rights phase', just as there were the fur trade and government phases. It is marked, however, by the first deliberate attempt by *Qallunaat* to systematically alienate Inuit from the resources they have customarily depended on for their cultural independence. The solutions to the problems that this has created are much further away than the simple return to the winter *aglu* with harpoon in hand that the animal rights movement suggests.

. . . [S]uch a hope on the part of animal rightists is unrealistic, but not because Inuit have for too long succumbed to the lure of modernity. Rather, the problems that modern life in the North presents to Inuit require more than a return to the material condition of an idealized past can accomplish. They require an appreciation on the part of Inuit and Euro-Canadians of just how complexly the interactions of both cultures have changed the human environment of the North.

Continuation of the northern seal controversy as it is presently being conducted does not bode well for either of the parties involved. Inuit remain faced by the prospect of reassembling the stability that seal, caribou, and other species offered the traditional subsistence system. In this regard, the solutions that are currently being imported, adventure tourism, commercial food harvesting, and further bureaucratization, are far from the mark. All are the product of non-Inuit imagination. Past experience with externally developed strategies for Inuit cultural 'development' suggests that even the best ideas, proposed without indigenous input, invariably produce little else but greater change.⁶

As for the movement, every escalation in the rhetoric it directs toward aboriginal peoples multiplies the risks it runs for itself and its message. For instance, the Inuit seal controversy, and, now, Native trapping, have brought the most uncompromising exponents of the animal rights philosophy to the fore of the public's attention. . . . The risk is that the rigid dogmatism this wing represents regarding Native society and culture may, as it receives greater exposure, weaken the important larger social influence the movement has obtained over non-Native issues.

Acrimonious debate with Inuit and Indians, who are themselves equally worthy objects of empathy, has already become an important matter of concern, affecting both the internal and external relations of the movement. So much so that, in the first case, some original seal protest actors, like Greenpeace, have chosen to disassociate themselves from further conflict with Inuit.

With regard to the movement's external relations, the arguments that animal rightists have flung back at Native critics, regarding economic complicity and cultural assimilation, have not served it well. Although the Native community (including sympathetic social scientists) was initially stunned by statements that linked the problems of modern aboriginal society exclusively to the fur trade and its own weakness, the past several years have shown Native Peoples to be both a resilient and powerful opponent.

These declarations have precipitated two unfortunate results. The first is that they have caused Inuit increasingly to reject parts of the movement's message with which they were once in sympathy. Inuit initiatives for compromise have been, and remain, based on the appeal that some aspects of this message holds for them.

Second, the movement's own dogmatic stance provided the basis for Inuit joining the fur industry and government in the countercoalition activists now face. In this regard, and as much as the movement may point an accusing finger at such an 'alliance', it was its uncompromising and culturally biased interpretation of what constitutes traditional aboriginal subsistence, its ethos of shared social solidarity, that led to the gulf that now exists between Inuit and animal rightists. This is the propriety of imposing a *Qallunaat* view of animals, whether it arises solely from within the movement or reflects a more generalized Western consciousness, on a people whose perspective has evolved in a considerably different cultural, ecological, and historical setting.

The New Inuit–Animal Rights Dynamic: Speculations and Conclusions

. . . It is impossible to predict what the final effects of the northern seal debate will be on Inuit or the animal rights movement. For Inuit culture, the past five years have meant exposure to one of the most intensive periods of externally directed change that it has experienced at the hands of *Qallunaat*. At the moment, there is little prospect for the weight of this pressure for culture change, whether unintended or deliberate, to abate. As for the animal rights movement, as long as it ignores the traditional socio-cultural relevance of the modern Inuit subsistence adaptation, it will remain a victim of the parallax view of Native culture that it has created for itself, at times a noble remanent of some hunter-gatherer ideal and others a social artifact perceived to be without contemporary merit. . . .

Inuit remain very much a traditional people living in the modern world. A part of this modern reality is the technology that has accompanied *Qallunaat* into the North. The animal rights movement has misconstrued, as others have, the presence of these new tools as reflecting the substance of contemporary Inuit life. In fact, it is *ningiqtuq* which is this substance.

In discussing Inuit tradition, hunting, and subsistence, consideration of artifacts often clouds cultural understanding. It is Euro-Canadian contact history which makes the snowmobile a useful tool in modern Inuit harvesting. It is the continuing social relevance of traditional *ningiqtuq* [sharing] practice that makes seal harvesting a valid component of contemporary Inuit subsistence culture.

Notes

1. R. Hunter, *Warriors of the Rainbow* (New York: Holt, Rinehart and Winston, 1979).

2. J. Livingston, "Roundtable Discussion on 'Aboriginal Societies and the Animal Protection Movement: Rights, Issues, and Implications,' " in *A Question of Rights: Northern Wildlife Management and the Anti-Harvest Movement*, ed. R. Keith and A. Sanders (Ottawa: Canadian Arctic Resources Committee, 1989), 118–22.

3. K. Bartlett, "A New Ethic or an End to a Way of Life?" *Animals' Agenda* 8 (1988).

4. J. Z. Z. Matowanyika, "Cast Out of Eden: Peasants versus Wildlife Policy in Savannah Africa," *Alternatives* 16 (1989): 30–39.

5. P. Watson, personal correspondence, 1985.

6. See, for instance, R. Q. Duffy, *The Road to Nunavut: The Progress of the Eastern Artic Inuit Since the Second World War* (Montreal: McGill-Queen's University Press, 1988).

Population and Consumption

QUESTIONS about the relation between population and environmental destruction have provoked passionate, even acrimonious, debate. Some people believe that global population must be brought under control at once if there is to be any hope of preserving wild nature and the very quality of life on the planet. Others believe that population is only a marginal concern, or even that the issue should not be discussed at all. It should not be surprising that the population question provokes such passions. What is at stake are very personal concerns about reproductive freedom and the authority of religious teachings, as well as deeply political issues involving the status of women, the global distribution of wealth and power, and the vast disparity in consumption between rich and poor. It is no wonder that for most of the past decade these questions were ducked by many governmental leaders.

Avoiding these issues, however, will not make the population problem go away. In fact, failure to talk about it virtually ensures the inevitable damage that an ever-increasing population will cause. In the next forty-five years, world population is expected to double from a little under 6 billion to well over 11 billion, and there is no guarantee that population will stabilize there. People disagree about how many people the Earth can support, but everyone must agree that there is some limit on our finite planet beyond which the quality of life and the health of the Earth are in grave jeopardy.

Biologists Paul and Anne Ehrlich argue that this limit has already been reached. Even though some parts of the world may not seem crowded, this is beside the point. They define overpopulation as a condition in which a population cannot maintain itself without degrading the environment to a point that it can no longer sustain the population over the long term. By this definition almost all countries, rich and poor, are overpopulated. Although the greatest population increase in the next four decades will occur in the poor nations, people in the rich countries will continue to make greater demands on the Earth's resources. For example, an American child born today will drive about 700,000 miles in his or her lifetime, using 28,000 gallons of gasoline. Americans consume 33 percent of the world's paper and 24 percent of the world's aluminum, and each individual American uses 300 times as much energy as a citizen of a developing country. It is clear that the planet cannot support very many Americans. Despite the overwhelming nature of the population/consumption equation, the Ehrlichs are clear on one thing—the population explosion will end, either humanely, by reducing birth rates, or violently, by increased death rates. The choice is ours.

Economist Julian Simon agrees that the choice is and should be ours, but his understanding of the issue of global population is very different from that of the Ehrlichs. Simon argues that decisions about how many children to have should be left to individual parents and their communities, since he regards population questions not as scientific questions, but as value questions. Because Simon believes that values are so complex, variable, and ultimately personal, he argues that population decisions are not the appropriate domain of scientists and policymakers.

Co-founder of the Institute for Food and Development Policy, Frances Moore Lappé, and her co-worker Rachel Schurman do not agree that these questions are strictly about personal values. They suggest that reproductive decisions are shaped by various "power structures," by which they mean "the rules, institutions, and assumptions that determine both who is allowed to participate in decisions and in whose interests decisions are made." Through their power-structures analysis, which takes into account such factors as women's status, economic and food security for aging people and the infirm, and access to health care, they suggest that a successful population policy can be implemented only if strong democratic institutions are in place. Without equal access to decision making about the quality of life, there is no way to solve the global population problem.

In the mid-seventeenth century, when the global population was about 500 million, a doubling of the population would have been of little concern. But today, with a population almost twelve times as large, and growing at an exponential rate, it would be irresponsible to look the other way. However the population question is ultimately answered, it must be addressed, as it is one of the most pressing questions of our age.

Further Reading

Bayles, Michael, ed. *Ethics and Population Policy.* Cambridge, Mass.: Schenkman, 1976.

A collection of essays by leading philosophers on various ethical issues about population size.

Hartmann, Betsy. *Reproductive Rights and Wrongs: The Global Politics of Population Control and Contraceptive Choice.* New York: Harper & Row, 1987.

An in-depth study of population-control policies and their effects on women.

Wattenberg, Ben, ed. *Are World Population Trends a Problem?* Washington, D.C.: American Enterprise Institute for Public Policy Research, 1985.

The proceedings of a symposium addressing the question of whether current world-population trends pose a problem for economic growth or environmental quality.

[From] *The Population Explosion*

Paul R. Ehrlich and Anne H. Ehrlich

IN THE EARLY 1930s, when we were born, the world population was just 2 billion; now it is more than two and a half times as large and still growing rapidly.[1] The population of the United States is increasing much more slowly than the world average, but it has more than doubled in only six decades—from 120 million in 1928 to 250 million in 1990.[2] Such a huge population expansion within two or three generations can by itself account for a great many changes in the social and economic institutions of a society. It also is very frightening to those of us who spend our lives trying to keep track of the implications of the population explosion.

A Slow Start

One of the toughest things for a population biologist to reconcile is the contrast between his or her recognition that civilization is in imminent serious jeopardy and the modest level of concern that population issues generate among the public and even among elected officials.

Much of the reason for this discrepancy lies in the slow development of the problem. People aren't scared because they evolved biologically and culturally to respond to short-term "fires" and to tune out long-term "trends" over which they had no control.[3] Only if we do what doesn't come naturally—if we determinedly focus on what seem to be gradual or nearly imperceptible changes—can the outlines of our predicament be perceived clearly enough to be frightening.

Consider the *very* slow-motion origins of our predicament. It seems reasonable to define humanity as having first appeared some 4 million years ago in the form of australopithecines, small-brained upright creatures like "Lucy."[4] Of course, we don't know the size of this first human population, but it's likely that there were never more than 125,000 australopithecines at any given time.

Our own species, *Homo sapiens*,[5] evolved a few hundred thousand years ago. Some ten thousand years ago, when agriculture was invented, probably no more than 5 million people inhabited Earth—fewer than now live in the San

Francisco Bay Area. Even at the time of Christ, two thousand years ago, the entire human population was roughly the size of the population of the United States today; by 1650 there were only 500 million people, and in 1850 only a little over a billion. Since there are now well past 5 billion people, the vast majority of the population explosion has taken place in less than a tenth of 1 percent of the history of *Homo sapiens*.

This is a remarkable change in the abundance of a single species. After an unhurried pace of growth over most of our history, expansion of the population accelerated during the Industrial Revolution and really shot up after 1950. Since mid-century, the human population has been growing at annual rates ranging from about 1.7 to 2.1 percent per year, doubling in forty years or less. Some groups have grown significantly faster; the population of the African nation of Kenya was estimated to be increasing by over 4 percent annually during the 1980s—a rate that if continued would double the nation's population in only seventeen years.[6] That rate did continue for over a decade, and only recently has shown slight signs of slowing. Meanwhile, other nations, such as those of northern Europe, have grown much more slowly in recent decades.

But even the highest growth rates are still *slow-motion changes compared to events we easily notice and react to*. A car swerving at us on the highway is avoided by actions taking a few seconds. The Alaskan oil spill caused great public indignation, but faded from the media and the consciousness of most people in a few months. America's participation in World War II spanned less than four years. During the last four years, even Kenya's population grew by only about 16 percent—a change hardly perceptible locally, let alone from a distance. In four years, the world population expands only a little more than 7 percent. Who could notice that? Precipitous as the population explosion has been in historical terms, it is occurring at a snail's pace in an individual's perception. It is not an event, it is a trend that must be analyzed in order for its significance to be appreciated.

Exponential Growth

The time it takes a population to double in size is a dramatic way to picture rates of population growth, one that most of us can understand more readily than percentage growth rates. Human populations have often grown in a pattern described as "exponential."[7] Exponential growth occurs in bank accounts when interest is left to accumulate and itself earns interest. Exponential growth occurs in populations because children, the analogue of interest, remain in the population and themselves have children.[8]

A key feature of exponential growth is that it often seems to start slowly and finish fast. A classic example used to illustrate this is the pond weed that doubles each day the amount of pond surface covered and is projected to cover the entire pond in thirty days. The question is, how much of the pond will be covered in twenty-nine days? The answer, of course, is that just half of the pond will be covered in twenty-nine days. The weed will then double once more and cover the entire pond the next day. As this example indicates, exponential growth contains the potential for big surprises.[9]

The limits to human population growth are more difficult to perceive than those restricting the pond weed's growth. Nonetheless, like the pond weed, human populations grow in a pattern that is essentially exponential, so we must be alert to the treacherous properties of that sort of growth. The key point to remember is that *a long history of exponential growth in no way implies a long future of exponential growth.* What begins in slow motion may eventually overwhelm us in a flash.

The last decade or two has seen a slight slackening in the human population growth rate—a slackening that has been prematurely heralded as an "end to the population explosion." The slowdown has been only from a peak annual growth rate of perhaps 2.1 percent in the early 1960s to about 1.8 percent in 1990. To put this change in perspective, the population's doubling time has been extended from thirty-three years to thirty-nine. Indeed, the world population *did* double in the thirty-seven years from 1950 to 1987. But even if birthrates continue to fall, the world population will continue to expand (assuming that death rates don't rise), although at a slowly slackening rate, for about another century. Demographers think that growth will not end before the population has reached 10 billion or more.[10]

So, even though birthrates have declined somewhat, *Homo sapiens* is a long way from ending its population explosion or avoiding its consequences. In fact, the biggest jump, from 5 to 10 billion in well under a century, is still ahead. But this does not mean that growth couldn't be ended sooner, with a much smaller population size, if we—all of the world's nations—made up our minds to do it. The trouble is, many of the world's leaders and perhaps most of the world's people still don't believe that there are compelling reasons to do so. They are even less aware that if humanity fails to act, *nature may end the population explosion for us*—in very unpleasant ways—well before 10 billion is reached.

Those unpleasant ways are beginning to be perceptible. Humanity in the 1990s will be confronted by more and more intransigent environmental problems, global problems dwarfing those that worried us in the late 1960s. Perhaps the most serious is that of global warming, a problem caused in large part by population growth and overpopulation. It is not clear whether the severe drought in North America, the Soviet Union, and China in 1988 was the result of the slowly rising surface temperature of Earth, but it is precisely the kind of event that climatological models predict as more and more likely with continued global warming.[11] In addition to more frequent and more severe crop failures, projected consequences of the warming include coastal flooding, desertification, the creation of as many as 300 million environmental refugees,[12] alteration of patterns of disease, water shortages, general stress on natural ecosystems, and synergistic interactions among all these factors.

Continued population growth and the drive for development in already badly overpopulated poor nations will make it *exceedingly* difficult to slow the greenhouse warming—and impossible to stop or reverse it—in this generation at least. And, even if the warming should miraculously not occur, contrary to accepted projections, human numbers are on a collision course with massive famines anyway.

Making the Population Connection

Global warming, acid rain, depletion of the ozone layer, vulnerability to epidemics, and exhaustion of soils and groundwater are all, as we shall see, related to population size. They are also clear and present dangers to the persistence of civilization. Crop failures due to global warming alone might result in the premature deaths of a billion or more people in the next few decades, and the AIDS epidemic could slaughter hundreds of millions. Together these would constitute a harsh "population control" program provided by nature in the face of humanity's refusal to put into place a gentler program of its own.

We shouldn't delude ourselves: the population explosion will come to an end before very long. The only remaining question is whether it will be halted through the humane method of birth control, or by nature wiping out the surplus. We realize that religious and cultural opposition to birth control exists throughout the world; but we believe that people simply don't understand the choice that such opposition implies. Today, anyone opposing birth control is unknowingly voting to have the human population size controlled by a massive increase in early deaths.

Of course, the environmental crisis isn't caused just by expanding human numbers. Burgeoning consumption among the rich and increasing dependence on ecologically unsound technologies to supply that consumption also play major parts. This allows some environmentalists to dodge the population issue by emphasizing the problem of malign technologies. And social commentators can avoid commenting on the problem of too many people by focusing on the serious maldistribution of affluence.

But scientists studying humanity's deepening predicament recognize that a major factor contributing to it is rapidly worsening overpopulation. The Club of Earth, a group whose members all belong to both the U.S. National Academy of Sciences and the American Academy of Arts and Sciences, released a statement in September 1988 that said in part:

> Arresting global population growth should be second in importance only to avoiding nuclear war on humanity's agenda. Overpopulation and rapid population growth are intimately connected with most aspects of the current human predicament, including rapid depletion of nonrenewable resources, deteriora-

tion of the environment (including rapid climate change), and increasing international tensions.

When three prestigious scientific organizations cosponsored an international scientific forum, "Global Change," in Washington in 1989, there was general agreement among the speakers that population growth was a substantial contributor toward prospective catastrophe. Newspaper coverage was limited, and while the population component was mentioned in the *New York Times*'s article,[13] the point that population limitation will be essential to resolving the predicament was lost. The coverage of environmental issues in the media has been generally excellent in the last few years, but there is still a long way to go to get adequate coverage of the intimately connected population problem.

Even though the media occasionally give coverage to population issues, some people never get the word. In November 1988, Pope John Paul II reaffirmed the Catholic Church's ban on contraception. The occasion was the twentieth anniversary of Pope Paul's anti-birth-control encyclical, *Humanae Vitae*.

Fortunately, the majority of Catholics in the industrial world pay little attention to the encyclical or the Church's official ban on all practical means of birth control. One need only note that Catholic Italy at present has the smallest average completed family size (1.3 children per couple) of any nation. Until contraception and then abortion were legalized there in the 1970s, the Italian birth rate was kept low by an appalling rate of illegal abortion.

The bishops who assembled to celebrate the anniversary defended the encyclical by announcing that "the world's food resources theoretically could feed 40 billion people."[14] In one sense they were right. It's "theoretically possible" to feed 40 billion people—in the same sense that it's theoretically possible for your favorite major-league baseball team to win every single game for fifty straight seasons, or for you to play Russian roulette ten thousand times in a row with five out of six chambers loaded without blowing your brains out.

One might also ask whether feeding 40 billion people is a worthwhile goal for humanity, even if it could be reached. Is any purpose served in turning Earth, in essence, into a gigantic human feedlot? Putting aside the near-certainty that such a miracle couldn't be sustained, what would happen to the *quality* of life?

We wish to emphasize that the population problem is in no sense a "Catholic problem," as some would claim. Around the world, Catholic reproductive performance is much the same as that of non-Catholics in similar cultures and with similar economic status. Nevertheless, the *political* position of the Vatican, traceable in no small part to the extreme conservatism of Pope John Paul II, is an important barrier to solving the population problem.[15] Non-Catholics should be very careful not to confuse Catholics or Catholicism with the Vatican—most American Catholics don't. Furthermore, the Church's position on contraception is distressing to many millions of Catholics, who feel it morally imperative to follow their own consciences in their personal lives and disregard the Vatican's teachings on this subject.

Nor is unwillingness to face the severity of the population problem limited to the Vatican. It's built into our genes and our culture. That's one reason many otherwise bright and humane people behave like fools when confronted with demographic issues. Thus, an economist specializing in mail-order marketing can sell the thesis that the human population could increase essentially forever because people are the "ultimate resource,"[16] and a journalist can urge more population growth in the United States so that we can have a bigger army![17] Even some environmentalists are taken in by the frequent assertion that "there is no population problem, only a problem of distribution." The statement is usually made in a context of a plan for conquering hunger, as if food shortage were the only consequence of overpopulation.

But even in that narrow context, the assertion is wrong. Suppose food *were* distributed equally. If everyone in the world ate as Americans do, less than half the *present* world population could be fed on the record harvests of 1985 and 1986.[18] Of course, everyone doesn't have to eat like Americans. About a third of the world grain harvest—the staples of the human feeding base—is fed to animals to produce eggs, milk, and meat for American-style diets. Wouldn't feeding that grain directly to people solve the problem? If everyone were willing to eat an essentially vegetarian diet, that additional grain would allow perhaps a billion more people to be fed with 1986 production.

Would such radical changes solve the world food problem? Only in the *very* short term. The additional billion people are slated to be with us by the end of the century. Moreover, by the late 1980s, humanity already seemed to be encountering trouble maintaining the production levels of the mid-1980s, let alone keeping up with population growth. The world grain harvest in 1988 was some 10 percent *below* that of 1986. And there is little sign that the rich are about to give up eating animal products.

So there is no reasonable way that the hunger problem can be called "only" one of distribution, even though redistribution of food resources would greatly alleviate hunger today. Unfortunately, an important truth, that maldistribution is a cause of hunger now, has been used as a way to avoid a more important truth—that overpopulation is critical today and may well make the distribution question moot tomorrow.

The food problem, however, attracts little immediate concern among well-fed Americans, who have no reason to be aware of its severity or extent. But other evidence that could make everyone face up to the seriousness of the population dilemma is now all around us, since problems to which over-population and population growth make major contributions are worsening at a rapid rate. They often appear on the evening news, although the population connection is almost never made.

Consider the television pictures of barges loaded with garbage wandering like The Flying Dutchman across the seas, and news stories about "no room at the dump." They are showing the results of the interaction between too many affluent people and the environmentally destructive technologies that support that affluence. Growing opportunities to swim in a mixture of sewage and medical debris off American beaches can be traced to the same source. Starving people in sub-Saharan Africa are victims of drought, defective agricultural policies, and an overpopulation of both people and domestic animals—with warfare often dealing the final blow. All of the above are symptoms of humanity's massive and growing negative impact on Earth's life-support systems.

Recognizing the Population Problem

The average person, even the average scientist, seldom makes the connection between such seemingly disparate events and the population problem, and thus remains unworried. To a degree, this failure to put the pieces together is due to a taboo against frank discussion of the population crisis in many quarters, a taboo generated partly by pressures from the Catholic hierarchy and partly by other groups who are afraid that dealing with population issues will produce socially damaging results.

Many people on the political left are concerned that focusing on overpopulation will divert attention from crucial problems of social justice (which certainly need to be addressed *in addition* to the population problem). Often those on the political right fear that dealing with overpopulation will encourage abortion (it need not) or that halting growth will severely damage the economy (it could, if not handled properly). And people of varied political persuasions who are unfamiliar with the magnitude of the population problem believe in a variety of farfetched technological fixes—such as colonizing outer space—that they think will allow the need for regulating the size of the human population to be avoided forever.[19]

Even the National Academy of Sciences avoided mentioning controlling human numbers in its advice to President Bush on how to deal with global environmental change. Although Academy members who are familiar with the issue are well aware of the critical population component of that change, it was feared that all of the Academy's advice would be ignored if recommendations were included about a subject taboo in the Bush administration. That strategy might have been correct, considering Bush's expressed views on abortion and considering the administration's weak appointments in many environmentally sensitive positions. . . .

All of us naturally lean toward the taboo against dealing with population growth. The roots of our aversion to limiting the size of the human population are as deep and pervasive as the roots of human sexual behavior. Through billions of years of evolution, outreproducing other members of your population was the name of the game. It is the very basis of natural selection, the driving force of the evolutionary process.[20] Nonetheless, the taboo must be uprooted and discarded.

Overcoming the Taboo

There is no more time to waste; in fact, there wasn't in 1968 when *The Population Bomb* was published. Human inaction has already condemned hundreds of millions more people to premature deaths from hunger and disease. The population connection must be made in the public mind. Action to end the population explosion *humanely* and start a gradual population *decline* must become a top item on the human agenda: the human birthrate must be lowered to slightly below the human death rate as soon as possible. There still may be time to limit the scope of the impending catastrophe, but not *much* time. Ending the population explosion by controlling births is necessarily a slow process. Only nature's cruel way of solving the problem is likely to be swift.

Of course, if we do wake up and succeed in controlling our population size, that will still leave us with all the other thorny problems to solve. Limiting human numbers will not alone end warfare, environmental deterioration, poverty, racism, religious prejudice, or sexism; it will just buy us the opportunity to do so. As the old saying goes, whatever your cause, it's a lost cause without population control.

America and other rich nations have a clear choice today. They can continue to ignore the population problem and their own massive contributions to it. Then they will be trapped in a downward spiral that may well lead to the end of civilization in a few decades. More frequent droughts, more damaged crops and famines, more dying forests, more smog, more international conflicts, more epidemics, more gridlock, more drugs, more crime, more sewage swimming, and other extreme unpleasantness will mark our course. It is a route already traveled by too many of our less fortunate fellow human beings.

Or we can change our collective minds and take the measures necessary to lower global birthrates dramatically. People can learn to treat growth as the cancerlike disease it is and move toward a sustainable society. The rich can make helping the poor an urgent goal, instead of seeking more wealth and useless military advantage over one another. Then humanity might have a chance to manage all those other seemingly intractable problems. It is a challenging prospect, but at least it will give our species a shot at creating a decent future for itself. More immediately and concretely, taking action now will give our children and their children the possibility of decent lives. . . .

Unequal Access to the Human Inheritance

Thus far, for simplicity's sake, we've mostly treated humanity as a single family squandering its inheritance. In many ways, that unitary view is accurate, but it leaves out one of the major features of global society: the division of the human species into haves and have-nots, rich nations and poor nations. Even that, of course, is still a simplification; countries like Argentina and

Portugal do not fit readily into either category, and almost all countries have both rich and poor segments in their populations.

The economic division of the world has changed somewhat in the four decades or so that we have been intellectually involved with population issues. In 1960, the rich–poor division of nations was sharper. In the 1990s, more countries are "semideveloped," and fewer of them still have the kind of total poverty typical of developing nations in the 1950s and 1960s. Still, the absolute numbers of people living in such poverty are much greater today, and the poorest of the poor have lost ground. Dividing humanity into rich and poor nonetheless remains a convenient simplification for considering how our one-time bonanza is being squandered. And recognizing the basic elements of the gross economic inequities that afflict the world is absolutely critical both to understanding the bind we are in and to finding ways out of it.

The numbers can be summarized briefly. Slightly over 1 billion people, less than a quarter of the world's population, live in nations whose standard of living—health, education, diet, housing, and quantity of material posses-sions—has improved dramatically over what the vast majority of the world's population enjoyed a century ago. But some 4 billion people don't. They live in nations where average per capita wealth is only about a fifteenth of that of the rich nations and where their babies are some five to twenty times as likely to die by the age of one. Of those, nearly a billion live in "absolute poverty"—defined as being too poor to buy enough food to maintain health or perform a job.[21]

Rich and poor nations also differ drastically in their rates of population increase. The poor nations, except China, are growing at an average rate of 2.4 percent a year, which, if continued, would double their populations in about twenty-nine years. The poorest populations are among the fastest-growing ones. In contrast, the populations of rich nations are growing at only approxi-mately 0.6 percent annually, which gives a doubling time of some 120 years. These numbers are, remember, averages—they conceal considerable differ-ences between nations within these groups, just as national statistics do not show the very different states of individuals within countries.

We must always also keep in mind that buried in dry statistics about differ-ences between rich and poor is an enormous amount of human misery, an endless series of almost incomprehensible tragedies. But, even if you don't care about starving children and overburdened parents who live without hope for a future, selfishness alone demands attention to the problems of the poverty-stricken. That is because the plight of the underprivileged of Earth is probably the single most important barrier to keeping our planet habitable.

Without the cooperation of the poor, the most important global environmen-tal problems cannot be solved; and at the moment the poor have precious little reason to listen to appeals for cooperation. Many of them are well aware that the affluent are mindlessly using up humanity's common inheritance—even as they yearn to help us do it. And all poor people are aware that the rich have the ability to bear the suffering of the poverty-stricken with a stiff upper lip. To remove such attitudes and start helping the less fortunate (and themselves), the rich must understand the plight of the poor not just intellectually but emotionally.

Our own *emotional* involvement with the sorrows of poor nations began with a visit to India in 1966. The desperate situation of that nation, exacerbated that year by the Bihar famine, left a lasting impression. There was no sign of profligate use of Earth's capital in the form of superabundant consumer goods, but there was abundant evidence of the loss of soils and biodiversity.

In 1989, Paul returned briefly to India and found some things improved, some much worse, and the situation of the world's largest democracy even more precarious. The population of 500 million in 1966 had expanded by 325 million, and the results in urban sprawl and poverty were horrifying. But other aspects of the nation remained impressive: the admirable qualities of the Indians, both peasants and sophisticates, with whom he had contact, the rise of a substantial middle class (widely evident in Delhi), and success in increasing agricultural production (people looked comparatively well fed).

But an Indian government report estimated that 2.5 million Indians live their entire lives in the streets and that, of the urban poor, 65 percent have no tap water, 37 percent have no electricity, and 50 percent must defecate in fields and vacant lots.[22] India has managed to "keep it together" better than many (including us) expected. Whether it will continue to do so even more overpopulated, with much less topsoil, groundwater, and biodiversity, and in the face of the greenhouse warming and other global ecological problems, is questionable. We cannot be optimistic about the future of that nation—or ours—if current trends are allowed to continue.

For one thing, some superficial differences between the two nations have faded. Among the shocking things we saw in our original trip to India were huge numbers of people living in the streets and an army of beggars. Now, in any large American city, one can see many homeless people sleeping in bus stops and on park benches and street gratings. Beggars in New York's Pennsylvania Station are as persistent as those in Old Delhi. In the wake of the Reagan years, several hundred thousand Americans are homeless, and the income gap between the rich and the poor in the United States has grown.

Many of the consequences of overpopulation in the United States, especially the plight of America's own poor and the nation's huge contributions to global environmental deterioration and resource depletion, are too easily overlooked. But, as we've noted, signs of too many overconsuming people, such as gridlock on freeways and city streets, severe air pollution, growing mountains of garbage, ubiquitous toxic wastes, and escalating crime rates, are increasingly apparent.

The United States and India, the rich and the poor, face the same basic choice: either to shift in an orderly, planned way to a sustainable human life-support system or to be brutally forced into that shift by nature—through the untimely deaths of large numbers of human beings. Population control in both rich and poor nations is absolutely essential. If that were achieved, and the rich chose to restrain themselves and to help the poor, the remaining nonrenewable resources could be used to build a bridge to that sustainable future. At that same time, the damage currently being done to nominally replenishable resources would have to be curbed and their replenishment encouraged. Otherwise, those resources will be capable of supporting even fewer people in the future. Sustainable development is needed not just in poor nations, but in rich nations as well (that certainly is *not* what they have now).

In short, human numbers and human behavior must be brought into line with the constraints placed upon *Homo sapiens* by the limits of Earth and the laws of nature. People who think those can be ignored or evaded are living in a dream world. They haven't reflected on the 4 *million* years it took for humanity to build a population of 2 billion people, in contrast to the forty-six years in which the second 2 billion appeared and the twenty-two years it will take for the arrival of the third 2 billion. They have overlooked the most important trend of their time.

Notes

1. The world population in 1990 was about 5.3 billion. Most demographic information cited is from *1989 World Population Data Sheet,* issued by the Population Reference Bureau (PRB), 777 Fourteenth Street NW, Suite 800, Washington, D.C. 20005.

2. Note that the U.S. population was growing much faster before then, spurred by substantial numbers of immigrants. It quadrupled in the six decades before 1928, turning a post–Civil War society largely restricted to the eastern half of the nation into a cosmopolitan world power spanning the continent.

3. This evolutionary blind spot is discussed at length in R. Ornstein and P. Ehrlich, *New World/ New Mind* (New York: Doubleday, 1988).

4. D. Johanson and M. Edey, *Lucy: The Beginnings of Mankind* (New York: Simon and Schuster, 1981).

5. Note that we are considering *Homo sapiens* as the latest human species and are applying the term "human" to all hominids since the australopithecines. Some people would restrict the term "human" to *Homo sapiens*.

6. When annual growth rates are under 5 percent, a working estimate of the number of years required to double the population at that rate can be obtained by simply dividing the percentage rate into 70.

7. Exponential growth occurs when the increase in population size in a given period is a constant percentage of the size at the beginning of the period. Thus a population growing at 2 percent annually will be growing exponentially. Exponential growth does not have to be fast; it can go on at very low rates or, if the rate is negative, can be exponential shrinkage.

8. P. R. Ehrlich, A. H. Ehrlich, and J. P. Holdren, *Ecoscience: Population, Resources, Environment* (San Francisco: Freeman, 1977), 100–104.

9. The potential for surprise in repeated doublings can be underlined with another

example. Suppose you set up an aquarium with appropriate life-support systems to maintain 1,000 guppies, but no more. If that number is exceeded, crowding will make the fish susceptible to "ich," a parasitic disease that will kill most of the guppies. You then begin the population with a pair of sex-crazed guppies. Suppose that the fish reproduce fast enough to double their population size every month. For eight months everything is fine, as the population grows $2 \rightarrow 4 \rightarrow 8 \rightarrow 16 \rightarrow 32 \rightarrow 64 \rightarrow 128 \rightarrow 256 \rightarrow 512$. Then within the ninth month, the guppy population surges through the fatal 1,000 barrier, the aquarium becomes overcrowded, and most of the fish perish. In fact, the last 100 guppies appear in less than five days—about 2 percent of the population's history.

10. Note that "doubling times" represent what would happen if the growth rates of the moment continued unchanged into the future.

11. S. H. Schneider, *Global Warming* (San Francisco: Sierra Club Books, 1989).

12. "Eco-Refugees Warning," *New Scientist*, 10 June 1989.

13. *New York Times*, 4 May 1989.

14. *Washington Post*, 19 November 1988, C-15.

15. Italy is not a freak case. Catholic France has an average completed family size of 1.8 children, the same as Britain and Norway; Catholic Spain, with less than half the per capita GNP of Protestant Denmark, has the same complete family size of 1.8 children. We are equating "completed family size" here with the *total fertility rate*, the average number of children a woman would bear in her lifetime, assuming that current age-specific birth and death rates remained unchanged during her childbearing years—roughly fifteen to forty-nine. In the United States, a Catholic woman is more likely to seek abortion than a non-Catholic woman (probably because she is likelier to use less-effective contraception). By 1980, Catholic and non-Catholic women in the United States (excluding Hispanic women, for whom cultural factors are strong) had virtually identical family sizes. See W. D. Mosher, "Fertility and Family Planning in the United States: Insights from the National Survey of Family Growth," *Family Planning Perspectives* 20 (1988): 202–17.

16. J. Simon, *The Ultimate Resource* (Princeton, N.J.: Princeton University Press, 1981) [this volume, 321–28].

17. B. Wattenberg, *The Birth Dearth* (New York: Pharos Books, 1987).

18. R. W. Kates, R. S. Cen, T. E. Downing, J. X. Kasperson, E. Messer, and S. R. Millman, *The Hunger Report: 1988* (Providence, R.I.: Alan Shawn Feinstein World Hunger Program, Brown University, 1988).

19. For an amusing analysis of the "outer-space" fairy tale, see Garrett Hardin's classic essay, "Interstellar Migration and the Population Problem," in *Stalking the Wild Taboo*, ed. G. Hardin (Los Angeles: William Kaufmann, 1978).

20. For a discussion of natural selection and evolution written for nonspecialists, see P. R. Ehrlich, *The Machinery of Nature* (New York: Simon and Schuster, 1986).

21. World Bank figures cited in World Resources Institute and International Institute for Environment and Development, *World Resources, 1988–89* (New York: Basic Books, 1989).

22. *Times of India*, 20 February 1989.

[From] *The Ultimate Resource*

Julian Simon

A SMALL number of scientists have convinced a great many politicians and laymen that rational population policies with respect to fertility, mortality, and immigration can be deduced directly from actual or supposed facts about population and economic growth. The persuaded politicians have come to believe it is "scientific truth" that countries should reduce their population growth. And the persuading scientists want the politicians to believe that such judgmental propositions really are "scientific." For example, the front page of the handbook of the population control movement in the United States, *The Population Bomb*, says "Paul Ehrlich, a qualified scientist, clearly describes the dimensions of the crisis . . . over-population is now the dominant problem . . . population control or race to oblivion?"

But it is scientifically wrong—outrageously wrong—to say that "science shows" there is overpopulation (or underpopulation) in any given place at any given time. Science can only reveal the likely *effects* of various population levels and policies. Whether population is now too large or too small, or is growing too fast or too slowly, cannot be decided on scientific grounds alone. Such judgments depend upon our values, a matter about which science is silent.

Whether you think that it is better for a country to have a population of, say, 50 million human beings at a $4,000 per capita yearly income, or 100 million at $3,000, is strictly a matter of what you consider important. And further, please keep in mind that if the empirical studies and my theoretical analysis are correct, the world can have a larger population and *higher* per capita income. This is just as true for less-developed as for more-developed countries. But the judgment about whether this is good news or bad news, and whether population is growing too fast or too slowly, or is already too large, depends on values. This is reason enough to say that science does not show that there is overpopulation or underpopulation anywhere.

Because many writers act as if population policies can be deduced from scientific studies alone, particular values enter implicitly into policy decisions, without any explicit discussion of whether the values really are those that the decision makers and the community desire to have implemented. For a leading example, because almost all economic analyses of "optimum" rates of growth take per capita income as the criterion, this criterion implicitly becomes the community goal and the guideline for policy makers. In some cases values are smuggled in consciously, though without discussion; in other cases the values enter without any conscious recognition.

Some Values Relevant to Population Policy

[1.] *The time discount rate*. The relative importance of the nearer versus the further future must affect every investment decision, and every judgment about the costs and benefits of resource use and population growth.

[2.] *Altruism versus selfishness*. Our willingness to share our worldly goods— either directly or, more commonly, indirectly through taxation—affects a variety of population-related policies, as has been discussed vehemently at least since Malthus. Should additional children or immigrants be welcomed into a community if there will be an immediate tax burden upon others? Should the poor be supported by welfare rather than left to die? Each of us has some limited willingness to contribute to others, but that willingness differs from person to person, and from moment to moment. In discussion, this factor usually gets tangled up with the matter of whether the transfers are a contribution or an investment.

[3.] *Space, privacy, and isolation*. This is the Daniel Boone/Sierra Club value. How much of your isolation in the forest are you prepared to give up so that others may also enjoy the experience?

[4.] *The right of inheritance*. Should only the blood descendants of the builders of a country be allowed to enjoy its fruits, or should others be allowed to come in and enjoy them, too? This issue is at the heart of immigration policy in the United States, Australia, Israel, Great Britain, and every other country in which the standard of living is higher than in the country of some potential immigrants. The issue also arises internally. For example: Are Native Americans or blacks morally entitled to partake of the benefits of social investments made by whites in past years? Do whites have a responsibility to repay blacks for the profits made by exploiting slave labor in previous centuries?

[5.] *The inherent value of human life*. Some economists and laymen believe that some people's lives are so poor that they would have been better off had they never been born. Others believe that no life is so poor that it does not have value. Still others believe that only the individual should be allowed to decide whether his or her own life is worth living. Surprisingly to me, this value, which is one of the most influential in population discussions, is rarely mentioned explicitly.

[6.] *The acceptability of various methods of preventing life*. To some people, abortion or contraception or infanticide are acceptable; for others any of these may be unacceptable.

[7.] *A value for numbers of people.* Both the Bible, which urges people to be fruitful and multiply, and the utilitarian philosophy of "the greatest good for the greatest number" lead to a value for more people, a value that many people do not share.

[8.] *Animals and plants versus people.* The Bible says, "And God said, Let us make man in our image, after our likeness: . . . Be fertile and increase, fill the earth and master it; and rule the fish of the sea, the birds of the sky, and all the living things that creep on earth" (Genesis 1:26–28).

In sharp contrast is the view of some environmentalists—for example, the "Greenpeace Philosophy" of the whale-protecting group: "Ecology teaches us that humankind is not the center of life on the planet. Ecology has taught us that the whole earth is part of our 'body' and that we must learn to respect it as we respect life—the whales, the seals, the forests, the seas. The tremendous beauty of ecological thought is that it shows us a pathway back to an understanding and appreciation of life itself—an understanding and appreciation that is imperative to that very way of life."[1]

[9.] *Eugenics.* Some have thought that the human race can be improved by selective breeding. This leads to policies encouraging fertility and immigration for some groups and discouraging them for others.

[10.] *Individual freedom versus community coercion.*

Now let's consider some of these values at greater length.

The Value of a Poor Person's Life

It is sometimes said that some people's lives are so poor and miserable that an economic policy does them a service if it discourages their births. It is a fundamental and unresolvable question whether the poorest person's life is worth living—that is, whether it is better for that poor person to live or to die. The view of many is that some lives are not worth living (they have "negative utility"). This implies that the sum of human happiness would be greater if people with incomes below the threshhold had never been born. My aim here is not to persuade anyone that all lives have value but only to show that the question is an open one, whose answer depends upon our values and view of the world.

The belief that very poor people's lives are not worth living comes out clearly when Paul Ehrlich writes about India.

> I came to understand the population explosion emotionally one stinking hot
> night in Delhi. . . . The streets seemed alive with people. People eating, peo-
> ple washing, people sleeping, people visiting, arguing, and screaming. People
> thrusting their hands through the taxi window, begging. People defecating and

urinating. People clinging to buses. People herding animals. People, people, people.[2]

But Ehrlich writes nothing about those people laughing, loving, or being tender to their children—all of which one also sees among those poor Indians.

There *is* misery in India. Intestinal disease and blindness are all around. A fourteen-year-old girl catches bricks on a construction job for thirty cents a day as her baby, covered with flies and crying, lies on a burlap sack on the ground below the scaffold on which the young mother works. A toothless crone of indeterminate age, with no relatives in the world and no home, begins with a cake of wet cow-dung to lay a floor for a "dwelling" of sticks and rags, by the side of the road. All this I have seen. And yet these people must think their lives are worth living, or else they would choose to stop living. (Note that to choose death does not require violent suicide. Anthropologists describe individuals—even young people—who decide they want to die and then do. People even die on their own schedules, frequently waiting until after weddings or birthdays of relatives to die.) Because people continue to live, I believe that they value their lives. And those lives therefore have value in my scheme of things. Hence I do not believe that the existence of poor people—either in poor countries or, a fortiori, in the United States—is a sign of "overpopulation."

When Is Coercion Justified?

Some people advocate forced birth control "if necessary." Again to quote Ehrlich, "We must have population control at home, hopefully through a system of incentives and penalties, but by compulsion if voluntary methods fail."[3]

The logic for having the state control the number of children we may rear has been stated as follows.

> In conditions of scarcity the civil right to have unlimited births simply does not exist. Such a claim is attention-getting and suspect. It is a favorite argument of minorities in support of their own overproduction of births. The right to have children fits into the network of other rights and duties we share and must dovetail with the rights of others. When all of us must curtail our production of children none of us has an overriding civil right of this kind. The closer we live together and the more of us there are, the fewer civil rights we can exercise before they infringe upon those of another. This adverse relation between dense population and personal freedom is easily documented around the world. It is time for people sincerely interested in civil rights to expose such special pleading, and to intervene when it is leveled against local or national programs.[4]

A briefer statement is that of Kingley Davis: "It can be argued that over-reproduction—that is, the bearing of more than two children—is a worse crime than most and should be outlawed."[5]

Many Americans have become persuaded of the necessity of such coercion, as these Roper poll results show:[6]

> Q. The population crisis is becoming so severe that people will have to be limited on the number of children they can have.
> A. Agree   47%
>   Disagree   41%

And the astonishing kinds of programs that have been suggested in the "population community" are summarized in [the accompanying table].

Some countries already have enacted into law coercive policies with respect to fertility. In India during the first Indira Ghandi period, in the state of Tamil Nadu, "Convicts . . . who submit to sterilization [could] have their jail term reduced"; and in the state of Uttar Pradesh, "Any government servant whose spouse is alive and who has three or more children must be sterilized within three months, pursuant to a state government order issued under the Defense of Internal Security of India Rules. Those failing to do so will cease to be entitled to any rationed article beyond the basic four units."[7] In the state of Maharastra, population 50 million, the legislature passed an act requiring compulsory sterilization for all families with three or more children (four or more if the children were all boys or all girls), but this measure did not receive the necessary consent of the President of India. And in other states in India, in Singapore,[8] and perhaps elsewhere, public housing, education, and other public services are conditioned on the number of children a family has. It is this possibility of coercion—by penalty, taxation, physical compulsion, or otherwise—that concerns me most.

I hope you share my belief that it is good for people to be able, as much as possible, to decide how to run their own lives. Such a desire for individual self-determination is quite consistent with giving people maximum information about birth control, because information increases their ability to have the number of children they want. It is also consistent with legal abortion. And it is consistent with public health and nutrition measures to keep alive all the children that people wish to bring into the world. I am unqualifiedly in favor of all these policies to increase the individual's ability to achieve the family size she or he chooses. But the same belief leads me to be against coercing people not to have children. By definition, coercion reduced people's freedom to make their own decisions about their own lives.

Though I would vote against any overall U.S. policy that would coerce people not to have children—including taxes on children greater than the social cost of the children—I do accord to a community the right to make such a decision if there is a consensus on the matter. If people recognize, however, that this decision is a matter of values, and that science cannot prove that we are overpopulated or on the road to overpopulation, people may be less likely to choose to coerce members of their own group not to have children.

Examples of Proposed Measures to Reduce U.S. Fertility, by Universality or Selectivity of Impact

Universal impact: social constraints	Selective impact depending on socio-economic status		Measures predicated on existing motivation to prevent unwanted pregnancy
	Economic deterrents/incentives	Social controls	
Restructure family: a) Postpone or avoid marriage b) Alter image of ideal family size Compulsory education of children Encourage increased homosexuality Educate for family limitation Fertility control agents in water supply Encourage women to work	Modify tax policies: a) Substantial marriage tax b) Child tax c) Tax married more than single d) Remove parents' tax exemption e) Additional taxes on parents with more than 1 or 2 children in school Reduce/eliminate paid maternity leave or benefits Reduce/eliminate children's or family allowances Bonuses for delayed marriage and greater child-spacing Pensions for women of 45 with fewer than N children Eliminate welfare payments after first 2 children Chronic depression Require women to work and provide few child care facilities Limit/eliminate public-financed medical care, scholarships, housing, loans, and subsidies to families with more than N children	Compulsory abortion of out-of-wedlock pregnancies Compulsory sterilization of all who have 2 children except for a few who would be allowed 3 Confine childbearing to only a limited number of adults Stock certificate-type permits for children Housing policies: a) Discouragement of private home ownership b) Stop awarding public housing based on family size	Payments to encourage sterilization Payments to encourage contraception Payments to encourage abortion Abortion and sterilization on demand Allow certain contraceptives to be distributed non-medically Improve contraceptive technology Make contraception truly available and accessible to all Improve maternal health care, with family planning as a core element

Source: Frederick S. Jaffe, "Activities Relevant to the Study of Population Policy for the U.S.," Memorandum to Bernard Berelson, 11 March 1969.

Do as I Do? Or as I Say?

"How can one call upon people in poor countries to reduce their birthrates if we in rich countries go on having many children?" This pious sentiment is frequently heard.

Some countries' populations may be growing so fast that on balance a reasonable citizen *might* want to slow down the birthrate. If the citizens of Singapore decide that immediately increasing the economic welfare per person is worth the price in slowed population growth, then someone with my values can accept most programs that will help them achieve their goals. I especially sympathize with the goal of enabling poor people to feel that, for themselves and for their children, the future will be economically better than the present. It is good to be able to believe that individuals and societies have a chance to get ahead economically, in my view. I am, however, strongly against Westerners telling Indians that "science proves" that fewer Indian births are a good thing, unconditionally. That is a lie, and an abuse of science. And I am against the United States putting pressure on other countries to adopt population control programs.

Yet some have added that we cannot ethically be in favor of lower birthrates in poor countries without also supporting strict control of population growth in our own country. There are several reasons why this argument is not persuasive. First, if peoples of all countries have a right to make decisions about social and personal population policies on the basis of what *they* want and what *they* believe is good for them, why should this not hold for us, too? Second, birthrates and growth rates in the United States are presently lower than those in most poor countries, and hence should give us no cause for embarrassment. Third, and most important, additional people in more-developed countries may well be of benefit, on balance, to people in poor countries. The positive effects include bigger markets for poor-country products, increased development of technology that poor countries can later use, and a larger pool of potential technical aides such as agronomists and Peace Corps workers. Of course the rich countries may not pay fair prices for the raw materials they buy, or may exploit the poor countries in other ways. Unfortunately, no one has yet even begun to analyze scientifically what the net effect is.

∾

Science alone does not, and cannot, tell us whether any population size is too large or too small, or whether the growth rate is too fast or too slow. Science can sometimes give citizens and policy makers a better understanding of the consequences of one or another decision about population; sadly, however, too often scientific work on this subject has instead only misinformed people and confused them. Social and personal decisions about childbearing, immigration, and death inevitably hinge upon values as well as upon probable consequences.

And there is necessarily a moral dimension to these decisions over and beyond whatever insights science may yield.

Notes

1. Greenpeace mailing, August 1980.
2. P. R. Ehrlich, *The Population Bomb* (New York: Ballantine, 1968), 15.
3. Ibid., prologue.
4. M. K. Willing, *Beyond Conception: Our Children's Children* (Boston: Gambit, 1971), 161.
5. Quoted in R. Elliot et al., "U.S. Population Growth and Family Planning: A Review of the Literature," in *The American Population Debate*, ed. D. Callahan (New York: Anchor Books, 1971), 206.
6. B. J. Wattenberg, *The Real America* (New York: Doubleday, 1974), 228.
7. International Advisory Committee on Population and Law (1977), 26, 174.
8. J. Salaff and A. K. Wong, "Are Disincentives Coercive? The View from Singapore," *International Family Planning Perspectives and Digest* 4 (1978): 50–55.

[From] Taking Population Seriously

Frances Moore Lappé and Rachel Schurman

SINCE 1950 the world's population has doubled, and 85 percent of that growth has occurred in the Third World, where today's population growth rates are unprecedented. . . . What set off this population explosion? And how can we defuse it to help bring human population into balance with the Earth's ecology?

To answer these questions, we present a "power-structures perspective," focusing on the multilayered arenas of decision-making power that shape people's reproductive choices, or lack of them. This perspective shows how the powerlessness of the poor often leaves them little option but large families. Indeed, high birth rates among the poor can best be understood as a defensive response against structures of power that fail to provide—or actively block access to—sources of security beyond the family.

When we ask what can be learned from the handful of Third World countries that have been extraordinarily successful in reducing fertility, we find this thesis reinforced. In each, far-reaching social changes have empowered people, especially women, thereby facilitating alternatives to child bearing as a source of income, security, and status. . . .

The Emerging "Power-Structures Perspective"

Over the past two decades, a sophisticated social analysis of the population problem has begun to emerge. It points to economic, social, and cultural forces that keep Third World fertility high: among them the low status of women, the high death rates of children, and the lack of old-age security. From this social perspective, high fertility becomes an effect more than a cause of poverty and hunger.

[Here we seek to] synthesize crucial insights emerging from this perspective, while adding a critical dimension: social power. By social power we mean, very concretely, the relative ability of people to have a say in decisions that shape their lives. To understand why populations are exploding in the Third World, one must understand how choices about reproduction—those most personal, intimate choices—are influenced by structures of decision-making power. These structures include the distant arena of international finance and trade, and extend downward to the level of national governments, on through the village, and, ultimately, to relationships within families.

"Power structure" is not a mysterious concept. It simply refers to the rules, institutions, and assumptions that determine both who is allowed to participate in decisions and in whose interests decisions are made. The decisions most relevant to the population question are those governing access to and use of life-sustaining resources—land, jobs, health care, and the education needed to make the most of them—and contraceptive resources.

Decision-making structures can most usefully be characterized as falling along a continuum from what we call democratic to antidemocratic. By democratic we mean decision-making structures in which those most affected by the decisions have a say, or that minimally include consideration of the interests of those affected. In no polity or other social institution is power shared in completely equal measure, but in our definition, democratic organization exists to the extent that power is dispersed and no one is utterly powerless. In contrast, antidemocratic structures are nonparticipatory when those most affected have no say, or unequal when power is so concentrated that a few decide exclusively in their own interests. Our thesis is that antidemocratic power structures create and perpetuate conditions keeping fertility high.

In Western societies one tends to think of democracy as strictly a political concept, and of power as exercised only in the political arena. We in the West also assume that because the communist state is the antithesis of political democracy, any use of the term *democratic* is inappropriate when describing communist societies. However, power is a critical variable in both political and economic affairs, as well as in social and cultural life. And the labels *democratic* and *antidemocratic*—describing structures of decision-making power in a multiplicity of social institutions—are most usefully applied not to societies *in toto*, but to the many arenas of life within societies.

Within any given society, power is not necessarily structured along the same lines throughout the political, economic, and social sectors. These varied sectors influence each other, but asymmetry is more the norm: a society might be highly antidemocratic in the way political power is wielded but might allow considerable sharing of economic control over essential resources. Take China. Under the former collectivized system, everyone had the right to participate in economic life and share in the fruits from the land. At the same time, political leadership was not freely chosen and people's right to political expression was not protected.

The converse is probably more common. In a number of societies—the United States is an example—political participation and expression are protected, but citizens' rights to economic resources are not. So a significant share of the population goes without enough income to provide adequate food, housing, and health care.

Structures of economic and political power differ by level as well: although they may be relatively participatory at, say, the national political level, they may remain grossly unequal at another level—for example, when it comes to relations between men and women within the family.

When this power-structures perspective is applied to the population problem, it reveals the ways in which structures of power—interpersonal to international—influence reproductive choices.

Power and Reproductive Choice

In largely agrarian societies, the most accurate indicator of the economic power structure is the control of farmland, for access to land determines a family's security.

What are the consequences for fertility when at least 1 billion rural people in the Third World have been deprived of farmland? In many countries, including Brazil, Mexico, the Philippines, India, and most of the Central American countries, landholdings have become increasingly concentrated in the hands of a minority during the period of rapid population growth. When the more powerful have an incentive to expand—such as the chance to grow lucrative export crops—and have military backing, they can quite easily seize the land of the less powerful. They might do it legally, by calling in the loan of a heavily indebted peasant family, or not so legally, by simply bulldozing the peasant's land and laying claim to it. The peasant family has no legal title or lawyer to back up its claim in court.

In this context, without adequate land or secure tenure—and with no old-age support from the government or any other source of support outside the family—many poor people understandably view children as their sole source of power. Indeed children can be critical to their very survival.

For those living at the economic margin, children's labor can augment meager family income by freeing adults and elder siblings to earn outside income, or by bringing in money directly. Furthermore, in most Third World societies, parents rely on their children to care for them in old age. Children's earnings also provide insurance against risk of property loss for many rural families for whom a bad crop year or unexpected expense can spell catastrophe.

Adding pressure for high birth rates are high infant death rates in the Third World, for to enjoy the possible benefits of children eventually, the poor realize they need to have many children initially.

Of course, the value of children to their parents cannot be measured just in hours of labor or extra income. The intangibles may be just as important. In community affairs, bigger families carry more weight and status. And for poor parents—whose lives are marred so much by grief and sacrifice—the role children play in fulfilling the very real human need for joy and satisfaction cannot be underestimated.

High birth rates reflect, moreover, the disproportionate powerlessness of women. With no say in many decisions that determine their role in the family, as well as in the society at large, many women have little opportunity for pursuits outside the home. Perpetual motherhood becomes their only "choice."

Women's subordination to men within the family cuts to the core of the population issue because it often translates into a direct loss of control over their own fertility. After several births, many Third World women want to avoid or delay pregnancy. But they simply do not have the power to act on their desire. As one doctor in a Mexican clinic explained, "When a wife wants to . . . [try] to limit the number of mouths to feed in the family, the husband will become angry and even beat her. He thinks it is unacceptable that she is making a decision of her own. She is challenging his authority, his power over her—and thus the very nature of his virility."[1] Patriarchal family and community attitudes may also pressure a woman to keep having children until she gives birth to a son, regardless of her own wishes or even possible jeopardy to her health.

The power-structures perspective helps explain the high birth rates where women are subordinated within the family and the society, but also it recognizes that the men who hold power are often themselves part of a subordinate group—those with little or no claim to income-producing resources. Denied sources of self-esteem through productive work and access to the resources needed to shoulder responsibility for their families, such men are likely to cling even more tenaciously to their superior power vis-à-vis women. In many cultures, men unable to earn enough money to support dependents feel inadequate and unable to maintain a permanent household. The resulting self-blame can contribute to a behavior pattern of men moving in and out of relationships, fathering even more children.

Taking the Broader View

Thus, the power-structures analysis stresses the impact on fertility of women's subordination to men, a condition that contributes to the social pressure for many births. But it places this problem within the context of unjust social and economic structures that deny women realistic alternatives to unlimited reproduction, structures that encompass far more than the family or even the community. From the level of international trade and finance, down to jobs and income available to men as well as women, antidemocratic structures of decision-making set limits on people's choices, which in turn influence their reproductive options. . . .

[A] discussion of the layers of decision-making power shaping rates of human reproduction might make the reader draw back with skepticism, for could not virtually every economic, political, and cultural fact of life be viewed within such a broad perspective? Our response is that to achieve a holistic understanding, one's view must necessarily be far-reaching. But such an approach need not lack coherence. The pivot on which our perspective turns is the concept of power. Without it we believe it is impossible to understand the complex, interrelated problems of poverty, hunger, population growth, and ecological stress, much less act effectively to address them. . . .

Taking population seriously means incorporating the concept of social powers as an indispensable tool of analysis and facing the logical consequences. It means learning from the historical evidence: without more democratic structures of decision-making power, from the family to the global arena, there is no solution—short of dehumanizing coercion or plagues—to the population explosion. The fate of the Earth hinges on the fate of today's poor majorities. Only as they are empowered to achieve greater security and opportunity—can population growth halt.

Note

1. Quoted in B. Hartmann, *Reproductive Rights and Wrongs: The Global Politics of Population Control and Contraceptive Choice* (New York: Harper & Row, 1987), 48.

— *Biodiversity* —

BIODIVERSITY is a difficult concept to understand. Indeed, this is probably part of the reason why, despite its profound importance, the issue of biodiversity loss gets so little attention. Generally, biodiversity refers to the variety and variability within and among organisms and the ecological systems in which they live. Because life is organized on many different levels ranging from the genetic to the ecosystemic, several different dimensions of biodiversity can be identified.

Genetic diversity refers to variety and variability at the cellular level, as in a specific gene pool. Species diversity refers to the number and variety of existing species. Ecosystem diversity refers to variety and variability at a higher level of organization, that of the ecosystem, which is a combination of plant and animal communities functioning holistically. Biodiversity is not constituted just by the numbers of species or ecosystems, but also by the varied associations and interconnections that exist between them.

One way of appreciating the extent of biodiversity is to contemplate the fact that 10,000 species of microbes may exist in a pinch of European soil, and 12,000 species of beetle may live in the treetops of less than an acre of Panamanian rain forest. Yet despite the vast amount that still exists, we are losing biodiversity at an alarming rate. Not only is biodiversity being destroyed, but so are the indigenous peoples who have been its guardians. Soon nothing will stand in the way of voracious, overconsuming industrial societies.

The biologists Ann Ehrlich and Paul Ehrlich provide an introduction to how much we are losing and why. One of their points is worth highlighting. Photosynthesizing organisms produce energy in excess of what is required for their own growth and life processes. Nearly 25 percent of the biosphere's excess productivity is now used for human purposes. This is energy that cannot be used by wild plants and animals. As human population and consumption increases, an ever-greater proportion of the biosphere's productivity goes to support human life. No wonder we are facing an epidemic of extinction.

Indeed, this epidemic may dramatically worsen. Most plants and animals cannot cope with rapid change. They have evolved in geological time, and their coping mechanisms are correspondingly slow. Yet human activity may be causing such rapid climate change that many plants and animals may not be able to migrate quickly enough to adapt. We can protect domestic plants and animals, and perhaps ourselves; but what will happen to animals that inhabit boreal forests when climate changes turn these areas into grasslands? Already there are reports of ozone depletion damaging various forms of life in the Southern Hemisphere.

The British scientist Norman Myers gives us some practical advice about what we can do to protect biodiversity. Developing countries can preserve more wild areas and do a better job of policing them than they currently do.

They can try to develop with nature rather than against it. Developed countries, whose hands are "also on the chainsaw," contribute to biodiversity loss through their overconsumption. They can and should pay for preservation programs in the developing countries.

It is one thing to say that biodiversity is being reduced and another to say what, if anything, is wrong with this. The American biologists Anne and Paul Ehrlich compare the loss of species to flying in an airplane that is losing rivets. One day we may lose enough rivets, or such an important rivet, that the airplane will crash, and this is not a chance we should take. The "rivets" metaphor is a powerful one, but in itself it does not constitute an argument.

The American philosopher Elliot Sober systematically examines the arguments that have been given for protecting biodiversity and, for the most part, finds them wanting. It is often argued, for example, that the species we are losing could have been economically valuable to us had they been preserved. But surely this is not true of all species, and if we do not know which species are valuable and how valuable they are, it is unclear how their value should figure in our decision making. The best argument for preservation that Sober can muster is aesthetic; but many environmentalists would think that assimilating the value of nature to that of human productions such as artworks, however wonderful they might be, is to miss the point of what is so important about nature.

It is ironic that the destruction of biodiversity, which may be the greatest of human crimes against nature, is also one of the least understood. We do not have a good philosophical account of why biodiversity matters, and the steps that would have to be taken to protect it are, in the present climate, politically impossible. Many people in developing countries want land for agriculture rather than preserves for plants and animals. The majority of people in America want to weaken the Endangered Species Act. Many people prefer maintaining jobs for loggers to preserving the northern spotted owl. Almost no one approves of transferring their tax dollars to other countries, whatever noble purpose is supposed to be served. And so the destruction continues.

Further Reading

Norton, Bryan. *Why Preserve Natural Variety.* Princeton, N.J.: Princeton University Press, 1987.

A philosopher's attempt to defend the value of biodiversity.

Wilson, Edward O. *The Diversity of Life.* Cambridge, Mass.: Harvard University Press, 1992.

One of the world's leading biologists explains the diversity of life and why it should be valued.

Edward O. Wilson, ed. *Biodiversity.* Washington, D.C.: National Academy Press, 1988.

Diverse authors discuss political, economic, cultural, ethical, and scientific aspects of biodiversity loss.

Extinction: Life in Peril

Anne H. Ehrlich and Paul R. Ehrlich

SUPPOSE you are about to fly to Brazil on Growthmania Airlines, an airline with the ambition of doubling its size every year until it eventually fills the entire universe. As you walk out to the jet, you notice a man on a ladder using a crowbar to pry rivets out of the airplane's wing. Curious, you ask him what he's doing. "I'm popping these rivets," he replies, "it's a good job. Growthmania pays me 50 cents for each one I pop, and they sell them for 75 cents each."

"You must be crazy," you reply. "You'll weaken the wing; the plane will crash."

"Relax, I've already taken 200 rivets out of this wing, and nothing has happened yet. Lot of planes fly with missing rivets. They build a lot of redundancy into jet aircraft, partly because they don't completely understand the materials and stresses involved, so nobody can prove that taking another rivet out will weaken the wing too much."

Now, if you have any sense, you'll walk back into the terminal, book a ticket on another airline, and, if you're civic-minded, report Growthmania to the aviation authorities. You know it is quite true that airplanes can and do fly safely with some missing rivets or some minor equipment malfunctions. But no one in his or her right mind would fly on an airline that continually removed rivets as a matter of policy, simply because no one can prove that popping one more rivet would lead to a wing's separating. The end of the rivet-popping trend is clear, but exactly when it will happen is obscure, both because the design of the wing is not completely understood and because the future stresses to which it will be subjected cannot be predicted.

Similarly, natural ecosystems—the communities of plants, animals, and microorganisms that live in an area and interact with each other and with their physical environments—are continually having their "rivets popped": populations and species of innumerable organisms are going extinct today, largely because of human intervention.[1] In the last quarter of this century alone, biologists have estimated, as many as 20 percent of the species existing at midcentury may disappear.[2]

335

No one can predict the exact consequences of those losses, just as the consequences of rivet-popping can't be predicted; exactly how an ecosystem works, what its most vulnerable elements are, and the stresses it may face in the future are unknown. But any biologist worth his or her salt can assure you that, if species are continuously removed, sooner or later a breakdown will occur.

Like the aircraft of responsible airlines, natural ecosystems ordinarily are under "progressive maintenance." The extinction of populations and species is a normal part of the evolutionary process, representing, in a sense, nature's failed experiments. When an organism with a particular genetic makeup leaves more offspring in the next generation than does another type, it's an evolutionary success story. Eventually, the less successful types go extinct. But these occasional extinctions are balanced naturally by the constant founding of new populations and the creation of new species through the evolutionary process of speciation—just as rivets are always being replaced and malfunctions corrected in properly maintained aircraft.

This process has been going on since life began on Earth perhaps 4 billion years ago, but during most of that time, more species were being created than were going extinct, ultimately producing the vast panoply of biotic diversity we see today. On a few occasions, each within a relatively short period of time, a "mass extinction event" occurred. At each of these times, a substantial portion of the existing complement of species disappeared from the fossil record. The last such event, about 65 million years ago, finished off the dinosaurs, among other major groups of organisms.

Some biologists think that in the last episode at least, and possibly the others as well, the extinctions were caused by a cataclysmic event. A giant meteor or comet striking Earth's surface would have raised a huge cloud of dust high into the atmosphere. Lingering for many weeks or months, the dust would have prevented sunlight from reaching the surface. With no sunlight, green plants, algae, and bacteria could not carry out photosynthesis, and many of them perished, as did many of the animals dependent on them for food. Regardless of what caused the extinctions, however, or whether the losses occurred within months or over millennia, it certainly took many millions of years for the biosphere to recover from the losses.

The Role of Humans

Now, unfortunately, another global epidemic of extinctions is occurring on a similar scale. This time, though, the agent is not some uncontrollable extraterrestrial body colliding with Earth: it is the behavior of a large and expanding population of one organism, *Homo sapiens*. To make matters worse, the same activities that are causing the extinctions are, if anything, suppressing the processes that normally give rise to new species and populations. The current rate of species loss can be only roughly estimated, but biologists think that losses of bird and mammal species in the last few centuries have been about 5 to 50 times the normal rate, while toward the end of this century they have risen to about 40 to 400 times normal rates.[3]

What have human beings been doing to cause the demise of so many species and how long has this been going on? Even before agriculture was invented, expert human hunters seem to have exterminated many of the large mammals that inhabited Europe, Asia, and North and South America—animals such as a huge North American dromedary, giant sloths, mammoths, aurochs, and the saber-toothed cat. In historic times, people have been responsible for the loss of the dodo, the Tasmanian wolf, giant moas, the passenger pigeon, and Carolina parakeet. And today, we are all aware of endangered species such as rhinos, elephants, cheetahs, tigers, wolves, ferrets, and numerous birds.

For these and many other species, hunting has been the primary direct cause of disappearance. Many less-conspicuous organisms such as rare cacti and other plants have also been pushed toward extinction, if not always quite over the brink, by human collectors. And some species have been targeted for extermination because they were considered pests; many large cats, wolves, grizzly bears, and even elephants are in this category—although the market value of the tusks of one elephant could support an entire African village for a year.

Still other species, such as predatory birds at the top of a food chain and some fishes, have been decimated by poisons intended to kill pests or by spills of oil or other toxic substances. Indeed, we may be underestimating the role of poisoning from various kinds of pollution in causing extinctions. Acid rain may prove to be an effective, if insidiously slow exterminator—especially in combination with other agents such as climate change and other pollutants.

But by far the most effective way in which human beings have caused extinctions is indirectly, through habitat destruction. People have modified to some extent more than two-thirds of the planet's land area—including much of the most productive land—and have had a significant impact on aquatic ecosystems, both freshwater and oceanic. Of Earth's land, more than 10 percent has been converted to cropland; perhaps 2 percent is paved over in urban development, roads, airports, and so forth; 25 percent is pasture; and the 30 percent still forested is rather heavily exploited or is just tree farms—monocultures of exotic (non-native) tree species.

This vast replacement of natural ecosystems with human-dominated ones, as human population has expanded in a few centuries from several hundred million to 5 billion, has inevitably spelled disaster for the organisms that share the Earth with us. Millions of populations of unsung, inconspicuous organisms—small plants, vertebrates, insects, and other invertebrates—have been pushed to extinction, or at least have been drastically reduced in range, genetically impoverished, and thus endangered.

Current estimates suggest the loss of three or four species a day in tropical moist forests alone. Even though tropical forests are far and away the world's most species-rich ecosystems, as well as among the most endangered ones, this is surely a gross underestimate. Earth's remaining tropical forests are being cut down or significantly degraded at the rate of 25 hectares per minute—a loss of an area about the size of North Carolina every year. There simply is no way to count the losses of myriad still undescribed tiny plants, insects (especially the millions of species of beetles dwelling in the forest canopy), nematodes, mites, fungi, and other obscure creatures that have been displaced. And further losses occur as vast unbroken tracts of natural area are reduced to small fragments that simply cannot support the variety of species that large ones do.

The change from a natural ecosystem to a human-directed one also commonly results in reduced productivity. Green plants and other photosynthesizing organisms have the ability to capture and use the energy in sunlight and convert water and carbon dioxide into carbohydrates; those materials are the source of energy on which virtually all other organisms, including ourselves, depend for life. This energy is known as net primary production (NPP); it is the sum of the energy produced through photosynthesis minus what the photosynthesizing organisms use for their own growth and life processes.

In just the last few decades, the conversion of forests and grasslands to cities, cropland, or pastures, and other processes such as desertification have reduced the worldwide NPP on land by an estimated 13 percent.[4] At the same time, the share of the planet's terrestrial NPP used directly by human beings and their domesticated animals (as food, fodder, and fiber, including wood) is about 4 percent; from the oceans the share is about 2 percent.

This seems modest enough, although disproportionate for one of as many as 30 million species with which we share the planet's bounty. But that 4 percent by no means accounts for all our impact on terrestrial life. By altering natural ecosystems or replacing them with artificial ones, we change the flora and fauna and divert most of the system's energy into a different array of organisms (some of which we call pests). Some NPP is destroyed in human-caused fires, and some is simply wasted.

When this cooption and diversion are calculated, humanity accounts for nearly 30 percent of the NPP on land and about 19 percent globally (including that 2 percent of the oceans' NPP). If the roughly 13 percent of potential NPP on land that has been lost because of human action is included in the calculation, human impact on terrestrial systems rises to nearly 40 percent, and that on the entire biosphere to about 25 percent.

Small wonder an epidemic of extinctions is occurring. *Homo sapiens* has literally taken the food from the mouths of other species and the homes out from under their feet (or roots). We use, lose, redirect, or spoil 40 percent of the energy produced by all of Earth's land ecosystems and wonder why our favorite birds, butterflies, or flowers are hard to find these days. Perhaps more relevant, the persistent and prevalent human poverty in certain regions is reinforced by both the reductions in productivity caused by the degrading or replacing of ecosystems and the limits to possible photosynthetic production in any one area.

The Importance of Biodiversity

Why is it so important to preserve species or different varieties of plants and animals, let alone microorganisms we can't even see? Many people want to preserve a particular species just because it is beautiful or interesting. People have probably always appreciated the beauty of such organisms as flowers, butterflies, and birds. The advent of the microscope enabled us to see and appreciate even more.

In the last century, it has also increasingly been felt that at least domesticated animals had rights and deserved to be treated well. Indeed, the gradual extension of "rights," exemplified at one extreme by animal rights activists, has also led to a belief that other organisms have a right to existence equal to that of human beings and that society has an obligation (because of its power to destroy) to preserve and protect other species—a stewardship duty.[5]

The aesthetic and philosophical reasons for preserving other life-forms besides ours are convincing to some people, but not the majority. There are hardheaded types who heed only pocketbook issues. If they could see the living things around them as resources—rather than just part of their surroundings, of no more consequence than roadside pebbles—they would find it easier to understand why preserving all species is essential for the lasting well-being of just one. All our food and the products we use every day originally came wholly or in part from a plant, animal, or microbe: consider for instance wool, silk, or cotton clothing and furnishings, paper, medicines, spices, rubber tires, oils in cosmetics and lotions, paints and dyes, shell buttons, ivory keyboards, or wooden houses and furniture.

Tropical forests in particular are rich potential sources of valuable foods, medicines, and products of all kinds—if we don't destroy them before their potential can be discovered. When we selectively remove species and damage or destroy entire ecosystems (as in deforestation), resources of enormous potential value are lost.

Tropical forests, more than other kinds of ecosystems, remain uncatalogued treasure houses. Of the approximately 1.4 million species that are known to science, only about one-third are in tropical forests. This is mainly because science has explored those forests less extensively than other environments. Although tropical forests occupy only about 7 percent of the Earth's land surface, they probably contain the great majority of the estimated 10 million to 30 million species on the planet. Of the tropical species so far recognized by

Western science, most are little known and their potential economic value is yet to be explored.

Another argument for the special value of rainforests is the high level of endemism—the occurrence of a species in only one or a few localities—that exists there. Forests in temperate zones, such as those throughout eastern North America, tend to contain the same dozen or so species of trees and a similarly limited array of smaller plants, mammals, and insects. But destruction of any moderate-sized tract of tropical forest is quite likely to cause the extinction of several species that exist nowhere else.

The human population today is increasing rapidly and is expected by demographers to double its current size before growth stops. About 20 percent—over a billion people—are chronically hungry and living in "absolute poverty." Since humanity is quickly depleting its resources, the logic of preserving species that could become valuable resources should be clear even to confirmed urban canyon dwellers. Yet even that argument is not persuasive enough to withstand the economic pressures behind the loggers, land-clearing settlers, and developers who continue to convert land to "more profitable" uses.

Yet there is an even more compelling, if much less widely understood reason to preserve other life-forms besides their intrinsic and potential economic values. Natural ecosystems, with their component species, are our life-support system. Since the Earth was formed over 4 billion years ago, other species have played an essential part in creating the conditions that permit human beings to exist and survive. Natural ecosystems are still actively involved in maintaining those conditions; they provide essential supporting services to civilization that we cannot do without and could not adequately replace even where we know how to do so.

Among these indispensable services are: maintaining the quality and composition of the atmosphere; moderating climates and weather; supplying fresh water; replenishing soils, cycling nutrients essential for life, and disposing of wastes; pollinating plants (including numerous crops); controlling the vast majority of pests and vectors of disease; providing food from the sea; and maintaining that vast "genetic library" of organisms from which has been drawn the very basis of civilization.

Most often we are not aware of these essential services until we lose them. People have noticed that the disappearance of a forest has often been followed by the drying up of formerly dependable streams in the area. When the forested area in the Virunga Mountain National Park in Rwanda was reduced by 40 percent in the 1970s, for instance, several streams that had provided water to the rest of the intensively farmed nation disappeared.

Similar observations have been made throughout the world, especially when mountain watershed forests were removed. A forest particularly, but any kind of vegetative cover, tends to soak up, slowly release, and recycle moisture through the atmosphere. Rainwater that falls on the Amazon forest, for example, is recycled an average of nine times as the moisture-laden air mass passes across the continent. With no forest to absorb and respire it, most of the water would simply run off the bare ground, washing away thin topsoil and flooding the river. Further downwind, the air would be dry, producing drought.

Deforestation or removal of other kinds of vegetative cover (such as scrubland or savanna) thus commonly leads to intensification of both droughts and floods. The frequent catastrophic floods of lowland India and Bangladesh are directly traceable to the deforestation of the Himalaya mountains in Nepal. The diminished river flow in the Nile in recent years, which threatens the agriculture of overpopulated Egypt, is due to deforestation in the watershed of the Nile's headwaters.

The same process is responsible for silting up the Aswan Dam, which will be rendered useless in a few decades. That silt is the result of accelerated soil erosion from the same deforested hillsides, a universal problem. Worldwide soil losses from erosion—much of it from deforestation and devegetation as well as from careless farming technologies and overgrazing—are an estimated 26 billion tons per year.[6] This is a loss civilization cannot afford. Soil erosion, although it can be temporarily masked by increasingly heavy applications of fertilizer, will sooner or later lead to declines in agricultural yields.

Desertification is the five-dollar word that covers the entire process of devegetation, soil loss, local climate change, and loss of productivity in arid regions; and the resultant degradation of the land is not reversible in practical terms. The impoverishment of the people dependent on desertified systems is among the great tragedies of this era. A prime example, and a possible harbinger for other vulnerable areas, is the continent-wide drought and famine in sub-Saharan Africa.

When we become aware of such changes, we can begin to have an inkling of our dependence on natural systems. When pest problems get out of control, and crops suffer attacks from blights and rusts, we notice the loss of pest- and disease-control services. A change in the weather (rarely for the better) is another clue that services have been disrupted. Most often, after deforestation, weather downwind becomes noticeably warmer and drier. Such changes can occur in any region, from the equator to the poles, but they are almost always most severe in the tropics.

Although these lessons have been clear since ancient times, when Greek philosophers recorded their observations and connected what they saw with the impoverishment of the land, they never seem to remain learned. The demise of any number of once-flourishing civilizations, from the Mesopotamians to the Khmers, can be traced to a failure to maintain ecosystem services. Perhaps every society must learn for itself that massive conversion of landscapes, the pollution of waters, and other abuses lead to losses of productivity in the long run.

Usually the motivating influence is a short-term gain or a very localized change made without considering the impact if many similar changes were made on a large scale (such as incremental forest-clearing for a series of farms). Nature most often is not vanquished in one mighty battle, but is taken in a series of minor skirmishes. Today we have a global civilization, a network of increasingly interdependent societies, heedlessly destroying ecosystems everywhere, one bit at a time.

If the ancient lessons are not applied soon, humanity just might follow the dinosaurs to oblivion. Only someone who did not know what rivets are for would knowingly patronize an airline with the rivet-popping practices of Growthmania, and only such a person would want to ride on Spaceship Earth when the rivets in its ecosystems were always being removed. But here we are, with no other spaceline offering transport, so let's educate the world to save those rivets.

Notes

1. P. R. Ehrlich and A. H. Ehrlich, *Extinction: The Causes and Consequences of the Disappearance of Species* (New York: Random House, 1981); L. R. Brown et al., *State of the World 1988* (New York: Norton, 1988).

2. Council on Environmental Quality and U.S. State Department, *The Global 2000 Report to the President* (Washington, D.C.: Government Printing Office, 1980).

3. Ehrlich and Ehrlich, *Extinction*.

4. P. M. Vitousek, P. R. Ehrlich, A. H. Ehrlich, et al., "Human Appropriation of the Products of Photosynthesis," *Bioscience* 36 (1986): 368–73.

5. D. Ehrenfeld, *The Arrogance of Humanism* (New York: Oxford University Press, 1987).

6. Brown et al., *State of the World*.

[From] *The Sinking Ark*

Norman Myers

DEVELOPING countries can do much to safeguard the global heritage in species. At least two-thirds, and possibly three-quarters, of all species on earth exist in the tropics, a zone that is pretty well made up of developing countries. Yet, while the tropics merit exceptional efforts at conservation, they have hitherto received exceptionally meager measures. Moreover, pressures of growing human numbers with growing aspirations are causing natural environments to be degraded at ever-more rapid rates.

So what can developing countries do to turn around the adverse trend? A long list of possibilities is available. They can set aside more wildland territories in order to protect representative ecosystems. They can clamp down on illegal hunting and trade in wildlife products. They can reduce conflict between wild creatures and domestic livestock. They can boost tourism as a support for parks and reserves. Above all, they can stem the wholesale conversion of virgin landscapes to croplands and the like by making sure that development projects are the right ones at the right time and right place. . . .

To be sure, a number of developing countries have already taken sizeable steps towards conservation of their species. Tanzania, with a government budget about as much as New Yorkers spend on ice cream each year, allocates a larger share of this impoverished national kitty to conservation of its wildlife than the United States spends by proportion on its bald eagle, mountain lion and other wild creatures. Tanzania's parks and reserves amount to 9 percent of the country, the equivalent of the United States setting aside California, Oregon and Washington states. When Peru received its first donations from the World Wildlife Fund and other outside organizations in the mid-1960s, these contributions almost equalled the entire funding allocated by the country to its conservation efforts. By 1975, however, Peru had invested sums of its own that totalled 50 times more than the total financial aid extended from outside during Peru's entire conservation history. Something the same holds true for several other developing nations, notably Iran, Costa Rica and Zambia, and their achievements may soon be matched by Venezuela, Zaire and Gabon, among other countries—all are establishing extensive networks of parks. . . .

True, developing countries are unlikely to look out for their forests merely in order to preserve 40–50 percent of humanity's heritage in species. However valid this motivation might be, it is not going to appear so pressing to developing countries' leaders as the urgent need to enhance their citizens' lifestyles. . . .

A Malaysian politician recently described how he was taken to task by an American conservationist over the logging threat to his country's Endau Rompin Park. Each hectare of the Park's forest contains around 60 m^3 of commercial timber, worth an average of $60 per m^3, which means that each square kilometer contains timber worth $360,000. Since one-quarter of the Park's 5,000 km^2 are threatened by logging, this means that the Park's survival in undisturbed form will deny the Malaysian economy $450 million in timber revenues. . . .

The United States as a Developing Country

To enable us to get a realistic grasp of what the alternative means, let us visualize how the United States would fare were it to be a developing country in the last quarter of the twentieth century. Instead of 70 percent of the populace occupying only 2 percent of national territory, at least as many would be living off the land. Most farmers, with a cash income of $300 per year, would be unable to afford the perquisites of high-productivity agriculture, such as mechanization and sophisticated technology. So their farming practices would be pretty wasteful in their use of the main arable areas, causing huge numbers of subsistence cultivators to spread into drier grassland zones, where each farmer would require a still larger plot to sustain his family. His family, responding to the sudden and narrow-focus infusion of medical aid from foreign sources during recent decades, would number eight to ten persons, and his offsprings' hopes for a steadily improving lifestyle would generate still further pressures for more land on which to support themselves. Indeed, demographers would point out that in view of the fact that over 50 percent of the populace was aged 15 or less (by contrast with around 20 percent in advanced nations), the parents of the future had already been born; and so even if the average American family were to come down to two children forthwith, the present total of 225 million Americans would grow to almost twice as many by the end of the century, with no prospects of zero population growth until well beyond the 500 million mark in another two generations' time.

Not that Americans would listlessly accept their lot. On the contrary, showing exceptional enterprise and willingness to work, they could well achieve economic growth rates to put them on a virtual par with "economic miracle" countries such as Japan and West Germany. Regrettably, these efforts would achieve little so long as America's access to the world's main markets was severely restricted at best. Result: America's citizenry would mostly remain countryside dwellers, and the over-loading of natural environments on every side would increase year by year. Indeed, the broad-scale disruption of virgin ecosystems would be plain for anyone to see, as the western forests made way for agriculture and new settlements, or were exploited for fuel, with the exception of the redwoods which were exported to cater for specialist and insatiable appetites in affluent communities overseas. One by one, the country's notable parks would fall to the hordes of land-hungry peasants, first the better-watered areas such as the Everglades, then the drier wildlands. Eventually, only Death Valley would remain. The only time the advanced world would pay much attention would be when it would wag a finger over the demise of the black-footed ferret and the California condor. . . .

. . . Who gains from conservation of earth's species and who pays for it?

In principle, everyone gains from survival of species. If Indonesia, Zaire and Brazil take steps to protect their threatened wildlife, the entire global community stands to benefit from the pragmatic purposes (modern agriculture, medicine and so forth) served by the genetic resources at stake. This argues that the entire global community should be prepared to share in the benefits. Equally to the point, it is developed nations, with their technological expertise, that currently make most use of genetic resources around the world and especially from the tropics, as underpinning for their agriculture, as sources of new drugs and as raw materials for industry. Were Brazil to maintain the forest habitat of its golden lion marmoset, and were this monkey to offer assistance to the anti-cancer campaign after the manner of the cotton-topped marmoset, the communities who would benefit most in the foreseeable future are those of developed countries where cancer is a scourge. People in Brazil, in common with the rest of the developing world, generally do not live long enough to contract cancer. To this extent, the benefits of saving the marmoset would be unequally distributed—and Brazil's efforts to safeguard part of the natural heritage of all nations amount, like the conservation activities of other developing nations, to a "resource handout" from developing nations to developed nations.

Equally to the point, it is developed nations, through their expanding appetites for hardwood timber, beef and other forestland products, and through the technological muscle of their giant corporations, that are unwittingly contributing to the destruction of tropical moist forests. Their hand is also on the chainsaw. . . .

. . . While the entire global community would hopefully contribute in support of its global heritage, it is reasonable that the main burden of the funding should be borne by those who stand to derive most immediate benefit through utilitarian application of genetic resources, and who disproportionately contribute to depletion of the earth's natural resources through their over-consumerist lifestyles. And when all else is said, the affluent nations are the only ones with sufficient wealth to pick up the price tab.

[From] Philosophical Problems for Environmentalism

Elliott Sober

Introduction

Preserving an endangered species or ecosystem poses no special conceptual problem when the instrumental value of that species or ecosystem is known. When we have reason to think that some natural object represents a resource to us, we obviously ought to take that fact into account in deciding what to do. A variety of potential uses may be under discussion, including food supply, medical applications, recreational use, and so on. As with any complex decision, it may be difficult even to agree on how to compare the competing values that may be involved. Willingness to pay in dollars is a familiar least common denominator, although it poses a number of problems. But here we have nothing that is specifically a problem for environmentalism.

The problem for environmentalism stems from the idea that species and ecosystems ought to be preserved for reasons additional to their known value as resources for human use. The feeling is that even when we cannot say what nutritional, medicinal, or recreational benefit the preservation provides, there still is a value in preservation. It is the search for a rationale for this feeling that constitutes the main conceptual problem for environmentalism.

The problem is especially difficult in view of the holistic (as opposed to individualistic) character of the things being assigned value. Put simply, what is special about environmentalism is that it values the preservation of species, communities, or ecosystems, rather than the individual organisms of which they are composed. "Animal liberationists" have urged that we should take the suffering of sentient animals into account in ethical deliberation. Such beasts are not mere things to be used as cruelly as we like no matter how trivial the benefit we derive. But in "widening the ethical circle," we are simply including in the community more individual organisms whose costs and benefits we compare. Animal liberationists are extending an old and familiar ethical doctrine—namely, utilitarianism—to take account of the welfare of other individuals. Although the practical consequences of this point of view may be revolutionary, the theoretical perspective is not at all novel. If suffering is bad, then it is bad for any individual who suffers. Animal liberationists merely remind us of the consequences of familiar principles.

But trees, mountains, and salt marshes do not suffer. They do not experience pleasure and pain, because, evidently, they do not have experiences at all. The same is true of species. Granted, individual organisms may have mental states; but the species—taken to be a population of organisms connected by certain sorts of interactions (preeminently, that of exchanging genetic material in reproduction)—does not. Or put more carefully, we might say that the only sense in which species have experiences is that their member organisms do: the attribution at the population level, if true, is true simply in virtue of its being true at the individual level. Here is a case where reductionism is correct.

So perhaps it is true in this reductive sense that some species experience pain. But the values that environmentalists attach to preserving species do not reduce to any value of preserving organisms. It is in this sense that environmentalists espouse a holistic value system. Environmentalists care about entities that by no stretch of the imagination have experiences (e.g., mountains). What is more, their position does not force them to care if individual organisms suffer pain, so long as the species is preserved. Steel traps may outrage an animal liberationist because of the suffering they inflict, but an environmentalist aiming just at the preservation of a balanced ecosystem might see here no cause for complaint. Similarly, environmentalists think that the distinction between wild and domesticated organisms is important, in that it is the preservation of "natural" (i.e., not created by the "artificial interference" of human beings) objects that matters, whereas animal liberationists see the main problem in terms of the suffering of any organism—domesticated or not. And finally, environmentalists and animal liberationists diverge on what might be called the $n + m$ question. If two species—say blue and sperm whales—have roughly comparable capacities for experiencing pain, an animal liberationist might tend to think of the preservation of a sperm whale as wholly on an ethical par with the preservation of a blue whale. The fact that one organism is part of an endangered species while the other is not does not make the rare individual more intrinsically important. But for an environmentalist, this holistic property—membership in an endangered species—makes all the difference in the world: a world with n sperm and m blue whales is far better than a world with $n + m$ sperm and 0 blue whales. Here we have a stark contrast between an ethic in which it is the life situation of individuals that matters, and an ethic in which the stability and diversity of populations of individuals are what matter.

Both animal liberationists and environmentalists wish to broaden our ethical horizons—to make us realize that it is not just human welfare that counts. But they do this in very different, often conflicting, ways. It is no accident that at the level of practical politics the two points of view increasingly find themselves at loggerheads. This practical conflict is the expression of a deep theoretical divide.[1]

The Ignorance Argument

"Although we might not now know what use a particular endangered species might be to us, allowing it to go extinct forever closes off the possibility of discovering and exploiting a future use." According to this point of view, our ignorance of value is turned into a reason for action. The scenario envisaged in this environmentalist argument is not without precedent; who could have guessed that penicillin would be good for something other than turning out cheese? But there is a fatal defect in such arguments, which we might summarize with the phrase *out of nothing, nothing comes:* rational decisions require assumptions about what is true and what is valuable (in decision-theoretic jargon, the inputs must be probabilities and utilities). If you are completely ignorant of values, then you are incapable of making a rational decision, either for or against preserving some species. The fact that you do not know the value of a species, by itself, cannot count as a reason for wanting one thing rather than another to happen to it.

And there are so many species. How many geese that lay golden eggs are there apt to be in that number? It is hard to assign probabilities and utilities precisely here, but an analogy will perhaps reveal the problem confronting this environmentalist argument. Most of us willingly fly on airplanes, when safer (but less convenient) alternative forms of transportation are available. Is this rational? Suppose it were argued that there is a small probability that the next flight you take will crash. This would be very bad for you. Is it not crazy for you to risk this, given that the only gain to you is that you can reduce your travel time by a few hours (by not going by train, say)? Those of us who not only fly, but congratulate ourselves for being rational in doing so, reject this argument. We are prepared to accept a small chance of a great disaster in return for the high probability of a rather modest benefit. If this is rational, no wonder that we might consistently be willing to allow a species to go extinct in order to build a hydroelectric plant.

That the argument from ignorance is no argument at all can be seen from another angle. If we literally do not know what consequences the extinction of this or that species may bring, then we should take seriously the possibility that the extinction may be beneficial as well as the possibility that it may be deleterious. It may sound deep to insist that we preserve endangered species precisely because we do not know why they are valuable. But ignorance on a scale like this cannot provide the basis for any rational action.

Rather than invoke some unspecified future benefit, an environmentalist may argue that the species in question plays a crucial role in stabilizing the ecosystem of which it is a part. This will undoubtedly be true for carefully chosen species and ecosystems, but one should not generalize this argument into a global claim to the effect that *every* species is crucial to a balanced ecosystem. Although ecologists used to agree that the complexity of an ecosystem stabilizes it, this hypothesis has been subject to a number of criticisms and qualifications, both from a theoretical and an empirical perspective.[2] And for certain kinds of species (those which occupy a rather small area and whose normal population is small) we can argue that extinction would probably not disrupt the community. However fragile the biosphere may be, the extreme view that everything is crucial is almost certainly not true.

But, of course, environmentalists are often concerned by the fact that extinctions are occurring now at a rate much higher than in earlier times. It is mass extinction that threatens the biosphere, they say, and this claim avoids the spurious assertion that communities are so fragile that even one extinction will cause a crash. However, if the point is to avoid a mass extinction of species, how does this provide a rationale for preserving a species of the kind just described, of which we rationally believe that its passing will not destabilize the ecosystem? And, more generally, if mass extinction is known to be a danger to us, how does this translate into a value for preserving any particular species? Notice that we have now passed beyond the confines of the argument from ignorance; we are taking as a premise the idea that mass extinction would be a catastrophe (since it would destroy the ecosystem on which we depend). But how should that premise affect our valuing the California condor, the blue whale, or the snail darter?

The Slippery Slope Argument

Environmentalists sometimes find themselves asked to explain why each species matters so much to them, when there are, after all, so many. We may know of special reasons for valuing particular species, but how can we justify thinking that each and every species is important? "Each extinction impoverishes the biosphere" is often the answer given, but it really fails to resolve the issue. Granted, each extinction impoverishes, but it only impoverishes a little bit. So if it is the *wholesale* impoverishment of the biosphere that matters, one would apparently have to concede that each extinction matters a little, but only a little. But environmentalists may be loathe to concede this, for if they concede that each species matters only a little, they seem to be inviting the wholesale impoverishment that would be an unambiguous disaster. So they dig in their heels and insist that each species matters a lot. But to take this line, one must find some other rationale than the idea that mass extinction would be a great harm. Some of these alternative rationales we will examine later. For now, let us take a closer look at the train of thought involved here.

Slippery slopes are curious things: if you take even one step onto them, you inevitably slide all the way to the bottom. So if you want to avoid finding yourself at the bottom, you must avoid stepping onto them at all. To mix metaphors, stepping onto a slippery slope is to invite being nickeled and dimed to death.

Slippery slope arguments have played a powerful role in a number of recent ethical debates. One often hears people defend the legitimacy of abortions by arguing that since it is permissible to abort a single-celled fertilized egg, it must be permissible to abort a foetus of any age, since there is no place to draw the line from 0 to 9 months. Antiabortionists, on the other hand, sometimes argue in the other direction: since infanticide of newborns is not permissible, abortion at any earlier time is also not allowed, since there is no place to draw the line. Although these two arguments reach opposite conclusions about the permissibility of abortions, they agree on the following idea: since there is no principled place to draw the line on the continuum from newly fertilized egg to foetus gone to term, one must treat all these cases in the same way. Either abortion is always permitted or it never is, since there is no place to draw the line. Both sides run their favorite slippery slope arguments, but try to precipitate slides in opposite directions.

Starting with 10 million extant species, and valuing overall diversity, the environmentalist does not want to grant that each species matters only a little. For having granted this, commercial expansion and other causes will reduce the tally to 9,999,999. And then the argument is repeated, with each species valued only a little, and diversity declines another notch. And so we are well on our way to a considerably impoverished biosphere, a little at a time. Better to reject the starting premise—namely, that each species matters only a little—so that the slippery slope can be avoided.

Slippery slopes should hold no terror for environmentalists, because it is often a mistake to demand that a line be drawn. Let me illustrate by an example. What is the difference between being bald and not? Presumably, the difference concerns the number of hairs you have on your head. But what is the precise number of hairs marking the boundary between baldness and not being bald? There is no such number. Yet, it would be a fallacy to conclude that there is no difference between baldness and hairiness. The fact that you cannot draw a line does not force you to say that the two alleged categories collapse into one. In the abortion case, this means that even if there is no precise point in foetal development that involves some discontinuous, qualitative change, one is still not obliged to think of newly fertilized eggs and foetuses gone to term as morally on a par. Since the biological differences are ones of degree, not kind, one may want to adopt the position that the moral differences are likewise matters of degree. This may lead to the view that a woman should have a better reason for having an abortion, the more developed her foetus is. Of course, this position does not logically follow from the idea that there is no place to draw the line; my point is just that differences in degree do not demolish the possibility of there being real moral differences.

In the environmental case, if one places a value on diversity, then each species becomes more valuable as the overall diversity declines. If we begin with 10 million species, each may matter little, but as extinctions continue, the remaining ones matter more and more. According to this outlook, a better and better reason would be demanded for allowing yet another species to go extinct. Perhaps certain sorts of economic development would justify the extinction of a species at one time. But granting this does not oblige one to conclude that the same sort of decision would have to be made further down the road. This means that one can value diversity without being obliged to take the somewhat exaggerated position that each species, no matter how many there are, is terribly precious in virtue of its contribution to that diversity.

Yet, one can understand that environmentalists might be reluctant to concede this point. They may fear that if one now allows that most species contribute only a little to overall diversity, one will set in motion a political process that cannot correct itself later. The worry is that even when the overall diversity has been drastically reduced, our ecological sensitivities will have been so coarsened that we will no longer be in a position to realize (or to implement policies fostering) the preciousness of what is left. This fear may be quite justified, but it is important to realize that it does not conflict with what was argued above. The political utility of making an argument should not be confused with the argument's soundness.

The fact that you are on a slippery slope, by itself, does not tell you whether you are near the beginning, in the middle, or at the end. If species diversity is a matter of degree, where do we currently find ourselves—on the verge of catastrophe, well on our way in that direction, or at some distance from a global crash? Environmentalists often urge that we are fast approaching a precipice; if we are, then the reduction in diversity that every succeeding extinction engenders should be all we need to justify species preservation.

Sometimes, however, environmentalists advance a kind of argument not predicated on the idea of fast approaching doom. The goal is to show that there is something wrong with allowing a species to go extinct (or with causing it to go extinct), even if overall diversity is not affected much. I now turn to one argument of this kind.

Appeals to What Is Natural

I noted earlier that environmentalists and animal liberationists disagree over the significance of the distinction between wild and domesticated animals. Since both types of organisms can experience pain, animal liberationists will think of each as meriting ethical consideration. But environmentalists will typically not put wild and domesticated organisms on a par. Environmentalists typically are interested in preserving what is natural, be it a species living in the wild or a wilderness ecosystem. If a kind of domesticated chicken were threatened with extinction, I doubt that environmental groups would be up in arms. And if certain unique types of human environments—say urban slums in the United States—were "endangered," it is similarly unlikely that environmentalists would view this process as a deplorable impoverishment of the biosphere.

The environmentalist's lack of concern for humanly created organisms and environments may be practical rather than principled. It may be that at the level of values, no such bifurcation is legitimate, but that from the point of view of practical political action, it makes sense to put one's energies into saving items that exist in the wild. This subject has not been discussed much in the literature, so it is hard to tell. But I sense that the distinction between wild and domesticated has a certain theoretical importance to many environmentalists. They perhaps think that the difference is that we created domesticated organisms which would otherwise not exist, and so are entitled to use them solely for our own interests. But we did not create wild organisms and environments, so it is the height of presumption to expropriate them for our benefit. A more fitting posture would be one of "stewardship": we have come on the scene and found a treasure not of our making. Given this, we ought to preserve this treasure in its natural state.

I do not wish to contest the appropriateness of "stewardship." It is the dichotomy between artificial (domesticated) and natural (wild) that strikes me as wrong-headed. I want to suggest that to the degree that "natural" means anything biologically, it means very little ethically. And, conversely, to the degree that "natural" is understood as a normative concept, it has very little to do with biology.

Environmentalists often express regret that we human beings find it so hard to remember that we are part of nature—one species among many others—rather than something standing outside of nature. I will not consider here whether this attitude is cause for complaint; the important point is that seeing us as part of nature rules out the environmentalist's use of the distinction between artificial-domesticated and natural-wild described above. *If we are part of nature, then everything we do is part of nature, and is natural in that primary sense.* When we domesticate organisms and bring them into a state of dependence on us, this is simply an example of one species exerting a selection pressure on another. If one calls this "unnatural," one might just as well say the same of parasitism or symbiosis (compare human domestication of animals and plants and "slave-making" in the social insects).

The concept of naturalness is subject to the same abuses as the concept of normalcy. *Normal* can mean *usual* or it can mean *desirable.* Although only the total pessimist will think that the two concepts are mutually exclusive, it is generally recognized that the mere fact that something is common does not by itself count as a reason for thinking that it is desirable. This distinction is quite familiar now in popular discussions of mental health, for example. Yet, when it comes to environmental issues, the concept of naturalness continues to live a double life. The destruction of wilderness areas by increased industrialization is bad because it is unnatural. And it is unnatural because it involves transforming a natural into an artificial habitat. Or one might hear that although extinction is a natural process, the kind of mass extinction currently being precipitated by our species is unprecedented, and so is unnatural. Environmentalists should look elsewhere for a defense of their policies, lest conservation simply become a variant of uncritical conservatism in which the axiom "Whatever is, is right" is modified to read "Whatever is (before human beings come on the scene), is right."

This conflation of the biological with the normative sense of "natural" sometimes comes to the fore when environmentalists attack animal liberationists for naive do-goodism. Callicott writes:

> . . . the value commitments of the humane movement seem at bottom to betray a world-denying or rather a life-loathing philosophy. The natural world as actually constituted is one in which one being lives at the expense of others. Each organism, in Darwin's metaphor, struggles to maintain its own organic integrity. . . . To live *is* to be anxious about life, to feel pain and pleasure in a fitting mixture, and sooner or later to die. That is the way the system works. *If nature as a whole is good, then pain and death are also good.* Environmental ethics in general require people to play fair in the natural system. The neo-Benthamites have in a sense taken the uncourageous approach. People have

attempted to exempt themselves from the life/death reciprocities of natural processes and from ecological limitations in the name of a prophylactic ethic of maximizing rewards (pleasure) and minimizing unwelcome information (pain). To be fair, the humane moralists seem to suggest that we should attempt to project the same values into the nonhuman animal world and to widen the charmed circle—no matter that it would be biologically unrealistic to do so or biologically ruinous if, per impossible, such an environmental ethic were implemented.

There is another approach. Rather than imposing our alienation from nature and natural processes and cycles of life on other animals, we human beings could reaffirm our participation in nature by accepting life as it is given without a sugar coating. . . .[3]

On the same page, Callicott quotes with approval Shepard's remark that "the humanitarian's projection onto nature of illegal murder and the rights of civilized people to safety not only misses the point but is exactly contrary to fundamental ecological reality: the structure of nature is a sequence of killings."[4]

Thinking that what is found in nature is beyond ethical defect has not always been popular. Darwin wrote:

. . . That there is much suffering in the world no one disputes.

Some have attempted to explain this in reference to man by imagining that it serves for his moral improvement. But the number of men in the world is as nothing compared with that of all other sentient beings, and these often suffer greatly without any moral improvement. A being so powerful and so full of knowledge as a God who could create the universe, is to our finite minds omnipotent and omniscient, and it revolts our understanding to suppose that his benevolence is not unbounded, for what advantage can there be in the sufferings of millions of the lower animals throughout almost endless time? This very old argument from the existence of suffering against the existence of an intelligent first cause seems to me a strong one; whereas, as just remarked, the presence of much suffering agrees well with the view that all organic beings have been developed through variation and natural selection.[5]

Darwin apparently viewed the quantity of pain found in nature as a melancholy and sobering consequence of the struggle for existence. But once we adopt the Panglossian attitude that this is the best of all possible worlds ("there is just the right amount of pain," etc.), a failure to identify what is natural with what is good can only seem "world-denying," "life-loathing," "in a sense uncourageous," and "contrary to fundamental ecological reality."[6]

Earlier in his essay, Callicott expresses distress that animal liberationists fail to draw a sharp distinction "between the very different plights (and rights) of wild and domestic animals."[7] Domestic animals are creations of man, he says. "They are living artifacts, but artifacts nevertheless. . . . There is thus something profoundly incoherent (and insensitive as well) in the complaint of some animal liberationists that the 'natural behavior' of chickens and bobby calves is cruelly frustrated on factory farms. It would make almost as much sense to speak of the natural behavior of tables and chairs."[8] Here again we see teleology playing a decisive role: wild organisms do not have the natural function of serving human ends, but domesticated animals do. Cheetahs in zoos are crimes against what is natural; veal calves in boxes are not.

The idea of "natural tendency" played a decisive role in pre-Darwinian biological thinking. Aristotle's entire science—both his physics and his biology—is articulated in terms of specifying the natural tendencies of kinds of objects and the interfering forces that can prevent an object from achieving its intended state. Heavy objects in the sublunar sphere have location at the center of the earth as their natural state; each tends to go there, but is prevented from doing so. Organisms likewise are conceptualized in terms of this natural state model:

> . . . [for] any living thing that has reached its normal development and which is unmutilated, and whose mode of generation is not spontaneous, the most natural act is the production of another like itself, an animal producing an animal, a plant a plant. . . .[9]

But many interfering forces are possible, and in fact the occurrence of "monsters" is anything but uncommon. According to Aristotle, mules (sterile hybrids) count as deviations from the natural state. In fact, females are monsters as well, since the natural tendency of sexual reproduction is for the offspring to perfectly resemble the father, who, according to Aristotle, provides the "genetic instructions" (to put the idea anachronistically) while the female provides only the matter.

What has happened to the natural state model in modern science? In physics, the idea of describing what a class of objects will do in the absence of "interference" lives on: Newton specified this "zero-force state" as rest or uniform motion, and in general relativity, this state is understood in terms of motion along geodesics. But one of the most profound achievements of Darwinian biology has been the jettisoning of this kind of model. It isn't just that Aristotle was wrong in his detailed claims about mules and women; the whole structure of the natural state model has been discarded. Population biology is not conceptualized in terms of positing some characteristic that all members of a species would have in common, were interfering forces absent. Variation is not thought of as a deflection from the natural state of uniformity. Rather, variation is taken to be a fundamental property in its own right. Nor, at the level of individual biology, does the natural state model find an application. Developmental theory is not articulated by specifying a natural tendency and a set of interfering forces. . . . The idea that a corn plant might have some "natural height," which can be augmented or diminished by "interfering forces" is entirely alien to post-Darwinian biology.

The fact that the concepts of natural state and interfering force have lapsed from biological thought does not prevent environmentalists from inventing them anew. Perhaps these concepts can be provided with some sort of normative content; after all, the normative idea of "human rights" may make sense even if it is not a theoretical underpinning of any empirical science. But environmentalists should not assume that they can rely on some previously articulated scientific conception of "natural."

Appeals to Needs and Interests

The version of utilitarianism considered earlier (according to which something merits ethical consideration if it can experience pleasure and/or pain) leaves the environmentalist in the lurch. But there is an alternative to Bentham's hedonistic utilitarianism that has been thought by some to be a foundation for environmentalism. Preference utilitarianism says that an object's having interests, needs, or preferences gives it ethical status. This doctrine is at the core of Stone's affirmative answer to the title question of his book *Should Trees Have Standing?*[10] "Natural objects *can* communicate their wants (needs) to us, and in ways that are not terribly ambiguous. . . . The lawn tells me that it wants water by a certain dryness of the blades and soil—immediately obvious to the touch—the appearance of bald spots, yellowing, and a lack of springiness after being walked on." And if plants can do this, presumably so can mountain ranges, and endangered species. Preference utilitarianism may thereby seem to grant intrinsic ethical importance to precisely the sorts of objects about which environmentalists have expressed concern.

The problems with this perspective have been detailed by Sagoff.[11] If one does not require of an object that it have a mind for it to have wants or needs, what *is* required for the possession of these ethically relevant properties? Suppose one says that an object needs something if it will cease to exist if it does not get it. Then species, plants, and mountain ranges have needs, but only in the sense that automobiles, garbage dumps, and buildings do too. If everything has needs, the advice to take needs into account in ethical deliberation is empty, unless it is supplemented by some technique for weighting and comparing the needs of different objects. A corporation will go bankrupt unless a highway is built. But the swamp will cease to exist if the highway is built. Perhaps one should take into account all relevant needs, but the question is how to do this in the event that needs conflict.

Although the concept of needs can be provided with a permissive, all-inclusive definition, it is less easy to see how to do this with the concept of want. Why think that a mountain range "wants" to retain its unspoiled appearance, rather than house a new amusement park? Needs are not at issue here, since in either case, the mountain continues to exist. One might be tempted to think that natural objects like mountains and species have "natural tendencies," and that the concept of want should be liberalized so as to mean that natural objects "want" to persist in their natural states. This Aristotelian view, as I argued in the previous section, simply makes no sense. Granted, a commercially undeveloped mountain will persist in this state, unless it is commercially developed. But it is equally true that a commercially untouched hill will become commercially developed, unless something causes this not to happen. I see no hope for extending the concept of wants to the full range of objects valued by environmentalists.

The same problems emerge when we try to apply the concepts of needs and wants to species. A species may need various resources, in the sense that these are necessary for its continued existence. But what do species want? Do they want to remain stable in numbers, neither growing nor shrinking? Or since most species have gone extinct, perhaps what species really want is to go extinct, and it is human meddlesomeness that frustrates this natural tendency? Preference utilitarianism is no more likely than hedonistic utilitarianism to secure autonomous ethical status for endangered species.

Ehrenfeld describes a related distortion that has been inflicted on the diversity/stability hypothesis in theoretical ecology. If it were true that increasing the diversity of an ecosystem causes it to be more stable, this might encourage the Aristotelian idea that ecosystems have a natural tendency to increase their diversity. The full realization of this tendency—the natural state that is the goal of ecosystems—is the "climax" or "mature" community. Extinction diminishes diversity, so it frustrates ecosystems from attaining their goal. Since the hypothesis that diversity causes stability is now considered controversial (to say the least), this line of thinking will not be very tempting. But even if the diversity/stability hypothesis were true, it would not permit the environmentalist to conclude that ecosystems have an interest in retaining their diversity.

Darwinism has not banished the idea that parts of the natural world are goal-directed systems, but has furnished this idea with a natural mechanism. We properly conceive of organisms (or genes, sometimes) as being in the business of maximizing their chances of survival and reproduction. We describe characteristics as adaptations—as devices that exist for the furtherance of these ends. Natural selection makes this perspective intelligible. But Darwinism is a profoundly individualistic doctrine.[12] Darwinism rejects the idea that species, communities, and ecosystems have adaptations that exist for their own benefit. These higher-level entities are not conceptualized as goal-directed systems; what properties of organization they possess are viewed as artifacts of processes operating at lower levels of organization. An environmentalism based on the idea that the ecosystem is directed toward stability and diversity must find its foundation elsewhere.

Granting Wholes Autonomous Value

A number of environmentalists have asserted that environmental values cannot be grounded in values based on regard for individual welfare. Aldo Leopold wrote in *A Sand County Almanac* that "a thing is right when it tends to preserve the integrity, stability, and beauty of the biotic community. It is wrong when it tends otherwise."[13] Callicott develops this idea at some length, and ascribes to ethical environmentalism the view that "the preciousness of individual deer, *as of any other specimen*, is inversely proportional to the population of the species."[14] In his *Desert Solitaire*, Edward Abbey notes that he would sooner shoot a man than a snake.[15] And Garrett Hardin asserts that human beings injured in wilderness areas ought not to be rescued: making great and spectacular efforts to save the life of an individual "makes sense only when there is a shortage of people. I have not lately heard that there is a shortage of people."[16] The point of view suggested by these quotations is quite clear. It isn't that preserving the integrity of ecosystems has autonomous value, to be taken into account just as the quite distinct value of individual human welfare is. Rather, the idea is that the only value is the holistic one of maintaining ecological balance and diversity. Here we have a view that is just as monolithic as the most single-minded individualism; the difference is that the unit of value is thought to exist at a higher level of organization.

It is hard to know what to say to someone who would save a mosquito, just because it is rare, rather than a human being, if there were a choice. In ethics, as in any other subject, rationally persuading another person requires the existence of shared assumptions. If this monolithic environmentalist view is based on the notion that ecosystems have needs and interests, and that these take total precedence over the rights and interests of individual human beings, then the discussion of the previous sections is relevant. And even supposing that these higher-level entities have needs and wants, what reason is there to suppose that these matter and that the wants and needs of individuals matter not at all? But if this source of defense is jettisoned, and it is merely asserted that only ecosystems have value, with no substantive defense being offered, one must begin by requesting an argument: *why* is ecosystem stability and diversity the only value?

Some environmentalists have seen the individualist bias of utilitarianism as being harmful in ways additional to its impact on our perception of ecological values. Thus, Callicott writes:

> On the level of social organization, the interests of society may not always coincide with the sum of the interests of its parts. Discipline, sacrifice, and individual restraint are often necessary in the social sphere to maintain social integrity as within the bodily organism. A society, indeed, is particularly vulnerable to disintegration when its members become preoccupied totally with their own particular interest, and ignore those distinct and independent interests of the community as a whole. One example, unfortunately, our own society, is altogether too close at hand to be examined with strict academic detachment. The United States seems to pursue uncritically a social policy of reductive utilitarianism, aimed at promoting the happiness of all its members severally. Each special interest accordingly clamors more loudly to be satisfied while the com-

munity as a whole becomes noticeably more and more infirm economically, environmentally, and politically.[17]

Callicott apparently sees the emergence of individualism and alienation from nature as two aspects of the same process. He values "the symbiotic relationship of Stone Age man to the natural environment" and regrets that "civilization has insulated and alienated us from the rigors and challenges of the natural environment. The hidden agenda of the humane ethic," he says, "is the imposition of the anti-natural prophylactic ethos of comfort and soft pleasure on an even wider scale. The land ethic, on the other hand, requires a shrinkage, if at all possible, of the domestic sphere; it rejoices in a recrudescence of the wilderness and a renaissance of tribal cultural experience."[18]

Callicott is right that "strict academic detachment" is difficult here. The reader will have to decide whether the United States currently suffers from too much or too little regard "for the happiness of all its members severally" and whether we should feel nostalgia or pity in contemplating what the Stone Age experience of nature was like.

The Demarcation Problem

Perhaps the most fundamental theoretical problem confronting an environmentalist who wishes to claim that species and ecosystems have autonomous value is what I will call the *problem of demarcation*. Every ethical theory must provide principles that describe which objects matter for their own sakes and which do not. Besides marking the boundary between these two classes by enumerating a set of ethically relevant properties, an ethical theory must say why the properties named, rather than others, are the ones that count. Thus, for example, hedonistic utilitarianism cites the capacity to experience pleasure and/or pain as the decisive criterion; preference utilitarianism cites the having of preferences (or wants, or interests) as the decisive property. And a Kantian ethical theory will include an individual in the ethical community only if it is capable of rational reflection and autonomy. Not that justifying these various proposed solutions to the demarcation problem is easy; indeed, since this issue is so fundamental, it will be very difficult to justify one proposal as opposed to another. Still, a substantive ethical theory is obliged to try.

Environmentalists, wishing to avoid the allegedly distorting perspective of individualism, frequently want to claim autonomous value for wholes. This may take the form of a monolithic doctrine according to which the only thing that matters is the stability of the ecosystem. Or it may embody a pluralistic outlook according to which ecosystem stability and species preservation have an importance additional to the welfare of individual organisms. But an environmentalist theory shares with all ethical theories an interest in not saying that everything has autonomous value. The reason this position is proscribed is that it makes the adjudication of ethical conflict very difficult indeed. (In addition, it is radically implausible, but we can set that objection to one side.)

Environmentalists, as we have seen, may think of natural objects, like mountains, species, and ecosystems, as mattering for their own sake, but of artificial objects, like highway systems and domesticated animals, as having only instrumental value. If a mountain and a highway are both made of rock, it seems unlikely that the difference between them arises from the fact that mountains have wants, interests, and preferences, but highway systems do not. But perhaps the place to look for the relevant difference is not in their present physical composition, but in the historical fact of how each came into existence. Mountains were created by natural processes, whereas highways are humanly constructed. But once we realize that organisms construct their environments in nature, this contrast begins to cloud. Organisms do not passively reside in an environment whose properties are independently determined. Organisms transform their environments by physically interacting with them. An anthill is an artifact just as a highway is. Granted, a difference obtains at the level of whether conscious deliberation played a role, but can one take seriously the view that artifacts produced by conscious planning are thereby *less* valuable than ones that arise without the intervention of mentality? As we have noted before, although environmentalists often accuse their critics of failing to think in a biologically realistic way, their use of the distinction between "natural" and "artificial" is just the sort of idea that stands in need of a more realistic biological perspective.

My suspicion is that the distinction between natural and artificial is not the crucial one. On the contrary, certain features of environmental concerns imply that natural objects are exactly on a par with certain artificial ones. Here the intended comparison is not between mountains and highways, but between mountains and works of art. My goal in what follows is not to sketch a substantive conception of what determines the value of objects in these two domains, but to motivate an analogy.

For both natural objects and works of art, our values extend beyond the concerns we have for experiencing pleasure. Most of us value seeing an original painting more than we value seeing a copy, even when we could not tell the difference. When we experience works of art, often what we value is not just the kinds of experiences we have, but, in addition, the connections we usually have with certain real objects. Routley and Routley have made an analogous point about valuing the wilderness experience: a "wilderness experience machine" that caused certain sorts of hallucinations would be no substitute for actually going into the wild.[19] Nor is this fact about our valuation limited to such aesthetic and environmentalist contexts. We love various people in our lives. If a molecule-for-molecule replica of a beloved person were created, you would not love that individual, but would continue to love the individual to whom you actually were historically related. Here again, our attachments are to objects and people as they really are, and not just to the experiences that they facilitate.

Another parallel between environmentalist concerns and aesthetic values concerns the issue of context. Although environmentalists often stress the importance of preserving endangered species, they would not be completely satisfied if an endangered species were preserved by putting a number of specimens in a zoo or in a humanly constructed preserve. What is taken to be important is preserving the species in its natural habitat. This leads to the more holistic position that preserving ecosystems, and not simply preserving certain member species, is of primary importance. Aesthetic concerns often lead in the same direction. It was not merely saving a fresco or an altar piece that motivated art historians after the most recent flood in Florence. Rather, they wanted to save these works of art in their original ("natural") settings. Not just the painting, but the church that housed it; not just the church, but the city itself. The idea of objects residing in a "fitting" environment plays a powerful role in both domains.

Environmentalism and aesthetics both see value in rarity. Of two whales, why should one be more worthy of aid than another, just because one belongs to an endangered species? Here we have the $n + m$ question mentioned [earlier]. As an ethical concern, rarity is difficult to understand. Perhaps this is because our ethical ideas concerning justice and equity (note the word) are saturated with individualism. But in the context of aesthetics, the concept of rarity is far from alien. A work of art may have enhanced value simply because there are very few other works by the same artist, or from the same historical period, or in the same style. It isn't that the price of the item may go up with rarity; I am talking about aesthetic value, not monetary worth. Viewed as valuable aesthetic objects, rare organisms may be valuable because they are rare.

A disanalogy may suggest itself. It may be objected that works of art are of instrumental value only, but that species and ecosystems have intrinsic value. Perhaps it is true, as claimed before, that our attachment to works of art, to nature, and to our loved ones extends beyond the experiences they allow us to have. But it may be argued that what is valuable in the aesthetic case is always the relation of a valuer to a valued object. When we experience a work of art, the value is not simply in the experience, but in the composite fact that we and the work of art are related in certain ways. This immediately suggests that if there were no valuers in the world, nothing would have value, since such relational facts could no longer obtain. So, to adapt Routley and Routley's "last man argument," it would seem that if an ecological crisis precipitated a collapse of the world system, the last human being (whom we may assume for the purposes of this example to be the last valuer) could set about destroying all works of art, and there would be nothing wrong in this.[20] That is, if aesthetic objects are valuable only in so far as valuers can stand in certain relations to them, then when valuers disappear, so does the possibility of aesthetic value. This would deny, in one sense, that aesthetic objects are intrinsically valuable:

it isn't they, in themselves, but rather the relational facts that they are part of, that are valuable.

In contrast, it has been claimed that the "last man" would be wrong to destroy natural objects such as mountains, salt marshes, and species. (So as to avoid confusing the issue by bringing in the welfare of individual organisms, Routley and Routley imagine that destruction and mass extinctions can be caused painlessly, so that there would be nothing wrong about this undertaking from the point of view of the nonhuman organisms involved.) If the last man ought to preserve these natural objects, then these objects appear to have a kind of autonomous value; their value would extend beyond their possible relations to valuers. If all this were true, we would have here a contrast between aesthetic and natural objects, one that implies that natural objects are more valuable than works of art.

Routley and Routley advance the last man argument as if it were decisive in showing that environmental objects such as mountains and salt marshes have autonomous value. I find the example more puzzling than decisive. But, in the present context, we do not have to decide whether Routley and Routley are right. We only have to decide whether this imagined situation brings out any relevant difference between aesthetic and environmental values. Were the last man to look up on a certain hillside, he would see a striking rock formation next to the ruins of a Greek temple. Long ago the temple was built from some of the very rocks that still stud the slope. Both promontory and temple have a history, and both have been transformed by the biotic and the abiotic environments. I myself find it impossible to advise the last man that the peak matters more than the temple. I do not see a relevant difference. Environmentalists, if they hold that the solution to the problem of demarcation is to be found in the distinction between natural and artificial, will have to find such a distinction. But if environmental values are aesthetic, no difference need be discovered.

Environmentalists may be reluctant to classify their concern as aesthetic. Perhaps they will feel that aesthetic concerns are frivolous. Perhaps they will feel that the aesthetic regard for artifacts that has been made possible by culture is antithetical to a proper regard for wilderness. But such contrasts are illusory. Concern for environmental values does not require a stripping away of the perspective afforded by civilization; to value the wild, one does not have to "become wild" oneself (whatever that may mean). Rather, it is the material comforts of civilization that make possible a serious concern for both aesthetic and environmental values. These are concerns that can become pressing in developed nations in part because the populations of those countries now enjoy a certain substantial level of prosperity. It would be the height of condescension to expect a nation experiencing hunger and chronic disease to be inordinately concerned with the autonomous value of ecosystems or with creating and preserving works of art. Such values are not frivolous, but they can become important to us only after certain fundamental human needs are satisfied. Instead of radically jettisoning individualist ethics, environmentalists may find a more hospitable home for their values in a category of value that has existed all along.

Notes

I am grateful to Donald Crawford, Jon Moline, Bryan Norton, Robert Stauffer, and Daniel Wikler for useful discussion. I also wish to thank the National Science Foundation and the Graduate School of the University of Wisconsin–Madison for financial support.

1. See, for example, J. B. Callicott, "Animal Liberation: A Triangular Affair," *Environmental Ethics* 2 (1980): 311–38.

2. D. Ehrenfeld, "The Conservation of Non-Resources," *American Scientist* 64 (1976): 648–56; R. M. May, *Stability and Complexity in Model Ecosystems* (Princeton, N.J.: Princeton University Press, 1973).

3. Callicott, "Animal Liberation," 333–34 (my emphasis).

4. P. Shepard, "Animal Rights and Human Rites," *North American Review* (1974): 35–41.

5. C. Darwin, *The Autobiography of Charles Darwin* (1876; London: Collins, 1958), 90.

6. The idea that the natural world is perfect, besides being suspect as an ethical principle, is also controversial as biology. In spite of Callicott's confidence that the amount of pain found in nature is biologically optimal, this adaptationist outlook is now much debated. See, for example, R. Lewontin and S. J. Gould, "The Spandrels of San Marco and the Panglossian Paradigm: A Critique of the Adaptionist Programme," *Proceedings of the Royal Society of London* 205 (1979): 581–98.

7. Callicott, "Animal Liberation," 330.

8. Ibid., 330.

9. Aristotle, *De Anima*, 415a26.

10. C. D. Stone, *Should Trees Have Standing? Toward Legal Rights for Natural Objects* (Los Altos, Calif.: William Kaufmann, 1974), 24.

11. M. Sagoff, "On Preserving the Natural Environment," *Yale Law Review* 84 (1974): 220–24.

12. See G. C. Williams, *Adaptation and Natural Selection* (Princeton, N.J.: Princeton University Press, 1966), and E. Sober, *The Nature of Selection* (Cambridge, Mass.: MIT Press, 1984).

13. A. Leopold, *A Sand County Almanac, and Sketches Here and There* (New York: Oxford University Press, 1949), 224–25.

14. Callicott, "Animal Liberation," 326.

15. E. Abbey, *Desert Solitaire* (New York, Ballantine, 1968), 20.

16. G. Hardin, "The Economics of Wilderness," *Natural History* 78 (1969): 176.

17. Callicott, "Animal Liberation," 323.

18. Ibid., 335.

19. R. Routley and V. Routley, "Human Chauvinism and Environmental Ethics," in *Environmental Philosophy*, Monograph Series 2, ed. D. S. Mannison, M. A. McRobbie, and R. Routley (Canberra: Philosophy Department, Australian National University, 1980), 154.

20. Ibid., 121–22.